THE LONG AND WHINING ROAD

SIMEON COURTIE

Enjoy the journey!

Sim

D1347868

A man and a van, a wife and three kids,
and their round—the—world road trip
as the world's worst Beatles tribute band.

THE LONG AND WHINING ROAD

First published in 2012 by Simantics Ltd.

Second Edition

www.simantics.tv

Printed and bound in Oxfordshire, England

ISBN: 978-0-9571980-0-5

To Jill, for taking the leap

I was holding my breath in the darkness of a desolate Italian churchyard. Holding my breath so as not to make a sound. Huddled with me in the clammy night air, squashed between the cemetery wall and the side of our VW camper van, were four frightened rabbits better known as My Family. We were hiding. My wife Jill had pressed me to take action twenty minutes earlier when the lights first went on in the church, but I'd dismissed the sudden illumination as a late-night visit from a priest who'd forgotten his cassock. Now, two cars had swung from nowhere into our dark hiding place, spotlighting Penny our camper van in their blinding halogen glare.

We were camping illegally. And apparently we'd been busted.

'The vicar's called the cops,' whispered Ella, my 13-year-old, helpfully. Bethan and Edie clung tighter to their mother. I could see in their eyes that the threat of arrest by the armed Italian Politzi would be almost as frightening to 11 and nine-year-old girls as a High School Musical sequel is to adults.

I heard a whimper. 'Come on, Jill. Don't be scared,' I whispered.

'That was Edie,' she spat under her breath. 'Now either you go and talk to them, or we're packing and leaving!'

The mysterious blinding headlights clicked off. Darkness once again engulfed us. An owl screeched. Several car doors slammed and heavy feet crunched gravel. I took a breath.

It was show-time.

How's it come to this? I thought. It had all seemed such a good idea back in Liverpool ...

That's where our story actually begins: Liverpool, the European Capital of Culture 2008. OK, so I teased you with that nail-biting encounter in the Italian churchyard as a flimsy attempt to try and grab you, like sticking the car chase at the beginning of a movie. The trouble is, when your camper van's top speed is 55 miles-per-hour, you don't get many car chases.

So, how did a radio DJ and part time comedy writer (that's me, putting my hand up) and his BBC journalist wife come to scoop together what little cash they had, buy a camper van and travel the world with their three kids? More worryingly, why did they feel the need to start The World's Worst Beatles Tribute Band and busk Lennon and McCartney hits in every country?

Well, as I say, it all started in Liverpool.

I spent my formative years growing up a Scouser, from the carefree laughter of a seven-year-old when we moved to the city in 1977 to the teen angst of 1984 when we left. My dad was a vicar, so that gave me a useful head start in school - if it's a race to see who can get beaten up the quickest. My mum was a writer. Cool if she'd written *Tainted Love*, or *Blackadder*, but she wrote books for the religious market - textbooks and funny books about being a vicar's wife, so again, character-building stuff for the playground that was best left under wraps. My parents were cool in other ways though. It was my mum's copy of *Rubber Soul* that got me into The Beatles, and it remains my favourite album of theirs.

Purists will argue for hours over the artistic integrity of *Sgt. Pepper* vs. *Revolver*, but you can't beat the memory of holding that big platter of precious black vinyl, inspecting the grooves for fluff, and your mum saying, 'Don't scratch that. I've had that since Christmas 1965!' *every single time* you play it. That's what cements a favourite.

I loved Liverpool and it was a wrench to move away when I was 14, but within a few years my schoolmates all scattered and we lost touch, so by 2008 I hadn't been back since I was a teenager. In the summer of 2008 we were visiting some friends near Manchester and, it being Liverpool's time to shine, we decided to spend a day or two seeing what a European Capital of Culture looked like. Jill wanted to 'do The Tate', and my own ambition was to visit the childhood homes of John Lennon and Paul McCartney, recently acquired by the National Trust.

What I'd feared might be a tacky experience aimed at Japanese tourists turned out to be a brilliant couple of hours which, quite incredibly, changed our lives. The reason it had such a bearing on our future was the impact the Liverpool visit had on Ella, Bethan and Edie. During the hour's drive into the city I'd done a potted history of The Beatles, playing tracks off my iPod, trying to engage the girls in what we were about to see. Neither Jill nor I thought they'd be very interested, but at least they were humouring me.

The tour was great. We were taken, in a group of only ten, to each house where original furniture and décor have been restored to their exact 1950s state. The NT guides live on site in their respective houses and are clearly massive fans. They showed us round, answered questions and told fantastic stories about the famous inhabitants' time there. Our girls stood and sang in Lennon's Menlove Avenue porch, where he and Paul used to work out harmonies because the echoey acoustics were so good. We crowded into the front room of Paul's tiny terraced council house, now adorned with original unpublished photographs that younger brother Mike McCartney took of Paul and the boys - none of them staged shots, just casual reportage moments in time. There's a black and white photo of John and Paul crouched with guitars on laps, John in the chair, Paul on the tiled fire hearth writing on manuscript paper.

'Look closely,' said the guide in his relaxed scouse drawl. 'They're writing *I Saw Her Standing There.*' And we were. Standing there. I got shivers.

The following days were full of questions and moments of discovery for the girls. 'How did they die?' 'Who shot John Lennon?' 'Paul's still making records?!' 'Ringo narrated *Thomas The Tank Engine*?!'

Edie, especially, was filling her seven-year-old mind with Beatles knowledge, and it was with no small amount of shock and awe that she learned her grandmother had known Ringo.

My mum, aged 18, had taken a summer job working as a chalet maid at Butlins in Pwllheli, North Wales. She bunked in the chalet next to the resident band that summer - Rory Storm & The Hurricanes - and got on famously with the lads, one of whom was their young drummer Richard who'd just adopted the stage name Ringo Starr. Among the tales she tells of her months there is the one about Ringo buying swimming shorts but finding them too baggy for the current fashion, and begging my mum to take them in a bit.

'So Granny Brenda has sewn up Ringo's shorts,' I concluded grandly, as we drove home, 'which makes you and him practically related.' Jill smiled. Edie's face was one of wide-eyed amazement. Somewhere inside she had just sworn allegiance to the Fab Four, and would be a stolid Beatles fan from that day on. A seed had been sown that would before we knew it, grow, becoming an unstoppable force propelling us around the world. Like Japanese Knotweed, the musical.

By the time we re-visited Liverpool a year later, we'd already hatched a secret plan to travel the world. Like all the best Top Secret schemes, it was born over a meal. In spy movies, plans are plotted over raw fish in a Tokyo sushi bar, or over canapés at an Ambassador's cocktail party in Geneva. Ours was over a plastic table and luke-warm fries at a fast-food burger chain in Banbury. Bethan, being a vegetarian, was idly peeling the contents of a cheeseburger apart to remove the meat when she made a bombshell announcement. 'I'm bored with Banbury,' she sighed.

Jill and I raised our eyebrows. 'Bored with Banbury, bored with life!' quipped Jill, cleverly misquoting Samuel Johnson, or possibly the *What's On* editor of the *Banbury Guardian*.

The cause of Beth's wanderlust? Blame the parents. We'd taken a fairly unusual holiday the year before, travelling from North Oxfordshire to Biarritz, South of France, using only public transport. We started at the bus stop outside our house and got to Europe's premier chic surf spot using nothing but buses and trains, each of us allowed to take only what we could carry. What had seemed like insanity when we were dragging cases up Paris Metro stairs and dashing, sweating and red faced, for trains we nearly missed was ultimately a triumph. The kids declared it The Best Holiday Ever and had returned home with the travel bug.

As the burger-bar conversation moved towards the inevitable subject of getting as far from home as possible and seeing something more interesting than Banbury Cross (yes, it really does have one as the nursery rhyme suggests. But, before you book a flight, it's not the original one), it became clear that all three children were really keen on my recurring idea of going round the world.

Ella, aged 11, looked from Jill to me and said, 'You always say we're gonna travel round the world, but you never mean it.'

'I would!' Jill replied. 'It's your father you need to convince.'

When I'd stopped choking on my free-refills cola, I begged to differ. We all knew that travelling the world was *my* dream, but that Jill would *never* take the risk. *I* was the risk-taker. *She* needed security. I saw a pile of stones and a roof worth hundreds of thousands of pounds that could pay for an amazing adventure. She saw a home for our children to grow up in. You can see how this debate had gone in the past. She pressed home her point: my career had taken off. I had a daily radio show paying good money and I'd never leave my comedy writing, not now I was being paid by one of the most famous satirical programmes on British TV. OK, I was only called in to write for them once in a while, but it was proper telly, proper comedy writing, and proper money in my bank account.

'You'd never go,' she declared.

Was she daring me? I brushed it off. 'Nonsense. I'd go like a shot.' I slammed my drink on the table dramatically, testing its plastic lid, as if a slightly creased cardboard beaker somehow sealed the deal. The girls looked from me to Jill, awaiting her reaction.

'Righto. That's settled then. When shall we go?'

Apparently, we'd just talked ourselves into it. The project would take another eighteen months to organise, but the decision had been made: *we were going round the world.*

Life went on. We gathered funds, ate fewer takeaways, paid off credit cards and started privately plotting our adventure. Jill made enquiries about taking a career break – a year of unpaid leave. I couldn't believe she was really up for it. Somehow, after years of pestering, I'd convinced her we should travel the world. She imagined posh flights and swanky hotels. Then I said the three words every girl longs to hear. 'Volkswagen camper van.'

'You're kidding, right?' she laughed.

'Think about it. We'll save a fortune on flights and hotels, and anyway we don't want to hop from boring airport to boring airport. This is all about the *journey.* Biarritz taught us that. It's the *travelling* that's fun. Meeting people, seeing places off the beaten track. Let's *drive* round the world!'

'Five of us? In a VW camper? Forget it.'

Admittedly, she would need some persuading. The kids were sworn to secrecy about our trip until we were *absolutely sure* we could make it happen, and once the initial thrill had abated they quickly returned to their normal lives of school, sleep-overs and, in Edie's case, The Beatles. After we'd tolerated the relentless barrage of pestering only a seven-year-old has the stamina to keep up, she succeeded in getting us to make a second Beatles-related visit to Liverpool.

She'd wanted to visit *The Beatles Story* ever since she'd spied it at the Albert Dock a year earlier, but had been cruelly dragged around The Tate instead. Finally, she got her wish, and we enjoyed every tiny detail of the exhibition, from Paul's first guitar to John's famous NHS wire-rimmed spectacles. Finally, my wallet relatively unscathed by an exit through the gift shop, I asked Edie if she needed the toilet before we left.

And that's where it happened.

The tiny spark that lit the fuse on this whole crazy idea.

Visitors to *The Beatles Story* may find themselves loitering outside the loos at the end. Male visitors mainly, I would wager, waiting for wives, girlfriends or children to do whatever it is they do that takes so long. The proprietors had kindly provided a diversion, adorning the wall with a massive map of the world, on which were many scattered dots of different colours. This caught Edie's eye. Closer inspection revealed that the map showed how many visitors from various corners of the Earth had come to the exhibition. And it was really interesting. South America, for instance, was quite cluttered with stickers because The Beatles are huge in Argentina, yet oddly they never went there. Weird. Edie spotted a couple of dots on Mumbai and pointed at the label.

'They know the Beatles in India?'

'Sure,' I mused, 'you can't move for buskers doing *While My Sitar Gently Weeps*.'

Nothing. Not even a smirk. Kids are harsh critics for a comedy writer. With a slightly doubtful frown she looked again at the map. 'Can we go there?'

'Of course we can. But not now. The ticket ran out on the car five minutes ago and we're late for Anfield.' And with that we all bundled into the car and headed to the home of the Greatest Football Club In The World, fully replete with Beatles history, facts and figures, and generally buzzing about how this was the best day we'd had in ages. I'd even got away with glossing over the fact that our future travel plans would apparently have to include a visit to India simply to prove the people there still loved The Beatles. A promise I was sure my youngest daughter would never remember. Right?

We were driving home when, somewhere between getting on the M6 and leaving the M40, the talk in the car turned to our Big Trip. It was the kind of idle chatter you'd expect. 'Where will we start?' 'What will we wear?' 'Are we near a services yet?' (That last comment was from me.)

And then Jill said something completely unexpected. 'Hilton Park's coming up.' No, just after that, she said, 'We should busk on the way round!' The idea of standing in the street and playing music for money would fill most people with dread. There was a moment of silence as the ridiculous concept sunk in. Then someone, it may have been Jill again (yes, let's blame Jill - it's a theme I'm warming to) went one better.

'Let's busk *The Beatles* on the way round.'

'What a great idea!'

'What a laugh!'

'What a great way to raise a bit of cash,' I suggested.

'For *charity*,' admonished Jill.

'Oh. Of course,' I nodded. 'Charity, naturally. Besides, it's probably best we don't fund a year of global travel relying on the generosity of some bemused locals in …'

'… Mumbai!' shouted Edie. Jill looked quizzical. I laughed at the mental image of us lot playing Beatles songs in India. The girls started to run with the idea.

'I could play the flute,' suggested Ella, who was a pretty decent flautist. 'It's small, too, so easy to pack.'

'I could play the trumpet!' shouted Edie, who had never played the trumpet in her life, but really wanted to. Beth stayed quiet. She played the cello. In the packing stakes, the odds weren't good.

What would I play? A guitar? No. This idea required wit, cunning, and something small enough to stow in a camper van. While Jill drove, I hit the Internet on my mobile phone. I had no idea how to play a ukulele or how much they were, but five minutes later at least one of those mysteries was solved. An entry-level soprano uke was £15 including postage. The eBay ad said 'Buy Now'. Who was I to argue? 'Kids, say hello to your band's ukulele player!'

Jill rolled her eyes (at least it wasn't the car). This idea had legs and she knew it. I could see the first tinge of regret across her face. By the time we reached home we were discussing a set list, a name (not the *Busking Beatles* - way too obvious) and had bought an antique German squeezebox from eBay for £35 which Bethan would learn to play.

We'd formed a band! And this band was gonna take on the world. In a camper van. One dodgy Beatles song at a time.

By August 2010, Jill had confirmed a one-year career break from her job at the BBC, I had resigned my post as breakfast show DJ on the British Forces radio station BFBS, and our three children were about to embark on a spell of absenteeism that would make Dennis the Menace look scholarly. We neared our departure from the UK in a disorganised panic. As we haphazardly attempted to throw together this complicated adventure alongside our already busy lives, it very quickly became clear that we were running out of time. A mere *week* before our ferry sailed from Harwich to Holland our house remained horribly full of belongings still to be stored, and horribly empty of potential tenants.

It seemed no amount of early mornings and late nights could clear the work still to be done. Time was slipping away and there were still more loose ends than in the DVD box set of *Lost*. One of those essentials on our 'to do' list was our launch gig. The plan for our epic quest was to busk from the Strawberry Field children's home in Liverpool, made famous in the song, to Strawberry Fields memorial garden in Central Park, New York. This meant some rather stressful 'band practices' as we attempted to learn at least a couple of Beatles standards, and required a day of our precious and ever-diminishing time to accommodate yet another jaunt up to Merseyside.

A few days before leaving England, we cleared one full day in the diary to drive to Liverpool and busk at Strawberry Field. We gathered at 7am for the three-hour drive, but there was a nervous tension in the air. Bethan was in a very bad mood. 'What's wrong Beth?' I asked.

'Nothing,' she growled.

I sat down next to her but she shunned me. 'Come on, darling, what's the problem?'

'What's the problem? I'll tell you what the problem is. Playing in the street is the problem. I don't want to do it. Why are you making us do this?'

'Come on Beth, don't skirt the topic. Something's definitely bothering you.'

She wasn't in the mood for jokes. The initial buoyant confidence we'd all felt when the busking idea was first suggested had long since evaporated. I'd sensed a simmering reluctance from the girls every time I'd suggested a band practice, but had brushed it off as nerves and ploughed on with the plan regardless. And now it was D-Day.

'Darling, we're all a bit nervous,' Jill said supportively.

'Don't make me do it,' Beth pleaded to her mum. 'Why can't we just be a *normal* family?'

Jill looked at her sympathetically. 'Because of all the daddies in the world, we got this one. Aren't we lucky? Now let's get in Penny.'

Penny (second name, Lane) is a 1989 VW camper van we'd bought on eBay for £4,000, and this trip to Liverpool and back was her first proper outing. She'd spent the last six months being upgraded: beefy suspension, larger water tank, a re-spray in yellow and white and of course, flowery curtains. The theory had been that if we accidentally turned left in Syria and found ourselves in Iraq and Afghanistan, she'd look too jaunty and cheerful to be deemed a threat. Of course, she'd also be a bright yellow target for a bored sniper and a magnet to kidnappers, but as we happily trundled north on the M6, turning heads and returning cheery waves, I chose to keep that thought to myself.

Strawberry Field, in leafy Liverpool 18, is an elegant sandstone house which though still owned by the Salvation Army is no longer a children's home. It was closed and had become the subject of a complicated planning and redevelopment wrangle. Consequently, no one would give us permission to gain access to the old house, which would have been such a great press conference backdrop for our newly-painted van and our ramshackle busking performance. Instead, we chose simply to rock up and try our luck.

Beaconsfield Road is very narrow, with a slender pavement's width between the road and the tall sandstone wall that surrounds Strawberry Field. It's also not very busy - a hopeless choice for *real* buskers, but as we couldn't consider ourselves anything near to that, we counted our blessings that not too many people would have to suffer our din.

Tucking Penny into the gateway, now much graffiti-ed as a shrine to Liverpool's most famous musicians, we piled out and tuned up. 'Strawberry Field?' asked Edie, looking at the small distinctive hand-painted sign on the gatepost. 'I thought it was Strawberry Fields, with an S.'

'Only in the song,' I said, getting our kit out of the van. 'Well, and in New York. They called the John Lennon memorial garden in Central Park Strawberry Fields, because of the song I guess.'

'Just think,' said Edie. 'A year from now we'll be there!'

Oddly, no gushing whoops of agreement were forthcoming from any of us. Bethan made a doubtful 'Hmmmmm' noise. It *did* seem impossibly far-fetched. I was trying to balance a video camera on a camping table in such a way as to capture our efforts when two ladies who were walking past stopped.

'D'you wanna hand, love?' asked the tall red-haired woman.

'Oh cheers mate, that'd be sound,' I replied. As always happens when I speak to native Liverpudlians, my own dormant Scouser is awoken and my vocal chords are once again possessed by the ghost of *Brookside*'s Billy Corkhill.

We explained to Linda and Joan what we were doing, and they happily hung around to video us doing our first ever public performance. They cheered at the end of *All You Need Is Love* and had to put the camera down to clap. Joan told us how, when she was a girl, her mum had worked at Liverpool's old Speke Airport and got tickets for them to be on the tarmac to welcome home The Beatles from New York after their famous Shay Stadium gig. We'd seen that black and white footage so many times of the fans screaming as the fresh-faced boys came down the aircraft steps, and here was one of those screaming fans. And she'd applauded us!

Then, when we told them we were busking to raise money for the children's charity UNICEF they plunged into their purses without hesitation and gave us a pound each. Our fundraising pot had started. All we needed were another 4,998 people like Linda and Joan, and our target would be reached.

Today, Speke Airport is John Lennon Airport (slogan - *Above us only sky*. Yes, really) but the sparkle in Joan's eyes as she recalled the noise and adrenaline of welcoming The Beatles home 40 years ago was joyous, and marked the beginning of a journey for us that would throw up a surprising number of these unusual tales of peoples' connections with the World's Biggest Band.

We chose to start our circumnavigation of the globe by heading East. It was a direction we were going to have to get used to, so we figured a ferry to The Hook of Holland was as good a start as any.

The ferry journey itself was a mixture of emotions. Any excitement at finally starting our quest was quashed by a thousand other thoughts and worries. We'd left the UK in such a mad rush that we couldn't help but be consumed by that nagging feeling, like when you set off to work and think you've left a tap running, or your hair-straighteners on, but times a hundred. This probably wasn't helped by the fact that we'd agreed to rent our home to a tenant we had met literally *ten minutes* before we locked the door for the final time.

As we were throwing the very last things we owned either into Penny, or into a box to lock in a shed, a truly remarkable sequence of coincidences happened. In the space of half an hour, a passing comment from a friend about a neighbour of hers who was desperate to move and was interested in our house, led to a man we'd never met before standing in our kitchen offering us what we wanted to rent our home. There then followed a surreal five minutes during which we talked terms, nailed a deal, explained everything he needed to know about the house – the kind of things an estate agent would drag out over several weeks - and bingo. We were landlords.

Landlords with greying hair and no fingernails, but all the same, a crisis had been averted. So having spent a large portion of the ferry crossing to Holland in Stena Britannia's wi-fi hotspot buying online membership to the Residential Landlords' Association and downloading the latest Assured Shorthold Tenancy Agreement, we bought a street map of Rotterdam in the Britannia Boutique, collapsed into a heap with the truckers and tourists in the Sunset Bar, located on the map the campsite we'd booked for our first night and admitted that we'd probably cut things a *bit* too fine with our preparations to leave home for a year. But that was behind us now. Assuming the tenants paid the rent, our biggest worry was over. Now we could relax, and look forward to our first night as proper travellers.

But we'd not yet seen the campsite.

I don't know why, but I'd always thought the Dutch were passionate about camping. It was a vague stereotype I'd talked myself into, like assuming all Canadians love ice hockey or all Italian politicians are corrupt. I'm sure at least one of those isn't true. I had nothing to qualify my theory, it was just a hunch - a tragically misplaced hunch. Stadscamping in Rotterdam had been well reviewed on a couple of blogs I'd read so I imagined a delightful Utopia of calm to ease us into our journey: pretty camping pitches surrounded by tulips and daffodils, overlooked by a sleepy canal, the occasional cheery cyclist and the soothing sails of a hilltop windmill.

In fact it's an over-priced muddy field under a six-lane flyover that backs on to the city zoo. If the traffic doesn't keep you awake, the murderous shrieks of feeding time in the monkey house will soon have you bolt upright at 5am. In our case we were awake that early on our first morning abroad anyway, thanks to the rain. This was August in Europe, peak summer-holiday season, which guaranteed two things: Prices would go up. Rain would come down. And boy, did it come down.

'Well, this is nice,' said Bethan hopping out of the van and over a puddle which had gathered in the centre of our adjoining clip-on frame tent. She was 11 years old, so sarcasm was her first language. I prodded a flap that let another sloosh of cold water hit the groundsheet.

'It's the first time we've used it. There are bound to be a few teething problems.'

'I can't get the fridge to work!' shouted Jill from inside the van. 'Did you plug it in?'

I rolled my eyes. 'Have I plugged it in? When these thieves are charging me for electric hook-up? Yes, I thought I should.' Now I was 11 years old, too.

'Well, it's not working. Cup of tea?'

'If there's nothing stronger,' I said, parking my camping chair in the middle of the puddle and trying to ignore the battering rain above us.

'Teething troubles. That's all,' said Ella, appearing from the depths of Penny in her pyjamas. Then Bethan leaned on our brand new camping table and a leg snapped off. She looked horrified.

'Oh. I'm so sorry. I just ... '

'It's fine, it's fine. Dawn on day one, and two things broken already,' I chirped, like it was the most normal thing in the world. 'If we keep this up we could break, ooh, seven-hundred-and-thirty different things in a year.'

An ominous cloud had gathered inside our damp, cluttered dwelling, only matched by the angry sky outside. As we gazed blankly through misty polythene windows, an even more depressing thought struck me. 'We've got to go into the city and busk,' I said, to no one in particular.

I can't recall the precise words that my family threw at me, but it was clear that this band was going nowhere. 'Maybe it'll clear a bit?' I offered, forlornly.

Jill draped her arm around my shoulder. 'Darling?' (Don't be fooled. I knew this tone. I wasn't about to be told something affectionate.) 'We're cold, we're tired and we're wet. We're living in a bog next to a motorway. I don't think any of us is in the mood to wear a happy smile and sing *Ob-La-bloody-Dee*. Not now.'

'Not ever!' added Bethan. They hunt as a pack when it suits them. I sighed. I considered the enormous price we had paid, not just in fees to camp in this squalor, but in our lives. We'd left jobs and schools and friends in a huge blaze of glory. There'd even been newspaper articles and television news items about us on BBC1 and ITV. We'd truly stepped into the breach and there was no going back. The wind whistled around the van, tugging angrily at the tent. Another surge of cold water lapped around my feet. 'Dear God,' I uttered quietly. 'What have we done?'

After visiting The Worst Campsite Toilets In Europe (they really deserved a plaque) we agreed on a compromise. We would put off the busking until tomorrow, but go into Rotterdam to recce.

'Get a feel for the place, pick a good spot,' I suggested as we folded down Penny's roof, unhooked the tent and guided her gently out of the quagmire.

Our first stroll through a foreign city was full of anticipation. We were global explorers, wide-eyed with curiosity at what the world had to offer. Countless new lands waited to be discovered, and here was the first. Where would Rotterdam set the bar for the many hundreds of exciting new cities to be explored on our adventure?

Low, was the answer.

Let's not pretend Rotterdam is a shining jewel in The Netherlands' crown. It boasts the busiest shipping port in Europe, so if miles of concrete industrialised container docks are your thing, it surely holds a special place in your heart. If you're an English tourist passing through, however, it's a bit like Swindon. But without the Magic Roundabout to add zest. Zest is not encouraged in Rotterdam.

Walking through the town centre we were approached by a homeless man who struck up conversation.

'You are a beautiful family,' he said from somewhere behind a matted ginger beard. The girls stopped in their tracks, slightly alarmed.

'Thank you,' I smiled. After all, there's no need to be rude. As I tried to walk on he rounded in front of us to engage us further in the tale of how he was trying to sell poetry.

'Good luck with that,' I offered, failing to brush him off. Soon he was reciting some shouty Flemish poetry at us and I was faced with my first moral dilemma of the trip. We'd never talked, as a family, about how we would deal with the inevitable begging we'd encounter on our journey. To be honest, we expected to experience it in India rather than Holland. So now I found myself cornered between the passionate, interesting-smelling Dutch gentleman, ranting his doggerel, and the expectant eyes of my children who were wondering what would happen next. Jill, I noticed, seemed to have found something fascinating to look at several safe steps away.

I interrupted the performer.

'I'm sorry mate. I'm not going to give you any money.'

He looked surprised. And a little hurt.

'Sorry,' I repeated and pulled the kids away.

'That wasn't very nice,' Ella commented.

'I know,' I replied. 'It didn't even rhyme.'

But they weren't in the mood for jokes. As we pushed on through the drizzle, we began, much earlier than anyone would have anticipated, our first discussion about begging. I pointed out that we were bound to be asked for money hundreds, possibly thousands of times during our year. We couldn't afford to give money to them all and there was simply no way we could decide who was more deserving. Therefore, we should refuse them all and take comfort in the fact that we were raising lots of money for UNICEF, a proper charity that will use the cash wisely. Jill talked about the begging gangs in India, about how kids are sent out to beg for adult gang leaders and are even deliberately injured so they'll earn more money. 'There is much worse to come,' she warned. I nodded earnestly and thought we'd made our point fairly well.

Then Beth said, 'But he was performing on the street and asking for money. Isn't that what we're doing?' and suddenly my actions seemed mean-spirited and cruel. If these were the kind of moral quandaries we were to navigate, this would be a complicated year.

The next day was gig day, and the rain had stopped. We drove back into the city centre and we'd picked our spot. The kind people in the Tourist Information centre had agreed that we could use their steps as a stage, facing a busy central square.

Well, it *had* been busy when we'd reccied yesterday. Oddly, it became a strangely peaceful square as we unpacked our instruments. Gone were the bustling shoppers, the young mums pushing prams and the strolling pensioners. My biggest secret fear was that, after what Beth had said, we'd be playing to the hobo-poet, shaking his head in disgust at my shocking double standards. So on the plus side, at least he was nowhere to be seen.

The biggest problem we had wasn't a lack of audience, it was a lack of confidence combined with a woeful lack of ability. Put simply, we were rubbish. Passers-by smiled, but kept walking. Songs fell apart, chords were forgotten, lyrics escaped us. Bethan, who had been slowly torturing herself about this moment all morning, was what psychiatrists might describe as 'in a very bad place'. (And they don't mean Rotterdam.)

I had cleverly constructed a sign made out of a pop-up goal bought on eBay for a fiver. It could twist into a flat disc to be stored in our instrument bag, but would spring out to become a three-dimensional triangular 'stand'. On what would normally have been the back of the goal was pinned a custom printed 'Beatnik Beatles' banner bearing our logo – a Beatnik Beatles button badge and a big apple, on which was a map of the world with our route highlighted. 'Busking The Beatles from Liverpool to New York for UNICEF' it proudly stated, and had our web address to make us look even more legit. The sign was designed to make us look 'the real deal'. More like professional performers, and less like ... well, hobo-poets.

Beth found a new use for it: a shield. She sat behind it, in fact *inside* it, filling its goal-mouth in the same way that an England keeper doesn't. Perhaps England's goal-keepers should try holding a squeezebox. She did look formidable. But not only could she not be seen, she couldn't be heard. Even when we coaxed her into the glare of the public eye, she scowled and played quieter than a tiny mouse who's run out of puff.

When we pulled ourselves together enough to do a passable bash at *All My Loving* a small boy left his mother to come and stand in front of us. *Brilliant! An audience.* We smiled to each other and felt the first glimmer of nervous enjoyment. Then the child let rip. He screamed. I don't mean an ecstatic scream of delight. This wasn't Beatlemania. There was no joy in his heart. It was the relentless piercing scream of a four-year-old whose primal reaction to our din was to join in. While his mother kept her distance, he screamed and screamed and screamed until we stopped.

There was no applause, just a welcome silence. The boy, happy with a job well done, toddled off. We hastily, and with no small amount of embarrassment, gathered up our belongings and called it a day, retiring to a nearby McDonalds to reward ourselves with coffee and ice cream. We had raised precisely zero cents for UNICEF. Edie, still holding the empty collecting tin, remained buoyant. 'We can leave with our heads held high,' she said. 'At least no one paid us to *stop* playing.'

The outcome of the de-brief was that a) we needed to practise more and get more confident, and b) we needed to structure our performance, like a show. All the girls agreed that they'd feel happier if I did some talking to the crowd, should we be lucky enough to get one, to make it appear more like an event. I was happy to oblige. Standing up and making a fool of myself is old territory to me, as High

Wycombe theatre-goers who endured my *Dick Whittington* will testify. Quite shameless.

It didn't change the fact that I spent the drive up to Amsterdam that afternoon wondering if this might all have been a colossally bad idea, especially when Beth said things like, 'Why can't we just be normal?' What was I putting these kids through? On the other hand, after we'd taken photos and video of our 'performance', Edie had said, 'Right, can we do it properly now, because we haven't raised any money at all?' She was really into it and would have stayed another hour I'm sure. Beth apologised later for being grumpy. We all knew how she felt. It was scary, standing up in public to play an instrument and sing. As we arrived in Holland's capital, I resigned myself to the truth that she'd either get used to the idea of doing something a bit silly for charity, and gain in confidence, or it would become increasingly difficult and we'd have to scrap the idea. Time would tell.

Amsterdam was beautiful. I was unimpressed with my Dutch experience up to this point, but Amsterdam won me over. Its tall, shuttered houses overlook winding canals, all criss-crossed with picture-book bridges, that give the city a relaxed, safe, peaceful charm. Driving Penny around its narrow streets was a challenge, and offered some memorable moments. I know my passengers will never forget the dawning realisation that at one point we were the only vehicle driving along a tramway.

'There we go,' I said cheerily. 'This road seems very clear.'

'Sim, we're on rails,' stated Jill. 'I don't think cars are allowed ...'

And then a tram appeared and I didn't catch what else she said, what with the bell ringing, the horn blaring and the kids yelling. Like I say, a relaxed, safe, peaceful charm.

Jill had bought tickets to visit Anne Frank Huis at 7.45 that evening. We filled the afternoon strolling through the old city centre heading towards The Vondelpark. With its neatly trimmed lawns, well manicured flower beds and pretty duck ponds it could be any of

London's royal parks, except for a couple of details. There's the constant jeopardy of bicycle versus pedestrian as a thousand cyclists of varying skill and ability weave their way through the crowds. And there's the thick haze of smoke lingering over large groups of students on the lawns. Amsterdam's lenience to drugs was well tested, and they were, in all senses, 'on the grass'.

'Look at all the smoke,' Edie said. 'They're having a barbecue!'

Our visit to Anne Frank's house was the first tick of the box for us making our world adventure educational. We'd had brilliant support from the girls' respective schools, both of them providing work to keep the kids on track while they were travelling, but we were determined to grab any opportunity to broaden their knowledge, and visiting the young Second World War diarist's secret loft was a must.

All three girls had read Anne Frank's diary at school, so exploring the tiny rooms proved to be moving and eerie. We were gripped by the tale of the Frank family's experience, so famously documented by Anne, and kept so alive in this tiny house-turned-museum. It was a superb, living experience that our girls won't forget.

** Spoiler Alert ** If you've never read *The Diary of Anne Frank*, then clearly, you must. But assuming you know the story, the museum concludes with footage from Belsen, where Anne and her sister ended up. This grainy black and white film was really upsetting and I got a bit choked up. It made my earlier worries about busking seem so ridiculously trivial, and I promised myself that I wouldn't get cross or bothered by petty problems any more.

When we got back to the campsite in Rotterdam it was 9.59pm. The campsite owners brought down a locked barrier at 10pm, so we were relieved to have made it, albeit without any dinner, back in time to park alongside our clip-on tent rather than outside on the street. And that's when we found a German family had ignored the entire empty space of the field and parked their motor-home *right next* to our awning, so we couldn't re-attach Penny. They'd apparently gone to bed. We had to walk around them to get from our van to our tent. And it was raining.

My earlier promise to myself had lasted almost two whole hours.

The 5am monkey-house alarm call was louder and more alarming than ever. I reasoned that the angry screams echoing from beyond the zoo wall were because, like me, the monkeys had woken to realise they were in Rotterdam. After affording them a moment's pity I sprang up to find the driving rain of last night had cleared to a mere persistent drizzle. Progress!

'I can't believe the very first time we use the awning it has to go away wet,' remarked Jill as we wrestled huge folds of slimy, clingy nylon into a muddy bag. The large clip-on frame tent is technically called an awning and it boasted a 'quick-erect' system. You can imagine how many jokes that provided.

'What, even in the cold?' friends would quip. 'Who makes it? Viagra?' I'd heard 'em all. The truth about the quickness of the erection was that even with its multitude of built-in hinges, clips and poles, the humungous marquee was still almost twice the size of the van and needed pegging down, a ground sheet pegging inside it, bedrooms (yes, two of them) installing and a multitude of zips, guy ropes and Velcro dealing with. It's an hour's work to get it up. And you'll never see *that* phrase on a pack of Viagra. Packing it away took about 40 minutes, the culmination of which was gathering all the various rolls of (wet) plastic, nylon, bits of string, poles and everything else that looked like it belonged, zipping it into what can best be described as a body bag for a very short, very fat corpse, and attempting to lift this on to the roof of the van.

In front of her pop-top roof that lifts up to provide extra headroom and a double bed, Penny has a roof well above the front seats – a small trough in which to stow luggage. It's about two metres off the ground, so is ideal for use by travelling professional shot-putters, or Highland caber tossers. For mere mortals such as you and me, here is how to use it: you must perform a precarious circus act involving balancing one foot on the edge of the open door frame (I suppose that would be the 'wheel arch' if you want to get technical) while calling for a beautiful assistant (or a muddy one) to hand you the body bag. Then, with one arm clinging to the roof, as the drum rolls and the crowd gasps, you twist towards the side of the van while the free arm hoists the dead weight majestically skywards.

The bag will fall well short of the roof, because you're not Iron Man. Some onlookers might sigh disappointedly at this point, and a small whimper from you is acceptable. This is where your beautiful (and slightly fed up) assistant rushes to your aid and pushes the midget corpse with all their might from below. Congratulations! With your combined efforts and much grunting and sweating, the awning will soon be located in the roof well, with only some minor bruising and a festering chronic spinal injury to show for it.

Already I was starting to question the wisdom of paying for my quick erection. I wondered how many other men had had the same regret.

There must come a time in every travel book when the author writes a line and thinks 'Boy, *that'll* go on the back cover!' This is not one of them: We left Rotterdam in the rain, destination Belgium.

It was while leaving Holland that we had our first encounter with a VW enthusiast. Penny had been getting quite a few admiring glances, but while we were sitting in a burger joint, allowing ourselves an unhealthy lunch to the usual chimes of 'We can't keep eating fast food all year' from Jill, I noticed a Viking circling the van. Despite being on the mature side of 60, he was every inch the Nordic warrior

– 6 feet tall, weathered face and a huge white moustache. He wore a baseball cap, because obviously a helmet with horns would bring unwanted attention, and he was poring over Penny's every detail, explaining them to his friend, a much shorter, less warrior-like fellow. He noticed me watching him and came striding towards us. Apparently no introduction was necessary.

'Is the engine a 401 or a 404?' he asked. I didn't know what he was talking about. I'd been invaded, I'd been caught off guard and I'd been found wanting. It was ninth century York all over again.

'Sorry,' he went on, 'I'm Gerrit. I used to build these vans.' His moustache stretched to reveal a wide, gleaming smile. He went on to explain that he'd been part of Holland's own *Air Cooled* club back in the 80s and had a business maintaining VW campers.

'Back then,' he said, 'you could run a business from the pavement. Everyone was doing it. Then they brought in laws, none of us could afford proper garages and the whole community disappeared.' His wistful nostalgia was something we would get used to. Penny had a habit of bringing that out in a person. I told him what I knew of her, that she was German and that VW had replaced her original engine with a 1.6 turbo diesel a few years ago. He nodded approvingly, then said the words we longed to hear. 'Keep her maintained, don't work the engine too hard, and she'll get you round the world no problem.'

And with that, Gerrit the Viking and his little friend bade us farewell, and strolled away to ponder why his ancestors could conquer whole lands and yet he wasn't even allowed to conquer a patch of pavement.

The first border crossing of our epic quest, entering Belgium from Holland, was utterly unremarkable, in many ways setting the tone for what was to come from the home of waffles and chocolate. The border crossing huts still exist, standing vacant, tatty and wrapped in weeds on either side of the super-smooth motorway that now sweeps south from The Netherlands. They're a tantalising remnant of what life must have been like before the European Union. As we sailed effortlessly past I remembered that my grandparents had once come to Belgium before I was born in 1970, a fact I only knew because as a toddler I'd been hysterically amused by a tiny Mannequin Pis ornament my grandad had bought there. It miraculously filled a glass potty with 'wee' when you held it in your hand. Hilarious. It was easy to imagine queues of 1960s cars, their passengers all dressed like my grandparents used to dress, waiting to show those huge old black passports to allow them to do what we had just done in the blink of an eye.

In making that small 'unremarkable' dig at Belgium just now, I don't feel entirely unqualified. I've visited the country several times and have a good friend who lives there. So, in the name of balance, let's first agree that Bruges is beautiful. Although, as a well-travelled friend once said to me, Bruges would be vastly improved if it wasn't so perfect.

'You long to see a prostitute leaning on a lamppost from time to time,' he sighed, and if you've been there you'll know what he means. It's a little bit Disney.

But on this journey we were heading straight for the capital, the European Capital, no less, to meet Edie's Godfather Simon and his family in Brussels. It turned out, by sheer luck, to be the perfect time to see the city as our visit coincided with the biannual Flower Carpet in the Grande Place. I don't find much to rave about in Brussels, but the Grande Place is stunning, and seeing its central square covered in an ornately designed carpet of flowers was impressive. After five minutes, of course, you've seen it and it's time to walk out to the unremarkable road junction on which stands the hugely *un*impressive statue of a urinating boy that somehow became the emblem for the city.

'I won't take visiting friends to see the Mannequin Pis,' Simon told us later. 'It's just too embarrassing. I can't bear to see their disappointment.'

The national icon for the European Capital is fantastically rubbish. The dirty statue is only a few feet tall, stands in a poky corner behind rusty railings, half obscured by a road sign. 'Girls,' I announced. 'If all goes well, in the next year you'll see the Taj Mahal, the Sydney Opera House, the Golden Gate Bridge and the Statue of Liberty. All of those are icons not just of a nation, but of a continent. Behold, as Europeans, this is ours.'

A gloomy silence fell upon us as we watched a crowd of Japanese tourists snap away, attempting countless angles of photography, only to review the pictures on their screens and shake their heads. It was always going to look a bit crap.

'I was actually really excited about seeing the little boy doing a wee, but now I'm here ...' Edie trailed off, lost for words, and possibly the will to live.

Simon was quite vocal about 'things Brussels got wrong', speaking with the infuriating passion you only get when you live in a place. 'You know they covered up the river?' he asked.

'They what?'

'It's true. That pedestrian shopping street you found. There's a river under there. What kind of city planner looks at a re-development proposal and thinks "Hmmm, a big river, I wonder how we could deal with that? We could build shops along the sides, we could build foot bridges over it, we could develop waterfront cafés ... or ... wait! We could slab over it and put a massive Next and H&M on top of it!" Brilliant.'

'To be fair, there is a River Island,' I pointed out.

By no means does Brussels have the exclusive award for Stupidest Planners, of course. My own home town of Banbury built a swanky new shopping mall on the side of a canal which included the dazzling idea of filling in a historic boat yard and turning it into a flower bed. Thankfully, a keen-eyed historian spotted the plans, started a campaign to save it, and it continues to be a profitable boat builder's yard. But it didn't stop the lobotomised planners building all the shops facing *away* from the canal. A stroll along the waterfront will now take you, not through the chairs and tables of chattering cafés, but past the overflowing industrial waste bins at the back of Next, Debenhams and all the rest. Genius.

But that's only Banbury. Who cares? Me and one or two others, and that's it. Brussels is big enough and important enough to know better. It's the seat of the European Parliament for goodness sake. Don't buy your city plan on eBay.

Our temporary home in Brussels was to be a campsite on the outskirts of the city in a place called Grimbergen. Despite its name, Grimbergen isn't grim at all. So neat and tidy are its roads and buildings, in fact, that as we cruised the well manicured streets Bethan got a bit spooked.

'This feels like the kind of town that lures you in, only to trap you for ever. We might never leave, or be heard of again,' she said.

It did feel a bit *Stepford Wives*. It was a vibe that permeated the campsite. I pulled up outside the reception hut, and popped in to find a stocky, angry looking man behind a counter. He was the owner, and checking in involved patiently listening to him berate the lack of respect people were showing his campsite these days, lecture me on how my children must respect the cleanliness of the showers by employing the squeegee to mop away the excess water after using them, and recall the tale of how when one man asked 'Isn't that what we're paying you for?' the owner gave him his money back and told him to find another campsite. Just yesterday, he went on, he had turned away a group of boys because of the way they wore their hair. I tried not to smirk. Clearly, respect was what this man demanded, and I was prepared to pay. I handed over my passport, agreed to a fee of €25 per night and returned to the van to drill the girls on the strict squeegee regime.

To his credit, we spent two nights on what I can confidently title The Cleanest Campsite On Earth. The washrooms looked like they'd never been used.

'Have you seen the toilets?' gushed Ella, running back to the van. 'They're so modern. It's like a film set!'

I don't think our own loos at home were ever as clean as the ones at Grimbergen campsite. We showered, we squeegied, we finally felt fresh again after the much grottier few days bog-bound in Rotterdam.

We spent a great afternoon with Simon and his family picnicking in the park and nattering. They asked the same questions we were getting used to.

'What are you most looking forward to?'

Syria seemed to be a popular answer.

'How will you do your schoolwork?'

Online, if we could ever find wi-fi, we moaned.

They showed the familiar sense of amazement at the notion that we could *ever* make it all the way around the world. On one hand, when people seemed completely flabbergasted that we were attempting such a journey, I thought, 'Yes, aren't we brave, fearless adventurers', or on the other hand I could think, 'Why are you amazed? Do you doubt we'll make it?' I suspect most people were thinking the latter, that we'd fail horribly and the next time they saw us we'd be on the TV news having been kidnapped on the border of Iraq or locked in a Syrian jail.

These suspicions were confirmed when, over a quiet beer later that evening Simon said, 'So, really, d'you think you're gonna do this?'

'Er, yeah. We *are* doing it,' I said, supping the frothy head on my pint.

'No seriously. I honestly can't imagine how you're going to make it. You'll have cash going out every day, and none coming in ... *for a year!*'

'Well, we're renting the house,' I reminded him, but he was delivering a message to which he'd clearly given some thought.

'Sim. If you run out of money, or time, and you don't get all the way round, don't see it as a failure, all right? It's OK to come home.'

I think I brushed it off at the time, hastily changing the subject to football, rugby or some other manly pastime, but those words stayed with me while I lay in the darkness of Grimbergen that night. It was the first time I'd actually considered that this might happen – we might *not* get round. Writing that now, I suspect you'll find that hard to believe, but it's true. A huge portion of what got this journey going was attributed to momentum, enthusiasm, and a blind faith that everything would be all right. We hadn't done a proper itinerary and we hadn't done a budget. We had a rough route planned and that was all. To say we'd done sums on the back of an envelope would be overstating it. We'd tossed a few numbers around in our heads and figured it was worth a shot. And here was a wake-up call, not from a doom-monger, but from a friend. I'd always trusted Simon's judgement. At that time he ran a TV channel, but when we first met he was my producer on Children's BBC. In short, he understood budgets and time-scales. It was his job.

I didn't sleep at all well that night.

'We'll be chasing the sun!' I'd confidently said many times when explaining our route around the world. 'Over a year without winter,' I would add with a smirk. And it should have been true, leaving England in the August heat, driving south east, all the way through the Middle East and then shipping to India, Thailand and Malaysia. We would then cross the equator to reach Australia at the end of January, the height of their summer, only to cross back into the northern hemisphere sometime around May, just as the Aussie summer was getting tired and the spring heat was arriving in the USA. It was foolproof.

'Chasing the sun, Daddy,' said Bethan, dryly, from the back of the van as we ploughed through driving rain into Northern France. I should have known that phrase would come back to haunt me.

'It *will* get hotter. It *has* to.'

'Yes but when?' asked Jill, equally fed up. 'India?'

Our destination was Arromanches, the town at the centre of the Normandy D-Day landings. A glance at the map showed that our route would also take us through the First World War battlefields of the Somme. I realised that, fresh on the heels of re-living Anne Frank's horrors, we might be in danger of over-egging the World War part of the girls' education, but what can you do? This stuff's too important simply to drive past, and those girls would just have to stand in that bleak rain-soaked First World War cemetery whether they liked it or not because one day they'd thank me. Once they'd got over their pneumonia and chest infections, obviously.

'At least we're driving south,' said Jill, looking forlornly skywards for a break in the clouds.

'Actually, I've got a bit of bad news there.'

We were in fact driving North West, precisely the *opposite* direction to that which our entire journey was meant to take. Even more depressing, when we looked at the map we realised that the French port of Caen was further south than we were.

'Do you realise,' said Jill with horror, 'that there are British holiday makers pouring off the ferry right now, yet to begin their drive, who are further south than us? And we've driven almost a thousand miles.'

I'll be honest, it was a low point. A low point only beaten that night, when we camped somewhere near Abbeville and decided the awning was just too much trouble for one night.

'We just need a small pop-up tent,' suggested Jill. 'We could either throw all the bags in it and all five of us sleep in the van, or we could spread out. You and I could have a night on our own.' Suddenly this seemed like a top-priority idea.

The French hypermarket we found didn't sell tents, so Ella suggested we improvise. 'Let's use the Beatnik Beatles sign. Pop it up into the goal shape, then drape a tarpaulin over it.'

A splendid idea, and with our bags stowed under our makeshift bivouac we settled in for a snug night in Penny's less-than-spacious accommodation. Jill and I were on the lower rock 'n' roll bed – the back seat laid flat - while Ella and Beth took the upstairs bed in the roof and Edie had her first night in the hammock bunk that snapped into place across the front cab. I'd only bought the bunk for emergencies.

'You'll hardly need it at all, Edie. It's just for those rare occasions when we're stranded somewhere and can't put the tent up.' She had given it her cautious approval. What none of us knew was how wide-of-the-mark my prediction would be.

It rained. A lot. Edie felt sick and got up, then came to sleep with us. The main sliding door was left ajar for ventilation - which meant hammering rain could find its way in while we snoozed. The tarpaulin contraption had not so much *shielded* the rain from the bags, but *funnelled* the rain on to them. We all woke damp, cross and tetchy. In a sullen mood we filled the van with wet stuff to carry further into Northern France's torrential weather and harboured our own private thoughts about whether ten days was too soon into the year to give up the whole debacle as a terrible idea and go home.

'This place is only famous for D-Day,' dismissed Edie after an hour in Arromanches.

Kids are hard to impress. Being at the centre of the biggest turning point in World War 2 just doesn't cut it. I could see her point though. By the time you've enjoyed your 'Liberation' pizza, 'Juin 6' ice cream and 'J Jour' candy floss, you might be sick of it all. Or just sick.

Behind the slightly gaudy seaside tourist tat, there's some great stuff in Arromanches, not least the remnants of the Mulberry artificial harbour - huge blocks of concrete out at sea, crooked reminders of Operation Overlord that constantly keep D-Day firmly stamped on the horizon. The museum was a bit uninspiring. It was a study of the complete operation to retake Northern France, military strategy and the like, rather than an attempt to evoke the emotion of those who took part. That was made up for in the 360° cinema at the top of the hill. A well made 20-minute film stitched footage from the June 6th landings with modern images of the area today, and followed the story through local towns and villages as paratroopers landed and French citizens were liberated - real *Saving Private Ryan* stuff. The kids particularly remember black and white archive footage of a soldier having his horribly wounded face stitched up among the rubble of a battle worn village. One soldier attempted to stem the flow of blood while a second attempted to stitch it up, unperturbed by the flies that kept landing on the cut. Nasty.

Back on the seafront Edie spent some of her pocket money on a football. 'But wouldn't a frisbee be so much more fun? And so much *flatter*?' I argued feebly, reluctantly accepting that I now had to find room in our cramped van for a large ball. Bethan felt very uneasy about playing on the beach.

'I'm not sure about this,' she said, chewing her lip.

'Oh come on Beth,' encouraged Ella. 'You're not *that* bad at footy!'

But Beth held back. Yes, she was rubbish at football, but that wasn't it.

'Hundreds, no *thousands* of men died here. Right here!' she proclaimed. 'It's like playing football on their grave.' The scene of so much bloodshed did suddenly seem an inappropriate place to kick a ball about. And as we all paused to consider her point, I did notice that the beach seemed uncommonly empty for a summer holiday resort.

'You're right. It is a bit weird,' said Jill.

'Hang on though,' I pitched in. 'Isn't this what all those blokes were fighting for? Isn't that the very reason those brave soldiers fought such improbable odds - so that children like you would be free to kick a ball? Or in your case, Bethan, miss it.' She smiled. After a short moment of contemplation, she agreed and her mood improved. Though not her game, sadly.

The next day after paying fleeting visits to rain-lashed Sword and Juno beaches we finally pointed Penny's nose *down* the map and headed for southern France. The journey to Italy would take us down France's West coast, via friends in Mortain, Saumort in the Vendée, Plassac near Bordeaux and then all the way across to the Alps. Staying with friends this early in the trip had once seemed like a strange idea. After all, wouldn't we be chomping at the bit to get on our great adventure? Well, no. We already felt so battered by the relentless rain of our first two weeks that any chance to sit in a warm house, take a hot shower and use a functioning washing machine felt like a Godsend. So much for the intrepid travellers. A whole fortnight in, and already hankering for a comfy bed.

We did camp for a couple of days in Brittany near La Baule where a mystical ball of fire appeared suspended in a curiously blue sky. For the first time since we left home, it felt like we were on holiday. We did all the classic family holiday activities - had a dip in the campsite pool, played on the beach, stood in a busy marketplace singing Beatles songs, you know the sort of thing. Guérande is a medieval town north of La Baule and we'd visited its bustling Saturday market many times on family holidays over the years. But never with this much trepidation. A conversation with Bethan had resulted in the decision to put The Rotterdam Experience firmly behind us and try a bit of busking once again, which is how we found ourselves carrying a large bag of instruments and a pop-up goal (sorry, professionally produced signage) around the town, scoping for a pitch.

This part of the process is more nerve-wracking than actually busking. You ask yourself 'Would *this* be a good spot? Or here, perhaps?' and your brain is shouting 'No, you idiot! None of these places make me want to stand up and start singing in front of all these people!' It's a challenging psychological battle. Eventually I settled on a wooden doorway outside a shop that was closed (so no one to upset there, then). As we cased it from a distance, umming and ahhing, a car drew up, from nowhere, and parked exactly where we were planning to stand. Thus began a hurried trend of market traders weaving their vehicles into the busy centre to de-rig their stalls. It was lunchtime. They were going home! If we didn't get a move on we'd miss the boat. Jill laughed as the car foiled our plans. Ella said 'It's a sign.' Next, I found the arched doorway of the central church. Acoustically brilliant ... until the bells started pealing.

'Honestly dad,' said Ella, 'how are you not seeing these signs?'

Undaunted, I found a third spot down the busiest pedestrian street leading off the square. We all agreed it was the perfect location ... and then Edie pointed out that a homeless man was begging there and she wasn't happy stealing his business.

'But next to him, we'll look great,' I suggested. No, we were moving on. Finally, the arched gateway in the city wall proved ideal.

We did our pre-arranged 'set'. Part of what had been bothering Bethan so much was the lack of structure – before she squeezed a single note out of that concertina she wanted a clear idea of what we would be doing. So it was agreed, *All You Need Is Love* ('cause everyone knows it and it's the one we know best), *Ob-La-Di* (because Beth had just learned it and really enjoyed it) and finally, if we've still got the enthusiasm, *All My Loving*.

From the moment we set up the sign we had some gathering interest. People paused, smiled and when we started singing, some even stopped and watched. Four people donated a Euro and we even got a round of applause. To call it a triumph might be a bit strong, but it was an important psychological victory, and considering we only did three songs, it was really rather splendid. Beth, especially, had enjoyed it. Phew!

As a reward, we treated ourselves to celebratory *gaufres*. There aren't many moments in life that can't be improved by a freshly made waffle.

As we progressed south through the Vendée Jill chose to drive for a while. She'd only had one go at the wheel of our left-hand drive van, and that was inside the large barn in Oxfordshire where Penny had been stored. Within a few minutes of guiding her down proper roads, we had a puncture. Jill, like the tyre, was deflated.

I, however, was gleeful and as we pulled on to a farm track I leapt at the opportunity to try out my new trolley jack. The trolley jack had been a controversial purchase, not owing to its cost (about £30) but because of its size.

'How come you can take a trolley jack but I can't take hair straighteners?' was the thrust of Jill's argument. Penny still had her original jack, which I'd wrapped in an old cloth and stuffed in a dark recess in the engine bay.

'Yer gonna need a trolley jack, Sim,' Blue, our mechanic, had advised. Blue ran a garage in the village we lived in near Banbury, and as Bodicote's finest spanner-swinger (alright, *only* spanner-swinger) shared a passion for T25 campers like ours and had been vital to our preparations. 'You'll need a trolley jack and a breaker-bar.' A breaker-bar is a 19mm socket for the wheel nuts mounted at the end of a long steel bar, providing huge leverage. 'If you've gotta flat in the middle of some slum, yer don't wanna be messin' around with that ol' VW jack. Yer wanna get the new wheel on pronto and get the bloody hell outta there.'

I'd nodded, sagely.

'And,' he added, 'the breaker-bar will be handy for fendin' off bandits while you're stranded.'

I was slightly alarmed at the thought of having to go head-to-head with bandits, especially if it came down to a tool-based spat. After all, I'd watched *Ross Kemp on Gangs* and had never once seen a gangster turn down a knife or a gun in favour of a Halfords voucher.

And so, some weeks later, here was my shiny chrome breaker-bar's debut. I unpacked the back of the van to access the hidden tool shelf above the engine compartment, lifted out the trolley jack and, reaching into the darkness, withdrew my Excalibur to present it, glinting in the sunlight. Jill watched in awe and wonder as I pumped the jack. The children gasped as Penny rose slowly off the road. Every 'crack' of each wheel nut under the magnificent torque of my silver weapon brought cheers and applause. Admittedly my memory might be embellishing the details a little, but speaking purely for myself, it was a beautiful moment.

Then the spell was broken. I removed her wounded wheel, rolled the spare one around, offered it up to the bolts and ... uh-oh. Penny was not high enough to accommodate the fully inflated spare. Further feverish pumping at the box-fresh jack ensued. I pumped, Penny jiggled. I cranked, she rocked. I sweated, she didn't budge. I swore a little under my breath.

'Everything all right?' asked Jill. 'How's that new trolley jack?'

'Brilliant,' I gasped. 'I, er, don't suppose you've seen a dirty old cloth bundle stuffed anywhere have you?'

The original rejected jack was drafted in, the sheepish and rather pointless trolley jack demoted to 'back-up safety jack' while 'old faithful' hoisted Penny high enough to get the spare wheel on. Job done, I repacked the tools, giving slightly more care to the old VW jack than I had afforded it before, and replaced the trolley jack with a look that I hope said 'hair straighteners would have been more use'.

By now we were all keen to get the adventure started. Even though we'd been on the road three weeks and driven over 1,000 miles, it all felt like a rehearsal for the big trip. Holland had felt like the first run through – a chance to try out the kit, realise how much of it didn't work, and get everything thoroughly soaked. France felt like the production meeting after the first run through – electrics were fixed, plumbing attended to and for a week or so it felt a lot like one of our regular family holidays. The comfort was welcome, but the itch to find adventure was growing stronger.

Buoyed up by our successful busk in Guérande, and by a riotous gig at our friends' farm in the Vendée (a private but rowdy affair to a house full of their mates that resulted in the UNICEF coffers being swelled by about 80 quid) we were ready to take on the world. Well, Italy.

After Bordeaux, with the Alps in our sights, it was time to head east. France is big. Clearly, it's not 'Australia big' or 'Alaska big', but it's easy to underestimate France's massive width. Bordeaux to the Italian border was what seasoned travellers would call a schlep. We wilted in 36°C heat as we drove through countless sun-baked villages devoid of human life, each one separated from the next by stretching fields of dead sunflowers. This became a two-day hit, and as we left our camping pitch next to a beautiful lake near Viam, west of Ussel, we all cheered as Penny's milometer clicked 2,000 miles since Liverpool. Then I turned on the sat-nav and the bubble burst. We'd originally decided to navigate our way around the world using maps, eschewing modern technology in favour of the 'old school' method of map reading, or, as it's more commonly known, arguing about which way up a piece of paper the size of a duvet should be.

But I had snuck in our sat-nav. It only had maps for Britain and France so would be useless after the Alps, but was invaluable for finding people's addresses while it worked. Beyond France, we didn't know anyone until we reached Australia, so had no addresses to find. It would be maps all the way and let the arguing commence.

On this morning though, I punched in the address of Jill's friend, John, in La Chambre, and the small screen informed us our journey time ahead was eight hours and 53 minutes. Through curiosity we re-entered the destination saying 'Yes' to toll roads which reduced the forecast time to four hours 30 minutes. OK – we would pay the tolls, but we all knew that four-and-a-half hours was complete poppycock. The sat-nav was basing its average time algorithm on something approaching an average car, in other words something that will travel at 70 to 80 miles per hour on a motorway. A sat-nav based on the velocity of a fully laden 21-year-old VW camper van should probably ignore satellite data and simply use a sundial.

A tedious slog of mind-numbing toll-charging motorway followed, and eight hours and 53 minutes later we arrived at John's place in La Chambre, a stone's throw from the Italian border. The scenery was stunning. I'd only ever been to the Alps in winter and it really doesn't do them justice. The winter blanket of snow, albeit beautiful in its own way, removes all the depth and detail from the mountains - the steep rocky inclines, thickly forested slopes, distant pockets of shining snow peeking from beneath high cloud. Everywhere we turned we were struck by ever more dramatic landscapes. I suddenly understood why summer walkers and climbers flock there in equal numbers to winter skiers. A washing machine and comfy beds for a night seemed minor bonuses next to the jaw-dropping land we had reached after our two-day slog. This was the first time we were awestruck by a new, previously unseen landscape. Suddenly, we were travelling!

'Of all the places we've seen so far,' said Ella, 'this is the one where I'd most like to live.'

It had started. We were already casing the planet for a new home and Ella had been the first to stick a flag in the ground. Of course, given that she'd just spent two long days on the road, she'd have plumped to live anywhere bigger than five square feet. That van can get pretty cramped.

The next morning we set off on what was the most impressive leg of our journey yet - across the Alps into Italy, destination: Turin, or Torino as the Italians know it. As I tentatively pointed Penny's nose towards the sky, climbing the first of many miles of twisty, precarious mountain roads, I had a sudden feeling of familiarity. Each hairpin turn, teetering on the edge of a drop to sure death – a stunningly picturesque death, but death none-the-less – seemed to ring a bell. Then it came to me. *The Italian Job* was filmed here!

The post heist getaway sees Michael Caine and his cohorts fling a coach loaded with gold bars around these very roads, ending in the greatest literal example of a cliff-hanger ending in movie history. I was explaining this classic final scene to the girls while Jill held her head in her hands and actually leaned over as if to try to stop us falling to a gruesome demise. At one point she yelped, only to be immediately echoed by a 'whoop whoop' from Edie sitting behind her.

'It's like a road they drive on *Top Gear*,' laughed Ella.

'I hate *Top Gear*!' shouted Jill.

The views were breathtaking and the only slightly disconcerting thing was that Penny seemed to be running hotter than normal. Very hot, in fact. We stopped to let her cool down a few times, and were a little perturbed to notice that she seemed to be belching a bit of black smoke behind her as we climbed. I got the impression she'd never been asked to do anything quite this strenuous before. Finally, after over an hour of crawling skywards we reached the plateau at a peak of about 2,000 metres above sea level and we could all stop holding our breath. She'd made it. We descended the steep twists into a new land, cheered as we passed the 'Italia' sign halfway down and while pausing once or twice to let the smell of burning brakes fade, we all agreed the old girl had coped admirably. And Penny had done well too. Yes, the vintage VW had had a hard day, got too hot and smoked a bit, but tomorrow she'd be fine.

Right?

(See what I did there? That was an actual cliff-hanger. It was no *Italian Job*, admittedly, but without half a ton of gold bullion and the services of Sir Michael, I did the best I could.)

Navigating Turin's ancient city's back streets using nothing more than a tourist street map meant that we rolled up to the youth hostel quite late. We hadn't booked. The girl on reception shook her teeth and sucked her head, or something like that, to indicate I was a fool for thinking I could swan in from nowhere and bag one of their esteemed family rooms. Seeing our plight though, she said she could accommodate us if we split up. Hostels, I learned, have strict rules on segregating the menfolk from the womenfolk. If you follow English cricket, I imagine it's much the same as being a member of the MCC.

So, men got the top floor, ladies the floor below. She looked at us and I could see her doing the maths. She had three beds free in a girls' dorm, and two in a men's. The solution was that Edie, being young and small enough to be classed an ickle girl, could share with me. The receptionist assured me that the two lads in our room were no trouble, and if I was happy to do that, we could stay. Jill, Ella and Beth would be in a six-bed dormitory with three French girls. Sorted.

To call it a learning experience would be diplomatic. It was fairly grim. Both camps were having their own night of torment. Jill insisted Edie and I share a bunk – literally, one bed. Yes, that left a free bed, but Jill was convinced a strange man would assault Edie unless she was sandwiched between me and a wall. And so, finding our room empty but for the possessions of two missing room-mates Edie and I opted for the bottom bed below the empty but bag-laden upper bunk near the door.

I can only assume that to increase the number of rentable beds the hostel owners had put our bunks in what had once been the sauna or the boiler room. We lay there in the darkness, still not having encountered our room-mates, dripping sweat and trying to avoid touching each other in a futile effort to keep cool. At around midnight I heard the door open. I lay perfectly still, eyes closed, a coiled spring, waiting as if on a hair trigger to leap into action should the forecast assault begin. Some minor shuffling of bags and clothes ended with the mystery room-mate climbing into the bunk above us. I relaxed. My breathing returned to normal after about an hour.

Suddenly, I was once again on high alert. The door latch woke me. The second man had returned to the dorm. I heard more shuffling in the darkness, and he left the room, presumably to go to the toilet. I stole the opportunity to find my phone and check the time. 2.43. *Quarter to three in the morning?!* I yelled in my head. *What are these people? Young, or something?* I heard him come in again and I must have drifted back to sleep by about 4. Oddly, when Edie and I woke up at 7, both the men had vanished without us noticing. I knew I hadn't imagined they'd been there, so obviously leapt to the only rational explanation for their early morning flit: we'd been robbed. However, a full check of wallet, phone, passport and a total of four fully functioning kidneys taught me to stop thinking the worst of people. We got up and went to meet the others for breakfast.

The girls' night had not been without drama. When they got to their room all three French girls were very much present ... and fast asleep in the dark. This meant Jill had to make beds (sheets get handed out at reception and you do the rest) by the dim light emitted from an iPod screen. Ella and Beth were too afraid to sleep alone so decided to 'top and tail' in one bunk. (Let's gloss over the question of why I was now paying for *two* unused beds). After a short time of silence, just as they were nodding off to sleep, Bethan had an involuntary leg movement resulting in her kicking Ella in the face, almost breaking her nose and causing fountains of blood to pour from it. I can only imagine the chaos that ensued, as they attempted to stem the flow, protect the sheets and find an escape route to the bathroom all by the light of a dim iPod and without waking three sleeping strangers.

Bruised, battered and deprived of sleep, we didn't feel very much like seasoned travellers next morning. Even Laurel and Hardy might have remembered to put a torch in their bag. We loaded the van with our rucksacks and decided to set off for Genoa, about two hours south of Turin on the coast, our spirits lifted by its alluring promise of an afternoon on the beach when we got there. As I turned the key, Penny seemed oddly reluctant to start. She'd never, *ever*, failed to start before. I turned the engine over a second time and after a few seconds she fired into life. We all exchanged a slightly worried glance. Ella looked almost tearful.

'Don't worry, darling, she's just a bit cold,' I reassured her. Then I remembered she wasn't tearful at all. She'd been kicked in the face and her eyes had been bloodshot all morning. My mistake.

We were out on the open road, driving south with the sun rising into a clear sky and an Italian pop station on the radio, chattering about the eventful nights we'd respectively had, when I noticed all was not well with Penny. Every now and then as we scooted along, there would be a blip in her power, a tiny lag that would vanish as quickly as it had appeared. More worryingly, it appeared to be getting worse.

By the time we reached Asti (of Spumanti wine fame) we all agreed she was definitely not herself. I was wracking my brain trying to diagnose the problem - she wasn't running hot, she wasn't emitting smoke, and when we parked she ticked over fine. It was almost as if she was 'choking' every now and again, suggesting it was a fuel problem.

Ella and Jill remembered that just before we'd got into Turin we'd stopped for fuel at a filling station where, before I could hop out of the van, an attendant had insisted I sit tight while he proceeded to fill Penny's tank. What glee we'd shared at this quaint, old world experience, completely new to the girls.

'It used to be like this in England,' we'd told them.

'Five quid it used to cost me to fill up my Yammy fizzer,' I reminisced.

'Your *what?*'

'It was a motorbike. Well, half motorbike, half hairdryer. The old man would come out of his hut opposite the Nag's Head in Wollaston and fill it up for me. I remember running out of fuel once and pushing the bike there. I was sweating and the old geezer, who'd never said more than two words to me before, said 'Heavy when they're empty, aren't they?' which I thought was quite a clever comment at the time, a bit like a riddle. What's heavy when it's empty?' The girls nodded.

'I almost regret telling him to sod off.'

They laughed. I hadn't really. I was a very polite teenage biker. Anyway, the theory Ella and Jill had, which I started to cling to, was that the Italian fuelmonger had put the more expensive 'Blue Diesel' in and maybe the mixture was messing up Penny's insides.

At this point, reader, I just have to step away from the computer for a moment and scream into a pillow.

Aahhh! That's better. The problem with Penny was in fact, so basic, so rudimentary and so ridiculously simple to fix that it physically pains me to recall the events that follow. However, I'm going to let you suffer. You'll have to wait to discover what that simple problem was. After all ... we did.

At a McDonalds on the edge of Asti (lovely town, by the way. Shut on a Sunday), we latched on to their free wi-fi and started to plan how we were going to communicate Penny's problem to an Italian mechanic. Using an online translator we started to cut and paste useful phrases on to a text document. For the sake of authenticity I shall paste the result below. As you'll see, what started as a sensible exercise soon became a fun game when Bethan took the laptop.

il motore perde il potere *(the engine loses power)*
intermittentemente *(intermittently)*
prego voi *(please will you)*
controlli il motore *(check the engine)*
quando premete l'acceleratore perde il potere *(when you press the accelerator it loses power)*
quanto ci vorrà? *(how long will it take?)*
quanto ha costato? *(how much will it cost?)*
QUANTO? *(HOW MUCH?)*
potete lo fate affatto più poco costoso *(can't you do it any cheaper?)*
come dormite alla notte? *(how do you sleep at night?)*
dovrei avvertire che io avete dato dei calci ieri sera alla mia sorella nel naso e gli avete reso il salasso. Può persino essere rotto. *(I should warn you I kicked my sister in the nose last night and made it bleed. It may even be broken.)*

We continued gingerly out of Asti towards Alessandria, because it looked on the map like a slightly bigger town, and therefore might have more garages to choose from. Also, it had a hostel, whereas Asti didn't, so if things got worse and the hours slipped by we could at least find a bed there. Ultimately, though, Genoa was still our goal.

But as the miles passed Penny just got sicker. We reached Alessandria and found that, when pootling around the town, she was OK, it was just when we tried to pick up speed that she died. And so we pootled. Our first task was to find the hostel. We roamed desolate back streets until we finally found, tucked in a corner behind a church, the daunting, medieval-prison-like facade of Ostello Santa Maria di Castello. I raised a response through the gateway intercom from a man who only spoke enough English to say 'No'. Nothing I said or asked got any other reply. If you've ever seen the slasher horror movie *Hostel*, believe me, at the sight of the massive wooden and steel doors you wouldn't even have pressed the buzzer. We were all quite relieved we couldn't stay there.

For an hour we coaxed Penny around the city looking for a hotel or a garage until, completely thwarted, we resolved to try to limp on to Genoa - a much bigger city with loads of campsites. It only took four miles to change our minds. Penny was refusing to play ball. Even the sight of an 'Autostrade' sign made her keel over. Maddeningly she would run fine, until you put your foot down. Then she'd rev with gusto before slowly getting weaker and weaker until she simply stopped. We'd passed an out-of-town hotel called Hotel Marengo, which sounds like it should feature in a Barry Manilow song, and to the rhythm of my mind's rendition of *Copa Cobana* I gently teased Penny back there. We made our first use of the Emergency Credit Card and checked in, our sadness at our misfortune tempered by the comforts of four-star luxury for a night.

Tomorrow, surely, we'd be on our way.

I've always loved the word 'turbo'. It reminds me of being a kid, because in the 1980s everything cool had a turbo. Not just cars, *everything*. It was the decade of power and excess, but only rich City traders or Formula 1 drivers had an *actual* turbo they could talk about. In my world, our family car was a Skoda (back when they were built from Eastern Bloc biscuit tins and were the punch-line to a thousand jokes) and turbo was an 'it' word, a five-letter zeitgeist that advertisers employed to sell stuff. Toy cars became Turbo Racers, vacuum cleaners bragged about 'turbo performance' and I'm pretty sure you could even get a turbo themed crisp.

My affection for its nostalgic allure was dented by a phone call from Alessandria's VW dealership, where I'd delivered Penny after three other garages had all turned me away. Here, Penny's poorliness had been diagnosed as a troublesome turbo. The fact she even *had* a turbo was distinctly at odds with her performance. You'd be forgiven for envisaging flames down her sides and an appointment to take on all-comers at Santa Pod Raceway, but in fact she was just a very pedestrian old lady, who happened to have a turbo. It's a bit like discovering your grandma has a pair of roller-blades. It's not something you'd brag about and it's almost certain to end in tears.

Since the moment we'd checked into our hotel I'd used the wi-fi to slavishly trawl the world's VW forums, and through various frantic emails and Vee Dub blog postings, I discovered Penny's engine - a VW 1.6 turbo diesel (a JX engine in Vee Dub parlance) - is useless without its turbo. It's more than just an 80s word to make it sound cool. Worse, I also learned that the turbos are no longer made. I cursed Alessandria's lack of any small mechanical workshop like our own small and friendly T&P Motors back in Bodicote, where I felt sure Blue would have had her fixed in a day or two.

I'd walked into the sleek, air-conditioned showroom of Zentrum Alessandria that morning, aiming a smile at the smartly-suited salesmen despite my sinking heart. There was no way these people would look at Penny. They had top spec executive über-rockets to sell. Then, as I was trying to explain my plight to a man who spoke no English, a stroke of luck walked through the door. Her name was Maria. She was stylish, tanned and chattering fluently to another colleague as they entered. He guided her over to me, where she exchanged some Italian with the bemused man I'd accosted, then turned to me and said, 'D'yer speak English?' in the most welcome Lancashire accent I've ever heard.

'Where are you from?' I asked with a grin.

'Burnley,' she smiled.

'I know Burnley! I spent a lot of my childhood in Padiham!'

We were away. Lost and stranded in a city where English was rarely spoken, I'd found a friend. She was born in Burnley but moved to Italy when she was 17, she commuted to work from Asti, had a long-term boyfriend in London and was my saviour.

'We'll 'elp yer, love,' she said, after I'd explained my woes, and with that the staff were all smiles. They arranged a lift for me back to the hotel and said they'd call when they'd looked at Penny. We spent the day using the hotel's wi-fi to do emailing, skyping and, much to the girls' horror, schoolwork. At about 3 o'clock, the phone rang. It was Maria, sounding a lot less chirpy. She broke the news of the 'torbo' as they called it and said they couldn't get the part because it was too old.

I sensed that, between the lines, she was saying 'That's all we can do'. I knew what a wilderness it was out there searching for mechanical help, and wasn't prepared to let this contact go.

'What if I got the part?' I asked hastily. 'Could your guys fit it?' She said they could, if it was exactly the same, and better still they were happy for me to leave the van safely locked in their secure car park. I didn't feel I could ask if we could camp in there too. We rushed a plan together. This was, undoubtedly, a blow. I'd hoped they would repair a gasket and we'd be on our way. A broken turbo was more costly, but also vastly more time-consuming to fix, which meant we had to find somewhere to stay. I felt my wallet wince.

First, I got a cab to Alessandria's only car hire company who furnished me with their cheapest car for a couple of days (a Skoda, which I noted had improved a lot since the 80s), then went to speak face-to-face with the VW mechanics who'd agreed to do the work. They made grumbling noises about the possibility of breaking the exhaust when they removed it but I could tell they were simply looking for reasons not to do it. Just like major dealerships the world over, they survive on new car sales and service contracts. Beyond changing the oil and spark plugs, they go to the laptop. A computer diagnoses everything and entire systems are replaced, rather than one fault repaired. The thought of one of their beautifully manicured mechanics having to physically undo some rusty turbo bolts on a 21-year-old van and make a new one fit in its place seemed abhorrent to them.

Even worse, Maria was off for the rest of the week - my only ally was flying back to London. 'Don't suppose you can pick up a reconditioned turbo for me?' I asked. She laughed. I was on my own.

We downscaled from four-star comfort to Alessandria's only campsite five kilometres outside the city, all slept in the awning, and with the enormous help of a Vee Dub collective back in the UK consisting of three vintage VW owners - mechanic Blue, my brother Gav and friend Sam - I sourced a newly reconditioned turbo. It would take five days to arrive, and so we spent a happy hour crunching numbers with the kids. It may not have been the kind of maths they'd have done in school, but it was very real-world logistical problem solving. The upshot was that the very cheapest way of us staying in Alessandria for the next week was to ditch the hire car and stay in the city centre. Not at a hotel, of course. We'd researched all of those. No, we would be checking in at ... Go on, guess. That's right. Ostello Santa Maria di Castello! The medieval-prison-scary-horror-movie hostel we'd been so relieved to have avoided days earlier.

Well, the fact that you're reading this book tells you that we weren't captured for use in a sadistic deadly game for the basis of a flimsy horror movie sequel. Surprisingly, behind its foreboding exterior, Alessandria's only youth hostel hides a quadrangle of arches, above which are wide light corridors with huge rooms going off them. An 'oasis of calm' might be how a guidebook would describe it, completely at odds with its façade. The family room had six beds, its own en suite (plush for a hostel) and even a little area with a sink for prepping food. It wasn't cheap at €87.50 a night, but it was the cheapest way of us staying in Alessandria, so we just had to hope the repair would happen sooner rather than later.

When you've spent two years of your life planning, preparing and building up to travelling around the world, it's very difficult suddenly to stand still. By day five in Alessandria we were bored, frustrated and depressed. We read books, we did schoolwork, we played cards. That makes it sound like we were in prison. 'But you were in an Italian city!' you might cry. 'How could you be bored?' The crucial, crippling fact of our being stranded was that it was costing us far more to stand still than to travel. Without the ability to camp, the accommodation costs alone were three times our daily budget. To compensate, all other spending was reined in and limited to essentials only. This did not run to hot meals. We'd lost our cooker (locked up at VW) and with no kitchen facilities at the hostel, not even the means to heat a pan or boil a kettle, we lived on salad, bread, cheese and cold meat. I like basil and sun dried tomatoes as much as the next man, and an antipasti diet may sound enchanting for a day or two. Try it for a week or more. You start to resent walking past restaurants. You hate pizza parlours, for tempting you with their fresh dough aromas. You look at family members and, as if in a cartoon, see a roasted chicken.

We were all in too foul a mood to busk, but in an attempt to make some constructive use of our time, and re-invigorate our enthusiasm for our own story, I tracked down the number of the local newspaper, *Il Piccolo*, hoping to set their next edition alight with the story of 'international fundraisers stranded in Alessandria', and 'Beatnik-mania gripping shoppers in city centre'. We even rescued the instruments from the van and bashed through some new material trying to seriously add some swing to the waltz of *She's Leaving Home*. I found a phone box and called the newspaper.

'Piccolo,' said a gruff voice.

'Hello. Do you speak English?' I asked.

'No.'

'But I've got a story!'

'Story?'

'*Si, si*! A story! For newsroom?'

I don't know what he said next, but it was rapid, Italian, and sounded a bit cross.

'English?' I asked feebly.

'No English.' Click.

And that was that. We hadn't even left our own continent and already the language barrier was enormous. We were sitting in the Lavanderia waiting for two loads of mixed cottons to finish when my phone rang. A very happy man from the VW garage said something about '*arriva torbo*' and Handel's *Hallelujah Chorus* burst from the heavens. He passed the phone to the only other person there with a shred of English who explained that the part I'd ordered had arrived and they would try to fix Penny next week.

'I would *love* you if you could do it on Monday,' I gushed. 'We are *desperate* to leave. No offence. It's a lovely town.' She laughed. Then there was an awkward pause. She hadn't understood a word of what I said.

Monday came and went. No one at the garage seemed very keen to explain when Penny would get repaired. More than a week had passed since we'd limped our poorly van into this city, and a strange thing started to happen. Like Bill Murray in the film *Groundhog Day* who hated Punxsutawney until he was stuck there for long enough to appreciate it, almost without noticing it I gradually started to feel the rhythm of Alessandria. Catching a bus in Alessandria? Don't expect to purchase a ticket from the driver. Don't even look for a conductor. 'An automated machine?' you might think. No, in Alessandria, you can't buy a bus ticket on a bus. You'll be asked to disembark. *Tobacconists* sell bus tickets. Obviously.

The fact that Alessandria had more tattoo parlours than hotels would once have irked me, but after eight or nine days there - who needs sleep? Ink me up! This strange place was weaving its spell on me. I'd wasted hours in the early days searching for a supermarket. A pointless waste of time. Here, they survive on *supermercadi*, little independent back street shops that shut for a three-and-a-half-hour lunch break and only seem to exist for the sole purpose of transporting you back to the 1970s. Bendy white Formica shelves hold an apparently random collection of objects from which you'll struggle to make a meal. You're as likely to find bed linen next to bread rolls and cat litter with the breakfast cereal. I hadn't shaved for a week when Edie eventually spotted a razor for me. A lone Gillette was on sale alongside tobacco pipes and sports trophies. A week earlier, that would have seemed absurd, but not now. *Now* I'd had Alessandria's logic ground(hogged) into me. Obviously that was the shelf for blokes.

After all, what self-respecting male, when replacing his razor, wouldn't also consider a pipe upgrade, and be tempted to award himself a plastic golden trophy for his quick thinking? I can only assume, therefore, that somewhere there was another shelf on which you'd find knitting patterns, sanitary towels and the Italian version of *Heat* magazine. (*Scorchio*, presumably).

As the days passed, calls to the VW garage got more frustrating. Even the intervention of an Italian speaking friend of a friend back home failed to establish any more than a grudging 'maybe tomorrow' from the garage. As our stay passed ten days I took the plunge and paid a cab to drive me over to the garage. My pleasure at seeing that our Burnley-born translator Maria had returned was short-lived. She translated the news that they were now planning on looking at the van the following Monday because the mechanic who looked at old vehicles was on holiday. I sighed, gritted my teeth and tried very hard not to shake her by the lapels, shouting 'Why couldn't you have told us this last week, or even the week before? If we'd known our stay would have been *this* long we'd have got jobs, bought a house and put the kids in school!'

Our third weekend in Alessandria coincided with our wedding anniversary. Penny was due back on Monday (we hoped), and Saturday marked 16 years since we were married. (Jill and I, not Penny and I. We're close, me and the van, but not *that* close.) To mark the occasion in celebratory fashion we rented the cheap Skoda again and headed to Genoa, the coastal city billed as 'the jewel of Italy's Riviera' that boasts Christopher Columbus as one of its sons. He trained to be a navigator there - not a great boast as he mistook America for India, but they don't talk about that. We would eat *gelato*, soak up the sun and play on the beach. Our Genoa visit remains memorable for one incredible fact. I wonder if you can work out what all these things have in common:

- The accomplishment rewarded with the 'Level 2' yellow swimming badge
- How far your football goes from the penalty spot to the back of the net
- 14 Nicole Kidmans lying end to end
- How far Usain Bolt runs in just under two and a half seconds?

That's right, they're all 25 metres. We can now add to that list 'the entire length of free public beach at Genoa'.

The sea front at Genoa is a curious thing. They have, like most rich coastal towns (Cannes, La Baule, Bognor), a line of large hotels and posh houses facing the ocean. In front of them is the coastal road, cross that and you find a wide promenade for pedestrians. No surprises so far, but then - walk towards the wall so you can look down on to the beach and you see - not a beach, but a shanty town.

Rusty corrugated iron rectangles jam against corrugated asbestos ones. A hideous eyesore of higgledy-piggledy roofs stretches down, almost to the sea. Beneath them are the countless bars, clubs and restaurants that own their few feet of beach. We tried, at two different points a five-minute drive apart, to walk down the steps to the beach only to be stopped and asked for our ticket. If I wasn't a member, or hadn't booked a table, it would cost us €7 *each* for access to the sea. Both wizened old women (it's always leathery old ladies minding the gate) pointed to the 'free beach'.

When we found it, our faces dropped as we saw a stretch of rubble squeezed between two roped off private areas on either side. I was so aghast I simply had to pace it out - 25 metres. You couldn't stretch out on the sand - because there wasn't any, but also because it was so packed with people stretching out painfully on the stones. There were no toilets, no showers, no lifeguards, but wait! What's this I see just beyond the fence? There's a lifeguard, over there! Look, he's got a red top on with, oh, STAFF written on the back. He's employed by the bar next door. I wonder if he'd leap into action if one of us on the paupers' side of the fence started to drown? I never got the chance to find out because he actually spent most of his time standing in the breaking waves making sure no mucky plebs from the public area wandered into his patch. Honestly - he turned children back so they didn't sully the sea for his paying customers.

Despite the disappointing beach experience, we ate ice-cream, toasted our anniversary in a rather lacklustre pizza restaurant and returned to Alessandria buoyed up for our imminent departure. On Monday, I resolved to spend *all day* sitting in the open-plan swish reception area of Zentrum VW as a constant niggling reminder that they damn well better get on with fixing Penny otherwise - well - I'd be returning the next day.

Cluttering up their tidy reception area all morning, I was a curiosity to the staff. They had to close at lunchtime, of course, so they invited me to join them at a local canteen. The chat was in Italian, but with Maria's help I joined in a bit. I spent most of the time though, looking at my watch and wondering when the hell they'd get back to work. Apparently a 90-minute lunch break was the norm. Finally, at 4.30 in the afternoon, I was invited outside to view the shiny new turbo in situ. A mechanic drove Penny around the block and deemed her health fully restored. I paid the €280 labour bill (I'd bought the part, of course, from the UK for £500) and did a little sum in my head. The total cost of our breakdown, when I added up the repair and the increased accommodation bill, was around £2,000 – a major dent in our budget that would certainly have an effect down the line.

'I think we can wave goodbye to Thailand,' said Jill when we calculated the impact later.

'Well, let's see,' I said, knowing she was right. We both knew that shipping direct from India to Australia, skipping Thailand, would save one shipping route and five flight tickets. But at the same time I couldn't quite bring myself to admit that Thailand, Malaysia and Singapore would elude us. *Not because of a turbo! Not this way, please.* The first harsh realities of our ambitious global trek were coming home to roost.

Putting all such thoughts out of our minds, we left Alessandria on Tuesday morning to cheers, folk songs and a ticker-tape send off. Or at least that's how it felt in our heads. Thanks, Alessandria, for your maddening, frustrating and curious ways. We despised you, but we learned to love you. Not a lot, but just a bit. And thank *you* reader, for sticking with me through Chapter 4. If it's felt in any way long, tedious and pointless, it's given you just a glimpse of what the 16 days felt like for us.

Let's get on with our journey, shall we?

It was half an hour later that Penny broke down.

We'd chosen to head east towards Parma, and to take things *very* easy for Penny, even paying the toll to take the *autostrade* - no steep hills, no stopping and starting, just a steady 55mph all the way. And there were no dramas. Not until thirty two minutes into the journey, anyway. Even then, when I detected the first tiny power-lag, I kidded myself it was in my head. Then Jill noticed the next one. Perhaps we were imagining it. No. There it was again, the undeniable tiny lurch of the engine stuttering. After a further ten minutes the engine was losing power in *exactly* the same way we'd experienced when we'd been so soundly scuppered by the failed turbo.

'A second turbo can't go, surely,' I said. 'Impossible. It just can't.'

I knew where these symptoms were leading and didn't fancy being stranded on the *autostrade*, so exited somewhere near Pavia. As we coasted on to a rural back road, I pushed the clutch in and the engine died - just as it had before the repair. *Everything was the same.* And, just as before, I could re-start the engine and it ran fine. It was like living in a recurring nightmare, only we were all wide awake. Apparently our 16 days in Alessandria had been wasted.

I interrupted Blue's busy morning at T&P Motors and, with the entire contents of the boot unloaded to expose the engine bay, and with a phone clamped to my ear, I listened as he talked me through some basic fault finding. He severely doubted it was the turbo failing. And that's when I found it. A stream of air bubbles coursing through the transparent fuel pipe. All the hose clips were tight, no crack to be found, but that was undoubtedly the problem. I thanked Blue, loaded up the scattered bags and family members and coaxed Penny to a VW garage in Pavia.

If the dealership back in Alessandria was posh, Pavia was positively regal. It was one of those VW garages that also sells Audis and Porsches. Unlike the impenetrable frost of Zentrum, though, here we encountered a warm welcome from a very friendly man, Luigi, who insisted he should take a look at Penny immediately.

He waved us, still in the van, into the workshop interior, where to our horror we saw we were being ushered towards a parking space between two very shiny and expensive Porsches, on a glistening, white showroom floor. Poor Luigi had no idea that one of Penny's charming features was a persistent oil leak from her rear end. Picture the faces on the gathering staff and customers as we piled out of the van and three blonde girls leapt into action with a packet of Wet Wipes to start mopping up our embarrassing gloopy black trail of shame.

'Stop! Stop! Iss fine,' called Luidi, laughing. 'We have someone take care of that.'

Luigi had the rugged, stubbly appearance of Hugh Laurie as Doctor House, and the girls got a bit giddy around him. All four of them. All he lacked was a limp and a team of young hot-shots in white coats with whom he could diagnose the mystery ailment after a few dead ends and wry witticisms. In fact, he had a smaller, fatter stubbly friend in blue overalls and they diagnosed the illness in five minutes: a blocked fuel filter. They showed me the thick brown gunk inside to prove it.

It had been new before we left England, so was just over two thousand miles old, but here's the diagnosis, as theorised by Luigi and seconded by Blue (joining in the debate on the phone). The fuel tank is old, it has lots of dirt in it. Italian diesel is, compared to what we're used to in the UK, a bit rough. So much so, in fact, that Italian truckers make it the norm to use more than one fuel filter to stop their engines clogging. The dirty fuel blocks the filter, the fuel pump sucks madly but can't get any fuel, so inevitably tiny air bubbles will be pulled in from somewhere in the system because the pump is causing a vacuum. Thus, air bubbles in the fuel pipe, engine able to tick over but dying when I put my foot down. According to Luigi, the only long-term solution was to replace the tank, but with regular filter changes and a careful eye on keeping the tank topped up above half full, we should be fine. Blue concurred, adding the fact that with the van sitting still for the last two weeks all the rubbish in the diesel will have had time to settle which is why we got 20 minutes into our drive away from Alessandria before she started coughing, once the tank had been sloshed around.

While we were all relieved to see Penny well again at a cost of just €50, and now empowered with the knowledge of how to fix the problem should it happen again (always carry a spare filter), you can guess the topic of conversation we quickly moved on to …

'So. Let me get this right,' said Jill to Luigi, with slow deliberation. 'It wasn't the turbo. We may have replaced a perfectly good turbo.' Luigi shrugged, not wanting to be drawn.

'What do you think Luigi, honestly?' I asked him. 'Would these exact same symptoms happen if the turbo failed?' He thought for a moment.

'No. I don't think it was ever the turbo.'

'Blue?' I said into the handset.

'Sim, if your turbo had gone you wouldn't have seen the road behind you. You'd have had more smoke coming out the back end than the Red Arrows.'

We thanked them all profusely and took to the road, our joy at being mobile highly tempered by the seething fury that Zentrum had misdiagnosed a problem as cheap and quick to spot as a blocked fuel filter for a two-week repair that had dented our pockets to the tune of two grand.

It put us in a tricky position. We quickly agreed the very last thing we wanted to do was return to Alessandria to take issue with them. We all wanted to get the hell away from there as quickly as our 55mph top speed could take us. It would be a battle to convince Zentrum they owed us some recompense.

'The thing is,' I complained to anyone who was still listening, 'at home, I relish these fights for justice. I'd get my teeth into this and make their lives a misery until they'd made amends for their cock-up.'

'We know,' said someone from the back.

'But while travelling? And in a foreign language? My heart sinks at the thought of it.' I sighed. 'I'll call them tomorrow.'

I'll summarise the outcome, dear reader, so we can both move on with our lives. Many weeks later the company I'd posted the old turbo back to, as part of their exchange programme, confirmed that there was no damage. It had been fine. A barrage of emails to Zentrum escalating in tone from friendly to 'I'm copying my lawyer in on this,' each in both Italian and English, and copied to branch and regional managers, gleaned no response whatsoever. After all, what did they care? They had their cash and I was hundreds of miles away and getting further. We were forced to consider it all part of the experience of driving around the world. I'm over it. No, really, I'm fine about it. My therapist says so. Let us never speak of the nasty incompetent garage again.

Whether you believe in God, or Karma, evidence for both was on the horizon.

We drove away from Pavia, cautiously paranoid that Penny was on the verge of collapse, anxiously waiting for another stutter, another random loss of power at full speed. But, of course, she was fine - completely cured. We made Piacenza our destination and started keeping an eye out for campsites. After an hour of approaching the city, touring the city, and then leaving the city without seeing a single sign bearing a tent, it started to occur to us that for the first time on this trip we may be forced to do some guerrilla camping - in other words, sleeping for free.

I'm sure there's a proper word for this, like when they call the posh tents at music festivals 'glamping', from the words 'glamorous camping'. I'd love to merge 'guerrilla camping' or 'gratis camping' to form 'gramping', despite it sounding like a naughty game teenagers might play – you know, sneaking up and goosing old grandads. As in, 'I'm bored, let's go out gramping.'

Police said Stanley Timmins, 70, was the victim of a drive-by gramping. 'They came from nowhere,' said the plucky pensioner. 'I didn't see them coming. But I certainly felt them. It's just not right.'

I coined the phrase 'framping' from 'free camping' for a while, until, lured by the egotistical notion that I may have actually invented a word, I Googled it. Unless some distinctly unsavoury and lewd pastimes are your bag, I'd advise against it. Take it from me, I've done the research. It'll save a lot of embarrassment all round if we stick to gramping. (And that's a sentence I never thought I'd write).

So, as we scoured suburban wastelands and remote farm tracks in the fading light, hoping to do some gramping, I remembered that in France they quite often provide free camper van car parks near ancient abbeys and other significant tourist attractions. Italy also has these car parks - we just couldn't find one. So we headed for a castle that was signposted, like a tourist attraction, and it took us mile after mile into the countryside until we'd all but given up on it. Dusk was upon us by the time we tracked it down, not really a castle at all, more a fortified courtyard that was now a private house. Next to it, however, was a church which had a rather attractive, secluded parking area at its rear.

'My dad's a vicar,' I told Penny, as I nudged her up on to the grass behind the building, far enough away from the road not to draw too much attention. 'So we're semi-qualified to be here.'

Within half an hour we'd made ourselves at home. The little two-man tent was up, and given the choice between inflating the airbed and enjoying a night on our own in the tent or simply throwing all the bags in it and sleeping in the van with the girls, Jill and I took the easy option and flung the bags inside. Ella got all the beds in the van ready, Velcro-ed the mosquito nets up and we were, after almost three weeks in this country, *finally* eating some home cooked fresh pasta. A bottle of wine was opened and spirits were high as darkness descended and we sat out under the stars polishing off the last of our supper. For the first time in what felt like weeks, we relaxed. There was no chance of us being disturbed at this most remote of locations at 9pm on a Tuesday evening. We were all alone. Bats flitted overhead. A large owl swept through the trees. A car drew up on the road next to the church. Someone got out and we heard its central locking blip.

Oh. Not *entirely* alone, then. Assuming you've read the gripping first page of this book, you'll know what happened next. Lights went on in the church. We skulked in the shadows. Jill got tense. The kids got scared.

'Go and talk to them,' instructed Jill.

'What?'

'Go in and ask if it's OK to stay here.'

'Why? That just gives them the opportunity to say "no". Why invite it? Much harder for them to come to us. Just sit tight. He'll be gone in a minute.'

An icy stalemate.

Suddenly we were bathed in light. Another car, no *two* cars, swept into the car park.

'OK,' I conceded. 'This is not what we planned.'

Rather embarrassingly, the new arrivals parked on the gravel just a few feet from us.

'Either you go and talk to them,' spat Jill in a furious whisper, 'or we're packing and leaving. Those are your choices.'

Car doors opened, headlights were extinguished, heavy feet hit gravel. Slam! Slam, went the doors in the darkness.

It was show time.

I took a deep breath and walked towards the dark silhouettes who were now reaching into the boot of one of the cars. In the dim light, cast from the lofty stained glass window, I clearly saw the unmistakable shape of a large violin case being pulled from the boot. I hung back, stalled by the realisation of what I was seeing. Either the contents of that case were meant for me, or worse, I'd stumbled into *someone else's* mafia hit. For a fleeting moment I remembered the 'breaker-bar and the bandit' scenario Blue had prepared me for, and cursed the stupidity of packing my tools away so tidily and inaccessibly.

Then the voices hit me. A gruff Italian-American accent growling, 'Tony's brought disrespect on the family name,' is what I half expected to hear. In fact, it was a group of ladies getting out of the car, chatting happily. If this was the hit squad, they'd turned it into a social occasion and were making a night of it. How very Italian. I stepped closer, into the light, and their faces turned to see me. Using the lightning-fast observation skills you only discover when in mortal danger, I quickly ascertained that there was a group of five young women, casually dressed, none of whom appeared to be 'packing' a gun, plus one young man who was holding what I now realised was in fact a guitar case. I smiled and used my trusty opener in these parts. 'Does any of you speak English?'

'*Si*, a little,' said one of the girls.

'I just wanted to check we're not in your way,' I said rather feebly. 'What's happening here?'

'We're rehearsing tonight, for a wedding. We're the choir.'

'And the band,' chipped in the man with the guitar.

Unbelievable I thought. *Of all the churches - nine o'clock on a Tuesday evening.* I tried to explain what we were doing there, which sounded pretty flimsy next to the rock solid reason of a wedding rehearsal. They smiled and one of the women said they hoped not to disturb us. I don't think she was being sarcastic. Then the man asked where we were from.

'We're from England,' I explained. 'We're driving around the world.' This always gets a reaction, and it stopped them in their tracks for a beat.

'Really? And you stopped here?'

'Well, we ran out of daylight and couldn't find a campsite. Actually, we're musicians too,' I half lied, and cheekily added that we'd love to listen to their rehearsal. They were delighted with the idea, so I hurried back to Jill and the girls who were still cowering in the shadows waiting for gunfire.

'Grab a blanket each. Don't worry about getting dressed. We're going to church.'

'I don't think any of us expected him to say that,' said Ella.

I hastily explained what was happening and moments later there we were, walking into a church that was suddenly bustling with people, our kids in their pyjamas, wrapped in blankets and clutching various cuddly bears, looking like the first refugees to seek asylum via choral singing since the Von Trapps. I got waylaid at the door by an elderly woman who engaged me in conversation - quite a feat as I don't speak Italian - and by the time I squeezed my way into the hubbub of the church, Jill was introducing me to the groom.

'This is Stefano,' she said.

'Congratulations!' I beamed, shaking him by the hand.

'Stefano's a dentist, and his fiancée Federica is over there. She's invited us to stay for cake at the end.' How did she do it? I'd only been separated from Jill for a moment, and she'd nailed an introduction to the bride, the groom, ascertained his career and gained an invite to share cake, all in 30 seconds. Incredible.

And so we sat in a pew, a respectful distance from the front, while the choir of about thirty, accompanied by a keyboard, guitar (the friendly chap who wasn't an assassin) and occasionally Stefano on a second guitar, belted out contemporary hymns. The female choir master drilled them through some pretty impressive harmonies, the happy couple picked up on little changes and tweaks, and it was obvious from the banter that far from being a formal church choir, these were all friends of the couple. The atmosphere was great fun. Federica came over to say hello and when we reiterated how grateful we were that she'd let us listen, she told us it was an honour for them. Her English was brilliant - it turned out she was an English teacher - and after we'd heaped praise on the quality of the singing she scooted up to the front to deliver the review to Stefano and the choir. We kept getting smiles and thumbs up throughout the hour or so rehearsal.

While we waited for the final song to start, Stefano, who also spoke brilliant English, joked that it would be very frustrating for him at the wedding on Sunday because he enjoyed playing the guitar, but would be otherwise occupied in the rôle of groom. He'd played in a few bands, he explained, and then he said something incredible. 'I played in England recently with my band. Do you know the Cavern Club in Liverpool? I am a Beatles fan so to be able to play there was very special.' I must have looked stunned. The last time a dentist saw my eyes that wide was when I got the bill.

'Did Jill tell you what we're doing?' I asked. 'While we travel around the world?' He shrugged quizzically, and grinned in amazement when I explained our own Beatles quest. A rapid-fire conversation followed about Liverpool, Beatles songs, the ukulele, until he was called back to the choir for the last song. After the practice, we graciously accepted their invitation to mingle with their friends and eat the most delicious moist apple cake in the world (we're good like that, always going the extra mile), and then Stefano said, 'Will you be here tomorrow? You should come for dinner at my house. It would be a great pleasure.'

We looked at Federica, we looked at each other, we looked stunned. They didn't know us at all. If anything, we'd gatecrashed their special evening, and now we were being invited to dinner. 'I'll call my parents to check,' he added. *Dinner with his parents!*

'Are you sure?' I asked. 'There are five of us.'

'No problem, there are five of us too. I have two sisters. They would love to meet you.' *Dinner with his entire family!* 'It will just be lots of pizza,' he added, as if it was nothing to get excited about. *Authentic Italian pizza with an authentic Italian family!* But I looked at the bedraggled state of my family. Tempting though the offer was, this was clearly the moment, having camped in their car park, gatecrashed their wedding plans and eaten their cake, to do the decent thing and politely decline.

Jill stepped forward. 'We'd love to come.'

So, with arrangements made to rendezvous back at the church the following evening, we spent the entire Wednesday in preparation for our exciting dinner invitation. We needed to do some jobs. We needed to wash clothes, find wi-fi, and above all we needed to shower. The latter was solved with a visit to Piacenza's swimming pool where I had something of an altercation with the lady on reception. It was a trifling matter regarding a rule about hats. Namely, that they had allowed us to enter the pool and do just one single length before calling us out and telling us we needed to purchase compulsory rubber swimming hats. I refused, and pursued the obvious course of action: insisted everyone have a hot shower, wash their hair and change into clean clothes before demanding my money back.

As we drove away, fresh, clean and aglow with my 'free shower' victory, Jill said 'You know what'll happen, don't you?'

'Go on.'

'That woman you just argued with will turn out to be Stefano's mother.'

The girls gasped at the thought of it and my tummy lurched a little. Wouldn't that be about right? Everything did seem to be going a little *too* well. I was probably due one of my Larry David *Curb Your Enthusiasm* moments.

Our date arrived at 7.15 to collect us from the church. (Another line I'd never expected to write when recounting our journey). We followed Stefano and his sister Francesca back to the leafy suburbs on the other side of Piacenza. Washed, spruced and more than slightly nervous we were ushered into the smart modern house that was the Milani family home. Stefano introduced us to his parents, Franco, a fit, handsomely tanned fellow with sparkly blue eyes, and Manuela, taller, willowy with thick blonde hair and a wide smile. Most importantly, she was *not* the receptionist from the swimming pool.

They greeted us warmly and almost immediately we were seated at a cosy dining room table around which would squeeze 11 of us – we five, five Milanis and Federica, the bride to be. Despite Franco and Manuela claiming not to speak any English (I'm sure they understood more than they let on) all fears that conversation might be stilted were quickly dispelled as we immersed ourselves in the busy hubbub of a typical Italian dinnertime: people came and went, Stefano's second sister Chiara arrived, the phone rang several times, Manuela and Franco kept leaping up to tend the cooking - we ate *nine* pizzas! All home made, all different. As quick as we could slice one up and eat it, a new one would appear from the kitchen, with toppings like thinly sliced courgette and herbs, Gorgonzola, anchovy, prosciutto and more. We talked about UNICEF - Piacenza has a link with the charity - we talked about the journey, we talked about the wedding, we talked about the van.

'Where will you sleep tonight?' we were asked at one point. 'Why not leave Penny parked where she is? You don't have to drive all the way back to the churchyard. Have some wine.'

We talked about the girls' schoolwork, Francesca and Chiara both spoke English and were telling us about their college work, Ella and Beth drooled over Francesca's 1972 apple-green Vespa and envied the fact that in Italy you can ride a scooter aged 14. We talked about our jobs. 'Jill's a journalist for the BBC,' Stefano explained to his parents, which sparked an animated chat among the family.

'We have a friend who's also a journalist,' he explained. 'But unfortunately he's away working at the moment, otherwise he could have come over to meet you. He's won a Pulitzer Prize for his writing.' We nodded our appreciation to Franco and Manuela. I'd once won The Neat Dive competition in the cub-scouts swimming gala, but neither of us could compete with a *Pulitzer*.

In short, we had a great evening. There was talk of getting the instruments out of the van to do some Beatles songs, but we seemed to get distracted while we relaxed in their living room discussing the route our journey was to take. We explained how we had always planned on going down to Rome, then across to the east coast and up the other side, through Venice and down into Croatia.

'But now we're two weeks behind schedule we were thinking of going straight across the top,' said Jill.

'Why not go to Rome then get the ferry from Ancona to Split?' suggested Manuela.

That option hadn't occurred to us. It would save time, delivering us half way down Croatia's Dalmatian coast, so probably be roughly equal, time-wise, to driving over the top. Then a TV game show moment happened. We put the decision in their hands.

'You tell us,' I said. 'Rome or Venice - we can't do both'. A huge family debate ensued, with heated arguments for and against each choice. Franco's heart was in Venice but Manuela argued for the capital. Their children also appeared divided. Eventually, a winner emerged. We were going to Rome. Ruled out because of unforeseen circumstances, Venice was the first sacrifice from our original planned route. She certainly wouldn't be the last.

The kids were getting tired. I checked my watch – 10:15. *Time to be making tracks*, I thought.

'Now,' said Franco. 'Beatles!'

Apparently the night was still young.

Stefano helped me fetch all our instruments from the van and another Beatnik Beatles impromptu gig was under way. He joined in on the guitar and the entire family sang along. We were a bit rusty but I'd cajoled the girls into some band practice earlier in the afternoon so we held our own - just. After the sing-song Franco discreetly handed me a hefty donation to UNICEF, which, considering the generosity they'd already shown, was a fantastic gesture. But that wasn't all.

'My father has made some calls this evening,' Stefano explained. 'He is friends with the Mayor of Piacenza, and the politician who's in charge of UNICEF fundraising. Unfortunately the Mayor is in Rome tomorrow, but another senior politician would like to meet you to do a press conference.'

They'd let us crash their wedding preparations, invited us into their home, fed us endless amazing pizzas and now organised a press engagement for us in the morning. And all just days before their only son was getting married. Was there anything these people wouldn't do for us?

'You should sleep here tonight,' Chiara said. 'We have plenty of room at the top of the house.'

Oh heavens, they just won't stop. Speechless, I knew we couldn't impose ourselves any further on this incredible family. They had already done so much for us. Time for a dignified exit.

Then Jill said, 'Thank you. We'd love to stay.'

She'd done it again.

So, having dragged all our bedding from the van up to the Milani's attic room, we settled down on various beds and scattered mattresses, still stunned by this family's generosity. A voice came from the stairs. It was Stefano.

'Dad says you can use the wi-fi - there's no key, just help yourself.'

'Thank you!' we chorused in unison. Again.

There followed a family discussion about whether *we* would have been as generous if the boot were on the other foot. If *we* were planning an event as significant as a wedding at our church in Bodicote and we turned up on the Tuesday evening to rehearse, only to find an Italian camper van at the door, would we have welcomed them in? Possibly. Would we have invited them to dinner? We had to admit that that was unlikely. Would we have then insisted they stay the night? The truth that we almost certainly wouldn't left us all feeling more humble than a tiny mouse eating the last crumb from the floor of Horace Mumble's Humble Pie factory.

At the risk of sounding like the closing two minutes of a 1980s American sit-com, there was a real life lesson being learned in that attic room. Why were we so cagey? We were, as a family, and perhaps as a nation, naturally suspicious and it was as if a revealing spotlight of open-hearted generosity had highlighted how unsavoury that particular trait was. I knew as I lay in that attic that the events of that day had changed us, maybe not perceptively, but deep inside there had been a shift. Now, I suspect you're thinking, 'Wait 'til a bus reverses into you in Jordan, then we'll see how open-hearted your generosity is,' or 'How charitable and loving do you feel when someone mentions a broken turbo?' And you'd be right. It wouldn't be easy, but isn't the unquestioning generous nature of the Milanis inspiring? A tiny piece of my cynicism had been extinguished, and in its place was a shining lesson in not being so defensive, and negative, and automatically thinking the worst, but instead to embrace opportunity and have the courage to plunge into the unknown. What kind of person invites a random family to dinner, organises their lives for the next day then asks them to stay the night? The kind of person *I* wanted to be, that's who.

(Cue cheesy American closing theme-tune – probably played on a saxophone.)

The next morning we were Quirky English Family in a typically busy Italian breakfast scene. Dashing, cereal, rushing, *Ciao*, coffee, debate, 'Morning!' cookies, plans, work, goodbyes, good-lucks, kisses. It was a blur. The upshot of it all was that Franco had the day off and would escort us to the Piacenza City Hall to meet the councillor for our press conference. Francesca would duck out of her college commitments to join us in town as translator. With the van re-packed we drove into the city.

What happened next was so slick, none of us had a moment to stop and think, or even speak to each other about what was going on. We were greeted by a welcoming committee at the City Hall and ushered into a plush council chamber where a group of about ten photographers and journalists were waiting expectantly. Giovanna Palladini, the Councillor for Social Politics, organised us in a row facing the press at the front. We were asked questions, with a translator on hand (although the journos spoke good English) and, as usual, I rambled answers that were far too long that would have had Jill kicking me in the shins if only she could have reached them. Suddenly at the centre of attention as a family, I kept thinking *what are the girls making of this?* But they appeared unfazed and just went with it.

Giovanna wrapped up proceedings by presenting us with the official pennant of Piacenza and a DVD explaining the historical highlights of the city, so the next time we came we'd know exactly where to go and could march straight there bearing our new pennant, as if we had the key to the city. Interviews and photos over, we breathed a collective sigh of relief. Then the translator said, 'The TV crew will be here in just a moment.'

We stepped into the morning sunshine to meet Italy's Most Glamourous Journalist waiting with a cameraman. She was tall, tanned, wearing designer sunglasses, skinny jeans, heels and, most eyebrow raising of all, a crop-top. You never see the BBC's Nicholas Witchell dressing like that. (Well, not at work). As before, events unfolded so quickly we were unsure whether Giovanna was explaining what *would* happen (I'll be handing them the flag, then this DVD) or whether this was actually 'the take'. Unlike UK cameramen who would have got their tri-pod set up, adjusted their white balance, taken some level etc., this young guy was flinging himself all over the place like we were at the centre of an MTV video. It was only when the councillor stopped talking and Posh Spice put her Liberta TV microphone in front of me I realised we were actually recording. Later, we reflected on her knowledge of English. Francesca suspected that she had pre-learned her three questions in English but didn't understand a word of what I said in response. She just smiled, nodded and waited for me to shut up. That happens to me a lot.

In a blink it was over. No re-takes, no 'one more for luck', just lots of kisses and 'ciao's, and, as quickly as we'd become stratospheric stars we were back on planet Earth, a regular English family in a regular Italian city. We stood, slightly dazed, and agreed Franco's idea of getting coffee and hot chocolate was a splendid one. The Piazza Duomo (Cathedral Square), where we sat and drank, had at its centre a huge column with the Virgin Mary looking down from the top. Franco told us it was erected after an incident in the Second World War. The square had been packed with people when a bomb was dropped right in the middle. Incredibly, the bomb failed to explode and no one was hurt. Divine intervention was the agreed explanation, hence the statue.

'What an amazing story,' I commented as we wandered through the square. And, almost as an afterthought, he added 'My mother was a girl in this square when the bomb dropped.' The statue looking down on us as we'd had our coffee was commemorating a miracle that, had it not happened, would have meant Franco wouldn't have *existed*. His mother would have just been another statistic of the war. As tour guides go, he certainly was compelling.

I can't remember at what point we were invited back to their home for lunch but somehow we all found our way around their dining table again where Manuela and Chiara had prepared fresh pasta for us all. We were invited to stay another day, and as I'm sure you now realise, they weren't just being polite. But we'd disrupted their lives enough. They had a family wedding to prepare for and not even Jill was going to accept any more generosity from these people. And yet even as we left, swapping addresses and phone numbers, Francesca gave a gorgeous model Vespa to the girls.

'Just until you get a real one,' she said with a wink.

We hugged, we kissed, we drove away slightly bewildered by the whirlwind of the last two days. The atmosphere in Penny as we drove through Parma towards La Spezia changed from excited chatter about the host of things that had happened, to a quiet glumness that it was all over. The anti-climax was cemented by a night at an overpriced campsite where Edie was sick and it rained all night. We were back in the real world, and by the time we set off for Pisa on Friday morning the entire Milani experience was beginning to feel like a strange but wonderful dream.

'You know what's happened?' said Jill. 'We've had our first proper travellers' experience.'

'And you know what?' added Bethan from the back of the van. 'If we hadn't been stuck in Alessandria for two weeks, we would never have met them.'

Bless her for giving our Turbo Torture Injustice a silver lining. She was right. Perhaps everything *does* happen for a reason. Perhaps there *was* a greater power at work. As I pointed Penny south, I felt slightly better about the two-week, £2,000 hole in our trip.

Just slightly.

Europe

Liverpool to Greece

North Sea

England
Liverpool
Harwich

Amsterdam
Rotterdam
Brussels
Germany
Berlin

Prague
Czech Republic

Arromanches
Paris
France
Guérande
Saumort

Switzerland
Austria
Hungary

Bordeaux

La Chambre
Torino
Alessandria
Piacenza
Italy
Slovenia
Croatia
Bosnia
Sarajevo
Serbia

Florence
Ancona
Split
Dubrovnik
Montenegro

Rome
Bari
Albania
Greece
Igoumenitsa

Mediterranean
Sea

N
W   E
S

Poor old Pisa. It appears that having innumerable tourists over many decades flocking to see a peculiarly tilted tower has never been quite enough to fund any regeneration of the surrounding city.

'There's not much to see in Pisa, beyond the obvious,' we were told by travellers and Italians alike. And they were right. If only Pisa could do *something* to try and keep people there for more than an hour or two, they'd be raking in the cash. But as it is, coach after coach-load of tourists are driven through miles of run-down dirty suburbs, dropped at the entrance to the walled church grounds, have their photo taken next to/in front of/pretending to hold up the leaning tower, and are whisked away to a more attractive place to spend the night. What a waste.

Florence, by contrast, won my heart - but not before a fight. Our first encounter, arriving amid the excited hubbub of a brisk, bright Saturday morning, was one of frustration and disappointment. The traffic system in Florence is deliberately designed to keep nasty diesel fumes away from all the beautiful buildings with their priceless façades, which is fair enough. After all, if Donatello put an extension on your house you wouldn't park your car in front of it. As a result I spent half an hour negotiating the slightly drab, lacklustre outskirts muttering things like 'Well, I'd hardly call it breathtaking,' before guiding Penny to a multi-storey car park that *did* take my breath away - with its prices.

We headed off on foot, our only mission: to do 'jobs'.

'We'll find wi-fi first,' I instructed the troops, 'then we can use it to find campsites, send emails, Jill can find some local media contacts for when we busk, and Ella can get her homework sent in.'

'Finally,' said a slightly grumpy 13-year-old, who was holding me responsible for her schoolwork being delivered late.

'We'll properly "do Florence" tomorrow,' I concluded.

Italy had been torturing us with the battle to get online, and Florence was more maddening than ever. The tourist information people gave us a map detailing the wi-fi hotspots but you needed an Italian phone to get the access codes. The same was true in McDonalds. We found a bar bearing the sign 'Free Wi-fi' on the door, we ordered a €23 round of drinks, only to find the Internet was not available. A second bar, a second sign. This time, I checked first.

'*Si*, Internet working,' assured the waitress. We bought drinks. Logging on revealed that the Internet was indeed free *if you have an Italian mobile phone number.* But wait! Tourists with international phones could buy the code for $2.50. My credit card details were dutifully and painstakingly entered, until finally ... 'Error loading page'.

'Where are we going to sleep tonight?' asked Bethan.

'Let's just get back in the van and drive the hell out of this evil city of fraudulent money-grabbing thieves,' I replied. I may not have been in the best of moods.

A healthy row was in the offing because Jill really wanted to see Florence, so to avoid us being the first couple to go to Italy's most romantic city and come away divorced, we decided to separate. Just in the city, not the marriage. Jill went back to the tourist information to get details of campsites while I took the girls to The Florence Dungeons. It was a tiny independent museum, not connected in any way to the Tussauds behemoth of the London Dungeons/Amsterdam

Holland

The first busk!
Strawberry Field, Liverpool

Rotterdam's most
reluctant street
performers

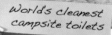

World's cleanest
campsite toilets

Contain yourself

Belgium

France

Trolley-jack: less use than hair-straighteners

Guérande, Brittany. Still learning to busk and smile at the same time

The Alps. Bad for camper vans.

Italy

A new turbo but another breakdown. We look relaxed, considering.

OSTELLO "SANTA MARIA DI CASTELLO"

"Hello? Is this the set of 'Hostel 3 - Slasher la Vista'?"

ITALIA

"Let's camp behind this church. We'll be completely undisturbed."

Florence,
Italy

Busking The Beatles
from Liverpool
to New York
in aid of UNICEF

Italy

www.beatnikbeatles.com

Being awarded the Città
di Piacenza pennant.

Makarska,
Croatia
(It's not a holiday)

Rigorous testing of new
masks and snorkels

Dalmatian coast road.
Not short of views.

Negotiating a deal for
the world's most
delicious satsumas

Doing schoolwork, but
ready for anything

Camping on the garage-deck

Discovering bougatsa - apples, pastry and sugar.

'Gramping' on a desolate beach, Asprovalta

Meeting a Republic Radio DJ while busking, Thessaloniki

The world's smallest cinema (with room for two more)

Drying laundry over Penny's engine

Lesson time, at the only power socket on the campsite

Dungeons/Hull Dungeons (I made that last one up). In fact, the main thing that drew us in was that on the ticket office was a recent photograph of film director Tim Burton on his visit there.

'If it's good enough for Mr Burton,' said Beth, and we nodded our agreement. The girls were patient enough with the audio guide explaining how rife typhoid, leprosy and the plague were during 14th and 15th century Florence, but if I tell you that we were back outside 15 minutes later and the most impressive thing the girls could say about it was that Tim Burton had been there, you'll realise that it was substantially less scary or even interesting than we'd hoped for. As we left, I looked more closely at the photo and saw for the first time a disappointment in Tim's eyes I regretted not noticing before buying our tickets.

Jill had had more success finding some campsites, so we headed back to Penny. It would be another day before we'd realise that we still hadn't seen Florence, not properly. Somehow, we'd managed to spend a couple of hours accidentally avoiding the historic centre. I was convinced the whole place was hugely over-rated and thought the Italians ought to set the bar a little higher if they were trying to impress anyone. From what I'd seen, Slough could compete.

It was after a proper day off, chilling out, washing clothes and using the wi-fi at Camping International, ten minutes outside the city, that Firenze (as the Italians call it) lay herself before us. With renewed vigour we took the bus into the city to be proper tourists for the day. We ticked an educational box by visiting the brilliant 'Leonardo Da Vinci - Machines' museum in the morning. Leo's early life, battling to make it as an apprentice artist in late 1400s Florence, was portrayed on film, and showed where his passion for engineering was born. Then large rooms displayed fully working machines built as precise replicas using Da Vinci's designs. Some were famous like the catapult, the glider and the military tank. Others, less so, like the buoyancy life-belt, the brilliantly simple but fiendishly clever interlocking temporary bridge which Ella loved, or Edie's favourite, the multi-pulley block and tackle gearing system, still used on construction sites today. It hardly sounds like the thrills and spills of a day at a theme park, I know, but the girls genuinely did enjoy pulling ropes and turning cogs and stuff. Honest.

It was after leaving the museum that we all got that slap in the face we'd had coming to us. We'd been in Florence three days and she had become impatient with us ignoring her. We ambled around a corner into Piazza Duomo. 'Wow!' I said, stopping in my tracks. I was a few paces ahead of the rest and turned around, watching them approach. They were holding hands, nattering and strolling. I waited, and watched it happen. They froze, their eyes widening.

'Woah!'

Florence cathedral will do that to you. To suddenly come up against a stunning towering structure of green, white and pink marble decorated in every available space with carvings from the greatest Renaissance artists in the world leaves you momentarily speechless.

'Aaahhhh,' said Edie, awestruck as I held her hand.

'I know. Incredible, isn't it?' I said, my neck craned back, trying to take it all in.

'Just look at that,' she said. I looked down at her. She wasn't looking at the cathedral at all. She'd seen a horse and cart. The collected works of two generations of the finest artists the world has ever produced versus an old nag.

'It's eating hay out of a sack!' she squealed in delight.

Michaelangelo, if you're listening, welcome to the *Britain's Got Talent* generation.

The inside of the cathedral is a complete contrast, being one of the most stark and bare cathedral interiors I've ever seen. I was grandly theorising about the theological juxtaposition between people praising God with their art on the outside but not wanting a distraction from prayer on the inside when Jill, who had a guidebook, said, 'They've removed all the art and put it in a museum. Look, here's a picture of Donatello's choir stall. You have to pay to see it now.'

I almost swore. 'They don't miss a trick, do they?' I hissed. 'If it moves, put it behind a ticket turnstile. Pisa could learn a thing or two.'

We cooed at the Ponte Vecchio bridge, ate overpriced ice-cream and were proper tourists for a day. Tomorrow, our journey would continue, but not before we had busked in this fine city to try to swell the UNICEF coffers.

A street-side artist we got chatting to told us that Piazzale Michaelangelo was the perfect place to perform. Up on the hillside, it's a tourist hotspot owing to its breathtaking views of Florence and so, as we climbed our way out of the city the following morning, we stopped to 'busk Italy'.

It was our favourite public gig yet. 'This busking lark is definitely getting easier,' commented Bethan after we'd done a few songs. The reception from passing tourists and locals was very smiley, and we soon got chatting to people, telling them what we were doing, turning down requests because we didn't yet know how to play them, and repeating the ones we did know. A Euro here, another there, and after about half an hour of playing, chatting and playing a bit more we had gathered a whole €12. Double figures! We met a Korean man who loved The Beatles and stopped to sing along with *Ob-La-Di*, a smartly-dressed American guy whose mother had worked for UNICEF, so he loved what we were doing, and a couple from Sheffield who, it transpired, had been visiting our home town of Banbury the week before. Small world, and all that.

By the time we drove south towards Rome even the usually reticent Ella was buoyant about our busk, saying she felt like doing more, and suggested we should learn some more songs.

'Yes, I think Lennon and McCartney wrote more than three,' I said, and as the milometer revealed we'd driven over 3,000 miles since Liverpool, for the first time I felt confident that the busk The Beatles around the world idea might actually succeed.

In some respects our journey was an unknown, and like all the big unknowns in the universe, it was in the lap of the gods. Or in our case, the Milanis. Back in Piacenza we had thrown our travel plans into the hands of our new best friends, and juggling between across the top (Verona, Venice) and down to Rome (Florence, Tuscany, Rome) they had directed us south. Jill took the wheel for the first time since a few weeks earlier in France, so obviously it wasn't long before we had our second puncture. Don't ask me how she does it. It's a gift.

Unfortunately, this time Jill had found the stray shard of steel/splinter of shrapnel/casually misplaced nail on a very busy and insanely fast *autostrade*. An Italian *autostrade* is like an English motorway or an American interstate, but with less hard shoulder and faster lorries. For added drama, the tyre met its demise just as we were entering the mouth of a tunnel.

Much inappropriate language was exchanged, as were the seating positions, and I gritted my teeth and gingerly drove Penny, a hideous, big, ten-mile-an-hour target for an 80-mile-an-hour truck to hit, through the tunnel until daylight greeted us a tense minute later. Until that day, the girls had got into a little game of singing every time we passed through a dark tunnel. But now, it seemed, a new craze had started. Nervously praying.

The slender hard-shoulder didn't offer enough room to actually change the tyre without risk to life and limb, so I pulled over far enough to allow me to jack up the front left wheel (why is it always on the side of the traffic?) and squirt Flat Mate emergency foam into the punctured tyre which would at least allow us to drive off the *autostrade*. Have you ever jacked up a camper van on the side of a busy motorway? As extreme sports go, it's a good adrenaline rush. The girls and Jill climbed to safety on the grass verge, and I busied myself with the jack and pondered my imminent death as an onslaught of Italian lorry drivers hooted at me.

'I've put the bloody triangle out!' I was shouting above the din. 'I'm not wearing this high visibility jerkin as a fashion statement! What do you want from me?'

The Polizia arrived, sirens wailing. *About flippin' time* I thought. But the police car zoomed past. Then another. I couldn't hear what Jill was shouting over the noise but she appeared to be thanking them for their assistance with an illuminating hand gesture. That prompted another lorry to honk back. Comedian.

'That was brilliant,' panted Ella as I rushed them back into the van so we could drive to a safe haven, my trousers covered in white foam and my eyes manic, like Doc in *Back To The Future*.

'31,' said Beth from the back seat. '31 honks!'

'You were counting?'

'Yeah,' said Edie. 'Beth started a game where we pulled our fists down like we were honking a horn to see how many truckers would honk back.'

'I thought they were honking at me 'cause I was about to die!' I shouted.

'One guy was on his phone,' Edie added gleefully, 'but he still waved, honked his horn *and* blew a kiss.'

'It did cross my mind', continued Beth, 'that it would have been ironic if he'd been so distracted he'd run in to you.'

I thanked them all for their concern, and we headed for the nearest decent size town to try to get a new tyre. That town was Grosetto. Rome was our destination, and Grosetto was only a two-hour train ride up the coast from the capital, so we decided to stop there, get *both* the front tyres changed (they were ready to be changed anyway) and let the train take the strain for our roam to Rome.

I dropped Jill and the girls in Grosetto town centre and drove to the nearest tyre replacement establishment I could find. While the tyre-fitter - a charming white haired old gent - was fitting Penny's new tyres, and telling me in his broken English how he had once visited Cornevalle (Cornwall), I inadvertently instigated the first major micro-technological malfunction of our journey. I dropped my iPhone.

As it bounced off the concrete floor the old man with the tyre wrench sucked his teeth. I hoped I'd got away with my clumsiness as the ridiculously expensive gadget, which despite the price was shod in a totally flimsy cover, had bounced and lived before. But not this time. I waved the friendly tyre chap farewell, and anxiously tried turning the phone off, then on again. Thoughts of what I might lose raced through my mind as I waited for the happy little fruit symbol to appear.

The contacts. Damn. The mileages for all our towns. Why didn't I back it up? The photos! Double damn. Why oh why didn't I back them up?

Nothing. The still intact screen showed the merest flicker of a white line, then nothing. If it were a medical drama, a doctor would have said, 'Call it. Time of death, 5pm.'

In life, there are certain rules you simply know make sense.
- Don't stick your head out of a train window
- Don't tease a snake
- Don't eat yellow snow

Well, add to that
- Don't perform surgery on an iPhone

After a day of grieving my loss I resolved to see if I could fix it. After all, *I'm just a man*, as Tammy Wynette almost sang. And it was only an iPhone. I happened to know that *iPods* come apart quite easily with just a plectrum, two thumbs and 14 swear words. Surely an *iPhone* would be much the same. Actually, no. Please don't try to open your iPhone with a plectrum and grunting brute force. Things snap. Important miniscule ribbon cables that have been crafted by tiny elves will tear, rip and break. Along with your foolish heart.

I parked Penny and trudged into the town to find Jill and the girls. The central square was tiny, and only one café appeared to be open so they were a cinch to find. After a few minutes of bereavement counselling over a cold Coke, we focussed on making a plan. We calculated the cheapest way of us seeing Rome before leaving Italy was to guerrilla camp - sorry, *gramp* - in Grosetto, get the first train down to Rome in the morning, return that evening and gramp again somewhere outside the town before driving across to the port of Ancona on the east coast.

The gramping was a bit of a nightmare. We'd just got settled in a massive car park on the edge of the city, where sleeping in a camper van was actually permitted, when Jill decided she didn't feel safe among the sound of rampaging youths, hot-hatches and squealing tyres. So we put the beds away, re-packed the van and moved into town, eventually parking in a residential area where a nearby house appeared to be training guard dogs to bark at anything slightly suspicious parked outside their house. And those dogs were good. None of us slept very much, but undaunted, as daylight appeared we found a country lane in which to wash and change (we were becoming real travellers now), found a café for some breakfast and then boarded the train to Rome.

To do Rome in one day is absurd. To do Rome in one day when we'd spent a full 16 days in *Alessandria* might confirm our insanity, but we were behind schedule, we had a ferry to catch, and we like a challenge. Rome blew us all away. We rushed it, clearly, and we all left wanting to go back and spend more time there. I want to walk through the Circus Massimo, now just a massive grassy oval, where once two hundred and fifty thousand spectators would watch chariot racing, and where the first Christian martyrs were thrown to the lions. Imagine a quarter of a million Romans yelling at the top of their voices, and today the oval Circus is still there, open for all (although lions are frowned on). Around every corner was another wonder. Yes, there's the Colosseum, and the Pantheon, and the Trevi Fountain, and the Vatican, and we saw them all and they are awesome. But it's the fact that *between* all of these jewels are crammed even more historic gems that makes Rome so stunning.

'Hey, there's an archaeological dig in the middle of the pavement,' said Jill. 'Oh, look, they uncovered a stunning mosaic floor a few metres down.' But no one was looking, none of the locals, anyway. A find that would get its own visitor centre and gift shop anywhere else in the world was barely given a second glance here, such is the proliferation of historical artefacts.

'See that archway, girls?' I enthused. They saw yet another arch covered in statues and carvings. 'It was built in 200 BC! It's over two thousand years old, and it's just standing there, among the people, and the traffic and the noise.'

It was incredible, and we loved it. Exhausted, we found Penny waiting for us at the railway station back in Grosetto at about 11pm, drove north towards Ancona for half an hour, then pulled off the main road to gramp on a large gravel clearing. It was only in the light of dawn that it became clear that the large gravel clearing we'd made home was in fact part of a major motorway construction project, and when I looked out of the window just after 7am I saw the orange flashing lights of diggers and earth-movers starting to stir.

The most energetic and fretful wake up routine followed, and amazingly we were all up, packed and organised enough to drive away at 7.30, exactly at the moment a man in a Land Rover with a flashing warning light came round to investigate what a yellow VW camper was doing in the middle of his multi-million Euro road-building project. We didn't have a chance to chat. We literally pulled away as he drove around the corner. We were laughing, but relieved.

'Man, gramping is stressful!' I said.

'Yes, but it's free,' reminded Jill, 'which we like.'

So, after four weeks in Italy we finally arrived at the ferry port in Ancona to continue our journey by crossing the Adriatic Sea. Out of curiosity I looked up our original itinerary, a rough 'guesstimate' of where we'd be and when - I had allowed three days for Italy!

'We're just going to drive straight across the top,' I had said, but Jill was having none of it. 'I've always wanted to go to Italy,' she had pined. 'You're not short-changing me with three days!' Eventually we'd settled on a week. I'm sure that a fortnight stuck in Alessandria wasn't what she had in mind, and a week on paper had become a month in practice. If our whole trip worked on that principle it was going to take us four years to get to New York.

As we reflected on our time in Italy, we agreed that we'd all loathed it initially, only to love it eventually. With Penny stuck in The Garage Of Doom we'd been under a cloud, but when the sun shone we saw real beauty: Piacenza, the Milani family, Florence and Rome. Next, it was on to Croatia. Despite the good times we'd had in our final weeks in Italy, we all felt a certain comfort as we boarded the ferry, safe in the knowledge that whatever else happened on this journey, we could, at last, put Italy behind us.

The fact that we returned to Italy a week later may prompt you to hurl this book out of the window in complete frustration. 'Dag nab it!' you may shout (if you're a Louisiana cotton farmer). 'These fools are too darned inept to manage even the simplest task – namely, to drive east!' And I wouldn't blame you. All I would say in mitigation is - imagine how we felt. Contain your urge to hurl and I'll explain. It's all to do with political unrest, a family row and the Eurovision Song Contest.

We enjoyed our overnight crossing on the vintage ferry from Ancona. Its oak panelled bar, and our tiny four bunk cabin built entirely from highly varnished wood, made it feel like a proper ship. Next morning I guided Penny from the darkness of the ship's bowels into the equally dark port of Split to find the sky had already done just that. Split.

Battering rain lashed us as we negotiated the precarious, mountainous coast road south towards Dubrovnik. Jill kept holding her breath and leaning away from the sheer drop beneath her as we wound through almost impenetrable rain. We got as far as Makarska, an hour or two south, before Jill's nerves could take no more. We had packed the tent away wet the morning we left Italy and so collectively agreed that unpeeling sodden nylon to camp in this horizontal rain was a bad idea.

The Dalmatian coast is dotted with towns that boast a clutter of 'Apartment For Rent' signs, most of them so homemade and badly written that you suspect the 'luxury holiday accommodation' is in fact a swarthy Croatian farmer's back bedroom. After a few 'er, I think not' false starts I found a reasonably priced apartment for the night. A perfect chance to stop, dry out and spread a huge map of the Balkans out on the table of our kitchenette to plan our route from Dubrovnik down to Thessaloniki in Greece.

I was very excited that the route which avoided the steepest mountain passes, and politically difficult Albania, would take us through a total of six countries. The list went like this: Croatia, Montenegro, Serbia, Kosovo, Macedonia, Greece. It was only when I presented Jill with this list that she went online to do some research on the FCO website.

The British Foreign and Commonwealth Office has a great website providing travel advice to Brits abroad. It's bang up to date, and even includes enlightening statistics like 'how many British Nationals required consular assistance in the past year', 'how many died', 'how many were injured' and 'how many formed a ramshackle travelling band'. It was FCO advice, for instance, that led us to avoid Albania. It said:

We advise against all travel to the north east border areas (the districts of Kukes, Has and Tropoje) between Albania and Kosovo because of the risk of unexploded ordnance placed during the 1999 Kosovo crisis and the poor condition of the roads.

Although public security is generally good, particularly in Tirana, crime and violence still represent a serious problem in some areas. Gun ownership is widespread.

(I particularly liked that last bit. Factual. Scary.)

We'd found, when planning the trip, that it was a similar story when we looked at driving through Pakistan or Afghanistan. The cities, particularly the capitals, are fairly secure - it's the borders that are a nightmare. And you can't avoid those if you're driving from country to country.

And the FCO was about to put another couple of spanners in our turbo, so to speak. First, Montenegro looked difficult. Paperwork was required that I hadn't prepared, and we would have to register with the police or be arrested trying to leave. These things alarmed Jill and, frankly, didn't show my planning skills in their best light. The only road left to us, then, was the one that dropped us down towards Pristina from Serbia through the north of Kosovo.

'The North Mitrovica area,' I said with confidence. 'Across the river Ibar.'

Jill read from the screen.

'We continue to advise against all but essential travel to the North Mitrovica area. On the night of 11 September 2010 law and order forces had to intervene to separate Kosovo Serb and Kosovo Albanian mobs on either side of the River Ibar - an international policeman and at least one Serb were injured as shots were fired and Molotov cocktails thrown. Tension remains high.'

Tensions were about to get even higher in our kitchenette. That incident was less than a week old.

'Did you plan *any* of this part of our journey?' asked the prosecution.

'Well. Sort of,' I replied. It wasn't a rock solid defence, I know, but I was still forming my argument.

'Sort of,' repeated the prosecutor. 'We have travelled, at some expense, all the way to Croatia. A country, from which, there is no overland route to Greece.'

'Well, there is a ...'

'Not,' she interrupted, 'unless Albanian gangsters, a prison cell in Montenegro and rioting mobs on the Kosovan border are part of your itinerary.'

(Dammit she's on a roll. Hang on, she hasn't finished.)

'Explain. What, exactly, *did* you do in the way of planning?'

An awkward silence descended. I knew she wouldn't like the answer. She raised her eyebrows expectantly.

'The Eurovision Song Contest.' It sounded weak. I could see that now.

'Sorry?' She wasn't sorry. She was pretty angry.

'Well, they all take part in the Eurovision Song Contest, don't they? So I just figured they must all be happy people. Friendly. If anything they're a little *too* friendly. The way they vote for each other is clearly not in the interests of finding the best song, it's because ...'

'You based a major and costly part of our journey - on the *Eurovision Song Contest?*'

'Well when you say it like that it sounds stupid. It's not like I sat down with the score sheet from the *Radio Times* and made a list, it's just ...'

'Did you?'

'What?'

'*Did you* sit down with the score sheet from the *Radio Times?*'

'No! It was just - y'know - a hunch. I'm sure I checked the FCO before we left. I couldn't have predicted violence that only took place a few days ago. We were in Alessandria!' That memory always cheered her up. She left the room. And in an open plan apartment that's not easy.

The argument was over. At least this round was. I won't bore you with the gory details of the many other rounds that followed on the subject of my lack of planning, but the upshot was that we now had a brand new plan to sail from Dubrovnik back to Bari in southern Italy, from where we'd catch another ferry across to Greece. Once the charged atmosphere had diffused a little, and we could talk about it again without anyone crying/throwing something/searching fruitlessly for a door to slam, we all agreed it was a darned shame that six exciting countries on our list were suddenly reduced to two. If I'd been on my own, or maybe with a mate on motorbikes, I'd have just pootled across and hoped for the best. After all, it's an approach that had got me this far. But even I could see that taking the children through a riot of Molotov cocktails, gunfire and unexploded ordnance could, by some, be seen as irresponsible.

'Back to Italy then,' said Ella, visibly tiring at the very thought.

'But at least we'll get to busk in Dubrovnik,' I chirped. Even that optimism, though, was doomed.

Our second punch in the ribs was potentially a lot more serious. After several weeks of living in our house back in the UK, our tenant still hadn't paid his first month's rent. He was blaming a banking error, promising to pay us something, but it never came. Jill, being a journalist, did some Internet research on our tenant to find that he openly talked on his website about how he'd been made bankrupt, but had picked himself up and was getting his life back together.

'Oh dear God, what have we done?' she said turning pale.

No amount of reassurance from me about how it could be a genuine mistake, and how he had given references to the agent prior to us meeting him, could change the facts: we'd left our house in the hands of a bankrupt tenant who had failed to pay his first month's rent. The implications were huge. Potentially, we'd be abandoning the trip. Not only might we have to deal with a messy eviction, we simply couldn't afford to travel without the rent money coming in. It was paying the monthly mortgage bill and providing some income for us on top. Without it, we'd have to go home and get jobs again, or go home until we could find new tenants. There were tears. My lack of planning was now compounded by our own naivety that we could just let the house out to a bloke who turned up half an hour before we left the country, and assume everything would be fine. We kept the bad news from the girls until we'd calmed down a bit, but told them the next day. We would continue as planned, and hope with all our might that the next month's rent got paid. If it didn't, it was game over.

Trying to put all this out of our minds, we continued south. The road to Dubrovnik was stunning. The twists and turns of the Dalmatian Coast road took us high above curving bays of clean, empty beaches and glistening sea, down through tiny fishing villages and across the massive flat expanse of the Neretva Delta. This mineral-rich valley was once under the sea, so is bursting with nutrients and is a fruit grower's paradise. Pomegranate orchards and mandarin orange groves stretch away from the coast towards the foothills of the inland mountains, and every few hundred metres another farmer sets up a roadside stall selling his wares. In our entire journey around planet Earth, nowhere did we taste better oranges than there. Perfect palm-sized mandarins that packed a flavour punch like nothing we'd tasted before.

An added bonus was that a tiny stretch of this coast road still belonged to Bosnia, who negotiated access to the coast when Yugoslavia was divided up. This meant a checkpoint, stamps in our passports, another country on our list and lunch of homemade, very salty sausages at a Bosnian café. Two minutes down the road we were back in Croatia again. We camped at a fairly woeful and overpriced campsite on the outskirts of Dubrovnik, and the next morning decided that we would park somewhere near the docks, sort out our ferry tickets, then take the instruments into the old city to fill the historic streets with badly executed Lennon and McCartney classics.

But Jill was having a bad day. She complained of stomach ache from the moment we woke and seemed lethargic to the point of horizontal. I used all my husbandly wisdom to make her feel better, saying things like, 'I'm sure it's nothing,' 'You don't *look* ill,' and 'Help me lift this massive heavy tent on to the roof.' But when I returned to the van after buying the ferry tickets, she was crying. I looked at the girls sitting in the back. They did that thing all kids do when their parents weep openly – they shrugged and glanced at each other awkwardly.

I put my arm around Jill to comfort her but she shrugged it off. 'What's up?' I asked in what I judged to be a caring and loving way.

'I want to go home.'

I didn't take this well. 'Brilliant. I've just spent 150 quid on ferry tickets to Italy! You couldn't have mentioned this five minutes ago?'

'I'm really sick of this,' she croaked. 'I hate it and I just wanna go home.' She was really crying now. I confess I felt more exasperated than sympathetic. Does that make me a monster? I'm not proud of what happened next, but you've read this far and deserve some warts and all honesty.

'I need the loo,' Jill grunted and leapt from the front seat, scooting away to find a toilet somewhere. She'd bailed out of the van, the argument and, apparently, the trip. I took the cue to have my own minor meltdown. 'You know what?' I said to the girls as we hung around outside the van. 'Forget all this.'

'What d'you mean?' asked Ella.

'I mean it's over. We're going home.'

'Really?'

'Looks like it. Actually no. Mummy's going home. I'm carrying on.'

'What?'

'Yeah why not? You lot can go home and I'll carry on on my own. I'll backpack around the world.'

She looked horrified. 'Are you serious?'

'This whole thing's not working,' I proclaimed. 'Jill hates it. That's obvious. And let's face it Ella, you're not really enjoying it. You hate busking. You're missing your friends. Let's just scrap it, while we still can. You lot go home. You can go back to school, see your mates, return to normal. The Beatnik Beatles thing was a stupid idea. Let's bin it.'

It really breaks my heart to recall how I picked this particular argument with Ella, and what a petulant imbecile I was. I was cross with Jill and I was cross with our tenant but I took it out on a 13-year-old. I'm sure I'm not the first parent to regret the way he's spoken to his daughter, but honestly, what a hot-headed idiot. I trust she will use her hormonal teenage years to reap her revenge. I'll give her that.

When Jill returned the drama took a new twist. She looked pale and very ill. I suddenly regretted my anger. Within moments of her explaining her tortuous search for a toilet (culminating in bursting into a café's private loo to be violently sick), Ella was tearfully spilling her guts. 'Daddy says we're going home,' she gabbled. 'He says he's carrying on without us,' which, as you might imagine, went down really well.

It was a low point, let me tell you. Emotions were running high, as was Jill's temperature. It quickly became clear that she actually *was* ill, and I was therefore on a fast-track to bagging an historic double of World's Worst Husband *and* World's Worst Father in one fell swoop. Her repeated vomiting and acute abdominal pain seemed serious enough for us to seek some medical help. Hospitals were located, but the patient wouldn't go.

'Let's just wait here,' she would whine. 'See what happens.'

None of us looked very sure of this idea, but Jill just wanted to sleep. As she closed her eyes she murmured 'And if you even suggest busking - you know where you can shove that ukulele.'

'You're gonna regret saying that if they turn out to be your last words,' I said.

A flicker of a smile. Maybe we'd be OK. We left her sleeping in Penny while we went to a café across the road which boasted wi-fi. The girls consulted Doctor Google to the point where they had Jill diagnosed with everything from a tummy bug to a lethal pulmonary embolism.

'Thank God for the Internet,' I said. 'Perhaps we should turn it off.'

'No seriously,' said Ella. 'Look at these symptoms for appendicitis. It could be that.'

I looked at the list. It did match. We decided to return to the patient and if things got worse, we'd go to hospital.

'Are we still going home?' asked Edie as we walked back to the van.

'No darling. Not today.'

'Tomorrow?'

'Tomorrow - is another day,' I said. 'That's from a famous film.'

'A James Bond film, isn't it?' asked Ella.

'No. It just sounds like it should be. It's from *Gone With The Wind.*'

'Sounds rubbish,' she said, and as quick as that we were back to normal. Jill awoke feeling less sick and strong enough to insist on going to see the old walled city. We failed to board two buses that were too full to pick us up so paid a fiver for a cab to drive us down into old Dubrovnik.

We found a beautiful walled fortress on the sea, sullied only by the *thousands* of tourists filling every square inch of space. Yes, yes, I know what you're thinking – 'That's a bit rich Sim, seeing as you were tourists too.' But we *weren't*, you see. We were *travellers*. There's a difference, and this was the first time we felt a bit snobby about the fact that we'd *driven* here and had *adventures* and met *people*. The hoards of thronging plebs filling Dubrovnik had poured off cruise liners. We'd seen two moored up near the ferry terminal and now their abundance of passengers had spilled out and been delivered, coach after coach, into the historic city. We noticed how all the shops sold the same trinkets and tat that we'd seen people snapping up in Florence and Rome. They're the same key-rings, fridge magnets and tea-towels, just bearing a different name. It all felt horribly commercial and artificial.

We headed back to Penny, slightly disappointed, but ready for our onward ferry journey back across the Adriatic. All talk of busking was banned. After all, we'd already narrowly escaped a visit to hospital that day and I didn't see the point in inviting a trip to A&E for an embarrassing procedure to remove a ukulele.

The ferry crossing to Bari was largely uneventful for all of us except Jill, who spent a large part of the night decorating the ocean from the back of the boat, but the crossing from Bari to Igoumenitsa in northern Greece was far more entertaining. When enquiring about the cost of the tickets, I must have reeled a little at the €110 price tag for a cabin because the Italian lady behind the booth window said, 'Or, you can camp in the garage. That's just €15.'

'What, you mean sleep in the van, on the *garage deck*?' I asked, trying not to sound surprised, and trying not to remember *The Herald of Free Enterprise*.

'Of course, if you would like to.'

And so, as with any roll-on-roll-off ferry, we drove up the boarding ramp into the oily gloom and were waved towards our parking area. Then, unlike on any other RORO ferry I'd ever taken, a burly Greek sailor asked if I wanted to hook up. Normally that might be an entirely inappropriate thing for a sailor to ask a chap, but luckily I knew that 'hooking up' is camper parlance for plugging into external power.

And that was our sleeping accommodation sorted. Up went the roof, down went the beds, and armed with a small card bearing the words 'Licence to Enter Garage' we had the run of the ship. Welcome to Greece. This joyfully lax attitude to security was echoed when we arrived in Igoumenitsa. The port authority's immigration controls were hilariously anarchic. As the ferry docked, cars, trucks and motorbikes started to gather at the top of the ramp inside the ship's campsite, sorry, garage. No uniformed disembarkation personnel pointed, waved or organised – it was a free-for-all. As the ramp touched the harbour, much pushing, squeezing, honking and shouting ensued until finally we all spilled on to the dockside.

Blinking in the morning sun, I expected to pursue the usual drill learned by any seasoned Brit abroad: follow the car in front. Imagine our surprise then, to see the four vehicles in front of us speed off in four *different* directions. The huge tarmac dock had no painted lanes, no exit signs, no customs buildings or passport control huts to be escorted through, just two slightly embarrassed-looking uniformed officials standing helpless in the middle of the car park while vehicles of all shapes and sizes streamed past them and off towards the Greek horizon. The Chuckle Brothers had apparently secured the Greek border. No passports were checked and we realised, as we explored our own route out of the port, that the Greek financial crisis, which by this time was really starting to bite, must have been worse than we thought: if you could afford a car, you were in. No questions asked.

Our route was simple – head for Turkey. This path straight across the top of Greece is a historic one. Today the rather grand and expensive Egnatia Motorway, completed in the mid 2000s, will take you all the way from north west Greece to the north eastern border with Turkey, but the road follows the exact route of an ancient Roman road that even until the late 1990s was regularly slogged by drivers who took 12 hours to navigate its wiggles from coast to border. That journey time is now cut in half thanks to hundreds of tunnels and bridges easing the passage through the Notia Pindos, and other inconvenient mountain ranges.

Obviously a six-hour journey time would involve being in something more modern than a 1989 VW camper, but we were happy to spend at least a week meandering across Greece.

The country's taxpayers forked out €3bn towards the €5.5bn price tag for the shiny new road, and given the financial precipice Greece found itself teetering on by 2010, I wondered how badly the Greek Government wished it could have its money back, and simply let us struggle up and down the old Roman road. So why did they do it? Tourism, for one thing. The main argument the Greek Government made to get the funding was that the road would bring much needed tourism to the more deprived north west of the country. Did it work? We got chatting to a hotelier in Kozani, about a third of the way along the 400-mile road and asked how he felt about the Egnatia Motorway.

'Everyone was very happy when they planned the new road,' he remembered. 'But none of us could see what would happen. Things are worse for us now. People pass through. They might stop for coffee, but then they carry on. Worse, local people will drive away to Thessaloniki for shoes or clothes or whatever because it's become easier. There's more choice. It's cheaper. So it's bad for our town.' It was a frank appraisal, but he didn't seem unduly concerned. 'We will adapt,' he added with a shrug.

As Penny's milometer registered 4,000 miles since Liverpool, we reached the busy sea front in Thessaloniki. It was hot and it was packed. Cafés and bars spilled punters on to busy pavements, apparently oblivious of any recession or financial crisis. We stopped to pursue what was by now becoming a familiar routine: find a tourist information place, get details of campsites, get wi-fi if possible, look for a laundrette. A curious fact about Greece that we were slowly learning was that they don't have public laundrettes. We'd failed to find anything like the coin-operated *lavanderia* of Italy, or what Americans call a laundromat. There were dry cleaners aplenty, but no one seemed to understand that we just wanted a washing machine. The tourist information office was shut so we resolved to stay smelly and head out of town to find a place to spend the night.

Fifteen minutes down the coast we found a beachside campsite that appeared entirely closed, apart from the fact that there was no gate stopping us going in. So we did. All the buildings were locked, but the restaurant next door showed signs of life, and eventually the owner appeared to unlock the primitive toilet block and take €20 off me. The weirdest thing here was the constant presence of stray dogs, marauding in packs. It was curious, and a bit scary. Particularly in the dead of night when Jill and I awoke in the pop-up tent (where we'd opted to sleep to get a bit of space) to hear what sounded like the vicious three-headed dog from *Harry Potter* clomping its mammoth jaws around some sort of dinosaur bone just inches from our heads.

'What the hell is that?' Jill hissed.

'Scary. Stay quiet.' I whispered.

We waited, and then I got even more freaked when it ran away, because it seemed to circle the tent, but rather than sounding like a dog, it ran on two feet. Two feet on short running legs.

'Bloody hell, it's some sort of child vampire and it's gone to get its friends!' I gabbled.

'D'you think we should go and sleep in the van?' she asked.

'Er - *yes!*' Cautiously we scuttled, by the dim light emitted by a mobile phone, from the tent to the van. The girls didn't seem unduly concerned at our arrival, so I kept my vivid theories about what was roaming outside to myself and let them sleep. The next morning we all agreed this place was a bit weird and it would be good to move on. So we had a quick rehearsal of a few Beatles tunes and planned to spend the day in Thessaloniki, get a busk out of the way early, then enjoy the city a bit before moving on.

To most Brits, and I included myself in this, Greece's second largest city after Athens was most famous as the airport destination you'd fly to before being transferred to one of hundreds of package holiday hot spots. So it was a pleasant surprise to explore Thessaloniki properly and find we really liked it. It can't compete with Athens for historical ruins I suspect, but it has a thriving, young, energetic quality that's infectious. A maze of bustling backstreets twisting through and around the occasional ancient arch or church contains countless interesting independent shops selling the kinds of things you didn't really see much of anymore in England, like vinyl records and coloured hair extensions (really, a whole shop of them). Even its 'posh end' seems understated. You barely notice boutiques like Louis Vuitton nestled among the chaos. It was really refreshing, different from any other city centre I know. And it was the chosen venue for our Grecian busk.

The seafront was even busier than the day we'd arrived here, which was encouraging, but we were fighting a strong breeze which threatened to swallow what little audible volume we could create. We also found to our dismay that our Greek audience wasn't half as smiley and curious as those in Italy or France. I don't know whether it was the language barrier, or whether we were just too quiet, but most people just walked past barely giving us a glance. Maybe it was the smell.

The music, we hoped, would be universal, but the language barrier was definitely getting bigger. Dutch, French, Italian - you can see similarities to our own language. You could at least hazard a guess. But Greek? It was funny when Ella first saw it written on a sign.

'They've got a triangle for a letter! And an M on its side. How are you supposed to say that?'

It certainly created a problem when trying to explain our mission to baffled passers by. We stuck at it for a good half hour and I was surprised by the girls' determination to carry on, but we only raised €7, which seemed disheartening after the fun and buoyancy of Florence. One good thing was that we were featured on a local radio breakfast show. The morning DJ from Republic Radio came and chatted to us and gave us some publicity on her show. So a bit of media interest was good, even if the locals were immune to our charms. 'Well, I suppose it's €7 UNICEF didn't have before we went out and made fools of ourselves,' I said as we piled into the van.

'Every little helps,' said Ella, who'd seen one too many Tesco adverts.

At least our spirits weren't too dampened by the experience, and importantly we were back on track after the Dubrovnik crisis.

That night we reached Asprovalta, about an hour east of Thessaloniki. The rain was lashing down as we arrived, but as we gazed through the misting-up windows at the churning Aegean Sea, the sky cleared. We parked on a stretch of the beach road that looked peaceful enough for some trouble-free gramping and headed out on foot into the tiny seaside town. We'd reached the stage in our journey where everything felt very out of season. All we were finding were chained gates at long-closed campsites and the ghosts of gleeful holiday-makers long since departed. Even a lot of the hotels were closed. There were clues all around of how busy these places must have been in the height of summer; shower points standing alone on the deserted beach, stacks of sun-loungers under tarpaulins, boarded up beach bars and brightly painted children's play areas abandoned, eerily desolate.

The locals were still around of course, and they had to eat, so one or two restaurants remained open. One empty bar in the ghost town promised nothing more tempting than those three syllables that had come to rule our lives: Free wi-fi. While Jill emailed and researched Turkey I got chatting to a local man who was enchanted by Penny. He'd lived in North Carolina for three years (hence his effortless English) and recalled with fondness his own purchase of a massive American motor-home which he'd driven across the States several times. I gave him our website address, told him of our adventure and that we'd busked earlier that day in Thessaloniki, but that wasn't what most impressed him. '*Five* of you?' he kept repeating. '*Five*? In that tiny van?'

It was a squeeze, but we were getting it down to a fine art. By this point we didn't even have to put up the small tent to make bag storage. We could stow all our luggage in the front underneath Edie's bunk, leaving the top bed (or 'upstairs' as we liked to call it, despite the glaring absence of any steps) for Ella and Bethan and the bottom rock 'n' roll bed for Jill and me. That might sound like 'hell in a tin box' (a phrase first coined by my wife on hearing I wanted to buy a camper van) but it's really not. That night, for example, we strolled back from the bar, cooked some risotto on Penny's little hob, put the beds in order, settled down to watch a comedy on the laptop before bidding each other 'G'night' in our own tribute to *The Waltons* and falling asleep to the rhythm of the breaking waves.

Bliss. Gramping can be great. And the price is right.

Mornings were trickier, I'll give you that. Blinking in the daylight you realise that the world has got up and is getting on with its busy day. Commuters pass by on nearby roads, and it feels as if someone has secretly moved your bed to the centre of a busy roundabout while you were sleeping. It was always an unsettling way to wake up. Also, of course, everyone wants a wee. If you can wait until the first coffee stop, or nip behind a tree, you get by. A shower is more difficult to find, but you'd be amazed at the all-over-freshness you can achieve with baby wipes. I'm sorry, were you eating? Well, I did promise you warts-and-all detail.

Approaching Turkey we paused for a few days at Alexandroupoli, just 34 miles from the Turkish border, where we found one of the few remaining campsites that was still open. It had free wi-fi which, to groans from the girls, meant two days of school work. Ella had loads of work to hand in through her online 'learning platform' so with parental tuition Bethan and Edie had to crack on with science and maths they'd not done for a week or so. I was given the choice between Edie's next science topic - the life cycle of a plant - or Bethan's next science topic. I bravely grappled with pollination while Jill spent the morning teaching our 11-year-old about human reproduction. Thank you. I accept your congratulations and shake you warmly by the hand.

A pause also gave us a chance to steel ourselves for our first proper border crossing. Turkey was the first country on our trip that required visas. These could be organised at the border, but we'd read contradicting info on vehicle insurance. Some websites said we needed Green Card insurance from our country of origin, others said we could buy it on the border. It was our first experience of how muddled all the information is that's out there on the various travel websites.

'Most of these accounts say to expect a three-hour wait to get visas sorted,' Jill reported from behind the laptop. 'Some talk about having to empty the vehicle for customs.'

I looked wearily at the chaotic state of Penny. 'They can help themselves. I hope they're good with a dustpan and brush.'

For its dramatic value, the border approach didn't let us down. Barriers were raised, passports were checked, armed soldiers waved us on to a bridge, and like Berlin's Checkpoint Charlie it had another barrier at the other side. As we crossed, the only thing sharing our bridge was a platoon of soldiers marching on exercise. More armed guards waved us onwards.

'Is that it?' we kept asking ourselves. The deserted road opened up. That had seemed easy. We rounded a bend. That wasn't it. Buildings, huts, barriers and guards greeted us, and beyond them, a prominent Turkish flag flew from a ridiculously high flagpole. At the first booth, a tiny window slid open and a gruff man who had been employed mainly for his angry, furrowed brow said, 'Passport.'

Jill, who for some reason had found herself driving this tricky stretch of the journey, handed them over.

He leafed through the first. 'No visa,' he grunted.

'No, we were hoping to buy that here,' Jill replied, her colonial English so perfect she might as well have added, 'my good fellow' at the end.

He leafed through the next passport. 'No visa.'

'That's right. We need to buy the visas here,' she pushed on. 'Where do we get the visas?'

Ignoring her, he started looking through the third. *Dear God, he's going to do this with all five.*

'No visa.'

'No. That's right. The thing is, you see, we need - to buy - the visas - here. *Here!*'

She was pointing and waving now. I looked on supportively from the passenger seat. Oblivious to her sign language, the man picked up the fourth passport. Jill sighed.

By the time he had ascertained that even Edie, a fully functioning nine-year-old, had failed to organise a Turkish visa for herself it was becoming obvious that this had never happened before. All those websites, guidebooks and forums had lied. This man was living proof that no one had ever turned up at his booth before without having a Turkish visa in their passport. We were screwed.

Finally he raised a finger and pointed at a hut just behind us. It had been obscured from view as we approached Mister Jolly's Happy Passport Booth. On it, a handmade sign read 'visa cash'.

'You go there,' instructed Mister Jolly and, refraining herself from saying, 'Why the bloody hell didn't you say that five minutes ago?' Jill parked up and we went to meet Mister Jolly's cousin, Harry Happypants.

His home was even smaller than Mister Jolly's. As all five of us battled a blistering gale to approach what looked like a grey steel Portaloo, I recalled the three hour wait we'd read about. My only experience of getting visas thus far had been getting our India ones which had involved two trips to London, an hour and a half of form-filling and three, yes *three*, different drafts of a covering letter until the authorities there conceded we were fit to visit. Imagining a similar rigmarole in these bleak, hostile surroundings, I gritted my teeth and tapped on the small dirty window, which slid open. 'We need five visas please,' I said pushing our passports through a wall of cigar smoke towards the shadow of a man in the fog. A calculator was tapped and its screen shown to me. 75.

'Each?' I asked horrified.

I heard a 'tsch,' and a wrinkled dark skinned face rolled its eyes. He tapped the calculator and spun it back at me. 15. He pointed at each of us.

'OK!' I shouted above the wind, raising my thumb to show him I understood sums. I pushed €75 towards him and expected a long, involved process of form filling to begin. I had come armed with reams of photocopied birth certificates, drivers' licences, international drivers' licences, marriage certificate - the works. In fact, what happened was this: he took my money and simply peeled five stickers from a large book. I couldn't see what the book was called, but I assume it was a brightly coloured children's book that read 'My First Visa Office' on the front. Each sticker was stuck in a passport, returned from the fog and the window slid shut.

My wallet was similarly relieved by the Green Card insurance broker who charged me €73 for a green sticker on an A4 sheet that would allow me to pass yet another smoking man in another tiny booth. He, in turn, sent me to (you guessed it) a fourth man in a fourth tiny booth who added his rubber stamp to my passport without even looking up from his newspaper.

And we were through.

Turkey, we quickly decided, was great. We encountered so many friendly people on that first day that we couldn't help but love it. Everyone from petrol station attendants to shop workers asked where we were from and where we were going and by the end of the day Edie had had her head stroked about twenty times.

Our destination was Istanbul, but we were realistic enough to know we wouldn't get there before dark, so our first night in Turkey was spent in yet another 'out of season' seaside town. Marmara Ereğlisi didn't have a campsite but, feeling flushed with the success of our first grueling border crossing, we offered a motel owner a reduced price for two rooms which he accepted. To save cash, Jill suggested we pop the roof up on Penny, now parked outside the motel in the middle of a small town square, and cook our own dinner. We were recounting the events of the day while pasta bubbled away under the bright strip light of Penny's kitchen when a car drew up. A man jumped out and came up to the window where our meal was cooking.

Jill slid it open, and the man reached into his pocket for some cash and seemed to be asking, in Turkish of course, what was on the menu.

Jill explained that we weren't actually selling the food, and with no more debate he hopped back into his car and drove away. It was only when the surreal moment sunk in a moment later that we kicked ourselves for not flogging him a bowl of delicious freshly made pasta in tomato sauce. 'What were we thinking?' Jill said. 'Forget busking – start cooking.'

To the echoes of our very first call to prayer from a distant minaret, the conversation that evening centered around the idea of selling food from Penny's side window. Pancakes, we decided, would be easy. By the time the girls had us selling crêpes in Istanbul from a newly sign-written van, the idea was running away with them. And we all know where that can lead. They weren't getting out of busking *that* easily. We went to bed, all of us giddy with excitement that we'd got into Turkey and that tomorrow we'd be driving into Istanbul, one of the cities we'd been looking forward to the most.

And what could possibly be wrong with driving in Istanbul?

Mark this point. This was the first morning we experienced a Turkish breakfast. The plates presented to us by the motel owner's wife bore sliced tomato, sliced cucumber, olives and a cold boiled egg. She placed a basket of fresh white bread on the table before stepping away a few paces to watch us eat.

'Is this lunch?' whispered Edie.

'I think so,' I whispered back. 'Don't say anything. Just eat.'

Apart from the surprise that the bread was *amazing* (Turks make great bread – much nicer than our British loaf or a French stick) it was exactly as you might expect a nice lunch salad to be. This breakfast, we later realised, is standard fare not only in Turkey, but in Syria and Jordan too. It was, therefore, the first of those Middle Eastern meals that we gulped down hungrily, naïvely unaware that it could ever be something we would tire of.

Our only mission that day was to get into, or at least near, Istanbul and find somewhere to camp. We wanted to spend a few days there, not only because, well, *it's Istanbul for goodness sake*, but also because one of the things we'd read on the Misinformation-net was that we could get our Syrian visas in Istanbul without having to do it in Ankara, meaning we could take a more interesting route south around the coast rather than cross the middle of the country. We also wanted to busk in Istanbul, even though the fact we hadn't heard *any* Western music on the radio at all filled us with busk-trepidation.

Jill had found three campsites, all located somewhere near the airport, and we were still searching for the first when we stopped, having battled huge traffic jams for an hour, to have a drink at a café in Yeşilköy, a small village on the fringes of Istanbul's suburbs. Again, the friendliness was overwhelming. The elderly café owner didn't speak much English, but understood I was looking for the campsite. He asked a young man who was his only other customer, who then insisted I wait while *he* phoned someone who would know. Between them, they wrote down instructions on how to get there. Then a third man arrived and joined in the debate. As we paid, and thanked them for their help, the third chap waved us over to his car. He wanted us to follow him.

So we piled into Penny and followed this random stranger, thinking the campsite must be just around the corner. 'He's probably got to drive past it on his way to somewhere else,' I said.

Ten minutes later, we were still following him. He stopped and jumped out at one point to ask a friend, who gave him further directions. 'We've got to give him something,' said Jill. 'What can we give him for all this trouble?'

'All we've got is a box of Turkish delight,' said Beth from the back. Then, after a pause added, 'That's probably the last thing he wants.'

He continued to escort us all the way to the hidden campsite on the outskirts of town before simply giving us a jaunty wave and driving off, back the way we'd come from. We hadn't even had a chance to thank him. It was what had by this time become known to us as a 'Milani moment'. I wonder, if I'd gone into a café in my home town to see a friend giving directions to a Turkish bloke about how to get to a campsite several miles away, whether I'd have jumped into my car and driven him out there. No, is the honest and slightly sheepish answer, I don't think I would.

We coasted through the gates of the campsite, relieved it was open. The received wisdom from guidebooks is that to gramp in Turkey is to tempt fate. 'Camping on the street or outside closed campsites is never worth the trouble,' one wrote, 'as the Police are very hot on moving you on.' The Turks were not at home to gramping, then. We'd already encountered some highly efficient parking wardens so official refuge was welcome. A security guard stepped out from a Reception hut to tell us the site was, in fact, closed. Furthermore, he explained, 'There is no camping in all of Istanbul now.' Oh dear. The next plan, then, was to find a hotel and ask if we could camp in their car park - something that apparently was not unusual in Turkey. And so we drove back through the friendly village of Yeşilköy and kept driving, deeper into Istanbul.

Four hours later we arrived, exhausted, ragged and spent ... exactly where we'd started in Yeşilköy.

A blow-by-blow account would drive you to tears, but suffice to say that for a city so massive, Istanbul offered a surprising lack of hotels. What it did have was a plentiful supply of traffic. Mad, insane, from-the-jaws-of-hell traffic. Oncoming lorries, one way streets randomly ignored, hand-carts sideways across two lanes, stray dogs, stray cats, stray children and suicidal scooters driving against the flow.

How we didn't die, I have no idea. To this day, so permanently is the near-death moment etched on our minds, we all still vividly recall a miracle millimetre miss with a head-on truck who swung the wrong way up our one-way street. There's a classic scene in the John Hughes film *Trains, Planes & Automobiles* where John Candy drives his car between two oncoming articulated trucks and, as sparks fly from each side, Steve Martin, terrified in the passenger seat, sees him as the devil. When they screech to a halt Steve realises he's been gripping so hard his finger nails are embedded into the dashboard. That's what it felt like in Istanbul - *for four hours.*

Every time we stopped at a petrol station to buy a map, there were none. And *twice* when we gesticulated and repeated, 'Maaap,' to the attendant we were offered a box of tissues. 'I know the Turkish for tissues,' I said, ploughing on into the throng. After ruling out the Holiday Inn as too pricey and the airport hotel because it was behind a locked barrier we found ourselves, as darkness fell, driving past the only other hotel we'd seen all day, back in Yeşilköy.

I'm sure my account of what happened next would differ greatly from that of my eldest daughter. I would describe events like this:

We, through great endeavour and tenacity, found a quaint little boutique hotel, the owner of which clearly wanted to help us, despite the fact that the hotel was in fact full.

'Have you got a car park we could camp in?' asked Jill. The bearded middle-aged man shook his head and continued perusing his heavily scrawled booking diary.

'I can put you all in one room tomorrow, but what are you going to do tonight?' he asked himself, stroking his beard. And that's when he, like the last inn-keeper in Bethlehem, offered a solution. Not a stable, but an attic.

Here's what the sequence of events must have been like for Ella:

Four hours in the car and we were exactly where we started. Unbelievable. At least Mum and Dad were so stressed they buckled and booked a hotel. Except the place they found wasn't a hotel. Not if your idea of a hotel is thick carpet, a revolving glass door and lifts. This was a house. A big, old, creepy-looking house. Inside, the walls were covered in weird little tapestries in frames and black and white photos of dead politicians.

The man said they were full, so we weren't staying, and even though the wind and rain had got worse, I fancied my chances back in the van. That's when the owner said something crazy. An idea so unthinkable only an idiot would take him up on it. And an idiot did. In the blink of an eye, we were traipsing up a huge spiral staircase to the top of the house to look at this guy's attic.

In the dark roof-space of this creaky mansion was a collection of tiny, single bedrooms. Little more than cupboards, really. There was no running water and by the look of the switches and wires Thomas Edison himself had installed the electrics. The man showed us five tiny doors. Behind four of them were cramped, old-fashioned cubby holes each with a bed. One had enough room for two little beds. I knew what my sisters were thinking: WHICH ONE OF US IS GONNA SLEEP ALONE?

'So we would have all these rooms?' my Dad asked, full of glee at the prospect.

'Oh yes,' said the man. 'Except this one.'

He pointed at door number five. It wasn't even a real door. More like half a door. A slim shutter you'd have to squeeze through. I could see light from under it. Someone was in. The owner pointed at me and my sisters.

'You need to realise,' he instructed, now quite serious, 'a man lives in there.'

There was a pause.

'But you are quite safe.'

With my heart in my mouth I heard the most terrifying sound I could have imagined. It was my Dad.

'We'll take it!'

Our new host David, was born in Chicago, married a Turkish girl and had lived in Istanbul for years. He laughed at the lunacy of us driving in the city. While he made us the now familiar Turkish breakfast we saw a local TV news item describe how the traffic had got so bad that locals were buying tiny boats and using the Bosphorus river to get to work. He pointed us to the local train that went straight to Sultanahmet, the old city.

The walk up the hill from the station takes you past Topkapi Palace, the Hagia Sophia and to the Blue Mosque. It beats the gasworks, believe me. The first thing that struck us was how calm and peaceful it was, despite the tourists. I had imagined Istanbul to be a constant cacophony of chattering, shouting, selling and bartering, but here you could wander the gardens and courtyard of the Blue Mosque and hear birdsong.

Following an insider tip we went from the Blue Mosque to the depths of the city, literally, descending into the cool darkness of the Basilica Cistern. This underground reservoir built by Byzantine emperor Justinian in the year 532 is visually and architecturally incredible. Over three hundred majestic columns support a stone roof spanning a 65m by 143m area. It once held nearly a million cubic metres of water, which was carried by miles of aqueducts to the Great Palace and its surrounding buildings. The cistern was eventually closed and apparently forgotten until a scholar called Petrus Gyllius was researching Byzantine history in 1545. He heard stories of locals who could lower a bucket from their basement and pull up water. Some were even catching fish. He dug around, literally, and rediscovered the cistern. But even the Ottomans didn't think too much of it and the cistern became a dumping ground for all sorts of waste, including dead bodies.

It's these facts that make a visit so enthralling, not just to see it fully restored, its beautifully lit pillars rising from the water, but to find those dark, unlit corners and imagine what it must have been like for old Petrus, discovering it by the light of a flaming torch and bumping into God-knows-what down there.

We had a popular fast food lunch of a fish sandwich in Eminonu under the Galata bridge. Hundreds of fishing rods protrude from both sides of the bridge and the dockside below as hoards of anglers aged five to 95 effortlessly pluck sardines from the water. It's a wonder the fish never learn. This constant supply not only feeds the fishermen, but also stocks a bustling row of restaurants whose speciality is simply grilled fish - sardines or mackerel are most common - in a chunk of fresh bread with some salad. A better example of self-sufficiency you couldn't hope to see, in a country that prides itself on being genuinely self-sufficient. Even in 2010, Turkey was able to grow and produce everything it consumed, which probably explained why the food was so cheap. The motorway service stations had better stocked delicatessens than most English market towns. Olives, nuts, spices and pulses were sold loose from barrels. Trays of fresh Baklava - delicious diamonds of honey, pistachio and puff pastry - lay temptingly alongside cheese counters and ... oh, wiper blades. You forget you're on a motorway.

Full of fish, as we negotiated the city on foot and on trams we were reminded of our Florence experience; how first impressions can be so wrong. The day before we would gladly have never set foot in Istanbul again. Today we loved her. Trying accurately to describe her size and sprawl is hopeless. Istanbul the city is bigger than Switzerland the country. We had an interesting conversation with Hollis, a New Yorker whose husband is Turkish, who compared Istanbul to the burgeoning mega cities of Cairo and Buenos Aires, cities that redefine what we consider a city to be. They're so big, their own suburbs feel like cities within a city. It was no surprise to her whatsoever to hear that we'd spent four hours driving around and had found neither the centre nor the edge of Istanbul.

Gaining visas for Syria was always going to be the biggest bureaucratic battle on this journey and our mission the next morning was to gather all our official paperwork and introduce ourselves to the Syrian Consulate. In 2010, after 20 years of being a police state, and just a few months before a revolutionary and bloody uprising, Syria was very cautious about who it let in. Consequently they did not issue visas at the border with Turkey - you had to get them in advance. The Syrian Embassy in London had made it very clear that travellers should obtain their visas before setting off. However, if more than three months passed between obtaining the visa in your country of residence and getting to the Syrian border, or equally important back *out* of Syria, getting your visa in advance would prove useless because after three months it expired. So what did people like us do?

We turned to the Internet, of course. Plus we consulted new-edition guide books and even called a few embassies. Welcome, reader, to the twisty, turny, Alice in Wonderland world of upside-down and inside-out contradictory information I like to call Syrian Border Control. At the time of our travelling all of these things were true:

- People *had* obtained visas at the border. Some people (from the USA mainly) had taken up to eight hours to process, others were through in half an hour.
- People as recently as a week earlier had been turned away at the border for not having a visa. No one knew why there was a discrepancy – it was apparently a game of chance.
- All guide books advised against leaving it until the border. The guide books and travel websites said we could obtain our single entry visas in advance from the Syrian Embassy in Ankara.
- The Syrian Embassy in Ankara said we couldn't. Only Turkish residents could.
- Non-Turkish residents *had* obtained single entry visas at Ankara. They had posted online accounts saying so.
- Non-Turkish residents had also obtained single entry visas from the Syrian Consulate in Istanbul.
- The Syrian Consulate in Istanbul *did not* issue visas to non-Turkish residents.

I know that last one is true because we tried. A very polite woman answered the door, three flights up an old office block in the Maçca part of Istanbul. It was as she explained that under no circumstances were they able to issue visas to non-residents, that I remembered a conversation we'd jokingly had with the girls months earlier. We had talked about Edie turning on the tears to get us through a difficult border crossing and she chose this moment to remember. While I was engrossed in trying to explain our dilemma to the Syrian woman, I noticed Edie dramatically throwing her hands over her face. The Oscar-winning gesture was only cemented further when Bethan clutched the poor waif into her chest, and stroked her hair as if to comfort her. Intriguingly, the woman's first advice to us was to get a visa at the border.

'Is that possible?' I asked.

'I have friends who've done it. It's quite common.'

'Really?' I beamed. This was great news.

'It is a risk though,' she added.

Ah. 'Can you contact the border and check with them?'

'No. We are nothing to do with them.'

'Can you phone the Ankara embassy and check if we can get our visas there?'

'No. We are nothing to do with them.'

'Can you at least give us a letter, or a note, just to say we've been here and tried to get visas?'

'No.' I heard a sniff next to me. Streep and Dench were taking it up a level.

'Wait a minute,' she added. 'Let me go and check with my boss about the situation at the border.'

We waited, shuffling our feet nervously, cluttering up the gloomy stairwell. Beth and Edie congratulated each other on a performance worthy of the Academy's attention. The lady returned. 'No. You cannot get your visas at the border.'

'But you just said that ...'

'You cannot.'

'But you know people who ...'

'I'm sorry.'

And then she added, helpfully, 'Perhaps you need to skip Syria. Goodbye.'

That was the solution from the Syrian Consulate: don't go to Syria.

We tried not to let the setback get us down, but the afternoon sights, sounds and smells of the wonderful spice bazaar and equally impressive, but much more touristy, Grand Bazaar were undoubtedly sharing space in our heads with Plans B, C and D.

That evening was spent getting quotes to ship Penny from Istanbul to Jordan, weighing up the price of one of us flying back to London to get the visas sorted there versus sailing or flying to Aqaba. There were lots of options.

'The offices are closed now,' I said. 'Tomorrow we'll get some definitive advice from the Syrian embassies in Ankara and London.' Jill and Ella exchanged a glance.

'Yeah, right,' they said in unison.

Besides, we needed another day in Istanbul in which to busk, and – although I didn't know it - for me to receive a nasty injury from an almost-naked angry man.

We were in a great mood the next morning because (pause for dramatic announcement) the rent money was in the bank! Our tenant continued to proclaim that he was pursuing the missing first month's rent after a banking error, but the payment for the *second* month appeared so we *weren't* going home. Phew! And what better way to celebrate than to stand in front of a bunch of Turkish strangers singing Beatles songs? I could tell the band needed convincing, so by way of an incentive, I promised Jill and the girls that we could all enjoy an authentic Turkish bath - *after* we had busked. It was three weeks since we'd picked up our instruments way back in Thessaloniki and the only cure for nerves was bribery. Advice from those who knew the city, like David and Hollis, was to perform in Taksim Square. I'd had my eye on all the tourist coaches serving up a ready-made audience at the Blue Mosque, but they begged to differ.

'Taksim is *real* Istanbul,' they'd enthused. 'It's the transport hub. Commuters, businesses, shops - always busy, and famous too. There's a big statue of Mustafa Atatürk. You can't miss it.'

And we didn't. As the bustling metro elevators pushed us up into the drizzle of Taksim Square, we were all momentarily lost for words, not through awestruck wonder, but through fear. It was *huge*. Metro stations, bus stops, tram stops and the short funicular railway all collide in a wide square lined with cafés and restaurants. (As a complete aside, two weeks later terrorists saw the same popular potential and a suicide bomber blew up a bus full of police officers there. Missing a bomb attack by seconds is a story. Missing one by a fortnight isn't. But it was a sobering reminder that so much of our journey was in the lap of the gods.)

David was right - this was real. Real Turks busily getting on with their real lives, getting real wet and looking real miserable. More than a little daunted we headed for the statue of Turkey's republican founder, where a couple of policemen sat in their car watching the gathered throng. A stage was being set up for a concert that evening. We tucked ourselves behind a large advertising board, obscuring us from the police's view, erected our pop-up sign and launched into our first number. Despite the drizzle, we raised a few smiles, and by the end of *All You Need Is Love* we'd drawn a crowd of about a dozen onlookers. As we played through *All My Loving* and *Ob-La-Di* several locals even donated, but when I spoke to them not one of them knew the songs. 'Well, that could be the way we're playing them,' I admitted. 'Have you heard of The Beatles?'

Blank looks. Something inside me lurched a little. It was the feeling explorers must get when they stumble upon a lost tribe in the Amazon.

I had wandered into a land that was oblivious to The Biggest Band In The Universe. We had taken our first tiny step out of the comfort zone of our Western world.

We wrapped our set when, during *Norwegian Wood*, the nearby stage crew started sound-checking their colossal speakers by playing Pink Floyd's *Brick In The Wall* loud enough to shake Atatürk to his concrete foundations. Without missing a beat, we started miming along. I knew the words, Ella pulled her flute into two silver drumsticks and Edie threw some 'rock' shapes. We actually went down quite well. It was only later that Jill pointed out the irony of this anthem to truancy being performed by the girls while their mates back home were stuck in Tuesday morning school. We met a few English speakers, another New Yorker and a guy from Cape Town who watched our full half-hour set. 'I love *Hey Jude*,' he said at one point.

'*We don't do that one*' is a phrase I should have had printed on a T shirt.

We raised about 23TL (Turkish Lira) - a tenner in English pounds, met some interesting people, gave some baffled locals a smile, and considered it a triumph. Time to pay the band.

But before the Turkish bath, lunch, and a couple of Embassy phone calls. A tiny café off Taksim Square provided the finest chicken kebabs we'd ever tasted – drizzled in home-made marinade and wrapped with a fresh mint salad in the freshest flat bread imaginable. I drool at the memory, even though I've long since stopped eating meat. The munching bliss was only sullied by three frustrating calls to the Syrian Embassy in Ankara. They started by saying they didn't issue visas to non-residents, then when I explained that I couldn't get a visa in my own country because it would have expired, there was a pause. I asked them what a traveller in my position should do to get into Syria, and they hung up. That happened all three times I called them. It made me laugh in the end.

The Syrian embassy in *London* - surely they could help. Guess what the first thing the man there asked me? 'Have you tried the embassy in Ankara? You should get it there.' Unbelievable. Not even the country's own consulates and embassies, knew what their own policy was.

By the time we were washing down our kebabs with huge glasses of freshly squeezed pomegranate juice (cheaper than water) we had decided on a plan. Drive to Ankara and try there. If it's a 'no', drive to the border and try our luck there. If *that's* a 'no' we would be stuck waiting for the embassy in London to process our visas – a two-week turnaround, plus the less-than-ideal situation of posting all our passports away.

But now wasn't the time for such trivial worries. We had busked in Turkey! It was time for a treat. An outrageous luxury, a frivolous expense: a genuine Turkish bath. The Hamam. We'd all seen it on the telly: Michael Palin getting smothered in clouds of bubbles, kids' TV presenters having buckets of water thrown at them (a natural reaction: they get that a lot). And here in the heart of Istanbul's ancient city was arguably the most famous bath-house of them all, the Çemberlitas Hamam.

This impressive suite of baths was built by the architect Sinan in 1584. No, I'd never heard of him either, but judging by the huge twin marble domes, ornate pillars and beautifully carved marble benches, I guess his quote was eye-watering.

The first bonus, on descending the steps into the peaceful reception area was finding that the kids were half price (about a tenner each), which, given that Edie only visits the wet end of a bathroom about as often as Halley's Comet visits the inner solar system, made it reasonable value.

There are three options for patrons (although prices may have changed by the time you're reading this) - for 35TL (£14) you can relax in the bathing area, lying on the heated marble platform and soaking up the calm for as long as you like. But you're washing yourself. No one's touching you. (In retrospect this sounds very appealing). For 55TL (£22) you get a sound soaping down, scrub, massage and wash from one of the Hamami attendants. For 95TL (£38) you get all that plus a half-hour massage involving oils, a table and a brand new friend who knows every inch of you intimately.

The leaflet was keen to stress that men and women each have their own identical bathing areas, but the level of nudity seemed a little vague. Guide books talked of 'wearing a bikini', an option which could provide me with two firsts in a day. The *Lonely Planet* guide instructed that one should only decide on whether to strip naked after 'gauging the atmosphere', a phrase that became something of a running joke in our family during the build-up to the event. 'Why, oh why, didn't I gauge the atmosphere?' we would joke, imagining the possible embarrassments that lay ahead.

After weighing up the price chart at the busy reception desk, just off the street, we opted for something a cut above blue stripe 'value range' but not as lavish as 'taste the difference' luxury, choosing the mid-price option.

Touching had been given the green light.

And so we parted, Jill and the girls to their soapy spa paradise, and me, on my own, being shepherded by a tiny wrinkled man in a loin cloth who may or may not have been Gollum, to what appeared to be a tiny 1960s holiday camp chalet.

This tiny box of a room had a slim door with frosted glass, just enough room for a junior size bed and a little table. I was instantly taken back to Butlins in Bognor, where I had gigged as a Children's TV (ahem) 'star' back in the 1990s and they had put me up in a room almost identical. If the Hamami attendant had suddenly produced a puppet aardvark on his arm, I probably could have done a glittering 45 minute set. Momentarily disoriented, I nearly missed Gollum explaining with the words 'change' and 'lock' that this was my cue to get my kit off and use this room as my locker. He handed me a tiny petemal - a printed cotton cloth about the size of a small hand towel - and graciously took his leave, leaving me to ponder Today's Big Decision.

As I toyed with the elastic on my boxer shorts, it was remarkably hard to 'gauge the atmosphere' from inside my Butlins chalet. *In for a penny*, I thought and stuffed them with the rest of my clothes into our instrument bag. (Yes, I really had visited the ancient Hamam carrying a ukulele, a squeezebox, a flute, sundry percussion instruments and a collapsed pop-up goal bearing our Beatnik Beatles signage. I bet Michael Palin never multi-tasked like this.)

I made my way back out on to the landing area rather sheepishly, wrapped only in the briefest of cotton tea towels, and leaned nonchalantly on the balcony's wooden rail. I instantly threw myself back against the wall, realising that this raised gallery overlooked the busy reception area one floor down, and anyone idly glancing up would glimpse a sight that was not entirely the Turkey they'd been expecting. Clinging to the wall as I shuffled along, I found the hobbit, who pointed me not to a wondrous glowing doorway billowing steam and golden sunlight from around its gilded edge, but back down the staircase to reception.

'There must be some mistake. I'm already changed,' I said, meekly stating the obvious.

He pointed down the stairs. There was no mistake.

Courtie you fool, I thought. *You could have been sipping coffee and eating Baklava in a charming café, but oh no, you just had to get your clothes off in public. Idiot.*

I took a deep breath and descended the stairs. Was I imagining it or was reception busier than normal? As the door to the street swung open again I saw a blustery squall was chasing pedestrians into the doorway for shelter.

'Afternoon,' I said, nodding politely to the anorak-clad crowds gathering at the ticket desk, who suddenly smiled at this surprise floor-show. I continued, exposed but for the briefest flapping cotton, towards a burly-looking Turk who was beckoning me over to another door.

I knew from the pictures in the leaflet what to expect. The central domed room has a large raised circular marble platform in the middle, on which bathers sit or lie gazing up at the tiny glass holes in the dome which let daylight puncture the gloom like tiny stars. Around the edge are stone arches that lead to smaller bathing rooms in which you can scoop hot water in large copper dishes and sloosh yourself down with the kind of gay abandon that in most other bathrooms would flood the living-room below.

As I felt the humidity hit me, my eyes adjusted to the dim light. The leaflet had pictured a few svelte girls, artistically lit, stretched out on the marble platform but I guessed, based on countless travel documentaries, that the men's section would be occupied by a couple of overweight Turks and possibly a middle-aged banker or two. Today, however, the Çemberlitas Hamam appeared to be hosting the wrap party for Elite Model Agency's *World's Top Male Model* contest. Female readers might be surprised to learn that we men, despite our bravado and gruff exterior, do actually notice how handsome/ugly, fit/fat other men are. You know that competitive comparison thing women have that makes them hate Kiera Knightley? Well, we're not that bad. It's almost unconscious, probably deep in our tribal instincts, a sense that reassures us that we belong. Or, in my case, that I didn't. Two dozen 20-year-old lads rippled two dozen washboard stomachs as I entered the arena, swiftly tensing my love handles. I didn't know what to do. It was like walking into a house party on your own but there was no kitchen to flee to. I'd been handed a yellow plastic tag at reception which was to show the bathing-attendants which services I'd paid for, but no one took it from me or seemed very interested, so I found a spot on the marble platform and shuffled uneasily into the middle to lie down.

The Elite Models were, like any bunch of lads in a slightly uneasy near-naked scenario, doing all they could to prove they weren't gay.

If it hadn't meant exposing themselves, they'd have been flicking towels at each other (although I did actually witness this in the showers later). They were splashing water at each other, arching their wet backs on the marble to make fart noises, some were even playfully rubbing each others shoulders, laughing in a 'wouldn't it be funny if we really enjoyed this sort of thing' way. Ironically they couldn't have looked more homoerotic if they'd thrown on a Kenny Loggins track and started playing volleyball.

I wandered over to a vacant side room and had a sloosh. I tried to catch the eye of the wiry old man who was washing and scrubbing a chap at the edge of the big platform, but there didn't seem to be a system for who got washed and when. I sat in the stone annexe surveying the central scene of joshing and hilarity and waited. I'd found my kitchen.

Soon, I was summoned to approach the platform by a walking mountain wearing a small white towel. He was the shape of Obelix in the *Asterix* cartoons and a man of very few words. 'Come,' he ordered, so I did. 'Lie,' he pointed at the edge of the circular platform, so I did. Probably out of nervousness, I tried to strike up a conversation with him as he donned a scrubbing mitt and started to rub me down.

'What is your name?' I asked. His stern face remained emotionless. 'Safad.'

And that's where the conversation ended because he was leaning on my chest so hard I couldn't speak. I don't think Safad was much of a talker. I was just pondering how Safad sounded like the name of a terrorist splinter group, when he removed the mitt, squeezed a cotton bag of soapy bubbles over me and started his own reign of terror. In becoming a hamami, Safad had clearly sacrificed a sparkling career as a cage fighter. What started as a vigorous rub down developed into what Safad would later call a 'massage', although The Hague War Crimes Committee might have taken an altogether dimmer view.

We got off to a bad start. I was on my back and Safad was pushing his rivet-gun thumbs deep into my thighs causing me such considerable pain that I was clenching my teeth, squirming and shouting 'Argh' quite a lot. Then a middle-aged bearded man came up and started arguing with Safad. He was in some sort of dispute over the colour of his white plastic tab, and was clearly venting his frustration in Turkish to the first person he could find who worked there. Safad was having none of it, and continued to pummel my deepest muscles while arguing with the aggrieved punter.

And then it happened.

I burst out laughing. It was completely involuntary. The ridiculousness of the situation I was looking up at coincided with a surprising twinge of pain from Safad's evil hands and I started laughing. The random guy looked down at me, furious. Safad was unrelenting. This made me laugh even more. I was now in that horrible place I call a 'church laugh'. Having a vicar for a father meant I spent a lot of my childhood in church. I also spent a lot of my childhood in whispered conversations with mates during services and know the perils of getting trapped in a 'church laugh'. It's when something hysterically funny happens exactly at the moment when you mustn't laugh. When a congregation is at its most silent, contemplating some enormous tragedy like Ethiopian famine, or the untimely death of a much-loved parishioner, that is when your entire body will be aching, bursting, throbbing to explode into laughter at some private joke only you and a friend are aware of. The fact you *mustn't* laugh, makes it all the funnier.

The angry man tried to continue venting his spleen at Safad, who continued to pummel ruthlessly while I laughed like a drain, hostage to the situation. It was horrible. Inside I was aware what an imbecile I looked, but I was out of control. The fact that the angry man may have thought I was laughing at *him* just made me laugh even more. The fact that I so desperately wanted to stop laughing just increased the hysteria. As the disgruntled customer stormed off, Safad took my mirth as a sign that I wasn't taking his work seriously enough and stepped up his campaign.

Now lying on my stomach, I took deep breaths and tried to get a grip, which is exactly what Safad was doing with my feet. He was pushing them so hard into the marble that I was squirming like a fish out of water trying to find a position where my bones wouldn't be crushed to dust. And still I giggled. What the hell was wrong with me? I considered that perhaps Safad had inflicted internal bleeding and I was experiencing the euphoria that is sometimes observed just prior to death.

Please let it stop!

By the time he had pushed my shoulder blades almost through my chest to touch the marble beneath, I was actually banging my hand on the warm wet surface shouting, 'I submit'.

He concluded his torture with a final wallop to my back and stood back, happy with a job well done. I tenderly picked myself up and looked around. A few of the Elite Models were glancing at me, unimpressed. I knew I was getting picked last for volleyball.

Safad the Life Squeezer showed me to a second room for more soaping of hair and slooshing with gallons of water, then bade me goodbye with a vice-like shake of my hand. 'Massage good?' he asked.

'Yes,' I replied, shakily. What else could I say? I wanted to say 'No. You clearly have anger issues. You hurt me, and furthermore, you appeared to take considerable pleasure from inflicting pain. You are a very bad man, Safad.' But he was much bigger than me.

'You tip good,' he said.

'Of course,' I said

'You look,' he added, not letting go of my hand. 'You find.'

'Yes, yes,' I urged. 'I will look for you when I'm changed.' *Dear God let me go.*

Look for him? Some bloody chance, I thought as I wrapped myself in dry towels and headed back to my Butlins chalet. It was creepy enough that I'd endured some sort of sadomasochistic humiliation.

Paying my torturer for the pleasure? What would that make it? Too weird, that's what. I gingerly got changed and headed for the stairs back down to reception where a cool drink and glossy magazines would while away the minutes until the return of the girls. I swung around the bottom flight, and who's standing at the foot of the stairs, hot and sweating with a face like a bulldog chewing a wasp? Bloody Safad.

I pulled 10TL from my pocket and stuffed it into his voluminous palm. I felt dirty. Which was ironic given where I'd just been.

And that's not the end of the episode. That evening, while my shirt gaped open at the neck, there was a cry of alarm from Edie. 'Woah! What is *that*?'

She was pointing at my chest. I looked in the mirror, and sure enough, she had reason to be perturbed. A large lump had appeared on my collar bone. It didn't hurt, but it certainly looked odd. As for all medical queries, I once again turned to Doctor Google for advice. What I was seeing, and what was making my entire family go 'eurgh', was my sterno-clavicular joint, where the clavicle (collar bone) meets the sternum (big bone in the middle of your chest). It's held in place by ligaments, I learned, and can sometimes dislocate forwards, usually as a result of car crashes or sports injuries. There was no mention of mountainous masseurs. Lots of people, I read, have visited their doctors with one clavicle sticking out asymmetrically only to be told, 'You've dislocated your sterno-clavicular joint. Live with it.' So I do.

It is my special lump and I call it Safad's Trophy. He tried to break me, and medically speaking, he did. But mentally, I'm a rock. I can even use a bathroom now without crying.

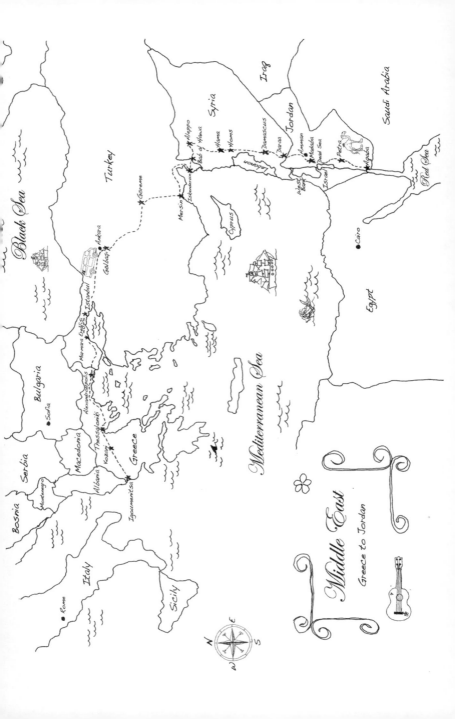

Middle East

Greece to Jordan

'*Getting Syrian visitor visas is a straightforward process in Ankara,*' claimed the superb and normally accurate Lonely Planet Guide. '*A single-entry visa costs €20. You need two passport photos and can pick up the visa on the same day you lodge your application.*'

Couldn't be simpler. Or indeed, further from the truth.

Having driven several hours of dull motorway from Istanbul to Ankara, we'd found the only camp-ground available, which was actually a bit of wasteland behind a rather posh hotel in Golbasi on the outskirts of the capital. It was far from anything approaching idyllic, but we were here for one purpose and one purpose only. So, armed with passports, cash, kids' birth certificates and letters from employers to prove we weren't Syria's greatest fear (busking beatniks), we found the Syrian Embassy.

Imagine a stunning white marble edifice glistening in the Turkish sunshine. Gleaming pillars frame a grand white staircase where a tanned, uniformed doorman shows you into a breathtaking lobby with deep plush carpets and ornate chandeliers. That's how I imagined the Syrian Embassy to be. It's not like that. We walked past it twice before we spotted a dirty brass plaque on a gate that was so grey, industrial and bound in barbed wire I assumed it was the entrance to a building site. A postman pressed a buzzer so I waited next to him for the gate to open, which it did, just wide enough to fit an envelope through, just long enough for me to say, 'Visa?' and get the gate slammed in my face.

The cheerful Turkish postie pointed us a few yards to the left where a small booth stood behind more barbed wire that had a hole cut in it just big enough to see the booth window. Through this tiny portal lay the land George W. Bush famously described as The Axis of Evil. I'd always disregarded that phrase as the paranoid ranting of America's least worldly president, so imagine my surprise to find, sitting inside the booth, The Axis of Evil himself.

From beneath a crop of ginger hair and behind an impressively bushy ginger moustache, glared Ankara's Most Angry Man.

'Good morning,' I chirped. I may not speak the language but good manners cost nothing. 'We are English,' I said, nodding over my shoulder to include the family. The look on his face read utter disdain. 'We are travelling to Syria and need a single-entry visa.' I smiled despite his immunity to my charms.

'You have Turkish resident's permit?' growled the moustache.

'No. We are travelling from the UK. We were told by the British Em ...'

'No tourist visas. I cannot help.'

'The problem we have is that we couldn't apply for our visas in the UK as they would have expired.'

'Passports,' grunted the hirsute one. This was progress. I eagerly shoved our passports through the hole in the fence and he took them. Leafing through the first one, 'No visa,' he said before casting it aside. He leafed through the next.

'No visa,' and it spun across the table to join the first. He picked up the next passport. *Good grief. I've been here before.*

'We don't have our visas. We were told to come here for them.'

By now all five passports were thrust back in my hand.

'How do we get visas?'

'Goodbye'

And with that, The Axis of Evil slammed the window shut and, just in case this was too subtle a signal that our conversation was over, stood up and left the booth.

'We'll take that as a no then!' shouted Jill after him. It was all kicking off with the Syrians, but before my punchy wife could start a proper diplomatic incident, he was disappearing into the embassy.

We returned to our bleak little campsite to find we were no longer its only residents. A mighty Toyota Land Cruiser had arrived emblazoned with logos and a cartoon rat. Neil and Silvie (with an 'i') were a South African couple on a mission to drive from Britain to South Africa as part of the Rambling Rat project that benefits the charity Street Kids International. The first thing they said after our 'hellos' was that they were in Ankara to sort out their Syrian visas. And guess who they'd been to see? The Malevolent Moustachioed Misery himself. Neil had even managed to get into a bit of a row with him, so it warmed my heart to know what a terrific day that bloke had had.

They had then gone straight to their own South African Embassy, where they'd been greeted enthusiastically by a man who was thrilled to find real South Africans in Ankara, and who assured them that with a nod, a wink, and a decent bottle of wine, an official letter could be produced that would get them a visa from the Syrians. They were sorted.

Jill called our own Embassy again where a man in the consular section told her that until just two months ago the British Embassy *could* have written us a letter that would have had the necessary leverage over the road in Syria. But for reasons unexplained the Syrians had changed their minds. That left us with the 'chance it on the border' option, or, following the advice of the Syrian Embassy in London, sending all our passports back to the UK to be processed.

'What would the British Embassy's advice be on the wisdom of an English family in Turkey sending their passports back to the UK?' Jill asked the chap on the phone.

You could almost hear the alarm bells ringing inside this man's head as he stressed *several* times that under *no* circumstances would the British Embassy advise us one way or the other on this course of action. For one thing, it would make us illegal.

'But what does that really mean?' she asked.

'Well, if you were stopped by the police, and you're in Turkey without any passports, and therefore without Turkish visas, you're breaking the law. It would be - awkward,' said the man, choosing his word carefully.

'But what other option do we have?'

'You could skip Syria. Fly to Jordan?' he suggested.

'We're driving.'

'Ah.'

So we made photocopies of the Turkish visa pages in our passports, as he had advised, and sent the precious originals with our paperwork and necessary fee to London courtesy of DHL.

We were now officially 'illegals' in Turkey. That's when we were joined on our little plot of land by another VW T25, just like our Penny. Max and Sylvie (with a 'y' - I know, you don't meet a Sylvie in years ...) were French and doing pretty much what we were - driving around the world. And guess what brought them to Ankara? You're ahead of me. They became the 8th and 9th members of our Syrian Visa Club. They, like us, ended up sending their passports back to their own Syrian Embassy in Paris and awaiting their return to the French Embassy a week or so later. We formed a merry little gang in that few days we all shared Ankara's only patch of camping ground, swapping notes on previous highlights and horrors, and debating when we should start taking anti-malarial tablets. The risk of catching malaria would start in southern Turkey, but you have to start the medication a couple of weeks before you're in the danger zone, so the five of us dutifully swallowed our first of what would be eight weekly doses. Over the following 24 hours the five of us dutifully ran to the toilet, acknowledging that the 'possible side-effects' were exactly as described on the box.

When I look back on the collective visa problems we were all having, and given what happened in Syria just a few months after this, I think our little clan must have been among the last foreigners to attempt to drive through the country before political instability and the Arab Spring uprising made all travel there impossible. It was maddening that no one at any embassy or consulate seemed to be able to help us, but I wonder now what was going on behind the scenes. I suspect certain authorities in Syria were already getting twitchy, and early defences were going up.

'Five thousand miles since home' clicked by and we reached Göreme, which you'll find nestled among the stunning and world-renowned rock formations of Cappadocia. The incredible landscape is a living science lesson in rocks and erosion. If you didn't know your sedimentary from your igneous, nature has kindly provided a demonstration of their differences in central Turkey on a massive scale.

The ancient volcanic eruption of Erciyes Daği deposited such a mix of mineral deposits that thousands of years of wind and water erosion have left clusters of 'fairy chimneys' (tall conical towers) for tourists to clamber around, and stunning valleys of rippling stone from which Byzantines cut houses, churches, whole cities which still exist. The most famous cluster of churches is now an Open Air Museum and a UNESCO World Heritage Site.

'Gosh Sim,' I hear you say in quiet awe. 'This place sounds wondrous. You discovered a fantastical lost land.'

Yes, I did. But so did about four hundred million other people before me. Cappadocia is one of Turkey's BIG tourist attractions. You can fly from the UK to holiday there. Tour companies bus hundreds of punters daily from as far away as Ankara, three hours north.

The 'I'm not a tourist, I'm a traveller' snob in me reared its ugly head again.

I know it's not a very nice trait, to look down my nose at those perfectly decent travellers of a certain age (and usually a certain size) who pour from luxury cruise ships into air conditioned coaches to be couriered, cocooned from the world around them, to the very heart of some ancient city (I'm looking at you, Dubrovnik) before ultimately, at some point (after many, many large lunches and countless all-you-can-eat buffet dinners), being disgorged into the tiny, hewn-from-bare-rock doorway of an 11th century monastic church to gaze in wonder at their lack of cell-phone signal while completely ignoring iconoclastic ochre paintings that they couldn't see anyway because THEY'RE BLOCKING THE LIGHT!

Sorry for shouting. Like I say, I'm not proud. I may have got a bit cross at the Open Air Museum and been heard to mutter, 'UNESCO has ruined this,' as we fought and battled with the throngs of apparently uninterested slack-jawed tourists who obediently jammed themselves into whichever tiny unlit church their tour guide told them to for their allotted five minutes before baaing and bleating in their mother tongue while their flag-bearing shepherd rounded them noisily onwards to the next impossibly narrow passage or doorway.

Of course UNESCO *hasn't* ruined it. That's illustrated by how badly the surrounding churches and houses, outside the UNESCO site, have fared with their graffiti and dilapidation. But I defy anyone to walk around the jewel in Göreme's crown and not imagine what it was like before 1985. Before the coach parties. Before the theme park landscaped pathways, with their rope fences, and their conveniently placed café stops, peeking from between historic treasures with their jaunty illustrations of coffee cups and burgers. Before the turnstiles and the market stalls selling Turkish tat and filling the air with electro dub reggae.

Far more enjoyable than the ticketed-entry World Heritage Site was the free fun we had exploring the miles of hills and valleys filled with the remains of ancient dwellings and churches. Off the beaten track, we often had entire settlements to ourselves, and would clamber up steeply eroded inclines to crawl into dark cave-houses where, once your eyes adjust to the gloom, you can find the beds, the fireplace, the seats, all cut from rock bearing the tool marks of a thousand years ago. Every now and then we'd discover a painting, the Virgin Mary, or Jesus, the red ochre flaking off the wall high above the reach of idle vandals' hands. Everywhere there were the ghosts of ancient inhabitants. It was incredible. It was like letting your kids climb over Stonehenge. Thrilling, and yet naughty enough for you to wonder why it's even allowed.

A pure fluke led us, two days after parting in Ankara, to share the same Göreme campsite with Neil and Silvie, the young 'Rambling Rat' South Africans. So reunited, one hot afternoon we all hiked down the Red Rose valley, a twisty, fertile cutting through the bizarre rocks we overlooked from our camping ground. Neil was a secondary school science teacher, so we counted that as a school day as he taught us about rock formation, erosion and gave us an insight into their passion - ornithology. He dished out binoculars for us all and Edie made a list of at least 15 types of birds we spotted, the most exciting of which, if you're a twitcher, were rock sparrows (very localised to that area), a Syrian woodpecker (I didn't get a chance to ask it about its visa credentials), and a long legged buzzard (or Cher, as she's better known).

During our four-day stay in Göreme, we found ourselves part of an exclusive group of 'overlanders'. The Kaya campsite was almost empty. It was just us, Neil and Silvie, a couple of Canadians and a Dutch couple. They were Margot and Charles, sporting a shiny modern VW T5, while Bill and Pam had flown from Canada and bought a T25 like ours in Europe.

'Hey, let's get together later and get the guitar out,' suggested Bill from behind his bushy grey beard. We'd told him our story and understandably (though mistakenly) he'd assumed we were musicians. His wife Pam was a musician, and when he told us she'd seen our website and read our blog, we were flattered, but agreed a campfire sing-song was out of the question on these cold evenings, plus campfires weren't allowed.

Phew, nicely ducked, I thought.

'Why don't we use the communal kitchen?' suggested Jill before I could wrestle her to the ground and stuff a sock in her mouth.

'Great idea,' beamed Pam. 'A cook-house sing-song!'

'Although you may not fancy it,' she added, looking at me. 'You look terrible.'

I was ill. We'd all got a bit poorly after our first dose of anti-malarials and my ailment had spun into a nasty cold. As Pam and Jill planned the evening's shindig I was sipping hot lemon and honey, blinking, bleary eyed, from within the 'underwater fog' you suffer with blocked sinuses.

'Dot at all. Itta be fud,' I heard myself saying, which is how, several hours later, the whole gang of us were sharing stories, songs and some rather sticky cake late into the evening. Despite our ropey health, Ella played the flute, Beth picked up her squeezebox and I bashed out chords on the uke. We shared the egg shakers and Edie's frog-and-stick around the group and were the raucous sing-along 'yin' to Pam's thoughtful folk song 'yang'. She sang beautiful songs about giant redwoods and broken hearts, we demolished Lennon and McCartney standards. She had us in captivated silence, we took the roof off. It was a good mix.

We left the hills of Cappadocia the next morning wrapped in whatever flimsy layers we could piece together from our rucksacks, having bought woolly socks and hats to get us through the night time frost (they had had snow the week before we got there), only to discover with some surprise that just two hours south, it was still summer. By the time we reached the Mediterranean coast at Mersin, we had gone from an 8°C morning chill to a sun baked 27°C in just 180 miles. The landscape changed from barren rock to endless miles of flat farmland, first given over to potatoes (being hand-harvested by small family gangs), then to cabbages, then eventually 'The Med' arrived: palm trees, cacti, sandy soil and sunshine.

We were planning on getting to a campsite near the Syrian border where we'd wait a week for our visas to arrive from London, but Mersin, a bustling Mediterranean port, seemed like a good place to stop in the afternoon. The central street we chose to park in was narrow, busy and had clearly never been home to a yellow VW camper van. Our arrival was big news. People stopped what they were doing, staring, pointing and then holding up traffic and directing us into a parking space. It was quite an entrance. I almost expected to step out of the van to a 'ta daaa' and crowds of applauding people, like Bill Murray in the final scene of *Ghostbusters*.

In fact I stepped out of the van - into a puddle of mysterious fluid. Looking down the street was like the moment in a cheap cop drama when they retrace the path of the wounded man by following the blood on the floor. It started just up there - splatter - in the middle of the road. Then, drip, drip, drip, that's Penny driving forwards, then splatter, that's where I stopped to reverse. Then drip, drip, drip - a lovely arc into the space she currently occupied. I looked under the van. She was haemorrhaging a steady trickle of something presumably quite important.

I slid a billy-can under the leak (it's not just for campfire cooking, Scouts; be prepared) and retired to the lobby of a hotel opposite to rub my chin thoughtfully. Jill, pouncing on the opportunity for a proper bed, did a surprisingly cheap deal with the receptionist and booked us in. After we bundled our backpacks into our room I looked down on the street, saw the tell-tale splashes of doom still glistening in the sun and a collection of onlookers discussing Penny. By the time I'd changed into my oiliest clothes and gone back to Penny her crowd had moved on. It was about 5pm and still incredibly hot. I bought a can of Turkey's favourite fizzy orange soda from a kiosk, took a swig of its cooling sugary nectar and set it down on the kerb beside the rear wheel. It was time to take a look.

There's no easy way to examine the underside of a VW T25 without a ramp, but I knew I was just about slim enough to squeeze between the tarmac of the road and the countless metal, pointy, sticky-outy things that would try to snag me from above. My first fears were allayed: the gearbox was dry. Penny had been particularly stubborn about finding reverse as I had parked and I worried gearbox fluid was leaking, but no. The fluid appeared to be dripping from a rubber hose joint that I quickly worked out was carrying coolant. My tiny moment of triumph at the thought that this might be such a simple problem to fix was punctuated by a crunching splat from somewhere near my ankles followed by a splatter of sticky spray.

A small boy had stamped on my Fanta.

'Oi!' I shouted. 'Thanks a lot! I was drinking that!'

I could see the culprit from my gloomy position, possibly the most surprised six-year-old boy I've ever seen. He squatted to gaze under the van, but he was still struggling to locate the source of the shouty foreign noise.

'That's right. You! You stamped on my Fanta!' I bellowed, still lying completely flat, sandwiched between van and road. He squinted some more, then shrugged and walked away. 'Oh that's right, walk away!' I yelled, but he was running now. 'You owe me a drink!'

He was gone. I extricated myself, scratchily, back into the sunlight, glanced sorrowfully at the squashed explosion on the floor and went to get a shower.

Something in my brain must have clicked while I slept because I woke early convinced I was kidding myself about the coolant, and in the clear daylight the liquid in the billy-can was obviously the pale ruby colour of hydraulic fluid, not the blue chemical colour of coolant. A push on the brake pedal confirmed it. I could feel nothing but fresh air under my foot. Penny had no brakes. Just a month or so since being stranded for a fortnight, we were stuck again. *Please don't let Mersin be the new Alessandria,* I begged to myself.

Then, an extraordinary sequence of events took place. A big chap who'd been enjoying a cup of çai (tea) and a game of backgammon at a pavement table introduced himself. His name was Arro, he spoke a tiny amount of English and with the help of the hotel's Internet and Google Translate understood that I needed a mechanic to fix my brake pipe. He then brought two more men into the discussion, the 'otopark' car park attendant from over the road, and a thin wiry taxi driver who was one of the backgammon and çai gang. The otopark man produced a business card bearing the VW logo. It was Mersin's answer to 'Zentrum Alessandria'. I fought the urge to inflict harm. I typed into the translator.

```
It's a simple repair. Any mechanic could do it.
```
Or, as Arro read it: `Basit  bir  onarim's.  Her  türlü mekanik Yapabiliriz.`

'OK,' he said. 'I call'.

No doubt he could see in me that universal fear any sane man has of paying dealership labour rates, and as he spoke to the VW garage on the phone, an awful lot of negotiating seemed to be going on. He put the receiver down and explained. They would send a pickup for Penny right away, for which I would pay half the normal rate (about £40) because he'd told them I was *not* a tourist, but a friend.

By lunchtime, Penny had been at the garage for a couple of hours and no one had called, so, with the benefit of my Italian experience, I resolved to get over there and pester them. I was just deciding this when Arro appeared from his bag shop opposite the hotel and asked me how it was going. When I explained I was about to go over to the garage he ushered me into his shop and picked up the phone. While he was talking to someone at the garage, the thin taxi driver came in. His name was Mustafa and we both sat at the tiny table in Arro's shop. Then a smartly dressed waiter appeared from the street with a huge silver platter of food, laid it on the table and, with a polite nod to Arro, unveiled two large flatbreads covered in tomatoes and pieces of spicy lamb, a massive salad and two glasses of white *ayran*, a Turkish drink of diluted yoghurt and salt.

Arro put the phone down and explained that I needed to go over there so they could fill out the work contract and get on with it. I gesticulated that I'd do just that using Mustafa's taxi, so would return after they'd had their lunch, but they wouldn't hear of me leaving, almost pushing me back into my seat to share their feast. It was delicious, and as we munched, Arro assured me the VW garage were going to give me a good deal. When we'd finished, Mustafa took me over to 'Opal VW', a half-hour's drive out on the other side of the city, and stressed to the garage, under Arro's instructions, *not* to give the van a full service - just fix the brakes. For my part, I nodded, smiled and said '*fren*' quite a lot, which I had learned was Turkish for 'brake'.

Paperwork was signed, a mechanic was shown the precise location of the leak, I was whizzed back to the hotel, Mustafa rounded the taxi meter *down* but I ignored him and gave him a tip anyway, and I rejoined Jill and the girls to get on with our day. While we wandered through the sea-front park we encountered a jolly old man who, after establishing we *didn't* want a ride on his boat, told us of his years living in London, where he'd owned a kebab shop. Then a group of young lads, about 12 years old, befriended us, desperate to try out their English. The littlest of the gang was the most fluent, and asked us where we lived in England, which football team we supported, laughed when we told him 'Liverpool' (everyone abroad supports Manchester United) and asked whether we were Muslim or Christian. It seemed odd that such a question should be on the mind of a 12-year-old boy. 'We learned at school. In England you are Christians,' he said.

Then as Jill and I gazed out to sea, pondering the possibility of being stranded in such a delightful place, the old man joined us again. He pointed at Ella, Beth and Edie sitting under a tree.

'Your family?' he asked. 'Three girls?' We nodded, looking at them proudly.

'USELESS CHICKENS!' he shouted. It was a shocking outburst, and we both started laughing. 'You need a boy,' he said putting his arm round me. 'What is your name?'

'Sim.'

'Sam.'

'It's like Sam, but it's Sim.'

'OK. Sam. Who will take your name?'

'Oh, I see. I need a son to call Sim.'

'Right! Sam! I am Ahmed. You are Sam.'

'Sim.'

'Sam. So, my son, he is called Ahmed ...'

Well, you get the idea. This conversation went on for about ten minutes. Eventually we said our goodbyes to the giggling boys and the old sailor and went to gather up our three useless chickens.

When we got back to our street Mustafa was very excited and fetched Arro, who explained that I should go to the garage and get the van. It was fixed! They had phoned *him* in his bag shop. They had my mobile number, of course, but why waste time trying to speak to the English bloke? Call the fella in the bag shop - he knows the score. Mustafa bundled me into the taxi and we were off. Good to their word, the VW garage had fixed the leak, replaced the pipe, and even washed several week's of dirt off Penny because that's what posh garages do. And all for less than £80. Within 24 hours of rupturing her brake pipe Penny was back, fully fixed and ready to take us onwards to Syria. As I parked her outside the hotel, Arro came out to see me and check I was happy with the work and the price. What an amazingly kind man.

The next morning, I poked my head out of the hotel window to see what the weather was doing. Down on the street below, Mustafa was polishing his yellow taxi. He looked up, saw me and waved.

'Good morning!' I shouted.

'*Merhaba!*' he smiled.

'You know what?' I said, turning back to Jill. 'We've made some friends in this town.'

'That's right,' she replied. 'Everyone knows Sam.'

We spent our final week in Turkey camping near Iskenderun, within an hour or so of the Syrian border at Reyhanli, waiting patiently for our passports to return with their newly added Syrian visas. It was an enforced break and we felt ready for it. You might raise an arched eyebrow when I tell you that travelling is exhausting, and sometimes you just need a holiday from it. We were the only people sharing a tropical jungle of a campsite with its owner, Fergin. We hung washing between a banana tree and a mandarin tree, used a shower under a palm-leaf roof and only had hot water if the sun had been out for a while. It was marvellous. Especially when a man from DHL arrived with our long-awaited package. We finally had our Syrian visas.

So it was with happy hearts that we took a boat trip with one of Fergin's mates along the Hatay coast where the Mediterranean looks stunning and where huge mountains drop straight down to the sea. We scuffed the boat ashore on a volcanic beach inaccessible from the land, but as we walked along a mile of dark, igneous, rocky beach where not a soul sets foot, all nature's beauty couldn't distract us from the fact that it was the most litter strewn beach we'd ever seen. Rubbish, not dumped by humans, but by the tide, was everywhere. Barely a square metre wasn't sharing space with a drinks bottle, some polystyrene or a plastic bag.

The dirt and the beauty had been a constant feature of our month in Turkey, and seemed to echo the collision of cultures – not just Asia meets Europe, East meets West, but also ancient meets modern. Alongside shopping malls were fields where kids and women hand-harvested potatoes. There was a huge tourist industry, yet some places didn't even have organised rubbish collections. Recycling was an alien concept. In 2010 Turkey was still trying to become a member of the European Union, and it was mainly her lack of infrastructure and poor environmental record that was being blamed for holding her back.

'Long may she remain independent,' I said, because for every thing the EU would improve, an unquantifiable chunk of Turkey's character would be chipped away. Yes, a few nicer roads might get built, but elsewhere, campsite owners would start insisting on holding your passports as they did in Europe (presumably in case you steal a tree) rather than just welcoming you with a smile and offering you a cup of tea. It would undoubtedly be safer if every motorcyclist wore a helmet, but would we also be able to pile aboard a little boat with only two lifejackets between five of us and pay a bloke a few quid to have a brilliant afternoon of sailing? No. The owner of the boat would need costly licences, public liability insurance, a first aid certificate and membership of an expensive association to get a special sticker allowing him to take paying passengers. It just wouldn't happen.

Throughout this country of contradictions, where Christians and Muslims rub along quite happily together, it was the warmth of the people that seduced us. There was the random stranger who jumped in his car to guide us to a distant campsite, David, the hotel owner in Yeşilköy, who didn't have any rooms free when we arrived late, wet and exhausted but wouldn't hear of us leaving; and Arro, the Mersin bag shop owner who made it his mission to get Penny repaired and even shared his lunch with me. There were others, too – Dr Akcam, the orthodontist professor in Ankara who, responding to an email from Jill, offered to adjust Ella's brace for her, but wouldn't take a fee, and there was the complete stranger, a man who took an hour out of his day to accompany me through the city to DHL, just because it was quite hard to find.

As we teetered on the brink of entering Syria, we all felt sad to leave a country that had so greatly surpassed all our expectations. Our month of succumbing to the Turks' laid-back, smiling attitude to life, letting our days tick to the regular rhythm of the minarets' echoing call had left a deep impression.

'What did we love about Turkey?' I shouted from the driver's seat.

'The people!' came a shout from the back.

'The bread. Even nicer than French bread.'

'The tea.'

There you have it, reader. Good bread, good tea and good people – that's all we require in our Utopia. I pointed Penny at Bab al Hawa, just beyond a large and slightly scary border.

Before I tell you about our border-crossing into Syria - a story of bribery, corruption and child exploitation (I was responsible for that last one) - I must furnish you with some essential facts about getting into Syria in 2010.

> 1. The Syrian authorities were deeply suspicious of journalists, broadcasters and writers. Jill is a journalist. I am a broadcaster and writer.

That's the end of the list of essential facts.

This information is vital to an understanding of how events unfolded.

We had learned from our research into applying for a visa, that Syrian officials required evidence of our employment in the form of a letter on headed paper from our employers. I actually had a letter from BFBS (the British Forces radio station for whom I had worked) confirming who I was and what I did, but all anecdotal evidence we gathered seemed to suggest that putting 'radio presenter' and 'British Forces' on a Syrian visa application would have been like putting 'Name: Bin Laden, Osama' on a USA visa form. So I simply created a headed letter from my own company and put my job title as

Commercials/Promotions. Well, I did have to create a promo trail for my show every day, so it wasn't a lie, just selective truth.

Jill, however, is as honest as the North Pole midsummer's day is long. So she dutifully included her letter from the BBC, which stated she was on a career break. You could look at this as a positive thing because it was an official letter saying she *didn't* work for the BBC. Surely that would be a *good* thing, right?

Three days after submitting our visa applications online and posting the supporting paperwork from Ankara, my phone rang. 'Hello. This is the Syrian Embassy. Can I speak to Jillian Moody please?' The helpful Syrians in London were concerned about Jill's BBC connection. They said we would face a long delay unless we resubmitted Jill's application removing all references to the BBC. 'For occupation just put "Year of leave",' they advised. 'And include a covering letter simply saying "I have left my job and am unemployed".'

The irony that this was Syria's own visa office telling us to be economical with the truth wasn't lost on us. And so a new application was submitted, and sure enough my brightly coloured visa, when it arrived, bore the words 'Occupation: Commercials', while Jill's read 'Year of leave'.

We'd heard that the process for leaving Turkey would be almost as tortuous as getting into Syria, so we were braced for lots of queuing at small windows getting passports stamped. As we approached, the first uniformed official, gun slung casually across his hip, waved us to a halt. Now is the time in this border-crossing tale to introduce you to The World's Worst Liar, a woman who also holds the coveted title of Girl Least Likely To Be Snapped Up As An MI5 Spy, and the equally prestigious Last Person On Earth You Would Choose As A Drug Trafficking Mule: my wife, reader, Jill Moody.

She wound down the passenger window and handed the tooled-up guard our passports. He smiled at the girls in the back and did a quick head count. 'Five?' he asked.

'Yes, five,' Jill replied.

'What you do?'

'Wha ... I'm sorry?' flustered Jill, as if he'd asked her bra size. 'I ... er ...'

'Sorry,' smiled the guard, apologising for his English. 'I mean, where from?'

'Oh, um ...'

'England!' I shouted helpfully, leaving Jill's crimson glow to blossom fully.

He handed the passports back and waved us on.

'Wow, Mummy, you're really red,' said Edie from behind us.

'I thought he was on to me,' she panted.

'Good job you're so calm under pressure,' I said, 'otherwise I don't think we'd have got away with it.'

It was clear the next three hours would be no picnic.

An hour later, we were finally released from Turkey to drive the 100 yards of no-man's land and knock on Syria's door. We were greeted by a cheerful chap with a round face who said he worked for the Government tourist office. I shall call him Mr Benn. He looked absolutely nothing like the two-dimensional fancy-dress-loving animated character of the same name, but his boss, who we shall meet in a moment, looked *exactly* like the fancy dress shopkeeper in the cult 70s pre-school TV show, so for the sake of the story ...

Mr Benn, who called everyone 'my friend' and thought the word 'hello' meant 'goodbye', assured us that he would make the complicated processes of form-filling, tax paying, insurance-buying etc a breeze. 'You go first to this counter, get two stamps in the passport, then come and find me in my office. Go! Go! Hello! Hello!'

This first counter was where a humourless uniformed officer peruses your passport and, despite the fact that you've clearly been vetted at great length by the Syrian Embassy to gain a visitor's visa, takes it upon himself to conduct further interviews. 'Where are you from?' he asked suspiciously, looking at the page in my passport that says I'm from the UK.

'England,' I said with smile.

'Where are you going?'

'Well, I was considering the Amazon delta, or possibly the Great Barrier Reef, but as I'm standing at the entrance to Syria being interviewed by a Syrian whose sole purpose in life is to let people into Syria I'm going to answer - Syria' ... is what I wanted to say.

'Syria,' is what I actually said, and even that sounded a bit sarcastic. To compensate for my tone, Jill pushed Edie up to the counter. It was now a well-tested fact that Edie was currency. It drove Ella and Beth mad for a while, but it became quite funny. Need to push into a lane of busy traffic? Not a hope. Get Edie to wave at a driver, however, and we were straight in. Literally every single day since we'd crossed the Bosphorus river into Asian Turkey she had been kissed, stroked or had her hair ruffled. People loved her, so we used her.

As she rested her chin on the counter, the officer smiled at her. *Bingo.* 'What is your name?' he asked.

'Edie,' she said, blinking her big blue eyes from beneath her blonde fringe.

'You like football?'

'Liverpool.'

The man laughed. (It was a tough season. We were getting that a lot.) Then, he dropped the smile and turned to me. 'What do you do?' he asked icily.

Here we go I thought. *He can smell 'media' on us.*

'Commercials,' I replied, following the script helpfully printed in my passport by the Syrian visa office. He looked confused. 'Like adverts,' I blurted, panicked by his furrowed brow. 'Promotions. Radio adverts.'

'Don't say radio,' I heard in a clipped whisper. It was Jill, chillaxed as ever.

'You know. Adverts.' I concluded. He still looked clueless.

'You reporter? Generalist?'

'I think, my good man, you mean *journalist*,' I almost said, but to belittle the immigration officer is to open the door to a small, windowless room, a pair of rubber gloves and a world of pain. So I told myself not to get distracted by what a cool job a 'generalist' must have, generalising about stuff all day – 'How was work darling?' 'Not bad. Made some fairly broad statements about women not being able to read maps and men being terrible listeners.' I'd be a great generalist.

I just said, 'No.'

I sensed the very mention of 'reporter' had increased Jill's heart rate to that of a frightened field mouse, and as the officer wandered off to stamp the passports I turned to give her a supportive smile. She was smiling too, but the teeth were clenched and by the distant look in her eyes I knew she'd gone to her happy place.

Then Haakim leaned over for a chat. You haven't met him yet but he's been standing next to this whole scene at his own glass window getting his own border-crossing affairs dealt with. Haakim informed me that he was a truck driver. He was returning to his home just outside Damascus and insisted I take his phone number so that I might call him when we reached the city. Just then the starchy immigration officer returned to hand all our passports back to me, but when he saw Haakim chatting to me his mood darkened again. He spoke to my new friend in Arabic, and then Haakim started asking me questions, and suddenly he didn't seem quite as friendly as I had first thought.

'What are you doing here? What work?' he asked, trying to stay jovial, but looking slightly uneasy.

'I'm not working. We're on holiday.' He glanced at the guard, who urged him on with his eyes.

'What do you do, at home?' Haakim pressed on. *Oh Lord, this again.* And then he said, 'What does your wife do?'

By this point I had the passports, duly stamped, in my hands and Jill was dragging the kids away. I kept smiling and answering his questions. 'She doesn't work. Unemployed.' But somehow I was digging deeper every second and sensed the pack, for that's what these men were now, was turning on me. I made a bold choice, and simply extricated myself with a smile, a shrug and a jaunty wave. It's the English way.

'Well that was weird,' I started to explain to Jill as we walked away at a quickening pace, but before I could get any further, as if by magic, a shop-keeper appeared.

A stocky gentleman in his late fifties with a small moustache and spectacles introduced himself as Mr Benn's colleague from the Tourist Office. Then, with Mr Benn eagerly clucking alongside him, they ushered us into their tiny office. The shop-keeper explained that he would be able to get our Carnet for the van stamped much quicker than if we joined the queue, and also that he could nip into the office to get the insurance and tax, saving us waiting with the crowds outside. 'First though, a couple of questions,' he said. I knew what was coming.

Any modern traveller who's driven into Syria hasn't done so without first reading a hundred Internet accounts of what to expect. That way, of course, information is shared. It's what the Internet is good at, and why countries like Syria didn't like it. I knew, therefore, that Syria charged US$100 'diesel tax' to drivers entering the country in a diesel vehicle. And then a further 100 for every week they were in the country. Petrol vehicles, or 'benzine' as they were known, were free. I also knew that lots of people lied about what fuel their vehicle used, to avoid this expense. I had texted Neil & Silvie-with-an-'i', our new South African friends, the day before as they'd already crossed into Syria, to ask if they'd paid the diesel tax on their Land Cruiser. 'No,' he replied. 'They didn't even check the V5 vehicle document. Just say benzine and you save 100 bucks.'

'Is the van diesel or benzine?' asked the shopkeeper.

'Benzine,' I lied.

'Good,' he said. 'Because it's expensive to have a diesel.'

'Really?' I shrugged, as if I hadn't spent weeks researching these facts.

As he left to get our paperwork seen to, Mr Benn started to point out some of Syria's beauty spots to Jill as displayed on several curly, faded posters. Edie leaned over and said to me, quite clearly, 'Daddy, did you say the van was *not* a diesel?'

Mr Benn seemed to momentarily lose his thread.

'That's right darling, diesel be brilliant places to visit, won't they?' I pronounced unconvincingly. We really were hopeless at subterfuge.

That's when Mr Benn first brought up The Tip. 'If you are happy with the work my friend has done you may give him tip,' he said with a smile. 'But only if you are happy,' he added, as if I had a choice. *Sigh.* And I had thought this assistance was part of their job as employees of Syria's tourist office. How naïve.

Five minutes later, when the shopkeeper returned with the completed paperwork, rather than just getting on with the process of getting us across the border he settled back in his chair and wanted to chat. He was hopeless at small talk, but he clearly was attempting to build up to some big question or other. 'How old are you?' he asked me. I was so thrown I actually forgot the answer. I think he realised by our puzzled looks that, rather than making charming small talk, he had just come across as insane, so he quickly cut to the chase.

'What is it that you do for a job?' he asked with a smile.

Oh my goodness. They're all in it together!

Eventually satisfied with my answer, and failing to see the relief in my face that he'd not started grilling Jill on the same subject, or to notice that she was digging her finger-nails into the arms of her chair like an eagle gripping its struggling prey, he moved on. 'You come with me now. Just you.' He ushered me out of the room.

This is it, I thought. *They won't be happy until they've given me a good pumping in the debriefing room.* Mr Benn, the shopkeeper and I walked a few yards from the office, where the shopkeeper said, 'I don't like to talk money in front of the family.' *Ah. The Tip.* I nodded knowingly and slipped each chap a crisp 200 Syrian Pound note (about £2.70). This was clearly an insult.

'We normally get $50,' said the shopkeeper, deadpan. I must have looked alarmed because he then started to justify his overheads.

'There is the customs chief. He wants his money. He will wave you through if you're with us. Maybe $35?'

Funnily enough, he knew I had $35 in my wallet as he'd given it to me in change after selling me the motor insurance. I gave him a 1,000 SP note (£13.50) for them to share, but I could tell that behind their smiles they were less than impressed.

I was just explaining all this to Jill and the girls as we waited in the queue of cars to get through customs, when Mr Benn appeared. 'You will soon be through. I have spoken to the chief. He will open the door of the van, just for the cameras, then you will be on your way. OK? Hello.' And he was off. Ahead, several cars were being emptied of their contents. The queue was going to take a while.

Then he was back again. 'My friend,' he enquired, 'Are you sure this is benzine? I can hear the noise of the engine.'

'It's very old!' I shouted. 'A bit rattly!' He seemed convinced. Jill was not.

'We should never have lied,' she hissed. 'I'd have paid 60 quid not to have this stress.' The customs official, as per the pre-arranged and paid-for drill, opened the door, said hello to the girls, closed the door and waved us on our way. Bribery works. In the hubbub of people around us, as the barrier lifted, we heard a voice shouting after us.

Oh God what now? Jill was about to hold out her wrists to be shackled, shouting, 'I'm a journalist and it's a diesel! A DIESEL I tell you! It's a fair cop!' when a face appeared at the window. It was Haakim.

'You call me tomorrow. I'll be waiting!'

'We're not actually in Damascus tomorrow,' I explained as we crept forwards. 'But I've got your number. Thank you!' I shouted as we picked up speed.

'I'll be waiting!' he hollered in my rear view mirror.

'Drive! Drive! Drive!' shouted Jill.

And we did. One journalist, one generalist, three kids and a rattly old VW - *diesel*.

Our first stop after fleeing the border in a cloud of (ahem) 'benzine' smoke was Syria's second capital, Aleppo. Our arrival at dusk coincided with the frenetic final local rounds of World's Most Insane Driver, and competition this year seemed particularly high. Goat Truck Going Wrong Way Around Three Lane Roundabout almost had the award in the bag until, as darkness fell, Taxi With No Lights Reversing Wrong Way Up Busy Slip Road clinched it. It was another proud day in Syria's glittering record of a car accident every three seconds (no, really, that's a fact), and we were thrilled to witness it first hand. Given the frantic pace at which terror unfolded at every turn, it was a real boon that it only took an hour or two for the children to be able to blink again.

Aleppo had the same throb and bustle as Istanbul, but with the notable difference that here *all* the women covered their heads with a scarf, and many wore black, despite the warmth. The east meets west culture was far behind us. Aleppo felt like the *real* Middle East. It has one of the greatest examples of a fortified citadel in the Arab world, its ancient souq has streets so narrow that donkeys are still used to carry traders' stock up and down the cobbles, and it has the Baron Hotel. Agatha Christie wrote the first chapter of *Murder On The Orient Express* while staying at the Baron, and it also gained fame as a regular haunt of T.E. Lawrence (of Arabia). They still had one of his bar tabs from 1914 on display in the Smoking Room. Apparently he enjoyed a large gin. The hotel traded heavily on its nostalgia, only in as much as its prices were high, but that didn't stop us having a drink in the bar.

The interior of the Baron felt like it hadn't been touched since Lawrence's bar tab was written. Paint peeled from the ceiling, wallpaper lost its battle with gravity and curled its way south, and once-pretty red felt lampshades were faded and frayed. I'd read guidebooks that regretted with sadness that the place was so dog-eared and tatty, but I really liked the fact it was lost in time. It was all the easier to imagine it in its heyday a century earlier. These days it sits among busy streets lined with tiny car-repair and tyre shops, but back in Christie and Lawrence's day it was yet to be engulfed by the city and was in open parkland. Guests could shoot ducks from their balcony! That's what I call a hotel. Try discharging a couple of live rounds in a busy Syrian city today and see where the old 'duck shooting' excuse gets you.

Of course, gunfire of an entirely less sporting nature was soon to be heard throughout Syria, and it's only with hindsight and the knowledge of the events that followed our time there that I could start to understand our own experience. A look back at my on-the-road blog reveals I wrote '*It's not easy to describe this place without slipping into what could be misread as xenophobia. The mood here is suspicious, aggressive and conniving. It feels threatening.*'

Well, given that a nation who'd suffered for decades under an oppressive police state was about to explode into revolution, I now have a glimmer of insight into why we felt that way. We were frustrated because all the guidebooks had waxed lyrical about how friendly the people were, but the truth of it was that we just didn't find that. Well, not for the first week we were there. It seemed everywhere we turned, from the moment we crossed the border, people were 'on the make'. Restaurants didn't have menus or prices, so we quickly found we had to nail down how much the food was going to cost before they brought it, or they'd simply charge whatever they liked, often 'accidentally' miscounting how many meals we'd had.

A hotel receptionist offered to go and put a parking ticket on our car so it wouldn't get clamped. Jill gave him 300 SP for three hours parking, but he put a *one* hour 50 SP ticket on the car and went home with the rest of the cash. He thought it was fine to leave our car to get clamped so he could cream 250 SP (about three quid) off some dumb

Brits. On another occasion I bought some drinks and a couple of chocolate bars in a shop. '150,' said the man. I give him 1,000 SP note. He gave me 750 change.

'You said 150,' I said, waiting for the remaining 100.

'250,' he said, and walked away.

This sort of thing happened all the time. At first it was shocking, especially after super-friendly Turkey, then it became annoying, but ultimately it just became wearisome to go into every single encounter expecting a battle for fair play.

This was also the point in our journey when we finally lost all patience with being stared at, pointed at, laughed at (yes, people really did laugh) and generally being the freak show in town. We drew a crowd if we so much as stood still, and not a crowd of welcoming, chattering, smiling Beatles fans. People would stop, stare, and sometimes take photos with their phones, not wanting to engage, but too fascinated to move on. The attention of strangers had been fun for a while back in Italy and Greece. It became more intense as we travelled further into Turkey, but by the time we'd spent a few days in Syria the constant unwanted attention made us feel like paparazzi-battered Beckhams, but without their bank balance. Or cheek bones.

Again, retrospect lends a very different slant to this uncomfortable experience. It later became widely known that plain clothes government informants were prevalent in Syria's major cities, reporting any unusual activity. People were afraid to speak their minds, let alone speak to such a highly visible group of Westerners. We would find just one brave soul who broke the mould before the week was out, but first we had to find the home of my saint.

I'd always thought Saint Simeon was very strange, and a bit comical, so was thrilled to find the ruins of his monastery and his famous pillar were just north of Aleppo. I was about seven years old when I first discovered him in a huge book of fantastic facts that belonged to my Grandad. Turning eagerly to the page about Saint Simeon must have been the 1970s equivalent of Googling myself. All

I remembered from those days was that my name-sake was 'the bloke who lived on a pole'. But the chance to visit the actual pole (or at least the stump that remained) meant swotting up on the great man.

Simeon was the son of a local farmer. He joined the monastery near Aleppo, but found monastic life was just too easy, so do you know what he did? Wrong, no poles were involved at this stage. He moved to a cave in the hills and lived as a hermit to be closer to God. But people would come and ask him theological questions, which annoyed him, plus he could still forage for food which was a bit cushy and not nearly tough enough. So what did he do? No, still no pole. He chained himself to a huge boulder to make getting out-and-about even more of a challenge. Then more people came to see him, and this made him really cross, so then what did he do? Wrong again. He wore a metal suit fitted with spikes on the inside that made him bleed. (These days we have a name for people who enjoy this sort of thing).

Well, incredibly, *even more* people came to see Simeon the wacky monk. He really was the David Blaine of his day. He hated it. All he wanted was a quiet life contemplating God. 'Here's an idea Sim,' his monastic brethren must have thought. 'If you don't want people coming to see you, QUIT WITH THE CHAINS AND THE BOULDER AND THE SPIKES, YOU NUTTER!' But I suspect they just rolled their eyes with a wry smile and said 'That Simeon, eh? He's a one.'

And so Simeon returned to the sanctity of his monastery, but had forgotten how annoying his brethren were (and perhaps how much *he* annoyed *them*) so chose to live on a stone pillar three metres high. Well, would you credit it? Again, people came from miles around to ask the wise pole-sitter questions about life, the universe and what the view was like. So Simeon, seeking solitude through altitude, commissioned a rebuild. His new pillar was nine metres high. Then 15 metres high. But still the punters flocked, craning their necks and shouting their questions, so he ended up living atop an 18 metre high pillar. His food was delivered from below once a week and, in a rare moment of clarity, he fitted a railing so he didn't fall off in his sleep.

And there he lived for 37 years, being 59 feet closer to God and handing down occasional pearls of wisdom to onlookers below - unless they were female. He refused to talk to women. Ever. Even his own mother, poor woman. 'That son of mine, eh? He's a one.'

I found my pillar amidst the 1,700-year-old ruin just as the evening sun was illuminating the orange stone with an ethereal, warm glow. Today its 18 metres of grandeur has been reduced to a few metres of stump.

'It says here,' announced Beth from behind a guidebook, 'that for hundreds of years countless pilgrims have been allowed to chip a bit off as a memento.'

'Grumpy old Simeon would have loved that,' I said.

Our wander around the arches and decrepit, sunlit walls of the old monastery tipped the balance of our experience, after a poor start, slightly back in Syria's favour. Yet still the culture shocks kept coming. The site was about to close for the day, and there were only about a dozen people meandering quietly through the serene ruin. If this had been a National Trust property in the UK, a kind old lady would have gently approached us saying, 'I'm afraid we're closing, but please, take your time.' Here, at this ancient site of enormous historical importance, a man rode a scrambler motorbike around and *across* the stones beeping his horn loudly.

'Classy touch,' I heard Beth say under the deafening rasp of the two-stroke exhaust.

Would we ever get used to this strange land?

I blame Hama. It was Hama that clinched it. It Hama'd the nail in the coffin. Every time we enter a new country, alongside the thrill and expectation of new peoples and lands to be discovered, we had the added excitement of pondering where in that country we should busk. It was, after all, our mission to busk The Beatles in every country we travelled through all the way from Liverpool to New York. A tall order, sure, but it's good to have a goal. Ever since entering Syria, though, the mood in the band had not been good. I was sensing a simmering reticence to performing on the street.

'There's no way we're busking here. Forget it,' Jill had said in Aleppo.

'No way!' echoed Ella and Beth.

'Just because we haven't seen anyone doing anything remotely like street performance, and just because we saw several police officers run after a man trying to sell towels, doesn't make it illegal,' I argued weakly.

'They held a foreign couple for questioning a few weeks ago *for using a laptop*,' baulked Jill.

'Yes, but ...'

'For eight hours! The military police were called and they had to get a translator and everything. I read it on their blog. They were only trying to download their digital camera photos.'

Turkey

Galata bridge, Istanbul.
Cast, catch, cook, eat.

Taksim Square. "What I need
after this is a nice relaxing
massage."

Big bottle + soap + water
+ bumpy roads =
washing machine!

Turkey

Turkey

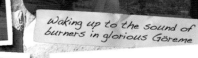

Waking up to the sound of
burners in glorious Göreme

Arro and Mustafa -
our saviours

Syria

A moment with my stump

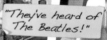
WELLCOME TO SYRIA

"They've heard of The Beatles!"

Aleppo Citadel

Syria

Damascus souq, with bullet holes.

Ennas leads the way

Happy birthday! Jelly?

Somewhere in there, Jill's getting directions.

Jordan

Jordan

اهلا بكم في
المملكة الاردنية الهاشمية
Welcome To The Hashemite
Kingdom Of Jordan

Climbing Mukawir to
Herod's party-palace

Jordan

'Welllll, they *say* they were,' I countered. 'Who's to say they weren't involved in some sort of illegal trafficking? Of towels, for example. The cops seem pretty hot on that here.'

But it was Hama that lost me the battle. Our journey from Aleppo to Damascus was broken by a stop. Hama time.

Hama is a town famous for two things: its large water wheels and a bloody massacre. The engineer in me applauded the ingenuity of the vast wooden wheels as they weren't designed to generate power, as is usually the case, but to transfer gallons of water in buckets from river level up to an aqueduct 20 metres higher, thus allowing gravity to supply fresh water to the town. I think the girls would have been interested too, had they not been constantly distracted by hoards of locals crowding around and touching them.

This is where Hama's second, darker claim to fame might be relevant. In 1982 the Syrian army, under the orders of President Hafez al-Assad (the current president's father, at time of writing), conducted a scorched-earth policy against Hama in order to quell a revolt against the régime by the Sunni Muslim community. Estimates of casualties vary from ten thousand to forty thousand deaths. Although we were there 28 years later, I wondered what effect this still had on the town. The atmosphere was like a pressure cooker, the whispered buzz around us more vibrant and suspicious than anything we'd experienced before.

With all four girls wrapped in headscarves and behind sunglasses, we braved the town for about an hour before their patience deserted them. For the safety of the locals, I removed my family from the scene. The circus had closed early. Back in the sanctuary of a rather dingy hostel room, I reluctantly agreed that preaching *All You Need Is Love* through the power of a haphazardly played ukulele would at best, get us arrested, at worst, be the overture to a highly charged sacrificial slaughter. The very idea that we would make any money was laughable. We'd already been advised that mentioning a connection with a charity was to be avoided as it leads to angry questions about converting people. Brow-beaten and ever-so-slightly depressed, we resolved to keep our heads down and press on south, or, as Jill put it, 'Get the hell out of this God-forsaken country as fast as humanly possible.' She was still on the fence, then.

So we took the road to Damascus – a bleak, barren, litter-strewn highway that offered none of the wonder I might have hoped for. St Paul's road to Damascus experience, converting him to follow Christ, is well known to anyone who went to Sunday School. The only dawning realisation a modern traveller might have, ploughing through the apocalyptic landscape, is that they should probably have turned around some time ago.

However, our mood lifted when we reached the capital. We camped on the outskirts of the city and shared the tiny site with our South African travelling buddies Neil and Silvie, who'd been there two days and were leaving the following morning. It was amazing how much better we all felt simply being able to share our similar experiences. Silvie had had a row with a dishonest fruit seller. I had too! Hooray! She had been groped by a nasty old man. I hadn't, but … brilliant! Neil had nearly had a fight with a lecherous slime-ball. Terrific! What a relief, to find it wasn't just us. It's curious but true; when everyone realises that everyone else is miserable too, somehow morale lifts. I've worked at companies who embrace this as a management technique.

The next day was Jill's birthday, and we'd all made funny cards. I'd found a picture of the Syrian president and given him a highly disrespectful speech balloon, but it was Edie's that caused tears to roll down Jill's cheeks: 'Who'd have thought it? 42! Well, you know the famous saying - 42 is the new 22!' It was so upbeat and chipper we somehow found it hysterical.

And things went from good to better. As we headed into Damascus on foot, looking every inch the lost tourists holding a map upside down, a woman who spoke good English approached us. 'Can I help? You are looking for somewhere?'

I confess, the girls and I rolled our eyes at each other. *That's all we need - another pestering local who'll want paying.* Jill told her we were going to the old city. The woman looked at the map, but quickly discounted it. 'I'll walk with you. It's not far.'

I heard a cash register in my head.

And so she strode ahead, leading the way and constantly chatting with Jill. The girls and I trailed behind exchanging worried whispers about where this might be leading, both literally and metaphorically. By the time we'd reached the walls of the old city, Jill and the mystery tour guide were getting on like a house on fire. 'This is Ennas,' Jill said, introducing us properly. 'She's a student at the university, studying English.'

We all greeted her politely and started to doubt our earlier snap judgement. Ennas insisted on taking us to the best entrance to the souq, weaving us through busy streets, deftly palming off street traders and expertly taking Edie by the hand when she wanted to stop traffic. *Wow, she's a professional,* I thought. I'd taken weeks to discover The Power Of Edie. This Syrian girl knew it instinctively.

When we mentioned that we hadn't eaten any breakfast, she led us not to any old café, but a full ten minutes' winding through the old Christian quarter of the city to find her favourite café. She spoke to them in Arabic, they knew her, and when we asked that she stay to have a drink with us she declined, saying she had to get to work. She swapped email addresses with Jill and left. We all sat down, stunned, a bit sheepish too, but also relieved. Syria was redeeming herself. Ennas had explained how she'd been studying English for four years, but that she'd never met any foreign family, let alone an English one. Suddenly I could understand why she was so keen to give up an hour of her time to chat and ask questions, but she hadn't ever come across to us as needy or suffocating like the overzealous people who'd leapt in our faces in previous towns. She was gracious, polite and genuinely generous with her time.

The day had got off to a cracking start and the birthday girl called the shots from then on. Whatever Jill wanted, went. A museum on the history of Arabic calligraphy? 'Yippee!' shouted the kids.

'Would you lot mind if we went inside the Great Mosque?' she asked.

'Just try and stop us!' we roared.

We window-shopped in the souq and discovered that even here you could enjoy the ultimate birthday food – jelly and ice cream. The souq in Damascus is a wide, cobbled street that had once been a Roman avenue leading to the Jupiter Temple, which in turn became a Christian cathedral, and then the Muslim mosque it is today. Now under cover, the high, corrugated arched roof of the souq 'street' tells its own story. Pin shafts of sunlight pierce the gloom of the market below - hundreds of bullet holes, still shining from the black roof, remnants of an uprising against French occupiers in 1925.

Another joy was that because Damascus is huge and used to international visitors, no one stared, pointed, spat (oh yes, we really had been spat at) or even batted an eye at us. Even the souq traders weren't too pushy. It was bliss. We went back into the old heart of Damascus that evening for some food and knew its twisty, wiggly back-streets like natives. As we wearily navigated our way through its ancient labyrinth back to bed we reflected on how, in just one day, Ennas and Damascus had redeemed Syria in our eyes. We'd experienced a complete U-turn in our thinking. Perhaps that litter-strewn highway had worked its magic after all.

'One day,' we agreed, 'we'll come back.'

Of course none of us knew how difficult that would become, or the dangerous turmoil Ennas and her family would face in the coming months.

We got horribly lost trying to leave Damascus, and stopped to ask for directions. Jill jumped out to seek assistance and was immediately surrounded by six men (including a policeman) who argued among themselves in Arabic before each pointed us in a completely different direction. Eventually we found our way to Daraa near the border crossing and were helpfully given directions by gangs of friendly and excited teenage students pouring out of a large school. Daraa seemed an inconsequential town to us, but would soon see protests that were the violent catalyst of the forthcoming Arab uprising against the Bashar al-Assad regime. Much later, we would watch news footage of massive protest marches filling the streets we'd driven through, watch soldiers open fire indiscriminately, and wonder with heavy hearts what became of those smiling teenage boys that jogged alongside Penny, wanting to shake our hands.

With one of the most unusual, enlightening, yet stressful weeks of our lives behind us, our shoulders relaxed and our smiles grew with every 'Welcome to Jordan' we received at the border. This border-crossing couldn't have been more relaxed if they'd offered us a comfy chair, slippers and a pot of tea. Guards smiled, children's hair was ruffled. Welcome to the Hashemite Kingdom of Jordan. Anyone who's read T.E. Lawrence's account of his time leading the Arab revolt in the desert will feel a frisson of excitement at the word Hashemite, for they were the army he led. Ahead of us, between the border and the Red Sea, lay the vast red deserts in which he lived, rode and earned his place in history as Lawrence of Arabia.

We'd read about a church in Madaba, just south of the capital Amman. The church was famous for a sixth-century mosaic on the floor of the nave, believed to be the world's earliest map of the Holy Land. Of more interest to us, they rented rooms in an adjoining building using the income to support the church school to which it was attached. For a small fee they allowed campers to pitch up in their car park and use the showers and wi-fi. Perfect. We had a history of camping next to churches, as you know, and the outcome had always been favourable.

The town was, like so many Middle Eastern towns we'd driven through, hot and chaotic on our arrival. Hooting cars, chattering crowds and a gridlocked mêlée greeted us as we crawled into the throng.

'Oh my God!' shouted Ella. 'Look at that!' I glanced around looking for the cause of the outburst. 'Out there, on the pavement. A cow's head!' Sure enough, plonked forlornly on the pavement outside the tiny door to what must have been a butcher's shop was a bloody bovine bonce. It wasn't casually strewn, but placed carefully upright, its horns reaching halfway up the door, its ears crusting in the heat, its white hair stained with blood. As we crept past in the van, it stared vacantly through a cloud of flies up at the girls. Bethan was slack-jawed, her vegetarian sensibilities appalled.

'Brilliant,' Ella laughed. 'What am I gonna do with this cow's head?' she mimicked. 'Oh, just pop it outside on the pavement. That'll look nice.'

Eventually we found St George's Orthodox Church and parked Penny in their safe courtyard, the only vehicle in the calm, walled square. On one side was the large church, two other sides were old two-storey stone buildings converted to become accommodation for staff and paying guests, and on the fourth side was a visitor centre and small café. The courtyard was busy with the regular traffic of students making their way to and from the school on the other side of the church, so rather than being in a secluded spot we felt slightly as if we were in a fishbowl, but it would be peaceful after dark and that's when it mattered.

Shortly after we arrived we were introduced to David, a tall dark American in his twenties whose Arkansas roots gave his voice a rich drawl and his vocabulary a natural ability to use words like 'folks', and 'y'all', without it sounding like he was spoofing the *Dukes of Hazzard*. He was an English teacher at the school and within a few moments of us explaining to him what our trip was about we all agreed it would be a terrific idea if we came into the school to talk to the pupils - and play some songs.

'We're not very good,' qualified Jill.

'Well I gotta slot at four,' he said, looking at his watch. 'Ya got two hours t'practise.'

Suddenly the girls needed the toilet. They hadn't been inside a school for almost five months and the thought of going into a *foreign* school and *performing* made their stomachs lurch more violently than when they'd encountered decapitated Daisy. Quickly, it was all systems go. Ella and Edie created an amazing PowerPoint presentation about who we were, where we'd come from and the journey we were taking - pictures of our house grabbed from Google street map, Edie's class photo showing the church school in our village. I reminded myself how a ukulele worked and Jill told Bethan to smile and not look so scared.

There's a moment in the film *Jaws* where Roy Scheider as Chief Brody thinks he sees a shark out at sea. Stephen Spielberg employed a marvellous 'contra-zoom' effect borrowed from Hitchcock to make the background rush away as Roy's eyes fill with horror. We had one of those moments when David walked us into the school. We had only seen a tiny fraction of the building next to the church and imagined it as a small primary school. 'How many kids are there here?' I asked as we turned the corner. A colossal modern edifice loomed into view.

'1,800 pupils,' he replied. *Whoosh! There goes the background.* Maybe he could see the girls' faces, because he quickly added, 'But my class will only be about 20 or so.'

'How old are the pupils in your class?' I asked innocently.

'Early high school, I guess.'

'11? 12?' I asked hopefully, as we passed a security man at a desk and climbed a wide staircase.

'14, maybe 15,' he said.

Damn. Tough crowd, I thought. I couldn't imagine a class of 14 and 15-year-olds finding a badly played Beatles song very entertaining at all. Objects might be thrown. When I was 14, if a man had come into my school, in the rough end of Liverpool, and tried to play a ukulele, he'd have been introduced to a unique new playing position and strung up at the gates as a warning to others.

I forced a smile at the girls, who hadn't blinked for some time. 'Stop worrying. We'll be fine,' I lied.

We arrived at a classroom half full of babbling teenagers and David called them to order. They all spoke brilliant English, having been studying it since they were four years old, but when they spoke they had a curiously Southern States accent. Funny that. David introduced us, I explained that the girls hadn't been inside a real school since July, so were naturally terrified, and the class warmed to them immediately. By the time we'd shown the presentation on the laptop, for which Ella received a round of applause, and answered a few questions - 'Is there any country you didn't like?' 'Before I answer that, is anyone here from Syria?' - it was time for a song.

The class was very relaxed, a few pupils drifted in late and none was told off by their affable teacher. Before playing, I was just running through the instruments we all played (not one of these kids had seen a ukulele before, so I considered that to be my contribution to humanity), when a skinny little boy bounded in and sat at the back.

'Hello. What's your name?' I asked.

'Ferris.' he replied.

'Great name. Welcome, Ferris,' I smiled. The reference to one of our favourite movies made Jill and the girls grin too.

'And Edie plays the frog,' I went on. 'Does anybody know the name we give to a type of instrument that you hit?' I asked, and then, as a private joke for our girls added, 'Anybody? Anybody? Anyone?' Our very own *Ferris Bueller* moment helped us forget our nerves, while the class played around with the word 'percussion'.

The class agreed that they had heard of The Beatles, and even if they hadn't, they did a very good job of picking up *Ob-La-Di* by the second chorus. We split the audience in half to teach them *All You Need Is Love* which was a bit of a riot because all the girls clung together in one half while all the boys stuck to the other. The result was the brilliantly choral line, 'All you need is love,' from one half, swiftly followed by a deep, reticent and frankly embarrassed, 'ya da da ta da,' from the other. There were gales of laughter and enough whoops and applause to make the rest of the school wonder who was having so much fun. Too soon, it was time to go. We posed with them for a class photo, they all keenly noted our website address and hoped that the words 'ukulele' and 'percussion' would feature in their forthcoming English exam.

Happy, relieved and feeling on top of the world, we treated ourselves to a slap up feast of hot sandwiches at a café across the road (no slaughtered cattle remnants to be seen) and basked in the re-living of our hour of fun at St George's Orthodox Church School and the brilliant people we'd met - and we'd only been in town a few hours. We were about to collapse into our beds later when David wandered from his room over to the van. He and a few church and school staff were about to serve tea in the corner of the courtyard. The evening was warm, and they wouldn't hear of us not joining them. Judging it would be impolite to refuse, especially as freshly made sticky cakes were mentioned, we sat, drank, ate, and were introduced to Brian, another young teacher from America, Bisham, a Cypriot who'd settled in Jordan and now made it his mission to look after us, a trader from Palestine, a few others whose names instantly escaped me, and Father Innocent, the bearded, twinkly-eyed boss of the church. We found ourselves warmly welcomed by the group and quickly ensconced in a mixture of debates, all heartily argued by the unorthodox Orthodox priest, including 'How the C.I.A. killed Princess Diana', 'What's wrong with the Catholic Church' and 'How George W. Bush pushed Christianity out of Iraq'.

Well, if you will camp next to a church ...

Jordan is rich in history. There's been civilisation there for thousands of years and a huge number of the biblical events I grew up learning about at school and church happened in Jordan. When John the Baptist baptised Jesus two millennia ago, I doubt either of them considered the long-term tourism benefits for the area. Years before that, when Moses climbed Mount Nebo to be rewarded with a view of the Promised Land, it can't have been further from his mind that one day people would pay to stand in the same spot. But here we are. Jordan, you might be surprised to learn, has no oil or anything much at all in the way of natural resources compared with its flush neighbour south of the Saudi border. How does it make ends meet? It gets financial help from the USA and Saudi Arabia, and as I write, is bringing in 13 per cent of its GDP from tourism.

Hidden gems - that's what David the Arkansas English teacher offered to show us when we met on the morning of his day off. Brian, his colleague from California, had his day off on the following day, so offered to do the 'big tick' hotspots of Jesus's baptism site and the Dead Sea with us then. So, we sat with them both over breakfast to plan our routes.

Breakfast hadn't changed, by the way, since somewhere east of Thessaloniki. Turks, Syrians and Jordanians all start the day on an egg (usually hard boiled) accompanied by bread, olives and cucumber. The only thing that had changed in 2,000 miles was the bread, which got flatter. Coffee was always Nescafé - I hadn't found ground coffee since northern Turkey - and the tea was always sweet. Looking back, this was good training for India, not that I knew it then. I remember specifying that I didn't want sugar in tea, but always being understood to mean I wanted *less* sugar. The idea of tea *without* sugar was unheard of. It was always black and always served in a glass. We'd left those mugs of dark tan PG Tips 'builder's tea' a long way behind us.

David, as well as being a teacher, was an archaeology student. Prior to getting his teaching job, he'd been to Jordan twice before on digs, and was planning to spend the next summer doing more of the same. Because of this, he knew of places we could go completely off the beaten track to witness Jordan's ancient history, newly revealed from beneath the ground.

'Tell Hesban' is not an instruction, it's a ruin on a hill five miles north of Madaba. We clambered from the road over rocks and through wiry, dusty weeds to the top of what is, in effect, a man-made mound. The reason Tell Hesban is on a hill is simply because so many different generations built their town on top of the ruins of the previous one. The result is an archaeologist's dream. With a bit of exploring you can see evidence of its time as a Bronze Age settlement, an Amorite capital (900–500 BC), a Hellenistic fortress, a Roman settlement called Esbus (63 BC–AD 350), a Byzantine ecclesiastical centre, an Umayyad market town (650–750), a regional capital of the Abbasids (750–1260) and the Mamluks (1260–1500) and, finally, an Ottoman village. They're all piled on top of one another, higgledy-piggledy, in an area no bigger than a couple of soccer pitches. We crawled into dark caves, balanced our way across ancient arches and had a brief tutorial in how archaeologists work. It's by digging, mainly. Consider that a free lesson.

East into the ever-hotter desert were the finest mosaics in Jordan, discovered at an archaeological dig at Umm ar-Rasas. We were finding the sun seriously intense, but it was pointless commenting on it. 'You should try summer here,' is all people would say. As the thermometer hit 30°C and we watched hot air funnels form dust twisters across the sand, we had to remind ourselves this was mid-November. Locals were bracing themselves for winter, and while we perspired and wilted we regularly saw natives wrapped in coats and hats against the chill.

The jewel in the crown among the collection of ancient churches discovered at Umm ar-Rasas is the Church of St Stephen, whose huge mosaic floor, still showing a brightly coloured, symmetrically patterned border around a central panel of hunting and fishing scenes, is the largest in Jordan. It dates from 785AD and partially overlaps an earlier church floor from 587AD. The entire area has been protected with a purpose-built roof and raised walkways from which to view the tiles, so a bit of tourism money's been spent, but we had the place to ourselves.

'See how the people in the mosaic have their faces all shuffled around?' David asked. 'Iconoclasts re-shuffled the tiles where faces should be, because they believed that people had started to worship the actual images rather than God.' This must have been one of the first examples of pixelating a person's face to obscure their identity.

'Jordan is so unbelievably well off for archaeological sites that there simply isn't enough money to protect them all,' David explained as we moved outside to stroll between pillars and under arches. 'So the sand we're walking on now is all that's protecting even more priceless mosaics that they've discovered underneath.' He stopped to get his bearings.

'See how these pillars are symmetrical?' he asked. We nodded obediently. 'We're standing in the central transept of a church, the altar would have been at the end in front of that semicircle. That's the apse. Let's take a look.'

He stooped down and started brushing the desert sand away with his hands. Sure enough, tiny coloured tiles appeared. An awestruck 'Whoa' from the girls led to more pushing of sand. 'It's a bunch of grapes!' shouted Edie. But the biggest 'wow' was still to come.

'See what happens when I do this,' David said, unscrewing his drink bottle. He sloshed the tiles with water and a glistening rainbow of gleaming, vibrant colours from a thousand years ago instantly shone into our world. I'm sure I heard a choir of angels sing. Our jaws dropped and you could suddenly see why archaeologists dig this stuff. Literally.

We stopped at Wadi Mujib, a huge gorge that's locally nicknamed Jordan's Grand Canyon, to enjoy the picnic lunch we'd gathered hastily that morning: fresh falafels with salad, rolled in flatbread – delicious and cheap.

While we munched, gazed and absorbed nature's beauty, I heard a sound I recognised echoing around the valley. It was a sound we've all heard in TV reports from war correspondents - the distant *brrrrrrap brrrrrrap* of machine gun fire. An old Bedouin, his chiselled face like tanned leather, was watching us with amusement, so I asked him where the gunfire was coming from. He illustrated with a mime that it was someone shooting birds.

'Hunting?' I said 'With an automatic weapon? Seems a bit unfair.'

'Welcome to Jordan!' laughed David. Although Jordan is seen as the peacemaker in the Middle East, it was a reminder that we were in a country whose neighbours include Iraq, Lebanon and the Palestinian West Bank. I imagine AK-47s are fairly plentiful. The old man took a piece of paper and a small pencil from his weather-battered tunic.

'What is word?' he asked in remarkably good English, and then offered the piece of paper to me so I could write it down for him. 'Hun – ting,' he repeated as he replaced the scrap of learning in his pocket. Then he went on, 'Hunting bird,' he said miming a flapping bird. Then, squirming his hand in front of me, he added, 'or fish.'

Ah yes, the delicate, patient art of the angler - tempting, teasing and luring his prey for as long as ... oh sod that. Pass the machine gun.

David had one last place he wanted us to see before our day was complete - Mukawir, the hilltop site of King Herod's palace where Herod's son (also called Herod) beheaded John the Baptist at the behest of his stepdaughter Salome. The sun had peaked, the heat was easing, and as the thin desert road wound through orange-brown hills, David pointed to a telegraph pole beside the empty road ahead. 'Just pull in there,' he said. 'We can fit this in before we get to Mukawir.' We got out and he led us under a flimsy wire fence and up a hill.

From nowhere appeared a city, dug out from the ground. This dig was one David had read about, the result of two months' work every two years over the past decade. There were no signs, no visitor centre, just an ongoing project he wanted to show us, mainly because of the incredible luck these volunteer archaeologists had had. To explain, here is your first proper lesson in How To Be An Archaeologist:

> 1. Dig a hole (we may have covered that earlier). It should be five metres square.
> 2. If you don't find anything of interest, start again somewhere else. If you *do* find something that makes you say, 'Oh, look at this,' dig a bit further.

There may be a couple more tiny details, but basically you can now consider yourself fully qualified.

In the case of this particular dig, they had sunk their first five metre square hole and, 'Oh, look at this,' stumbled upon the altar of a three thousand-year-old Moab temple. I once found a Victorian inkwell when digging my garden. Now I'm not so proud.

'This may not look much,' said David. 'But you're standing in the oldest temple in Jordan.' It was incredible that something 3,000 years old was simply left open to the elements year in, year out. Even more alarming was that we were able to climb all over it.

'This place is *amazing!*' said Beth, and it was.

Mukawir was reached just as the sun was setting. We shunned the path around the edge of the hill and took the direct route, climbing the steep shale. It's only the adventurous few who make this choice, but the reward is that you can find the prison cell cut into the rock where John the Baptist was held and ultimately killed. Again, we were completely alone – no tourists, no tickets, no turnstiles. We squeezed ourselves through the narrow opening in the hillside, switched on the torches David had sensibly told us to bring, and found two low rooms carved out of the soft rock. It was very eerie, stooping, touching the damp walls and being transported back 2,000 years, imagining John the Baptist's final hours.

With the sun dipping fast beyond the Dead Sea, we scrambled higher up the steep slope to reach the top for the last few minutes of a stunning sunset. We sat on the fallen remains of pillars marking where Herod's 'party palace' had once stood, tired, reflective, and imagined Herod's drunken parties and the view they'd enjoyed. 'What a venue,' Jill said.

'Imagine living back then and being invited to a party up here,' said Bethan, looking at the red, glistening Dead Sea below.

'Imagine if you'd offered to bring something,' I commented. 'I wouldn't want to climb that hill carrying a trifle.'

The bar had been set pretty high for poor Brian. We were still gushing about our amazing day the next morning when we set off with him to see a few of the more obvious tourist sights. Like David, he was in his early 20s and employed to teach English at the church school next to where we were camping. A little shorter than David, he had the lean build of an athlete.

First stop – Jesus's baptism site. Before you imagine a heavenly scene borrowed from a stained glass window, let me tell you what it's *really* like. First, there's no river. The river Jordan has receded to such an extent that the exact spot where historians agree John baptised Jesus is now a muddy ditch between the reeds, some 200 metres inland from the river. Even when it had been wet, it was never in the main river. I'd always pictured (probably thanks to illustrated Bibles of my youth) Jesus walking up to his waist in a big river. In fact it's more of an inlet, or an offshoot of the Jordan. I guess it had less current. Safety first.

The river Jordan is the natural boundary between Jordan and Israel, and is the no-man's land between them. The only section of the river you can reach without first meeting a high barbed wire fence is the internationally agreed 20 metres of bank, where, from the Jordanian side, you can look across the rather meagre, muddy six metres of water to the plush, marble steps of the Israeli side. You're free to dunk your feet in the river, but always under the watchful eye of armed soldiers on either side.

This entire experience will remain more memorable, however, for another reason. Just before the small shuttle bus took us towards the protected site, our new friend Brian broke his arm. I'd love to tell you he was prising apart a fight between Israeli and Jordanian guards, or wresting a baby from a pack of wild dogs, but in fact he was going to the loo. He tripped on a branch, broke his fall on some handily placed rocks and fractured a bone in his wrist. Once the wooziness had passed he insisted on carrying on with the day. After all, no actual bone was poking through the skin, and he'd broken it twice before so ... onwards! I made a sling out of one of the girls' headscarves (ever the boy scout) and he bravely marched on. What a guy.

From Mount Nebo we looked out at the Promised Land Moses had spent a lifetime searching for. On a clear day you can see Jerusalem, but through the haze we could only just make out Jericho. By contrast, we ended the day 1,300 feet below sea level. The Dead Sea isn't actually a sea at all, fact fan, but a saltwater lake. It has a salt content of 33 per cent, which, as you know from your science lessons, increases its density to a point where you float effortlessly at its surface without the need to swim or tread water. What you may *not* know is that the salt and minerals it contains are nothing at all like table salt. They are incredibly bitter to a point where getting water on your lips is instantly regrettable and getting it in your eyes will have you crying like a baby.

What I can guarantee you never got told by Norris McWhirter on *Record Breakers* is that if you spend more than ten minutes bobbing about in its viscous mineral soup, it will start to sting in less expected regions of the body. How can I put this? Where you have an orifice, no swimming costume will stop the Dead Sea finding it and working its prickly evil. Just another amazing fact they didn't teach you in Sunday School. 'It's agony if you've got a cut,' shouted Edie to Jill, across a few locals enjoying the rejuvenating mud. 'I think I've got a cut on my ...'

'NO! No you haven't,' Jill interrupted. 'We're all feeling it down there. Time to get out.'

Driving back to Madaba, with Brian nursing his injury in the front seat, we got chatting about his life in Jordan, his home in California and his parents. 'If you're going anywhere near California, they'd love to meet you,' he said.

'You might regret saying that,' I joked. 'Or *they* will. We're planning on shipping Penny to Los Angeles sometime around next May. You better warn them.'

He told us he was a keen runner but found it hard to train because no one runs for pleasure in Jordan. Locals viewed it with great suspicion, and some thought he was an American spy. When he mentioned he'd run a Marathon, Jill and I told him about our own Marathon experiences in New York and the Medoc respectively.

'What time did you do?' I innocently asked him.

'Two eighteen,' he replied, matter of fact. I almost drove Penny off the road.

'Two hours eighteen minutes?' Jill and I repeated. To put that in context, as I write, Paula Radcliffe holds the women's Marathon world record with a time of two hours, fifteen minutes.

'Yeah, it was my first Marathon,' Brian went on. 'And I won. I'd been really into cycling but never had a go at distance running.'

'Turns out you're pretty good at it,' I said.

'Apparently. That time made me third fastest in the U.S. The reason I've gotta keep running while I'm here is that I've got a place in the Olympic try-outs.'

'Oh God,' said Jill, her eyes wide. 'We've just broken the arm of America's next Olympic hopeful.'

Brian laughed. 'Not at all. *I* broke the arm of *one of* America's Olympic hopefuls.'

'Yes, but on our watch,' I said. 'I'm really sorry.' He just laughed and kept telling us what a great day he'd had. Several months later,

Brian returned to the States and had to make a choice between staying in America to pursue his running, or returning to Jordan to take up a more senior teaching post in Amman. His love of Arabic and the Jordanian people drew him back. He assures us his injury during our day together wasn't the turning point. Honest. Sorry, Team USA.

It was mid-November, and as we reached Petra a couple of hours south of Madaba it was the start of Eid al-Adha. Known simply as Eid, it's the Islamic festival that marks the end of the Haj - the pilgrimage to Mecca - and celebrates Allah's sparing of Ibrahim when he was about to sacrifice his son, but couldn't, then didn't have to, and killed a sheep instead. Christians know the story of Abraham too - it's one of those Old Testament stories that both religions agree on. In Jordan it means a week off work, a slap up meal and a bleak outlook for our woolly friends. Twenty three thousand sheep were imported to Jordan for this week. In every town there were people browsing pens of sheep and goats on the roadside. Having picked their animal, it's either taken care of while they wait, or taken home where its dispatch will be a family affair.

We saw a happy family scene in front of a small house near Petra in which the women were skinning a sheep while dad sharpened a knife and young son held sheep-number-two by the scruff of the neck, awaiting its Sweeney Todd demise. Yes, it was gruesome, but there was an honesty to it we lack in our Western pre-packed freezer-ready world. And you can't deny it's fresh.

Arriving at the gates of the ancient city of Petra on that November morning, visitors were struck by three things: The Indiana Jones Snack Bar, the price board displaying an eye-watering entrance fee of 50 Jordanian dinar (about £47) per person, and us, spinning on our heels and walking away. The shock that almost floored us when the ticket man asked for 100 JD to go and look at Petra was partly because of the ridiculous leap in inflation they'd just awarded themselves: the *Lonely Planet Guide*, published just months before, told of admission at 21 JD. The man at the booth confirmed that had been accurate, but that the price had gone up two weeks ago. 'More than double?' I baulked. 'Seems a bit unfair.' He shrugged, unable to explain it. '50 quid to see a historic city?' I still asked, as Jill dragged me away.

As we walked back to Penny we pondered how that compared on the World Scale Of Seeing Historic Stuff. Stonehenge - about seven quid. The entire contents of the Louvre - roughly the same at €9. Rome's Colosseum – €12. And that's just the ones we could think of that charge a fee. The majesty of Giza's pyramids, the breathtaking splendour of Florence cathedral, the entire contents of the British Museum - all free. Just bowl along and have a gander. In what bonkers world did we leap from that, to expecting a couple to pay £100 to see some rather impressive masonry work? Of course, holiday makers who've made Petra their destination and dream will begrudgingly pay up, but when you're travelling the world on a budget you have to consign it to the 'not this time' bin and vow to write a stiff letter to the Jordanian Tourist Board advising them to stop offering mind-altering drugs at their pricing strategy meetings.

Instead we went to Little Petra, which is a Little Cheaper, being free. It too has small temples cut into the distinctive orange rocks, still has paintings on the ceilings dating back 2,000 years, and even better, you're free to clamber up the rocks, discover hidden rooms and ultimately ascend to a dizzying plateau overlooking the breathtakingly impressive valley of rocks that links Petras 'Big' and 'Little'. And the very best thing about Little Petra? Almost no one goes. We had it to ourselves and ate a picnic sitting on a ledge that felt like the edge of the world. A day that had started with the promise of little more than some mild sightseeing had delivered adventure and surprises. No real drama, though. Not yet.

We continued south from Petra across mountains, deserts and through spectacular thunderstorms. Wadi Rum, if you're unacquainted with Jordan's various wadi (which means water, though most are now dry) is the most famous pocket of desert in the country. It's just north of Aqaba and is where visitors go to live the Bedouin dream, pretend to be Lawrence of Arabia, trek into the desert on a camel, cook on an open fire and camp under the stars. Despite it being a tourist magnet, everyone assured us we *had* to witness its beauty. Even David, who'd shown us Jordan's *real* hidden jewels said we must spend a night or two in Wadi Rum. And that's from a man who unearthed 3,000-year-old Moab pottery before our very eyes. In fact, we didn't go there to camp with the Bedouin, bankers and barristers. We were there for the camels. The idea of riding a camel had possessed the kids since back in Syria, and if you're only going to ride a camel once in your life, Wadi Rum is as good a place as any. It beats jumping the fence and attempting to rustle your own at the Cotswold Wildlife Park.

The enormous desert is a protected park, and while I was in the Wadi Rum Visitor Centre finding out where to buy a ticket to enable us to drive Penny through the gates, I heard a voice calling from the distance. 'Daddy! Daddy!'

Hark. The angelic song of my eldest daughter. What news brings she from the desert car park? 'A massive bus has hit the van!'

Brilliant, I thought. *I leave them alone for two minutes …*

The scene that greeted me in the car park was chaotic. Sure enough, an enormous tourist coach had reversed into our nicely parked and fully occupied van, and indeed, Penny now sported a huge dent in her side. Around this were many gabbling children (some of them mine), lots of Arabs, a bus driver and a man clutching his hair and screeching like a castrated barn owl. Oh, that was me.

I may have overreacted a tad. I asked the bus driver where his eyes were. I asked why he was smiling. I asked if he understood how a mirror worked. I asked if he'd ever driven a bus before. I was hyperventilating. I was asked to calm down. Soon the police wandered over. A diplomatic incident was about to occur. We were all ushered into the back room of the ticket office where, two hours later and with the help of several budding translators, an acceptable arrangement was arrived at. Simply reporting the incident to *Jett*, the bus company, and claiming from their insurance wasn't the best plan. For one thing, it would involve several hours of filing a report with the traffic police in a town many miles away, but also the driver would lose his job. He wanted to pay for the damage out of his own pocket, but how much? All my talk of … not wanting a back-street bodge … and … getting a VW garage to do it … was ultimately pointless - there wasn't a VW garage in Jordan.

Then, an esteemed businessman who owned several hotels in and around Aqaba happened upon the scene. When he walked into the room, dressed impeccably in full-length white robes, everyone stood up, even the coppers. He introduced himself. 'Hello Sir. My name is Osama. I have a friend who runs the best garage in Aqaba. They repair Mercedes, all the best cars. I can arrange for them to repair this. It will be perfect.'

Finally, a written agreement was signed by all concerned stating that the bus driver would pay for the full repair and any overnight accommodation if the garage needed the van for more than a day - he was being assisted in this by Osama.

'At least no one was hurt,' people kept saying, and that was true. If I could choose between a ten-tonne bus reversing into Penny and the burning, rolling, animal-related road smashes we'd seen on Middle Eastern roads, I'd pick the bus. It was generally agreed that the repair would cost about 250JD, and later, as we tidied up the paperwork, the driver thanked me for not making an official complaint. He had six kids and brought home 200JD *a month*. He wasn't trying to make me feel guilty, he was genuinely thankful this hadn't cost him his job. I shook his hand and told him not to worry, and suggested that one day, if he saved all his money and didn't eat for a whole fortnight, he could take his wife to see Petra.

Of course I didn't. But honestly - what a day of contrasts. None of it seemed right, or sat comfortably with us. We had a bashed up van, a struggling bus driver had a month's wages to scrape together and we were all putting our faith in a bloke called Osama.

We made a plan. We'd spend a couple of nights in Wadi Rum before driving the 30 miles south to Aqaba where we would get Penny's dent repaired and arrange shipping her to India. We woke early after gramping in a car park, and spilled out of the van to go and make use of the loos in the campsite. A 'stealth wee' in someone else's toilet block is all part of the fun of camping for free. If you're feeling confident you can even have a 'stealth shower' like I did, at which point you're probably ready to turn pro and take your own VW around the world.

Our late arrival after dark, due to the crunch the night before, rewarded us with a gob-smacking view to wake up to. We were in a desert! This really was Lawrence of Arabia country, the very desert where the British officer galvanized the Arabs to fight the Turks from here all the way to Damascus. There were huge, red, mountainous rocks towering behind us, and ahead were miles of orange sand, more even bigger rock formations, and - that's what we'd come for – camels. The tiny desert village felt like one of those one-horse town prospector settlements in old cowboy films. While I was scouting it for some breakfast and to get the lowdown on the current rate for renting five camels, Jill met a man. She does this. It's a gift. None of us mind.

Saleh was wearing classic Arabian robes, headscarf and sandals, plus, oddly, a leather bomber jacket. Well, this was November, the temperature would only reach 35°C today. He had offered Jill a deal on some camels, but also a 4x4 tour of the desert to see the ruins of a Beduin outpost known as Lawrence's House, some massive sand dunes to climb and a couple of cool rocks to clamber up. I negotiated his fee down to about £40 and he and his camels were ours for the day. But first he insisted we came over to his house to have tea with his wife and meet his kids.

'Go on, go on,' he urged, pointing it out across the sand. 'I will meet you there with camels.' When we walked into his back yard a young boy of about seven and girl aged about nine greeted us and went to call their mum. An old lady dressed in black robes, grandma I assumed, smiled and waved from the corner as a man in front of her expertly butchered a goat, strung up by its hind quarters with some wire flex. Smiling, I took the girls over to say hello. Being Eid week, goats were being eaten everywhere. The man smiled, stopped for a moment and went to shake my hand, then realised it was covered in blood so stopped himself and laughed. Ella pointed at the pile of bloated internal organs slumped on the dusty floor and Edie noticed the decapitated goats head, staring vacantly at Bethan a few feet away. Bethan was strangely quiet.

Saleh's wife appeared clutching a young toddler and smiling broadly. 'Welcome, welcome. Come in, come in.' We sat in their living room on cushions scattered against the walls. The large room had no furniture at all, but a huge rug at its centre, cushions around every wall punctuated by camel saddles to lean on and a central ceiling fan to alleviate the heat. The walls and ceiling were painted in vibrant symmetrical patterns forming borders around the ceiling and around pictures on the wall. A large flower had been painted around the ceiling fan. It was a very cheery room, and soon the children were showing our girls their toys while we drank sweet rosemary-infused tea.

When Saleh arrived he joined us for tea and when I commented on the impressive butchery in the yard he invited us to join them for dinner. I was only making conversation, but he was genuine about his invitation. If you remember Piacenza, you can guess what happened next. I was just about to politely decline when Jill said, 'We'd love to.' The girls and I exchanged a glance. I knew what they were thinking. They'd met the menu face to face.

Putting such concerns behind us, we went to meet our camels. As anyone who's ridden a camel will know, the real drama is when the camel stands up or kneels down, so there was a chorus of 'Whoa!' 'Aaargh!' and general hilarity as we were each catapulted skywards by our desert steeds. Then began our steady plod to Lawrence Spring (you're noticing a theme with these desert landmarks) about an hour from town. Each camel was initially led by a boy from the village. Jill asked her young lad 'What's he called? My camel?'

'Jemela!' shouted the boy.

'Aah. That's a nice name,' she said, and when I plodded along next to her she said, 'Mine's called Jemela. What's yours called?'

'I haven't asked,' I said, then shouted down to the boy leading my beast. 'Excuse me, what's my camel called?'

'Jemela,' he replied.

'Thank you,' I shouted cheerily. There was a pause while we computed this coincidence.

'*Jemela*'s the Arabic for camel, isn't it?' smirked Jill.

'I think it might be.'

Soon they handed us the reigns to our *jemela* and precisely nothing changed. It was a gesture to make us feel in control, but the truth was, those camels did that route all the time and any thoughts a rider might have had of galloping off into the horizon to raise an Arab army and defeat the Ottoman empire would have been futile. It was blisteringly hot in the sun, but brilliant fun, and we all discovered muscles we didn't know we had somewhere deep in our inner thighs.

Saleh met us at Lawrence Spring, which doesn't actually have a spring any more, but does boast a solitary tree, so there must be water underground somewhere. The next few hours were spent touring the Wadi Rum desert sitting in the back of his open pickup, an old Toyota Land Cruiser, stopping here and there to explore. We were so glad we'd paid to do more than just ride the camels to the spring. From the car, we could see how close to the village it was - we had barely scratched the surface of the vastness of this desert.

Regularly stopping to get out and explore, we climbed up, then ran down, colossal sand dunes in huge flying leaps, conquered steep rock faces to stand on frighteningly high natural bridges formed between pillars of sandstone, and saw carved drawings of camels at old trading posts dating back a thousand years. As we hurtled back towards the village, the wind whipping our headscarves, the sun finally dipping low enough to be pleasant and give the desert a terracotta glow, we all agreed it may have been the best £40 we'd ever spent.

'Where you sleep tonight?' asked Saleh, back at his house.

'In the car park again. It's free.'

He shook his head. 'You don't want to sleep in desert?'

We explained that we'd looked into it but decided to spend our money on camels instead, but he was having none of it. He said he only had a few tourists staying at his camp that night, and if we wanted to join them we'd be most welcome. 'You must sleep in the desert. You can eat dinner out there, we'll have a barbecue, then sleep in a tent, some breakfast in the morning cooked on the fire ...' It did sound great, but we just couldn't afford it. By the time he'd dropped the price to one third of the going rate, however, I could bear my family's pleading faces no more. 'Please, I must insist,' whispered Saleh, 'don't talk about the money with the other guests. They are paying full price.'

Our lips were sealed.

And so we found ourselves sharing barbecued chicken (I was a little disappointed it wasn't goat) under the stars with Saleh and his kids. Also with us were Manuel, a Spanish geologist, John, an American language student, and Javier, a Spanish voluntary worker who had spent six months on a UNICEF project. A few more guests arrived later, but we were all in bed (sorry, 'on mat') by 9 o'clock, exhausted. The highlight was when Ella got up at 4am to go to the loo. Well, that in itself wasn't the highlight; it woke me, which allowed me to leave the tent, grab a seat, plonk it in the sand outside our camp and gaze at the stars. Before bed the bright moon had washed out the sky, but now it had disappeared beyond the horizon and the sky was black, littered with stars. To see the night sky from a desert is something I've always wanted to do, and it lived up to my expectations. The complete lack of light pollution made the view stunning. In the first 30 seconds of sitting out on the sand I saw two shooting stars. I cursed my lack of astronomical knowledge, only being able to identify the Plough (flipped almost upside down compared to our view at home) and Orion. I saw Jupiter and the dim red flicker I assumed was Mars, which I hadn't seen yet that year. After half an hour when the shooting stars had totalled five, I returned to bed. Mat.

After a campfire brekky of freshly made flatbreads and an egg dish we christened 'scramlette', we hurtled in the open pickup across vast, majestic sands back towards the village, and our dented van. Our clothes stank of camp-fire smoke and we had sand in every crevice, but we were happy.

In Aqaba, the temperature hit 38°C. We were the only camper van on a small campsite facing the sea, and as we couldn't raise Osama on the phone we decided to relax for a day or two. I tried not to get stressed about the fact that the benevolent businessman who'd stepped in to try to resolve the Big Bus vs. Penny clash was not answering his mobile phone, and as a distraction agreed to take Ella and Beth snorkelling. We covered up, as is the custom in Jordan - even men wear shirts in the sea – and, armed with the snorkels and masks we'd bought back in Croatia, stepped cautiously into the Red Sea. We had the beach almost to ourselves, but walking into the clear water all that seemed to be underfoot were pebbles and the occasional piece of litter. We soon walked out beyond pebbles on to smoother sand and were up to our waists, plunging our masks under water to survey what lay below the surface. Then Ella yelled, 'AT HOOVED!' It's not easy to form your words through a snorkel. We all pulled our heads up.

'What?'

'That moved. Down there,' she panted, pointing at my feet.

I pushed my head under again. Even under the water I could hear Ella scream, 'Daddy, you're standing on it!'

I danced my sandalled feet up as if doing a crazy sub-aqua Irish jig and tried to tread water in about four foot of sea before panic gave way to logic and I simply swam on my belly facing the sea-bed below. Sure enough, I'd disturbed a panther ray, about 30 centimetres from wing tip to wing tip. Its two tiny, black pebble eyes were all that gave it away under the sand, until eventually, disgruntled at my flapping, it rose majestically and swam underneath me. You can imagine the excitement gushing from us when we regrouped above the surface. We ventured further and had all but given up the ray as a lone visitor to these shores when we spotted several black-spotted puffer fish, each the size of a man's fist, their tiny wispy fins propelling their bulbous bodies gently along.

Soon, we were out of our depth, both literally and metaphorically. The coral reef was still quite a way out, according to a local boy we met out there, and then Beth said the words guaranteed to rattle an ill-equipped, nervous father while out at sea. 'A ray and a puffer fish. This close to the shore. Imagine what else is out here.'

Then Ella said, 'Can we get out? I think I've been stung on my arm.'

We'd observed the spotter's boards on the beach and knew the Red Sea was rich in life including sharks and jellyfish, so the thought of sharing our space with a gently floating school of jellies soon propelled us racing back to the shore. I won. 'That was amazing!' I shouted, finding my feet again.

'Are you all right?' I asked Ella, looking at her arm. She held out her wrist and we couldn't see anything wrong. She pointed to where she thought it hurt, but quickly decided it didn't.

'That was scary out there,' said Bethan.

'Yes it was,' I agreed. 'Let's go back and tell the others. I'm not going any further without a wet suit and someone who knows what they're doing.'

I never claimed to be Steve Irwin. But I learned from his ray-related folly.

Finally, on Sunday, we tracked down Osama at his hotel in Aqaba. He was the perfect gentleman, offering us tea and juice, explaining that he'd been in the desert for three days and promised to get Penny repaired as quickly as possible. He told of how The Captain's Restaurant had been opened by his father in the 1980s with just twelve seats. Now, the seafood restaurant is arguably the best in Aqaba and has spawned a newly built luxury hotel next door. Osama and his brother Rafiq had helped in the restaurant as boys, and now ran two hotels and two restaurants for the family firm. Osama had studied in Rome where he'd learned a lot about business, and even more about good restaurants. He was on a mission to change local people's attitudes to working in the service trade from one of shame to one of pride. In a cutting edge concept for Jordan, he shared 10 per cent of all his profits with his staff, on top of their wages, in an attempt to empower them.

'Are attitudes changing?' Jill asked.

'Yes, of course,' he smiled confidently. 'But I can't do it alone. You can't clap with one hand.'

He was trying to persuade other businesses to follow his lead in paying local people while training them - something they weren't used to - and was proud that his head-chef was from Aqaba.

Then he said he would not be pursuing the bus driver for the money to repair Penny. 'I believe that punishment with words is more effective than financial punishment,' he explained. 'I know these drivers, and he will already feel bad enough about what happened. I don't want his money.' He talked over tea about the charity project he was involved in, working with children from Aqaba and neighbouring Eilat in Israel, which aimed to show them that a peaceful future could be achieved. Kids from both cities formed a football team that Osama took to a tournament in Italy, and he glowed with pride when he told us that they'd beaten several Italian teams. He was a gentle, polite, humanitarian. Undoubtedly he had a razor sharp business mind, but he never for a moment betrayed any ulterior motive than to do well for his family and help his fellow man.

While the van was being repaired, Osama put us up in a lovely suite with five beds and by 5.30 the next evening Penny was ready to collect. In the evening gloom I could see she was straight again, and even the colour match looked almost perfect. I thanked the repairman profusely and paraded the whole family down to see Osama for a final goodbye. Once again, a complete stranger had extended us an unbelievably generous gesture. The accident had literally nothing to do with him, yet he stepped in and sorted it entirely at his own expense. To mix my world religions somewhat, good karma surely awaits.

India beckoned. Soon we would fly to Delhi and Penny would be on a ship. Travelling without her required a whole new mindset. We pared our clothes down to just those essential for three weeks of backpacking, and agonised about carrying our instruments, but all agreed that, though it would be great to use the three weeks as good press opportunity time, it was just too much to carry on foot. We'd found a shipping agent, a gaunt, wiry, chain-smoking Arab whose favourite English phrase was, 'It is better for you.' He agreed to ship Penny on a container ship from Aqaba to Mumbai for a fee of about £700. 'Pay in cash,' he instructed. 'It is better for you.'

It was, by contrast, incredibly inconvenient for us, but this was our first introduction to the ancient, unswerving customs of the global shipping trade, where deals are done on a handshake and cash rules.

We packed Penny for her journey and observed with a smile the almost-the-same yellow panel where her dent had been. The metal was impressively straight, the boot closed properly again and, unless you were looking for it, you probably wouldn't notice the slight colour difference. My favourite part was a drip. I doubted our mechanic Blue, or the original paint sprayer John, could have borne a paint drip on the bodywork but to us it was a battle scar - a reminder of a remarkable few days and the generous, smiling people we'd found ourselves sharing tea and tales with.

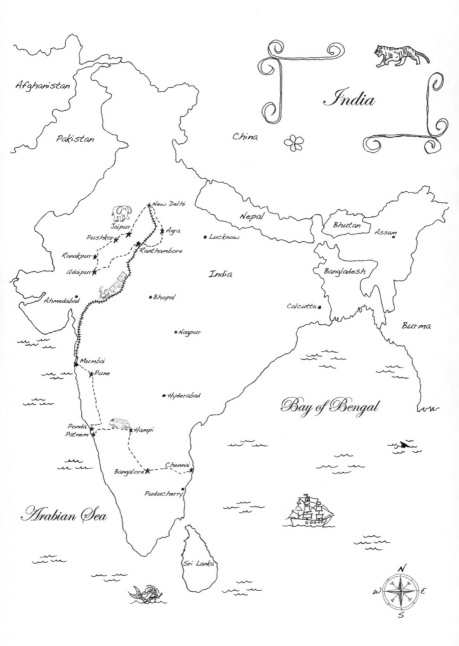

Afghanistan

Pakistan

China

India

Nepal

Bhutan

Assam

New Delhi

Jaipur

Pushkar

Agra

Lucknow

Ranakpur

Ranthambore

Udaipur

India

Bangladesh

Ahmedabad

Bhopal

Calcutta

Nagpur

Burma

Mumbai

Pune

Hyderabad

Bay of Bengal

Ponda
Patnem

Hampi

Bangalore

Chennai

Puducherry

Arabian Sea

Sri Lanka

N

W   E

S

Nothing on Earth can prepare you for India. I suspect even people who are born there must occasionally find themselves startled, confused and discombobulated by the rush, colour and chaos. Having left Penny safely stowed in a container in sleepy Aqaba, awaiting her sea journey to Mumbai, we flew to New Delhi with a plan to backpack our way south to meet her when she docked in Bombay - as sailors still called it.

Our introduction to India was a baptism of fire. We'd booked a budget hotel in the middle of Delhi's bazaar area and the pre-arranged cab that took us wasn't a car in the conventional sense of the word. It appeared to be made of Meccano and cardboard. Doors didn't latch, wheels wobbled perilously when its speed passed walking pace, and every lurch and bump was accompanied by an alarming screech or scrape from below. I sat in the front, squeezed next to the cabbie, our faces lit by a plastic disco-Hindu-temple flashing brightly from the dashboard. Jill and the girls squashed into the back, one wide-eyed in horror, three almost instantly asleep. After about 40 minutes we reached the kind of back streets we'd only seen in Danny Boyle's *Slumdog Millionaire*.

It was almost seven in the morning and our corner of the capital was already heaving with life. Dogs, hogs, camels and cows shared rammed alleys with rickshaws, cyclists, traffic and tuk-tuks - the tiny gas-powered three-wheeled rickshaws that fill every gap in every street. Cooking smells merged with the stench of litter, drains, heavy incense and an open trench being used as a gents' loo. There was simply no point of reference for our sheltered Western psyche. No high street banks, no car parks, food shops, bars or fast food outlets. All these services existed, of course, but in a form unrecognisable to our English eyes. Food was available everywhere, but not in branded packages or chain-store shops. Downtown Delhi felt like the design of a child who drew all his streets with a big fat crayon and filled them with his favourite vehicles, shops and animals, before handing the plans to his younger brother, who didn't rub out the original, but simply added more, until several generations later we had the finished product - a multi-coloured chaotic scribble of noise and mayhem.

The hotel was cheap. Not the cheapest, but cheap enough to have damp beds and swift mice. We got moved to slightly drier quarters, but I think the mouse on our landing had resident's status. We sank into an uneasy jet-lagged sleep until mid-afternoon, when I persuaded my family to brave the crowds and see Delhi. A walk through the bazaar's hectic streets brought the same level of pestering we'd been used to in Syria, but it was obvious from the start that we wouldn't be quite so isolated in the crowd. There were other westerners here, not coach parties, but every now and again the white face of a traveller wearing relaxed hippy clothing and an SLR camera would drift by. The pestering hawkers were keen, but not aggressive, and as Edie noticed quite quickly, they almost all wore similar clothes to ours - jeans and tee shirts. We'd stuck out so much more in Syria because almost everyone there wore robes.

It was still a lot to take in, and by the time we'd battled our way past Delhi's train station mêlée and had been approached a dozen times by people offering to take us wherever we wanted to go, Jill buckled. 'Let's go back.'

'But we haven't got there yet,' I whined.

'Got where?'

'Connaught Place. It's a big circle with loads of shops and stuff.'

Simply standing still to have this conversation invited at least two random strangers to stop, listen in, and offer their advice. 'Connaught Place is just up there,' offered the first.

'No, no, come with me,' interjected the second. 'You must bear left.'

'I will take you,' insisted the first.

'No, really, we're fine,' assured Jill, but a polite refusal wouldn't shake them, so we strode onwards, and even then they followed us. Finally, after they'd lost interest and drifted away, the only thing stopping us from reaching our destination was the six-lane outer ring road of Connaught Place. All the traffic lights on the main road had been switched off. Installing them had been a waste of time, according to one local, as no one on India's roads adhered to any rules apart from one: keep going. As a result, all six lanes of one-way traffic were fused into a writhing monster of cars, motorbikes, tuk-tuks and rickshaws, none of them sticking to a lane, but all weaving, dodging and constantly edging into any gap that might give them an advantage over their competitors.

We grabbed the children's hands and waited, forlornly, for a break in the scrum. After a minute or so of white knuckle half-attempts that saw us scurry back to safety, a boy of about 15 joined us. 'Come with me,' he said, his gleaming teeth smiling broadly. 'It takes practice.'

He stepped out in front of a speeding Ambassador - an ancient car based on the old Morris Oxford, prolific in India and built like a tank. I held my breath, the kid held his nerve, the car held back. I dragged Ella and Bethan with me in the boy's wake as he progressed, expertly timing each step to perfection so that we wove through the onslaught like salmon defeating the rapids. In the 1980s I'd played a computer game called *Frogger*. Now, we were living it. Relieved and joyous, we reached the other side and thanked the boy who simply said, 'No problem'.

'Wow,' I said, turning to Jill. She was nowhere to be seen.

'Oh no!' shouted Ella, laughing. She was looking across the cacophony of traffic to the distant figures of Jill and Edie, still stranded on the other side mouthing, 'Help.' Did she really think I was going to fight my way back to get them? I'd just been helped across a road by a 15-year-old boy - I'd lost any shred of pride at lane two.

Seeing the situation, the lad effortlessly dodged back through the deafening traffic to rescue them, guiding them deftly across the path of an oncoming truck while Ella, Bethan and I witnessed Act Two of the circus from the safety of the stalls. It was only when I watched as a spectator that I realised there was a zebra crossing on the road.

At the next do-or-die crossing a young man of about 18 told me he could never remember the traffic lights having worked here, and that it took most visitors at least a fortnight to master crossing the road. His name was Bahrat and he was on his way to buy cinema tickets for a later showing of a new Bollywoood film he'd arranged to watch with his girlfriend. His family ran a restaurant in Delhi, he told me, but he had the night off - Friday night was date night. When I told him we were getting around by train, and commented that our afternoon of Internet searching had proved frustrating, as most of the trains were full, he said, 'Always full online. You need to go to the rail office. They have a tourist quota they hold back.'

The rail ticket office was just opposite the cinema, so he showed us there, then nipped off to buy his Bollywood tickets before re-joining us in the office in case we needed any help. The upshot of our investigation was that although we could get from Delhi to Mumbai quite easily, filling the next fortnight touring Rajasthan would be almost impossible by rail. The stations weren't placed near the places we wanted to go and the fact that we'd always be buying five tickets forced the rail representative to reluctantly admit it would be much cheaper for us to hire a car. The thought of battling the madness outside in a hire car with a £500 damage waiver hanging over my head didn't really appeal, but that's not what he meant. Most tourists book a car *and driver* - it's cheaper than hiring a car because you're not paying huge insurance premiums and far cheaper than repeatedly buying five rail tickets and numerous cab fares. Soon a deal was done and we had secured the services of Naresh-the-driver and we were planning days in Agra, Ranthambore, Udaipur and Jaipur before returning to Delhi to catch the overnight sleeper train to Mumbai – a long held dream of mine. We thanked Bahrat for his friendly help, swapped email addresses and, as we'd spent a significant few minutes discussing Bollywood, promised to visit Asia's biggest cinema when we got to Jaipur. 'It is a palace,' he beamed. 'You will love it!'

So now we were tourists. Being without Penny for the first time was not only inconvenient because we missed having our own transport and cheap beds for the night, but it also felt, after three months together, like we'd lost a family member. Worse though, was that we'd lost our credibility as overland travellers. No amount of explaining to people that we were driving around the world and our van was on a ship could change the fact that we were just tourists now. Backpackers, sure, but we needed transport and accommodation just like every other holidaymaker from the west. This didn't sit very easy with any of us, so Jill made a mental adjustment. 'Let's treat it like a holiday,' she said. 'We can't get on with our journey until Penny gets here, we've got transport, we've got hotels we can stay in - OK they're not exactly luxury, but all the same - it's a holiday. Let's be tourists.'

'Good plan,' I agreed.

'I'm getting a guide,' she added.

'What?'

'Narash can get us a guide in Agra to show us the Fort and the Taj Mahal. It's only a fiver for the day. I'm going all "cruise ship".' She was living the dream. She'd be having a spa treatment next.

So we started the next day in Delhi seizing the opportunity to cover some world history with the girls by visiting Indira Gandhi's house, now a museum, which tells the story of her life and of her assassination. Most interesting to the girls was the macabre display of the sari Indira was wearing when shot by her own guards in 1984, grizzly dark brown blood stains still clearly visible around the bullet holes.

At the Mahatma Gandhi memorial we learned about the various periods of India's history, including the British occupation which was painted in a predictably poor light. Again, it was his violent end that captured the girls' imagination. You can walk in the great man's final footsteps from his bedroom to the prayer ground where he was shot, and read an eyewitness account of how events unfolded. There are quotes dotted around the site, some from Gandhi: 'My life is my message,' and 'I don't preach a new message. Truth and non-violence are as old as the hills,' are a couple I recall. Then Jill spotted one. 'There you go, girls,' she said. 'You can say that Albert Einstein quote when people ask why you missed school for a year.'

Ella read from a display board. 'The only thing that interferes with my learning is my education.'

Agra is as busy, colourful, noisy and polluted as any large Indian city, but has one massive unique selling point: the Taj Mahal. India's most popular tourist attraction was built by Mughal Emperor Shah Jahan in memory of his second wife Mumtaz, whose death in childbirth in 1631 is said to have turned the Emperor's hair grey overnight. It's often described as the most extravagant monument ever built for love, and is a must-see for any visitor to northern India. Its design is clever in that, as you approach, you can't see it from outside its symmetrically placed gates, so only when you pass through one of the mighty arches do your eyes meet its dazzling splendour.

It's breathtaking. Really, it is. Jill nearly cried. First of all, it's much bigger than you think. All those travel brochure snaps, and 'that' Princess Diana picture don't do any justice to its scale. When you walk into its gardens and see how tiny the people are at its distant doorways, you do a double take. The white marble appears to change colour throughout the day - pink at sunrise, white in the daylight, golden orange at sunset and a milky cream by moonlight. We were there at sunset, so having taken the obligatory family snaps at the latest 'must-see' in our growing tick list of global landmarks, we sat down against the west wall's mosque and watched the crowds – almost entirely Indians - milling about. The Taj's dome, walls and towers assumed a warm orange glow as the sun slid away. It was a trip highlight.

As we strolled away through the surrounding parkland, entertained by tame monkeys playing on the grass, the feelings of uncertainty that had overwhelmed Jill and the girls back in Delhi slowly ebbed away. At the next busy street I hailed a tuk-tuk to get us back to our hotel, and as we raced through the night - the four girls squeezed on top of each other in the back while I hung out of the front seat perched next to the driver - the wind rushing through our hair, we weaved and beeped past crowd, cows and camels through the busy Agra streets and allowed ourselves several whoops of delight. Giddy and laughing we piled out, and for the first time agreed that India might be quite cool after all.

When we planned that our world tour would include India, one of the things we dreamed about was the prospect of seeing a tiger in the wild. Ranthambore National Park in Rajasthan is widely regarded as the best possible place to witness such a thing and from Agra it was, in Indian terms, a short drive – at just seven hours.

We checked into another cheap and cheerful hotel – one with huge hand-painted elephants on the bedroom walls - and woke before dawn to embark on our own tiger safari. Wrapped in layers of our flimsy travellers' clothes against the 6am chill, we boarded a 'canter' – like a school minibus with the roof peeled off – and drove through the freezing mist into the wild bush-land. We picked up a few other tourists on the way into the protected park and there was an excited buzz among us at the prospect of glimpsing one of nature's rarest predators, that ancient Indian symbol of courage, the tiger. Slowly, our vehicle crept through long grass, under trees and alongside lakes, the hushed passengers not wishing to betray their growing impatience. After an hour of this, the glory of a tiger-less wilderness was losing its lustre.

'There! On the lake,' our guide whispered with reverence. 'An egret!'

An egret! I shouted in my head. *Brilliant. We've crossed umpteen borders over two continents to see a bird I could have seen in Poole flippin' harbour.*

'What next?' I whispered to Jill in awestruck wonder. 'A pigeon?'

The 1,000 rupees (about £14) *each* I had invested in our safari (which actually comes from the ancient Swahili word saf-a-ri, meaning 'expensive disappointment') proved fruitless. Beth did her best to look on the bright side, saying things like, 'It was nice to see the peacocks. And the deer. They were nice.'

Peacocks! Deer! It's not Blenheim Palace! I wanted teeth and claws and roars and at the very least a dangerously close encounter with a cobra or two. We did see a crocodile. It was some distance away, and the fact it lay entirely motionless while we watched meant I couldn't help thinking it might have been made of fibreglass. I blame Disney. I've seen too many theme parks. That damned mouse has robbed me of my wide-eyed wonder.

The following day we travelled on, bravely shouldering our crushing disappointment, towards Udaipur, a pretty city on a large lake. Naresh, our driver, was still failing to grasp that we were travelling for an entire year on a strict budget, and insisted on referring to our time together as, 'the holiday of a lifetime,' and insisting we visit every single pay-as-you-view tourist attraction on route. A large fortified town, several temples, an ornate tower on a hill, a 15th Century palace, a few more Hindu temples - they became a blur. We started to suffer from a phenomenon that here, in this book, risks making us sound aloof, condescending and superior. Snooty, even.

It was a malaise that can best be described as 'travel weariness', a creeping apathy that needed arresting and throttling as quickly as possible. A disease that, if left unchecked, risked turning me into the only guy who'd turn up at The Grand Canyon and sigh, 'Not bad. Bit like Jordan's Wadi Mujib but with more tourists,' and I didn't want to be that guy.

By now we'd all privately agreed that getting the driver was a mistake. Naresh was a nice enough bloke, but we constantly felt we were letting him down with our reactions. He'd offer us sightseeing opportunities that we felt we couldn't say no to, only to see him crestfallen when we'd return to the car after 15 minutes. 'You not like Chittogargh? Why so quick?' he would plead. It's not that we didn't like ruined forts, or old palaces and ornate temples, but *we had seen so much.*

'Look here,' a guide would say. 'Seats of ancient theatre where emperor would be entertained.' *Not bad, but I've stood in the Colosseum.*

'This jug from fifteen hundreds,' one would whisper dramatically. *I've picked up discarded pottery that pre-dated Christ.*

'These walls are dating from eleventh century.' *I've blown dust off a three thousand year old Moab altar.* I'm aware this sounds awful, I feel horribly guilty admitting it and, yes, we were very lucky to be seeing such treasures, but it's an honest insight into our mental state. Finally, as we reached our destination, Naresh announced, 'Welcome to Udaipur, the Venice of the East!' and I couldn't stop myself saying, 'I thought that was Norwich.'

At dinner that evening - vegetable biryani, vegetable pakora, zera aloo (potato and cumin) and naans - Edie asked how long the next drive would be. 'About three hours,' said Jill, to which Edie replied,

'Can we please not stop at a fort?' I'm ashamed to admit it, but there it is, travel weariness had us in its grip.

We stood still for a few days and grew fond of Udaipur. Our hotel wasn't at all expensive but had a brilliant rooftop restaurant, from where we could see the crazy clutter of all the other rooftop bars and

restaurants and enjoy the sun shimmering off the lake, with its famous island hotel that appeared to float. We watched traditional Rajasthani dancers and puppet shows and, suddenly conscious that it was December, snuck into tiny shops of treasures to do some discreet Christmas shopping. Hand-painted cards, pretty hand-embroidered blouses, and even hand-made perfumes were bundled up for Father Christmas to deliver later in the month.

On our journey through Rajasthan we noticed two unique tricks Indians did, that we often attempted with comedic results. One is the Indian squat, a resting position adopted by any man, woman or child who is simply waiting for something. They squat down, folding their legs so tightly that their knees locate in their armpits. The difficulty, and this is your challenge, reader, should you wish to accept it, is that the feet should be *flat* on the floor. The first thing *we* do when we squat is rise up on to the balls of our feet. Indians have the knack of folding themselves into a squat that sits happily on flat feet, perfectly relaxed, seemingly for hours. Try it, as we did, and prepare to roll over in giggles.

The second trick we noticed was their knack of drinking without their lips touching the receptacle. Whether it was a glass of water in a restaurant, or a tin cup of water scooped from a bucket, people *poured* into their mouths leaving a vital air gap between lips and cup, rather than sipping as we do. Despite the fact that a billion people drink like this every day, even tiny toddlers, it's much harder than it looks. Try it. Have a towel handy.

At Ranakpur is India's biggest Jain temple. Jainism is the chosen religion of fewer than 1 per cent of Indians, yet they have beautifully carved ancient temples all over the place. In simple terms (for they suit me best) Jainism is a bit like Hinduism. The essence of Jainism is concern for the welfare of every being in the universe and for the universe itself. Jains are strict vegetarians and live in a way that minimises their use of the world's resources, so in some respects they were aware of their carbon footprint about two thousand years ahead of their time.

Their temples are covered, floor to ceiling, in carvings depicting devils, elephants, dancers and one or two examples of the Karma Sutra – 'Move along, children, nothing to see here.' The Ranakpur temple is crammed with decorated pillars supporting several similarly carved domes and is undoubtedly a fine example of the ancient Jains' talent and dedication.

But we won't remember it for that. I'm afraid it's time to raise the thorny issue of tipping. To tip, or not to tip, is a tricky dilemma whoever you are and wherever you live, whether you're rounding up the bill at your local carvery, writing a Christmas card for your milkman or planning a doomed bank heist, as depicted in the opening scene of *Reservoir Dogs*.

Tipping in India is regarded as a right, rather than a privilege earned for good service. Every toilet at any restaurant, petrol station or café seemed to have a man or woman in the shadows thrusting a paper towel at you with one hand while holding out the other for cash. In one of our budget hotels we had breakfast included - defined as toast and butter. Once served, a second waiter brought a serving of jam, then waited expectantly for a reward.

The debates surrounding tipping are complicated. 'But Sim,' you might cry, 'the average wage in India is £238 a year - cut them some slack.' On the other hand, there's Steve Buscemi's point of view in the aforementioned *Reservoir Dogs*: Why should some people get tipped, and not others? Did you tip the man or woman who built the computer or printing press allowing you to read this? In our house we tip our postman and our milkman at Christmas, but not our bin men. I don't know why. I can drive a car, but am drastically under-qualified to drive a train. If I take a train the driver doesn't expect a tip, yet if I take a taxi ...

Well, it just so happened that when we got to this place, we put the 'poor' in Ranakpur. We were completely cash-less. I had failed to understand just how remote it was, and as the nearest ATM was over 20 kilometres away, we found ourselves penniless until we could drive to the distant town. Thankfully, entry to the one tourist attraction we'd been driven here to see was free. We removed our shoes next to the 'Remove Shoes Here' sign, only to be shouted at by an old man who angrily told us to bring them over to *his* shoe rack on the other side of the steps, a ruse I was used to by now - getting them back would require paying him the reward for good service we've been talking about. We took our chances with the other two dozen pairs of shoes strewn around the sign.

On entering the holy site, a white robed young man introduced himself. 'Hello,' he smiled. 'I am a priest here.' Jains don't have priests, they have monks and nuns, but I let it go. 'What a beautiful family,' he continued. 'Can I show you around the temple for ten minutes?'

'Great, but we haven't got any money,' I grinned, expecting a jovial knowing wink from our host and an arm around my shoulder, acknowledging my wry observation of life as a tourist in India. Instead, the look on his face was one of creeping disgust, as if he'd just set eyes on a family made entirely of excrement. Unable to speak his reaction, he simply gazed at my feet. I thought perhaps I'd trodden a dead raccoon into the place, but no, he just didn't want to converse any more.

'I'll take that as a "no", then,' I muttered and we went on our way. What I should have said was, 'I thought Jainism was the religion of self help, not help yourself,' but lines that pithy only come to people like Oscar Wilde or Mark Twain, and they probably had team writers. We didn't think he'd displayed a terribly holy way of conducting himself, but later saw him slouched in a corner on his mobile phone, spitting out of a window, so I don't think he was a particularly pious man.

When we walked through the gardens to a smaller temple, I sat outside with Ella and Edie while Jill and Beth wandered in. Apart from the uniformed security guard outside we had the place to ourselves. He made some polite conversation about the weather, and when Jill reappeared he offered to take our photo. Having taken the snap, he held out his hand. I raised my eyebrows and laughed. He smiled. 'Money?' he asked. I was beyond subtlety by now.

'You want paying?'

'Yes please. Just fifty rupees.' My family were walking away, as was the normal drill by this stage, but I was engaged. I just couldn't let this one go. 'Twenty rupees, then,' he suggested. 'Ten.'

'We have no money,' I said, which was true.

'You from England - I'll take Euros.'

He'd take Euros. Apart from his obvious misunderstanding of British currency, what next? Plastic? That was the final straw. I went a bit Basil Fawlty. 'Right. You. Look here,' I ordered, holding the camera to his face. 'See? Picture. Watch. Gone. Deleted. You should *not* trick people by taking their photo and then asking for money,' I admonished. Then, in very plain English, as if he was four years old, I said, 'You are a very bad man.'

And with that I spun on my heels and walked away, content that my British pride was intact and that I might just have taught the scoundrel a lesson in good manners. Having read that back, you should know I wasn't wearing heels. It wasn't that sort of place. You're probably not the least bit surprised to hear that he wasn't even slightly embarrassed. A few minutes later he was trying to give us directions to another temple. 'Do you want paying for that?' I asked, my unfortunate reflex sarcasm getting the better of me.

'Yes please,' he replied, without a hint of irony.

We still had a lot of acclimatising to do.

Pushkar is home to the *only* temple in the world dedicated to the Hindu god Brahma, and has at its centre a lake surrounded by several hundred other temples. It's been a pilgrimage destination for hundreds of years, and the small town survives solely on tourism. Beth was a bit under the weather when we got there so Ella, Edie and I explored the streets, the snake charmers and the temples, and found the lake. It's regarded as holy water, hence people wash in it, bottle it, and scatter petals on it as a gesture to Brahma, which we did, as is the tradition, only to watch a monkey scoop up our petals and eat them, which is less traditional. In the evening Beth made the ultimate sacrifice anyone with a poorly tummy can make, and agreed to accompany us to an Indian cookery class. She's got a will of iron, that girl.

Fiona is an Australian who met an Indian, Praveen, and together they ran a small hotel in Pushkar, while also running an occasional school at their home teaching curious guests the mysterious arts of concocting the perfect curry. We joined another group - also from Australia - and the ten of us had a fantastic evening, first buying all the ingredients from a veggie stall on a street corner in town, then seeing the tiny 'hole in the wall' miller's shop where locals got their own grain milled into flour while they waited. The secret, we learned, to the perfect chapati, is fresh flour. Remarkably, there's nothing else in them but flour and water, kneaded, then kneaded some more, before finally being soundly shown who's boss with some more kneading.

We all threw ourselves into chopping, peeling and prepping the veg, the ginger, chilli and garlic that would, with the addition of spices like cumin, turmeric and coriander seeds, become glorious Indian cuisine. Fiona's kitchen filled with wondrous smells as we made Masoor Dal, Garga Mattar (carrot and peas) and Bengal style sweet and sour eggplant. We learned such pearls of wisdom as, 'dry spices first, until they pop, then wet spices - garlic, ginger and the like - then vegetables', and, 'crush coriander seeds to make powder because pre-bought coriander powder loses its flavour very quickly in the cupboard.'

The ultimate reward, of course, was eating the results. We sat on rugs and scooped the delicious food up with chapatis, not always perfectly round (made by us amateurs), but perfectly cooked over a naked flame by Praveen. 'This is nothing like an Indian dinner party,' said Fiona. 'If an Indian family invites you round for dinner they will all cook and serve you, as you are the guests, but not eat with you. After the meal you may catch your hosts glancing at their watches, waiting for you to leave, as only after you've *gone* can the famished hosts eat the leftovers.'

The final stop on our tour of north west India, before returning to Delhi to get the sleeper train to Mumbai, was Jaipur. The capital of Rajasthan, Jaipur is famous for its pink city, now slightly grubby thanks to its less glamorous claim-to-fame as Rajasthan's most polluted city. You can basically divide it into three distinct areas: the *old* city - narrow streets, noise, tuk-tuks, cows, pigs and litter, the *new* city - slightly wider streets, noise, tuk-tuks, cows, pigs and litter, and the *pink* city - narrow streets, noise, tuk-tuks, cows, pigs and litter but with a pink/grey hue. It felt like Delhi, but for us it had three significant features: a big charity, a big screen, and big elephants.

First, UNICEF has one of its headquarters in Jaipur, so we wanted to arrange a meeting, tell them what we were doing and learn about their work in India. Secondly, as the state capital is home to Asia's largest cinema (Bahrat's fact from back in Delhi), I was excited about taking in some Bollywood action, sharing an auditorium with 1,500 Indian film fans. Thirdly, the kids were equally excited that it was here that Jill would be forced to make good on a hasty promise made a week earlier: by way of softening the blow of the tiger safari, notable for its absence of stripy growly things, Jill had offered to stump up for an elephant ride. It had worked. The thrill of potentially riding nature's biggest land mammal now eclipsed all tiger-related matters.

From the foot of the Amber Palace - a huge hilltop fort whose walls spread far around the surrounding mountain ridges, silhouetted against the sky like a mini Great Wall of China - you can ride an elephant up the long ornately-walled path to the palace gates, entering the courtyard in the grandest possible fashion. You can get two people on an elephant, plus driver, and the going rate to rent your portable pachyderm was about a tenner. So we had two, and Jill chose to play fast and loose beneath the elephant's legs as chief photographer. As you'd expect, this whole racket is 100 per cent for the tourists, and not by any stretch of the imagination a slice of normal Indian life, but I endeavoured to get some local insight from our driver Sanjay. I was trying to ask him how he got a job as an elephant driver - I'm always keeping my options open for future employment - but he didn't understand me. What I *did* learn was that it wasn't his elephant. All the beasts were owned by one company that looked after them, thus controlling the animals' welfare. 'I am just a taxi driver,' smiled Sanjay. 'With very big taxi.'

We were giddily high, tossed from side to side, and laughed like drains when our elephant broke into a jaunty trot up the hill - earthquake mode – and laughed again when the elephant in front went to the toilet in transit. After using a handy wall to disembark, the girls spent time feeling the skin of the mighty mammal. The huge leather wrinkles of the elephant's hide, dotted every few centimetres with a single, thick brown hair, were warm to the touch. We weren't expecting that. My elephant driver application form is in the post.

But our mission, when we weren't having fun on elephants, was to busk our way around the world raising money for UNICEF. We may have been temporarily parted from our instruments, but we could use our time in Jaipur to see how some of the money we raised might be used. UNICEF are very active in India and when I phoned the Rajasthan office I was put straight through to Anuradha who was delighted to hear of our journey and our fundraising, and immediately scheduled an 'all staff' meeting for us in their conference room the next day. 'It will be a great opportunity,' she said, 'for them to meet the people raising the funds they are using. I'm afraid we can't give you more than an hour,' she explained. 'It's approaching our end-of-year, and we are up to our eyes in final reports, planning budgets and a million things that must be done by Christmas.'

I was grateful they could see us at all, and couldn't help thinking that there might be several very important people sitting in a conference room the next morning feeling a little let down that they'd left a red-hot phone and creaking in-tray to meet a family who fool around playing Beatles songs in a haphazard way.

Ella got to work. It was like the Madaba school gig all over again, as she grabbed the laptop and started creating a PowerPoint presentation about our trip. We had photos of us busking, screen grabs of the UNICEF donations page; it was a fine piece of work. So, by 10 o'clock the next morning we were in front of 15 people who'd gathered to witness this strange English family that had landed. I told them about our trip, where we had started, where we were going, explained what 'busking' means (a word no one outside of the UK, Australia or America seems to know) and tentatively asked them if they'd heard of The Beatles. There was good reason for my caution. A few days earlier I'd asked our driver Naresh, a 35-year-old man who seemed pretty switched on, whether he'd heard of The Beatles. 'Yeah, sure,' he enthused. 'Beatles are very popular here.'

'See Edie?' I said eagerly. 'I told you they would be.' I turned back to Naresh. 'You know their music?'

'Sure! Music, parties, weddings, night clubs - Beatles very common.' This seemed incredible. They were bigger than at home! 'Salted, spicy,' he went on. He was miming eating something. Edie laughed.

'Beetles? Beetles you eat?' I asked.

'Of course. You want some?'

'Er ...'

'They start at maybe 20 rupees for poorer people. But richer people pay 200 rupees a packet.'

'What's the difference?'

'The more expensive beetles are cleaned better.'

The girls had grimaced. So, in the UNICEF office I was braced for a rush of enthusiasm for bug-based cuisine. 'Oh yes. Of course!' they chorused. *Phew! They understood it was a band.* 'If you mean *the* Beatles,' one woman said. 'I've never heard the Beatnik Beatles, what are they like?'

'Nothing like the Beatles,' was the honest answer. And so, gradually, they learned of our unique approach to fundraising, asked lots of questions about our route, the people we'd met, and then the UNICEF officer in charge of education asked how the girls were keeping up with their schooling. They were curious about Ella's school's distance learning technology, using an online Learning Platform, and you could see cogs turning as they envisaged how that technology could be used so well in rural India. They wanted to hear about where we lived - 'How big is your village?' 'Do you have a doctor?' They were building a picture of our lives at home, I suppose so they had a benchmark by which they could better explain what life is like for Indian children.

Back at home, we'd all seen TV charity fund-raisers like Comic Relief and watched films about kids in poverty. But somehow sitting in that small office in India with projects happening within a few miles of us made it all seem very real. During the meeting Jill reverted to journalistic type and sat with a pen and paper while firing questions at the assembled throng. The Indian Government, we learned, had money to spend. UNICEF used its technical skills and knowhow setting up projects on a regional level, and if they worked, then the Government invested, rolling them out across India.

Three of the people we met were in charge of education, health and nutrition for children under five. Our girls had already been affected by toddlers knocking on the car window asking for money, and seeing girls of nine or ten walking along the roadside with huge piles of branches on their heads, taking them home so they could cook a meal. I'd heard Edie say to Bethan, 'I think being a child here is a really hard life, isn't it?' The UNICEF staff mentioned a child labour project they'd set up, so Jill asked them to explain the typical lives these children lead.

Every year 150,000 thousand Rajhasthani children aged between six and 14 were sold to cotton farmers in the neighbouring state of Gujurat. Their families got 2,000 rupees (about £28) per child, who would in turn earn about 40 rupees (56p) a day. They were away from their families for four months during which time there was no schooling. Many children were horribly abused while they are away from their families. In a short film we watched about the project, a woman wept as she described the wounds she had found on her daughter's body, after being told by the men running the work-gangs that the girl died of a disease. It was clear, explained the distraught mother, that she'd been sexually abused and murdered.

UNICEF set up a project explaining to families why their kids needed to go to school, and the Government started initiatives where families received pensions and some social services, relieving the need to send children out to work. Schemes were set up to help keep the children going to school. Some of the children, for example, would have to walk six miles for lessons, so UNICEF paid for the Indian equivalent of a school minibus – a large tuk-tuk – to pick them up every day. Half a million children in the state benefitted from this scheme, set up by an office of just 22 UNICEF workers in Rajasthan.

We were humbled by their work, and when we got up to leave they all seemed genuinely grateful that we'd gone to see them. 'Meeting fundraisers makes us work even harder,' said Anuradha, 'because we can see where the money has come from.'

Suddenly looking silly for half an hour in a Turkish square singing *All You Need Is Love* didn't seem such a sacrifice. I felt moved to publish our experience on the blog, preaching that the money we were raising was making a real difference to children's lives, and we saw our website's online total pass the £1,000 mark.

Now, didn't we have a Bollywood film to watch? In the heart of the city, the Raj Mandir opens its brightly-lit door four times daily for Jaipur's entertainment-hungry film fans. To watch a Bollywood feature in such a famous cinema was the stuff of dreams to me. As a very junior dogsbody when I was first getting into radio, one of my more pleasurable jobs had been answering the telephones for BBC Radio Northampton's *Asian Magazine Programme* presented by the always-delightful Jona Kotnis. That's where I was indoctrinated into the mysterious world of Bollywood. Every track she played came from a film soundtrack. These weren't 'records' or 'singles' as we knew them. They were moments of high drama, passionate declarations of love or sorrow, clipped from a much larger tapestry of colour, dancing, conflict and morals that make up the classic Bollywood picture.

As a film fan I later learned that Bollywood had existed long before my late 80s introduction. Black-and-white films from the early 50s had the same staple ingredients found in Bollywood pictures today - huge co-ordinated dance numbers, heartbroken leading ladies who *must* have a tear-filled big close up and wear the shiniest lipstick on Earth, and muscle-bound leading men who are not afraid to dress inappropriately and dance in public. There'll be a fight, a wrong will be avenged, and we'll have to suffer some tragedy before we get to a happy ending. Not much had changed, so I was confident we'd all be able to follow the plot of whatever film happened to be showing at the Raj. And besides, what's not to love about those bhangra beats?

As we arrived under the green glow of the Raj Mandir's grand façade, our excitement grew even more to see that the film it was showing was a film we'd actually heard of. *Guzaarish* means 'request' and was creating all sorts of buzz - and scooping lots of awards – because, contrary to all the prejudices I've just told you about - it was a Bollywood film that dared to be different. It starred bona fide 'A' lister, Hrithik Roshan who, rather oddly, Naresh-the-driver kept insisting I looked like. I didn't, but it did little to dampen my secret dream of becoming a Bollywood star. His leading lady in *Guzaarish* was ex-Miss World Aishwarya Rai, and the movie promised all the classic Bollywood ingredients - songs, dancing, love, regret and euthanasia.

Yes, euthanasia. That was why *Guzaarish* was making waves, and it was a good film. Hrithik Roshan's acting was worthy of awards and Aishwarya got to wear the shiniest lipstick and weep into so many big close-ups she must have been thrilled. One of the curiosities about big Bollywood movies like *Guzaarish* is that the dialogue switches from Hindi to English and back every few lines. I noticed the same thing on TV commercials and radio shows too. It must be a nightmare for the actors, but audiences love it, and thankfully it allowed us to keep up with the gist of what they were all saying. Our most joyous memories of the evening are those of Naresh, our soon-to-be-let-go driver, who leapt at the opportunity to join us in the auditorium. 'Are you sure you won't join us, Naresh?' I asked politely, as Jill reached the ticket booth.

'No, no. This is your evening,' he replied.

'Five tickets, please,' said Jill into a small window.

'Make that six!' boomed a man's voice across the crowd. Naresh turned to me, caught up in the excitement. 'I have seen it twice! But I will see it again!'

He sat next to Jill, delivering huge stage whispers to her of forthcoming plot points that he simply couldn't contain. 'That is in fact his brother,' we all heard, long before the reveal, and, 'He will ask her to marry him,' and the brilliant, 'He will die.' It should have been annoying but it was amusing. Beautifully shot, set among the fields and beaches of Goa, Bollywood whetted our appetites for the parts of India we were still to discover. What none of us could have known, as we poured from the cinema with the masses, was that before we would find Goa, Bollywood would find *us*.

It happened at the Gateway of India - a fitting monument from under which a monumental opportunity should arise.

We'd travelled to Mumbai on the overnight sleeper from Delhi. Since watching Michael Palin go *Around the World in Eighty Days* on the telly, grappling with the Indian railways back in the late 1980s, I'd wanted to experience them for myself. The film *The Darjeeling Limited* only strengthened my desire. I'd already assumed that the wonderful 1940s, wooden panelled, four bunk compartments on the picturesque Darjeeling line would have been superseded by more modern carriages on the Rajasthan Express, so wasn't too disappointed to find a 'British Rail circa 1970s' plastic palace. The accommodation system on Indian rail is complicated and offers almost a dozen options, from 1AC at the top of the scale (air-conditioned sleeper in a four-bunk booth) down to unreserved sleeper class where, even after buying a ticket, you're not guaranteed a place on the train until boards are published on the platform bearing the names of the lucky. We'd chosen the third rung down, 3AC, which meant sharing in a booth of eight bunks. The most surprising thing about the journey (apart from the price - about £21 each for a 1,500-mile trip) was the constant food we were brought. We only discovered after settling in and chatting to one of our Indian booth-mates that the Rajasthan

Express was the *only* train line in India that provided food included in the ticket price. First, at 4:30pm, we were brought afternoon tea - a sandwich, a samosa, a cake and tea or coffee. However, we thought this was our main meal and, as we hadn't eaten since eight that morning, tucked in with such gusto that when our neighbours offered us their unwanted samosas and sandwiches we heartily unburdened them. It was with some surprise, therefore, that two hours later we were served cups of spicy tomato soup. 'Delicious,' we said. 'This must be supper before bed.'

Ten minutes later another tray was brought for each of us: dal, paneer masala, rice, pickle, papads, nan, and still our travel companions were offering us more.

'You want?' asked bunk six (Kohe, a Japanese student) offering me his nan bread. I was new to sleeper-train etiquette, but imagined vomiting was frowned upon, so declined. We bravely battled on, doing our level best to clear our trays, before collapsing in a bloated sweat.

'Amazing,' we panted.

'Brilliant,' we gasped.

'Why don't Chiltern Railways do this?'

And, just as Ella groaned, 'I couldn't eat another thing,' the porter reappeared.

'Ice cream?'

'Ooh, yes please!'

Mumbai is a 16-hour train ride from Delhi, but it felt a world away. In place of the narrow chaotic smoke-filled streets of the capital, we found wide boulevards lined with trees and with bright, blue skies above. Traffic stopped at traffic lights, there was barely a cow to be seen, and certainly no hogs, camels and piles of burning trash on every corner. The architecture was stunning; a glance to the left and it's Georgian London, while to the right there's a gothic church sandwiched between tenements reminiscent of New York. The buttresses, domes and stained-glass windows of the Victoria Terminus have prompted descriptions such as, 'to the British Raj what the Taj

Mahal is to the Mughal empire' - a stunning mixture of Victorian, Hindu and Islamic styles and now a World Heritage Site.

Its relatively obedient traffic and its occasional smart café or swish gallery made Mumbai feel cosmopolitan. We met a few travellers there from all over the world, and allowed ourselves a quiet feeling of smugness to hear their alarm at the noise, pace and sensory overload of landing in Mumbai from Australia, Italy or London. One chap from England used a phrase Jill had used herself in Delhi.

'It's just a complete lack of order,' he exclaimed.

'Try Delhi,' we would smile, grateful now for our toughening up in India's fire-pit. Only one foreigner we met, a girl from Portugal, had been to Delhi and she described it as her 'least favourite city in the world', which made me laugh. That was a bit strong, but it was reassuring to know it wasn't just us who felt a wave of relaxing calm on arriving in Mumbai.

Having installed ourselves in the YWCA, it was time to explore. The YWCA, by the way, is a fantastic place to stay; clean, cheap with breakfast and evening meal included. Best of all, it requires membership, so it was with much pride that I, a 40-year-old man, accepted my Young Women's Christian Association member's card. 'I'll keep it with my Brownie uniform,' I said to the lady on the reception desk, who returned my smirk with a bemused but polite smile.

It was a lazy Sunday morning. Mumbai's streets were surprisingly quiet and we planned to cross a tiny stretch of the Arabian Sea to visit Elephanta Island, where, confusingly, there are no elephants, but plenty of monkeys and ancient Hindu statues. I was buying the ferry tickets in the shadow of the Gateway of India when it happened.

'Hello, I'm from Bollywood,' said the voice. 'Would you like to be in a Bollywood film?'

I laughed out loud. Now I'd heard them all. Hawkers are constantly bombarding you with lines – 'Excuse me sir,' 'Hello, how are you?'

'You want taxi? Hop in!' 'City tour? Sir! Wait!' Eventually you get immune. But this was a new one.

'Please, I'm serious,' said the man, and he looked it. *Everything about this should be a scam*, I thought, but I recognised the look in his eyes. It was the look of an exhausted production assistant who'd been tasked with the impossible. 'I need to find 20 people who look English for filming tomorrow,' he explained.

'Where's your card?' asked Jill. The man was taken aback. So was I.

'Er, it's in the car.'

'Let's see it, then,' she demanded.

As he scurried off to get his business card, Jill explained. She'd read about this happening, which is how she knew the drill - get their card, ask the terms, where the shoot is, all the details. It's not uncommon for Bollywood films to recruit Western tourists as 'background artists' ('extras' to you, me and Ricky Gervais) in the hope of adding some glamour to a movie on the cheap.

'Glamour? Clearly he's more desperate than we thought,' I said.

And so it was, that at eight the next morning we were picked up on the Bollywood Bus - destination: destiny.

At this stage I need to make a few things clear. The casting agent, Imran, who had found us at the ferry terminal (or 'the bottom of the barrel' as it's known in casting terms) had told us the film title, who the star was, and that we could all be employed. We'd get to meet the star, take lots of photos and be well looked after with lunch and drinks thrown in. Also, we'd be paid the handsome figure of 500 rupees each for our trouble.

'Seven pounds for a day's work,' I'd said to Jill later. 'It's a bit of a cheek, isn't it?'

'Hmmm. Like you wouldn't have *paid them* to do it,' she pointed out, knowing me far too well.

'And what will we have to do?' I'd asked Imran.

'Just dance,' he smiled.

'Well, we're all *brilliant* dancers,' I lied. 'Will we be shown what to do?'

'Just freestyle. It's a party scene.'

'Freestyle. My favourite!' I beamed.

We had duly researched the movie that would herald our big screen début, and if anything it upped the stakes. It's called Ra.One (pronounced 'Rah one' as opposed to 'Ar ray one', which was a shame because 'Ar ray' is a scouse term of disagreement, as in 'Ar ray dat's cheat'n!'), and is a sci-fi movie that, at time of writing, enjoys the impressive accolade of being the most expensive Bollywood movie ever made. It stars Shahrukh Khan who is Bollywood's 'numero uno'. As well as being the Brad Pitt/Johnny Depp of India, he's the founder of two production companies (one of which, Red Chillies, was making what from this point forward shall be called 'my film'), is considered to be one of the world's most successful movie stars thanks to fans numbering billions, and has a reported net worth of 540 million US dollars. He was also listed in *Newsweek's* 'Top 50 most powerful people in the world'. I was slightly shamed to admit I hadn't heard of him.

When we arrived at the 'lot' (that's what us movie stars call the studios, plural), we were escorted into an empty 'stage' (that's what us movie stars call the studio, singular) where brightly coloured fabric walls had been erected on bamboo frames, making separate areas for 'makeup and wardrobe' (that's what us movie stars call makeup and wardrobe).

While an eager gang of us 20 or so tourists waited expectantly, a girl with a clipboard, earpiece and wearing a Batman tee shirt pointed at people, beckoning them inside. *Oh no! A selection process!* Before I had time to fully gather what was happening she pointed at me.

'You. Inside.'

I stepped forward, but suddenly felt that awkward twist in my stomach, like the immigrant men who, trying to enter America, had been separated from their families at Ellis Island. *I couldn't leave them, could I?* I looked back at their faces. They looked just as uncertain as I did. But none of them reached out to stop me, so I ran towards the light.

Having had some slap applied by Santosh - conversation limited:

'I've covered your spot.'

'Santosh, you're a wonder.'

'Next!' - I was bustled into wardrobe. Girls who just minutes earlier had been bleary-eyed travellers in rag-tag clothing were now tottering about on precarious heels wearing little more than glittery string. Clearly by 'Western glamour' Bollywood meant 'Western flesh'. One girl asked if she could wear something that covered her up a little more and was told 'Oh no! This is what London girls wear.' The Batman girl reappeared.

'What shall I wear?' I asked, wondering if I'd fit into those heels. She shouted to a man next to a rail of shiny shirts, and shoved me towards him.

'You're behind the bar. Bar tender,' she said.

'That's uncanny. You have a gift,' I replied, and was squeezed into a bar tender's outfit that couldn't have been more camp if it had boasted ostrich feathers.

Reunited with my family in my shimmering satin shirt, crotch-clenching pants, golden bhangra braces and a sequinned (yes, you heard me) tie, I judged by their laughter that they weren't too sore about not being in the film. Ella, Bethan and Jill were repeatedly offered the chance to dress up and go 'on set' (that's what us - oh forget it) but the sight of what all the other girls were wearing - or *not* wearing - put them off. They installed themselves in the wings to read, play cards, watch TV and laugh at me.

The scene was in a London nightclub and the set was impressive - a central illuminated dance walkway and circular stage, raised tables and seating around the sides, huge video walls leading to a wondrous bar at the back. Behind that bar was a less-than-wondrous barman. In fact there were two. A long-haired guy from Norway and an English bloke in unfeasibly tight trousers.

Because the scene was a music number, it was shot in little chunks, the entire jigsaw being precisely built, tiny piece by tiny piece. This meant 20 minutes of setting up a shot - the first four bars of the song, for example - and then about ten takes of those same four bars. After each take, the music stopped, everyone stopped dancing, the director shouted 'Re-set!' and we all hung around again until the cry went out 'AC off!' (air conditioning off - that's so they could use smoke-machines) 'Dry ice!' and then 'Sau sau!' which was the director's way of asking for 'Sound'. Once again the first beats of a banging bhangra dance tune would start. 'Let's go!' shouted the director loudly. 'Energy!' and the room would burst into life, I'd allow myself a small amount of grooving and do a fine impression of Tom Cruise in *Cocktail* but without the bar skills or juggling talent.

A standard shooting day in Bollywood is 12 hours. I got to know pretty much every other extra there that day, including Indian models who do it for a living and even an English girl from Norwich who lived in Mumbai and did agency acting to make a bit of cash. There had been some unrest in recent months when Indian actors threatened to strike because of studios using tourists as extras, a fact brought sharply into focus when I chatted with Gordum, an Indian model, at my bar. He was pleasant enough and we talked for about half an hour about films and music and books, but that was only after he'd quizzed me on my visa status and what I was being paid. I think the locals still resented white-skinned Westerners walking into a day's work. He was earning ten times what I was, though, so there were no hard feelings.

There were regular breaks, but by 8pm we were all shattered, and silently begging the director to shout 'wrap'. Jill and the girls were a lot less bored than I feared, and grateful they'd not been on the set where hanging around doing nothing was driving me crazy. At least they had their laptop, and books to read. Our scene had got about as far into the song as the first verse. Shahrukh Khan had made an appearance for about an hour to do one shot, where he beckoned the singer Akon over from the edge of the dance platform and pulled him off the stage. I never saw him after that, so got no picture of me with one of the top 50 most powerful people in the world. My Norwegian bar tender buddy, however, shared the toilets with him.

'Shahrukh Khan, a man worth $540 million, uses the same loos as us?' I asked, amazed.

'Apparently,' he shrugged. This was quite some revelation, given the typically Indian quality of the facilities. The cast and crew were flagging, and the floor manager was doing his best to motivate the party people. 'Come on! Let's go! It's a party. Keep the energy up. And that includes the barmen.' *I'd been noticed!* Maybe not for the right reasons, but still …

With renewed verve, by half past eight I was getting gung-ho with my moves. Years of working in TV weren't wasted as I spent every shot making sure I was within sight of the camera lens, and lacking the permission to use the bar props (the bottles were all fake - props guys made whisky by diluting cola) I was tossing an empty chrome cocktail shaker in the air with casual aplomb. I doubted it would distract the viewer from the scantily-clad female dancers in the foreground who appeared to be burdened with an enormous amount of 'booty' to shake, but I was having fun.

Again, and again, and again we did this shot. *When will it end? Let me go home!* Once more the music started. Once more Akon started singing about a girl who was apparently 'criminal'. And once more I smiled jauntily as I spun the chrome flask into the air. I winked at a girl, because I think detail matters and De Niro would have done it. I dropped the shaker.

CLANG!

Everyone near the bar turned round. The director shouted 'CUT!' I held my breath.

'That's a take!'

Of course it was. Twelve hours of barman solid gold and they take the shot where I drop the cocktail shaker. They asked me back the next day to continue shooting the scene but I declined. I didn't want fame to change me. By the time you read this *Ra.One* will be out on DVD. I'm afraid it's not very good. Almost a year after these events took place, on a rainy afternoon in Oxford, I took Jill to see 'my film' on her birthday (because I know how to show a girl a good time). We left at the interval, not having the strength to bear a further hour-and-a-half of Shahrukh Khan pretending to be in *Terminator 2* or *The Matrix*, while delivering the most butt-clenching, cringe-worthy script we'd ever gritted our teeth through. My scene, however, which turned out not to be a 'nightclub', but a launch party for a new video game, was brilliant. All the main characters mime to Akon's song, while dancing in a line: it's what Bollywood does best. Am I in it? Well, I certainly recognised those first ten seconds or so of the scene, and we both thought we glimpsed me throughout the sweeping camera shots and fast editing, so if you do ever have the misfortune to find yourself watching it, keep an eye out for Barman 2, at the back, on the right. And if you don't see me, just listen for the clang.

It was time to collect Penny from what the shipping industry still called the Port of Bombay, two hours away from downtown Mumbai. At this point in our journey we had driven through 12 countries, and the number of officials' signatures it had required to cross those borders totalled six. The number of signatures I had to gather just to drive Penny out of the docks in Mumbai was a staggering *twenty-three*.

The entire three-day process of reclaiming Penny, two of which I spent at the port, was surreal. My clearing agent, John, repeatedly begged me to complain to my Embassy about the process, in the hope that one day it might improve.

'No one sees how ridiculous this has become,' he would moan. 'Because no one person is overseeing the import of a vehicle under Carnet, it is falling to many, many people, none of whom sees the full procedure. If you drove the car into India,' he went on, 'one man would stamp the Carnet and you'd be through. But because it comes on a ship, we have all this.'

'All this' involves running around and between two large buildings at the port (a tuk-tuk ride apart, just to make it more of a challenge), persuading a total of 23 people to sign various forms, each in the correct order, and almost all needing to be told why they have to sign it. The only reason the entire pantomime only took three days rather than the threatened four or five was because John used my white Western face to push us past crowds of other clearing agents and get to the front of the queues.

'If they see a foreigner they will deal with us quicker,' he said. He also knew exactly who to bribe along the way - most people, as it turned out - and when no one appeared to be taking the promised action of finding our container and delivering it to the customs inspector, I went and searched for it myself.

This was highly unorthodox behaviour, but after two days in Bedlam I was throwing caution to the wind. At the risk of putting several men out of a job, skipping an entire layer of bureaucracy and therefore bringing the whole house of cards crashing down, I strode out into the dusty heat. 'I'll find my own flippin' box,' I muttered, and in a surprising triumph for a man who can't even find a jar of Marmite in the cupboard, I stumbled across Container UACU3222307 after about ten minutes. Many, many pieces of paper later I was opening the container, Penny started first time, and eventually we were free to leave and drive through Mumbai's rush hour traffic at nightfall - a modern and convenient way to reduce your life-span by several years without the costly need for cigarettes or drugs.

This was my first experience of a game I would be playing for the next few weeks called 'dodge India's policemen'. John, sitting in the passenger seat guiding us back into the heart of Mumbai, instructed me to avoid being seen by the cops. 'Stay behind this truck, then the police won't see us,' he said.

'But I haven't done anything wrong, have I?'

'No, no,' he assured, 'but you are very visible, and left-hand drive. That will be enough. They will want paying.'

I'd read that India's police were corrupt, and the topic of corruption in India was being talked about more and more. I'd even seen signs asking readers to report corrupt officials, but it didn't seem to be working. The next day, blissfully reunited with Penny, we crossed a busy junction along with lots of other cars, tuk-tuks and cabs, and a traffic policeman blew his whistle and waved at us. We were lost, so pulled over to ask him for directions. He looked at the map and told us the way, then told us he needed 500 rupees. 'Penalty,' he smiled. 'You crossed a signal. Dangerous driving.'

'Er, it was green,' I corrected, 'and we crossed with everyone else.'

'No, no, no. 500,' he insisted.

Jill stopped me arguing with the bent copper and offered him 100 (about £1.40), which he took happily. A little later, while we were driving through the suburbs in a line of traffic a police motorcycle pulled alongside my open window. 'Where are you going?' asked the young officer. I genuinely couldn't remember the name of the place, so simply shrugged.

'Dunno.'

'Pull over!'

'No thanks.' And still he stuck with us.

'Pull over up here!'

'I haven't broken any law,' I insisted. He dropped back, but then reappeared.

'Pull over!'

'Stop distracting me,' I calmly instructed. 'I'm trying to drive.'

At which point he dropped away, turned round and headed back to his territory. A third traffic cop tried to wave us down as we pulled across a junction with all the other traffic but we just ignored him.

The only other time I did eventually stop for a policeman was a few weeks later in Chennai, and that was only because I had an Indian man in the van who was genuinely afraid of the consequences. So, I dutifully stopped, put up with the rigmarole of waiting ten minutes before the aloof, power-mad bobby took his 100 rupee bribe and waved us away. Apart from that, a strict policy of 'avoid and ignore' was adhered to. 'The only trouble with that,' Ella pointed out, 'is how will we ever know if a policeman *really means it*. If there's a real problem?'

'Yeah, what if one of our wheels is falling off?' asked Beth.

'Or we have an angry monkey on the roof?' added Edie.

'We keep going,' I replied, with a slightly manic glint in my eye. 'No amount of waving and whistle-blowing is stopping this big yellow bus!'

It was only two days till Christmas, and after looking at the map we decided that rather than attempt to make it to Goa, which is where we'd always imagined we'd be spending Christmas, we'd spend it at 'The Y' in Mumbai, and make tracks on Boxing Day. The extra time gave me the chance to explore the Dharavi slum.

This is the triangle of land the same size as London's Hyde Park, framed by two of Mumbai's major railway lines and a main road, that is home to a million people and was made famous in the film *Slumdog Millionaire*. 'Reality Gives' is a Mumbai charity set up by a Brit - Chris Way from Birmingham - who realised while staying in Mumbai that Dharavi, which was already famed as India's biggest slum long before Danny Boyle's film, was misrepresented. Keen to promote it for the positive people and values he found there, he gathered the various tribal elders from the different religious districts within the slum and proposed 'Reality Tours'. These small, unobtrusive tours offer visitors the chance to explore the slum and meet the people, while profits are ploughed back into the community. Since they began in 2005 'Reality Gives' had paid for a kindergarten and the training of twenty local pre-school teachers, a high school with 33 pupils and a community centre where computer skills are taught.

The dilemma about taking the tour was obvious: it's a fine line between expanding your social awareness and voyeurism. I justified the visit by the fact that cameras weren't allowed, and also because I found a few online articles in Indian newspapers that backed up the charity's claims about the way the community was benefitting.

There were only three on my tour - two Australian women and me plus our Indian guide, so we didn't stick out too much in the throng and were able to spend a couple of hours winding our way through the slum, seeing and smelling slum life close up. In some respects it was exactly as you'd imagine: cramped, dark dwellings lining a maze of endlessly twisting alleyways and cut-throughs. Smoke filled the air and you had no idea what you might be stepping in. Yet in other ways it was full of surprises. Industries such as pottery, clothing manufacture and leather tanning thrived. Plastic and metal recycling businesses occupied another quarter. Beneath the corrugated metal roofs and plastic tarpaulin shelters was a hive of productivity. Dharavi's commercial output statistics were astounding - the annual turnover of the slum was estimated at about 650 million US dollars. Its social statistics also confounded expectation – 80 per cent of children went to school. That was significantly higher than most of the villages in Rajasthan we'd been talking about with UNICEF.

The most surprising discovery of my visit was how *happy* everyone was. I had naïvely associated slums with misery, yet Dharavi was the opposite. In fact, it was the least threatening place I'd been to since arriving in India. No one was begging - something impossible to consider outside the slum, where from Delhi to Mumbai and in every town in between we'd encountered beggars at almost every corner. It was a genuine shock, and demanded a mental readjustment, when children ran up to me and *didn't* ask for money by thrusting one hand towards me while putting the other to their mouth to mime eating.

Instead, they wanted to talk. They were all taught English from the age of four and were thrilled to see a white face they could try it on.

'Hi! What's your name?' was the chorus as they offered to shake hands, a gaggle of grinning faces. The first child I saw in the slum wasn't interested in me; she was a girl of about six, neatly dressed in a smart school uniform and she was dancing and skipping through the alleyways ahead of us. She swung every corner knowing this gloomy alien world like you know your own back yard. She stopped, shouted up to her mother and quickly scaled a ladder to reach a single room on the second level. The door was a flap of thick plastic. This was home, and this girl was as happy as any I'd ever seen. If a group of ten-year-old boys approached you in Delhi, you'd brace yourself to march through a barrage of begging and sleeve pulling. In Dharavi a similar gang surrounded me - to show me their toys. A wooden spinning top expertly propelled into life with a leather cord was the current craze. They insisted I had a go - laughed at my efforts and insisted I held out my hand so they could place the quivering, spinning top in my palm, as if to show how easy it was. It seemed an odd reversal of gestures that in the midst of this chatter and laughter, I was the white guy in the slum and I was holding out my palm to them.

It wasn't without its poignancy. My spinning top tuition took place at one edge of the slum in the shadow of two high-rise concrete towers built by the Government in the 1990s to re-house some of the slum dwellers. Our guide had been there in 1995 when Prince Charles had officially opened them. 'This area,' he remembered, 'was a beautiful playground. The grass was like The Oval.' Now, it was a rancid rubbish dump. 'The Government tidied it up for the Prince,' he went on. 'But now they just send a truck every few months to collect the rubbish.'

As he spoke, in front of us a young girl of about four was hitching up her pretty dress and defecating on the litter. Yet even here, no space was wasted. Behind the preoccupied girl there were animal skins, spread across the mounds of waste, drying in the sun. The output of these leather workshops is exported to Europe, and at least two major Italian fashion labels use their hides. I smile now when I see one of those designer leather jackets, its owner unaware of the prestigious garment's humble beginnings on the little girl's toilet.

After Dharavi was made a legal slum in 2000, the Government piped in mains water for three hours per day, and most dwellings also had electricity. However, only 1 per cent of homes in Dharavi had a toilet. Most people use communal facilities, which are massively over-burdened. I don't know what the ratio is in your house of people to toilets, but if you live in Dharavi it's 1,500 people per loo. Even in those conditions, though, Dharavi comes with a price tag. Dwellings were rented for the equivalent of about £28 per month, and people could only get them if they knew someone living or working there who could vouch for them. Even in India's biggest slum, demand outstripped supply and capitalism was the result.

It was a fascinating experience, and vital in getting a better understanding of the city. It took about a day for the sensory onslaught to sink in, and the overwhelming feeling I had when I left is the one that stays with me now - that contrary to the menacing squalor of Boyle's *Slumdog*, Dharavi was one of the most uplifting places I've ever visited.

Christmas in Mumbai was like none we'd experienced before. It *is* celebrated, because although Hinduism is the most prevalent religion in India (about 80 per cent of the population are Hindu), Christianity accounts for almost 3 per cent, about double the number of Sikhs, which surprised me. The greatest thing about spending the weeks leading up to Christmas in a largely non-Christian country is the complete lack of build-up and hype. More specifically, it was the absence of Slade.

To go an entire season without hearing *any* 'xmas standards' was bliss. No Roy Wood wishing it could be Christmas every day, no festive Shakin' Stevens and not once did Noddy Holder ask if I was hanging up a stocking on my wall. Instead, we pushed our way through a seething, sun-baked market place in the Chor Bazaar and bought tinsel and streamers with which to decorate our room at the Y, and went to the Nine Lessons and Carols service at St Thomas Cathedral on Christmas Eve. It was strange to walk into a 300-year-old Anglican church in the heat of bustling Mumbai, and sing familiar carols while ceiling fans whirred madly overhead. But these were the first Christmas songs we'd heard all year, and as we grabbed a tuk-tuk back to the YWCA we felt truly festive.

We had an email that day from some great friends in the UK telling us they had bought us all a night in a five-star hotel on Christmas night! So for our last night at the Y, we decorated the room, sang Christmas songs (even Slade was allowed), and stuck up a two-dimensional Christmas tree Ella had drawn so we had something to put presents under. The next morning Santa *had* managed to fill three stockings, and after breakfast we opened the gifts we'd bought each other - typically 'budget' and very Indian - tops, sandals, a fake Rolex for me (from Jill, whose father had worked for Trading Standards) and the surprise hit - traditional string puppets bought in Rajasthan. Ella and Edie loved them.

'I can't believe it,' I said to Jill. 'We spent all that money on *Beatles Rock Band* for the Nintendo Wii last year when a puppet would have done.'

We asked a splendid Canadian woman called Marilyn who we'd met at the Y to join us for lunch at a café we'd found that was serving English Christmas dinner - a slap up feast of turkey, mash *and sprouts*. Brilliant. Then we drove through Mumbai's terror-traffic to our swish hotel near the airport. We encountered only two impacts on the journey, which locals assured me was a remarkably incident-free drive through Mumbai. One bus simply ignored us while changing lanes, scraping our plucky wing mirror all the way down his side, and a dozy driver in a surprisingly new car pulled out behind us, got his timing wrong and scraped the back of the van – the same panel that had been repaired after the bus incident in Jordan. There was no point stopping to deal with these minor scrapes; no one has any road insurance and we'd witnessed much worse bumps resulting in a shouting match in the street before both injured parties simply drove away. At home they call it knock for knock. In Mumbai it's dog eat dog.

After a blissful night in five-star luxury we gorged on a Boxing Day breakfast buffet that reached beyond our usual Indian cuisine. Porridge, bacon, sausages and hash browns were eagerly enjoyed as a welcome change to sweet toast and jam – the staple at our cheaper digs. We must have looked a curious sight to the swanky hotel's wealthy guests as we trooped out through the marble-walled reception in our travellers' clothes, heaving our tatty back-packs into the back of Penny, who had left her customary puddle of oil on their pristine driveway.

Penny needed a service, and her oil leak was getting worse, so when we arrived in Pune I went on the hunt for mechanical assistance. I found several garages whose mechanics spoke no English, but could make it clear that they wouldn't touch Penny because they only ever worked on cars and trucks badged Tata - India's omnipresent vehicle of choice. By the end of the day, though, I'd found a man who, though unable to source the parts for a service, was confident he could repair the leak.

I spent a happy morning with Dhanbahadur Chatri and his brother Vinod, up to our elbows in oil while we dismantled Penny's engine in the search for the source of the drip. Dhan operated his small workshop out of the garage of his house, and we worked while many friends came and went, his busy wife brought us sweet chai, and children played games around us. He found the leak - a broken oil seal behind the timing belt pulley – but after several phone calls confirmed that he couldn't get the replacement part – a simple rubber

O-ring, but not a *Tata* O-ring. We'd have to live with it until we could find a bigger town with a VW garage.

'It's a shame,' I commented. 'We leave a pool of oil wherever we park. It's a bit embarrassing if it's on someone's driveway.' But Dhan and Vinod laughed.

'You don't need to worry. This is India. Everything leaks a bit!'

Dhanbahadur talked about how India was ruined by corruption, a subject I was surprised he raised. He told of how the police pulled people over all the time and took cash bribes as opposed to writing tickets, so I was able to tell him of our own experiences. He spoke passionately about how he believed that his own honesty would bring its own rewards. His father had worked in security and been a stickler for 'playing with a straight bat' – a typically Indian cricket analogy - constantly resisting the temptations his uniform put his way. He went on to become a priest.

'Would you like to speak to him?' Dhan asked, and started to dial on his oily mobile phone. 'Hello father,' he announced into the handset, while still lying on his back underneath Penny. 'I'm with a foreign man working on his car. We were just talking about you. Here he is.' And so I enjoyed a five-minute chat with Terry the priest, who, incredibly, had lived in Liverpool and still had family there.

'We're driving around the world from Liverpool to New York,' I told him excitedly.

'Oh my God!' he exclaimed, then added, 'May God protect you,' because it sounded more priestly, I think.

The final bill for three hours of labour was 300 rupees plus 190 for oil. That's about a fiver in British pounds. When I insisted he take 600 rupees, Dhan refused. 'God has sent you to me,' he smiled. 'If I do a good honest job he will send others too.'

With Goa in our sights, we had some decisions to make. We'd imagined India would be one of the cheapest countries on our trip, but it was becoming the most expensive, mainly because of the mounting hotel bills. We were struggling to find anywhere to camp because the concept was alien to Indians. Why would you camp? You might as well sleep with a sign above you saying, 'Dinnertime, tigers!' or 'Snakes - warm bed this way!' No one we met in India had ever seen a van like ours, and in that first month, and over the many hundreds of miles we'd travelled across Rajasthan and Maharashtra we didn't see a single campervan or motor home. Campsites, therefore, didn't exist. The bigger challenge was explaining to hotels that we wanted to sleep in their car-park because we wanted to be safely off the street, but we couldn't afford their room prices.

That was the one constant factor in every single day: making choices that were governed by our budget. Even something as major as our route was being affected. Something we'd feared way back in the gloom of Alessandria came true. As we'd stewed in that Italian town for over a fortnight while our crippled van was in VW custody, watching our savings peter away on the youth hostel costs, we'd darkly predicted that the £2,000 bill which the whole sorry affair racked up might ultimately cost us Thailand, and we were right.

I can't just blame the buffoons who misdiagnosed our faulty turbo. I'll admit that we were surprised by the hidden costs of shipping. For example, the actual freight cost of shipping Penny from Aqaba to Mumbai was just US$235. That's all the shipping company charged to chug that box all the way across the ocean. A bargain. But the *total* cost of that operation, from delivering her to the agent in Jordan to driving her away from the port in Mumbai, once all the many extra charges were added up, was *eight times* that - over £1,200.

Our original plan to ship from Chennai to Bangkok, drive down through Thailand and Malaysia and then ship from Singapore to Brisbane was now way beyond our means. We *could* go to Thailand, but then could we get as far as Australia before going broke? Or we could go directly from India to Australia and hope to make at least one last shipment from there to the USA, which would at least give us a shot at getting to New York.

The BBC phoned for a radio interview while we were in Pune and the presenter asked if I'd do the trip again. I laughed, because we'd so often said in jest, 'Next time we do this, we'll do it differently.' Then he made the mistake of referring to the trip as a holiday. 'It's not a holiday,' I corrected – a saying that had become a family catch-phrase. 'It's not all rubbing shoulders with elephants and riding Bollywood stars,' I said to silence, my comic inversion falling on stony ground. 'It's nail-biting, worrisome and consumed with thoughts like, *Will Ella pass her ICT coursework? Did Penny always have that knocking sound?* and *Why, oh why, do all shipping agents insist on being paid in cash?*'

'What do you call it, then, if it's not a holiday?' he asked.

'An adventure. An incredible, eye-popping, once-in-a-lifetime, exhausting adventure that tests *all* of our resolve and resourcefulness daily.'

'Will you get all the way round, d'you think?'

I paused. 'I just don't know,' I answered honestly. 'We're getting through the cash much quicker than we thought. We've already decided to skip Thailand and Malaysia and ship straight to Australia from Chennai. I think by doing that we'll just about scrape through all the way to New York.'

What he didn't know, and I didn't say, was that Jill had just hatched a cunning plan that would get us around Australia and New Zealand for very little expense whatsoever.

Having said all that, the very next thing we did was take a holiday. There's something about South Goa that makes it difficult to apply yourself to do anything apart from the task of doing nothing at all. It could be the clean, soft, sandy beaches, the gentle rustle of the swaying palms, the warm clear sea ...

India's top tourist state isn't *all* like that. We arrived in north Goa in time to spend New Year's Eve in Ponda. The small town barely gets a mention in any guide books, being overshadowed by Panaji, the state capital, just 15 miles up the road, but we'd already spent time in the city and found it charmless and horrifically overpriced (this was the very peak of India's tourist season) so we returned to a cheap but clean hotel we'd already reccied in Ponda. Hence, while Goa's north coast throbbed to the rhythm of a hundred New Year's Eve beach parties, we spent the last night of 2010 in a landlocked town watching a movie with the kids and fighting to stay awake until midnight. 'Low key' would sum up the dawning of 2011, the most unusual aspect of which was to wake up on 1st January with a completely clear head. Literally, a New Year's Eve to remember.

We drove south on the N17, a road that was constantly in the news because of its accident rate. 'Safety measures must be put in place,' preached the newspapers. 'Something needs to be done.' No one ever seemed to suggest that it might be the quality of the *driving* that pushed the death toll ever higher. This single carriageway road twists and winds up and down hills for several hundred miles from Mumbai all the way to Kerala. Applying safety measures in the form of speed cameras or traffic calming would be useless, as our average speed between Panaji and Patnem was about 25 miles per hour. The journey wasn't boring though. We were constantly entertained by the giddy madness of cars, bikes, buses and trucks all fighting to overtake each other (and us) regardless of blind bends, brows of hills or even clearly visible oncoming traffic. Many times, the oncoming traffic would also bring its own *Wacky Races* overtaking to the party, meaning vehicles *four abreast* would hurtle, face to face, head-on towards each other. Wing mirrors flew, horns blared, and it was incredible that in all this, we only got scraped once. That was by a man who was too busy rowing with the *first* bloke he'd run into to realise he was continuing to drive into *us*. That's a real talent - encountering your second impact while still arguing about the first.

The reward for surviving Death Race 2011 was Patnem. This quiet, unspoilt idyll was the destination for some friends of ours, Al and Mel, who were starting their holiday in India here. The anticipation and excitement we'd all felt about seeing them was huge. The last 'friends from home' we'd seen were in France - was that four and a half months ago? It was. The chance to spend a few days with friends in this paradise prompted the grand announcement, 'This is a holiday.' We gave ourselves a week off. No driving, no school work, no blog writing – it was bliss.

Sitting in a beach café in the shade of huge coconut trees and spotting Al and Mel wander in was amazing, and surreal. We beamed, we hugged and they produced a jar of Marmite for us. Suddenly the Earth was back on its axis. Their generosity reached far beyond potted yeast extract. They'd rented an apartment in nearby Rajbag and offered us the second bedroom, so we had some free accommodation for a couple of nights - the girls in the bedroom while Jill and I slept on the balcony. Our garden-furniture-bed took on a wondrous lustre once a mosquito net was draped over it, and the sleeping bags I'd brought up from the van were never used - even outdoors it was hot and humid all night, utterly unlike any other New Year's Day we'd known.

We slipped with ease into the routine of doing nothing but lounging around on the beach all day, while our friends put their 'hooray we're on holiday' energy to good use exploring all the local beach coves, hidden restaurants and markets. 'Have you bartered much?' asked Al when they'd first arrived.

'All the time,' we assured them. The kids had got so used to it in Rajasthan that by the time we were in Mumbai they were confidently knocking 50 per cent off sandals, bags, anything they had their eye on, and would ruthlessly walk away if the trader wouldn't meet their offer. Al and Mel were soon doing the same and I saw his skill first hand when, late one night, after leaving a deserted beach restaurant they'd found for us all, we struggled to find a tuk-tuk to get us home. We walked into the dark Goan countryside, roughly aware of which direction to take, sure a tuk-tuk would soon appear. We chatted, and walked, and walked some more. Soon, we were away from electric lights and in pitch darkness with only the glow from a mobile phone screen to show where the sides of the road were.

Still not a tuk-tuk was seen or heard. Then came the dogs. One piece of safety advice that Goa guide books offer their readers is that you should never walk alone at night, for fear of marauding packs of wild dogs. Just the previous night, Jill and I had been woken on the balcony in the early hours by barking and the blood-curdling howls, yelps and snarls of a pack of dogs apparently tearing another unfortunate dog apart. It was frightening.

In the dim glow of my phone's light, we all saw that a pack of about 20 dogs were sniffing around in the road ahead. They weren't 'marauding', and we too were a 'pack' of five people (Jill and Edie had stayed home, cleverly) but it was slightly scary. I held Ella and Beth's hands tighter and we strode towards the dogs, a couple of which showed passing interest, while most ignored us. Onwards we walked, leaving the panting behind us, into the thick darkness. Then, after another 15 minutes of walking, the happy buzz of a distant tuk-tuk warmed our hearts. Soon we were bathed in the yellow light from its single headlamp as we waved him to a halt.

'How much to Rajbag?' I asked.

'One hundred,' replied the young driver. (That's about £1.40)

As quick as a flash Al shot back, '80.'

That boy learns fast, I thought as I ran after the tuk-tuk begging him to stop.

I didn't really. I paid 100 and jumped in before the driver could have any second thoughts.

Penny turned a lot of heads in India. In Goa, where there are tourists from all over the world, she was the constant recipient of admiring glances as we tootled into the nearby town. Even parked on the road near the beach hut we were sleeping in, she attracted attention. I found a note written on a paper napkin tucked under her windscreen-wiper and as I tugged it free, it ripped, but I pieced together the delicate pieces to see a request to play at a local bar. We hadn't played for about six weeks, and nothing focuses the mind quite like a deadline. The note suggested the gig was part of an 'open mic' night that very evening, so we dusted off the uke, squeezebox, flute and frog and had our first band practice in a long time.

We weren't too bad in the confines of our beach hut, and even arranged a recorder part for Jill to play in a new song - *You Won't See Me*, one of my favourites from *Rubber Soul*. As evening fell we made our way along the beach to Crunch Bar, ordered some drinks and waited to see what unfolded. 'Let's just gauge the atmosphere,' Jill said, remembering that timely Turkish Bath advice.

The open-air bar was filling up as we ordered some food, and the audience appeared to be mainly ex-pats who wintered in Goa, with a healthy smattering of holiday-makers and locals among them. The man who'd left the note on the van was Graham, who took the stage and kicked things off with a couple of covers and a couple of his own songs, ably strummed on a Fender Stratocaster plugged into a small amp. There was a single microphone and a music stand. It all looked quite professional to a bunch of buskers who were more used to street corners. The mood was jovial and we all decided this would be a great place to do some songs, despite the fact we were a bit rusty and Bethan had forgotten to bring her music. She was confident she could remember the three songs we would do.

'Sure you don't want to do the new one?' I asked them.

'No. Stick to three. Leave them wanting more,' ordered tour manager Jill. I suspected her earlier recorder confidence was languishing back in the beach hut.

Graham gave us a great introduction and we piled up on to the stage before about 60 expectant faces. Very quickly, I resolved *not* to leave the instruments in the van when she was shipped to Australia in a few weeks. A month without them took its toll. Not on the girls - they were brilliant, effortlessly remembering every song note-perfect. I, however, had a total brain freeze halfway through *All You Need Is Love* and forgot the words, the chords and what my own name was. Somehow we got through it despite my best efforts to sabotage the song, and the audience were the type of friendly crowd who sing along no matter what, so that was a blessing.

They threw themselves into *All My Loving*, which made my brain locate the right gear again, and somehow, through the sweat and panic, we got cheers and applause to lift us into *Ob-La-Di* which went down a treat. We were just settling into it by the end, but stuck with our agreement and left the stage to much applause. Best of all, Edie went round with the UNICEF tin afterwards and we raised 1,275 rupees (£18.75). Loads of people wanted to talk to us about our trip, and the music and how long we would be staying. I got the impression that if we hung around in south Goa we could become a weekly spectacle. And once again, our journey prompted other people to share their Beatles stories. Tony, known as 'Hobo' on stage, was tall, sported a black cowboy hat, a warm smile and a thick Leeds accent.

He was a fellow ukulele player, but played the guitar most nights around Goa.

'I only saw them once,' he recalled. 'Leeds, 1963. I was 16 and queued for hours to get a ticket. They were pretty good, too. It was just before they became huge.' Then he added, wistfully, 'They never came back.'

I can't claim that our performance will be so fondly remembered in 48 years, but for about 48 seconds, we were the talk of the town.

We were driving through the tiny, market-stall-lined streets of Patnem when a persistent moped who kept beeping at me finally pulled alongside.

'Nice van,' said the cockney rider, who had the blond hair, stubble and well-worn sun tan of a man who had been on the road for more than a week or two. 'I'm Mark,' he said reaching through the passenger window to shake Jill's hand. 'You don't wanna camp round here, it's nuts. Heaving with tourists. Go about 15 minutes up the coast to Agonda. There's a bunch of us camping on the beach. A little community of overlanders from all over the place. Germans, Swiss, big trucks, little vans, there's a couple of families too so the kids would love it.'

'Sounds cool,' I said. 'We'll see you up there.' And off he sped. This was a pleasant invitation that had dropped into our laps, so we planned to head up there, case it out, and if it looked all right spend at least one night there before we continued south towards Mangalore.

And so began one of the strangest, most beautiful weeks of our year. Yards from an almost empty beach, tucked in the shade of tall palm trees, we shared a forest clearing with wild pigs, cows and a small collection of other overlanders – those people who choose to travel long distances over land. I don't know what the collective noun is for people driving around the world. A gasket, I think. Life in what many would consider paradise was so idyllic that the common tale was of travellers who'd planned on staying on that Agonda beach hideaway just a few days, only to find weeks had passed before they could tear themselves away. We'd reckoned on a one or two night stop-over and it became eight. We waved off a Swiss couple who'd arrived for a two-day pause - six weeks earlier. The only other English people there when we arrived in that first week of January were Mark, the moped-cockney we'd met earlier, and his partner Jo, who'd been there for three months.

'When will you move on?' I asked him. He sucked his teeth, looked at the sun and checked his watch.

'April?' he mused.

So constant was the camper van community, that each morning an entrepreneurial baker would visit to sell bread and pastries, as did a drinking-water van who also offered beer. And this peculiar, multi-lingual community rubbed along not just with each other, and the cows and pigs, but with the coconut oil man who appeared each morning and again at dusk to expertly climb the towering palms and tap the valuable juice, the tourist yoga groups who gathered to out-bend and balance each other before a morning swim, the martial arts group who thrusted, grunted and postured in the grey light of dawn, and the regular weekend gatherings of Indian party people. Cars, and sometimes coaches, of young men would arrive each Saturday and Sunday to swim, play volleyball, drink Kingfisher beer and dance (with each other – no girls allowed) to Indian-Western-fusion-pop rattling from distorted speakers powered by a car battery. And without fail, as dusk fell, they were gone.

Yet, surrounded by these sporadic moments of high entertainment, and amidst surroundings that could barely be more blissful, we had some difficulties and sadness. The first was a shining example of poor parenting that I feel duty bound to share with you. I had hired a moped from the owner of a tiny sweets and tobacco kiosk on the beach. For ten quid I could use his daughter's moped for a whole week, so it became our daily transport to and from Agonda village for the fetching and carrying of supplies, thus enabling the van to be left in 'sleep mode' rather than 'packed away and driving mode'. The girls had all had a go on the back of the moped, and then the inevitable happened.

'Can I have a go on my own?' Ella was the first to ask. So, on a wide piece of empty grass a few minutes from our van she and Beth both enjoyed the occasional figure of eight at the helm of their own powered steed – a thrill I can still remember from my own first go on a motorcycle. I'd been aged 11 then, so thought this was quite normal, especially in carefree India, where no one even wore a helmet. You can guess what's coming, so I won't spin it out. Beth had an accident. Despite her exquisite control, a metal sign tied to a fence caught a breeze, flapped up towards her and in her alarm she pulled the brakes and put her feet down while wobbling into the sign. Her sandalled foot scraped between the plastic fairing of the scooter and the smooth metal against the fence.

'I'm fine,' she quickly said as I jogged over to her. I checked her hand, thinking she'd bashed her little finger against the sign, but it looked normal.

'I'm OK,' she reassured again. Ella and Edie looked her over. She did look fine. 'I banged my foot,' she said, and when I looked down I could see a bruise on her ankle, and what looked like a nasty rub that would turn into a painful friction burn.

'Ouch, that looks sore. Can you move your foot?'

'Yeah, I'm really OK,' she said.

'Er, Daddy, she's bleeding,' interrupted Ella. I looked again at the ankle, but there was no cut.

'What? Where?' I asked. Then I saw it. Not the cut, but the result. Her lovely glittery sandal bought in Mumbai was filling with rich, dark blood, which began dripping rapidly on to the dusty floor.

'Oh God!' said Edie clasping her hand to her mouth. I was momentarily baffled, but when I craned my head around her leg saw a long, deep slice along the inside of her foot. I quickly became 'reassuring dad' while burying my inner panic deep inside.

'Ah. That's OK. Come on, let's get you back. You'll be OK darling. Hold tight.'

I slid behind her, reached around to grip the handlebars and twisted the throttle.

'I'll see you two back at the van!' I shouted to poor Ella and Edie as I sped away with the patient. Arriving back at Penny, we found Jill reading a book with her feet up.

'We've had an accident,' I said as we pulled up. 'We're gonna have to go to hospital.' It's an indication of how well my wife knows me that her first reaction wasn't 'What?' 'How?' or 'What happened?' She threw her book down in exasperation and said, 'Bloody hell!' as if it was only a matter of time before this sort of thing unfailingly happened on my watch.

A few minutes of feverish activity resulted in cockney Mark agreeing to lead the way to the local hospital, a random Indian man being cajoled into driving Beth and Jill there, and me acting as out-rider on the Scooter of Doom. Ella and Edie were left at the van to mop up blood. Beth didn't cry at all, which was astounding, but I later found out something that breaks my heart to this day - that while lying in the back of that stranger's car she'd looked up at Jill and asked, in all seriousness, 'Am I going to lose my foot?'

I'm filling up even now as I write that. Poor kid. Idiot dad.

One marvellous doctor and seven stitches later, all was well with the world. I'd learned that responsible parenting was still an elusive craft just out of my reach, and Beth had learned that iodine generously sloshed on an open wound hurts like nothing you could imagine.

It was also in the idyllic surroundings of our Agonda heaven that we received sad news about a friend in Kansas who we were planning to visit later on our journey. Lisa had been battling breast cancer for six years, about as long as we'd known her, and we learned from her husband, Ty, that she was seriously ill and that we wouldn't reach her in time. It was a punch in the stomach for all of us, as you can imagine. Dealing with news like that, in a place as beautiful as that, makes a person grasp for meaning from it all. Our only conclusion was that, put simply, bad stuff happens, wherever in the world you happen to be. Taking a year out doesn't make you immune. Be it the health of a friend or the stupidity of a carefree father, life goes on. We knew it would, of course, but it was unsettling when it happened.

Only weeks later would we learn that the biggest gut-punching news we'd receive was still unfolding at home.

I said it was a strange week, and as if to underline a catalogue of peculiar events, we were asked to do a gig for our little Agonda community. Jill, buoyed by the success of our recent stage performance at Crunch Bar, saw it as a great chance to bolster our UNICEF funds with a few rupees and entertain our new friends. It was our last night with this strange mixture of international travelling buddies, and we put a bit of effort into a proper show: six songs with planned 'talky bits' in between, a full half hour that brought our mission to life, told of UNICEF's work and a few jokes along the way. Jill even played the recorder. Our audience were a delight, singing, clapping and hollering for more. We sat up late into the night with them, laughing, trading stories and saw Beth revel in her bike accident kudos. It made driving away the next morning, back into 'real India', very hard indeed.

Our slightly longer-than-planned stay in south Goa was at the cost of seeing the northern tip of Kerala – just another of those places we'd written into our original schedule that fell off the itinerary owing to unforeseen circumstances. Besides, none of us really minded that the doctor had asked us to return Bethan's foot for him to look at (with Beth still attached, preferably) five days after the accident. Kerala would wait for our next visit to India. With a shipping date looming in Chennai, 1,300 miles east, we headed straight across the width of India.

Bangalore was a half way point in our sights, and on the way there we realised we could fairly effortlessly spend one night at Hampi, the site of the famous Virupaksha Temple and yet another World Heritage site to tick off our list. It wasn't a pleasant experience, partly because Edie was so ill. She still recalls with great clarity that she was sick 14 times in that one day, a fact I had mysteriously erased from my memory. A tourist trap village had sprung up in the midst of the precious ruins of the Vijayanagara Empire, full of hawkers, flimsy stalls of tee-shirts and tat and lots of aggressive young men trying to charge us for parking. We made a swift exit and retreated to a nearby municipal hotel, which was basic, but functional. I've since read that the local district authorities have torn down the offending village, so Hampi may be more attractive now.

It was memorable to Ella and Beth for a different reason. 'Daddy lost it,' they will tell you. Leaving Jill and Edie in their sick-bay hotel room, the two older girls and I decided to go and explore. As well as a few architectural ruins we found, where we walked around unhindered, we had great fun exploring the hills which abound with large boulders, many of which were used to make statues of Hindu deities. It was on one of these hills that I blew a fuse. A group of four lads aged between about 16 and 19 spotted us and came running over. Our hearts sank. We didn't feel threatened, we were just sick of being the centre of attention.

'How can I help you?' the first boy asked.

'We're fine, thanks,' I said, walking away. But soon they were surrounding us, a phone appeared and they were taking photos of us. In fact, no, they were taking pictures of the girls. That's when seven weeks of pent up frustration and lip-biting exploded. I grabbed the phone from the startled paparazzo. I showed great restraint in not stamping on it, I thought, but Ella and Beth will tell you 'restraint' wasn't what it looked like from where they were standing.

'Delete the pictures,' I instructed, holding the handset towards him. The boys laughed – they'd never met an English psychopath before. I grabbed the chap closest to me, pulled his head next to mine so that I might speak directly into his ear, and introduced him to some illuminating Saxon expressions that I hoped would suggest I wanted him to leave. Then, stepping back from the baffled fellow I said, 'How would you like it if I came banging on your door and snapped a load of pictures of your family without asking, huh?' I think I may have adopted my 'angry scouser' accent, too, which must have been weird. By now they were backing away with their hands in the air, which was a tad over-dramatic given I hadn't pulled out anything more lethal than a Liverpudlian turn of phrase.

As we walked away, Ella asked, 'What did you say in his ear?'

'I just asked him to leave.'

'Really?' they both asked, not buying it for a second.

'I feel a bit stupid, now,' I sighed. 'I've just had enough of this country.'

'I know how you feel,' said Beth.

'Let's not talk about that unpleasantness again,' I said. And they didn't – until we got back to Jill and Edie.

'Daddy went nuts at some lads,' they burst out gleefully.

We arrived in Bangalore as dusk fell over gridlocked traffic and choking smog. In search of a hotel, but with no hope of penetrating the city centre, we used our travellers' nous and headed out to the airport. After all, you'll *always* find a hotel near an airport. Except in Bangalore, where there are none. There were proudly displayed signs announcing the first hotels would be ready in five years' time. So we drove the 20 minutes back towards the city, and stopped at the only hotel we'd seen in over two hours of cruising the capital of Karnataka.

We were losing patience with India, and as if body follows soul, we were all losing weight and feeling exhausted. Jill seemed to have caught Edie's stomach bug, so cashed in a 'duvet day' to spend two nights in the relative luxury of the three-star, laughably named, Airport Hotel – well, even at 12 miles away, it really *was* the closest accommodation to the airport.

While we attempted to recoup some energy and vitality, I tinkered on the van, fixing rattles and niggles that had built up over the bouncy Indian roads. The girls did schoolwork, though wi-fi wasn't available so it was mainly English assignments from books – 'jingoistic writing' from the Second World War for Bethan and 'iambic pentameters' for Ella.

And at this time our mighty plan was born. (Sorry, I couldn't help myself - a small nod to the iambic pentameter fan in you.)

Our aim, as I think I've mentioned, was to busk our way from Liverpool to New York. Surprisingly, despite 18 months of planning, that's about as detailed as our mission got. Being under-prepared, under-rehearsed and under-funded was what made it exciting. Making plans day by day, learning to play our instruments and trying to make our cash stretch were all daily realities to be embraced. But with the next leg of our journey through Australia and New Zealand looming, and with funds diminishing, we realised we needed help - and we knew exactly where we could get it.

The funny thing about Australia was, as we travelled and told people our route, it was the *one* place about which people said, 'I've got a friend in Oz if you need somewhere to park your van for the night.' And when we'd reply, 'Yes please! Can we have their address?' people didn't look even slightly alarmed. We knew that wild camping was a big no-no in Australia and that the cops were quick to move on stray campers, so the idea of camping on the drive of various strangers had lots of appeal. We'd get to meet new friends. Friends with a toilet. And maybe even a washing machine.

'What if you threw it out there on the blog?' suggested Jill, forming her idea. 'And what if we offered something in return?'

'A song?' I suggested.

'Hmmm,' said Beth, arching an eyebrow. 'Hardly Charlie's golden ticket, is it?'

'Yeah all right! I was thinking out loud,' I retorted. I knew she was right, though.

'I suppose I could bake a cake,' she said.

'That's it!' said Jill. 'We'll offer a traditional English afternoon tea.'

'Oooh,' we all responded, eyes wide at the prospect of cake.

'Cucumber sandwiches, crusts cut off, a pot of tea and *our* Betty's cake,' she went on (Beth's lemon drizzle cake was as good as anything served in the famous Betty's Teashop in Harrogate). 'We can buy the ingredients pretty cheaply, and if people let us use their kitchen, we're sorted.'

And so, project *Put Us Up Down Under* was born. I posted it on the Internet.

If you know anyone living on the east coast of Australia who might like a visit from us, a delicious English tea and, if they're really unlucky, a song, then put us in touch! Email them NOW with a link to our website.

From Cairns in the north down to Melbourne in the south, we're making it our aim to try and get all the way down Australia just using 'friends of friends' power. As well as saving us money on campsites and hotel rooms, UNICEF can benefit too. One 'friend of a friend' who's been in touch is organising a gig. Brilliant!

So spread the word, ask around, and 'Put Us Up Down Under'. It's the ultimate feel-good gesture that'll give you that yummy warm feeling inside, almost as good as the feeling your friends will get eating Betty's lemon drizzle cake!

At this stage in our trip the blog had over 12,500 hits, so surely *someone* out there would help us out. It was a shameless experiment in harnessing the power of the online community to see if we could travel 2,500 miles of Australia's east coast just by hopping between one reader's friend and the next. Whether it would take off, we just had to wait and see.

By the time we had negotiated our way out of Bangalore, thanks to the help of hundreds of different Indian men who all pointed us in different directions, we had driven over 18,000 miles since leaving home. Penny was faring well, but with Chennai in her sights she faced her toughest test yet on the road to Chittoor. What had looked like the most direct route to Chennai was a road shunned by most motorists and used almost exclusively by trucks: a road so rutted, bumpy and potholed that for long sections lanes were abandoned and all traffic shared the only narrow, passable sections on the verge, regardless of their direction of travel. For over two hours we didn't reach more than 15 miles per hour. We rocked, rolled, winced and swore, deeply regretting our choice of route and waiting for something ominous to snap as Penny was pummelled. Incredibly, nothing went wrong.

Then, a few hours later on much smoother roads approaching Chennai, her brakes failed. I had slammed on the anchor seeing an oncoming, potentially crippling, speed bump rather late, and her 22-year-old brake pipe ruptured, leaving little more than fresh air under my right foot. We coasted to a halt on the dirt alongside some fortuitously placed workshops, where a couple of local lads leaning on their mopeds interrupted their chat to show me where I could buy some hydraulic fluid. Filling the brake reservoir and asking Jill to press the pedal pushed the very same red liquid out on to the dirt from somewhere behind the front right wheel.

I could see the new central pipe, replaced in Turkey, but all the other sections were rusty and old. This was not a minor glitch that could be fixed in a trice. The shrugs and shaking heads of the small crowd of Indians that surrounded us told us this was not going to be fixed anywhere near here. 'What are we going to do?' asked Jill. I looked around. We were miles from anywhere, next to a tiny strip of huts and stalls that served a community of what looked like no more than a hundred people.

'I think we can rule out the RAC,' I replied. I thanked the lads for their help and climbed back into the driver's seat. 'We'll carry on to Chennai.'

'With *no brakes*?' she asked, slightly horrified.

'Well, almost none,' I corrected. 'There's a tiny bit of friction on the wheels when the pedal is right against the floor.' I demonstrated by moving off, then slowly coasting to a halt again. 'See?' I looked around at four disbelieving faces. 'Honestly, we'll be fine,' I reassured them, and we were off.

It was another 90 miles to Chennai, and after a few miles of incident-free (if slightly tense) driving, Jill laughed. I looked at her quizzically. 'What?'

'What's that old joke about a good substitute for brakes being a loud horn?'

'Oh no,' I groaned, realising why she was laughing. Our horn had broken two days earlier. 'Do you think someone's trying to tell us something? Ninety miles through Tamil Nadu with no brakes and, just for laughs, no horn.'

As you might expect, to drive in India, and in a city as busy as Chennai, with no brakes and no horn sent our stress levels to an exciting new high. Crossing busy junctions at which pedestrians, bicycles and tuk-tuks all crossed in front of us assuming we'd brake, but with us knowing we simply couldn't, gave all of us a fresh new perspective on how precious life is. Many locals were also left touched that day by the moment they faced their almost-certain demise just inches from an English couple waving manically at them in wide-eyed terror.

We spent almost a week in Chennai, living in the YWCA, attempting, but failing, to get Penny literally 'ship shape' for her journey to Australia. Chennai's VW garage suffered from the problem that India, which ran almost entirely on cars made by Tata, had only had Volkswagens for two years. Presenting them with a 22-year-old camper van was entertaining for them, but disappointing for me. Despite their assertions that they could repair a simple brake pipe, after three days it became clear they couldn't. 'We will do temporary repair,' assured the boss, when I turned up for the third time to see how they were getting on. 'I'm afraid we couldn't get the part.'

'Part? It's just some brake pipe!'

'We looked, sir. I'm sorry.'

And so the mechanic gave the pipe a wipe with an oily rag and carried out the obvious repair any professional technician would do. I dare say the Formula 1 guys operate in much the same way to keep Vettel and Hamilton on the track. He looked hard at the ruptured pipe and proceeded to wrap some electrical insulating tape around it. I started to laugh.

'That's not going to work.'

'Wait wait,' urged the boss. And the mechanic smeared some grey Play Dough over the bodge.

'That's it? That's your repair? There is no way that'll hold the pressure of a brake pipe.' I said, stating the bleedin' obvious.

'It will hold the pressure,' lied the boss. I sighed. I'd lost the battle.

I drove Penny back to the Y, her brakes as useless as ever, and we resigned ourselves to getting her fixed as soon as she arrived in Oz. This plan was only slightly flawed by the fact that Australian ports have extremely strict rules on the import of vehicles. Not only do they have to be spotlessly clean, and devoid of any mud, shoes and food, they need to be free of oil leaks *and* pass a road-worthiness test. No amount of spring cleaning was going to stop Penny dripping oil, and no amount of pressing the brake pedal was going to stop her once she was moving. The idea of a uniformed official taking her for a spin around Brisbane docks and returning, white as a sheet, eyes like saucers, was one I tried not to think about.

In many ways, the few days it took for me to arrange the shipping, get Penny to the docks, through her Customs checks and finally driven into her sealed container for fumigation and transportation to sunny Brisbane, gave all of us a restful few days to reflect on our time in *Incredible India* (as it's billed in the brochures).

From beggars and bribery to the breathtaking wonder of the Taj Mahal and Goa's beaches, how do you sum up the chaotic contradictions of India? The acid test of the 'traveller' as opposed to the 'holidaymaker' is to be able to answer the question, 'What did you think of the people there?' and we found smiling, welcoming faces almost everywhere. Admittedly, sometimes those faces were poking their heads *inside* the van and jabbering to their friends while remaining somehow oblivious to our presence, but at least they were smiling.

A curious thing I noticed was that of the many, many Indians we met who asked about our trip and where we'd been, almost none of them asked what we thought of their country. I was starting to suspect they didn't want to hear the answer. Then, in Chennai, I met a man called Raj. He was helping to translate my tyre needs into Hindi for a local tyre shop, when our conversation revealed that he was a member of UNICEF. He enthused about our adventure and was only the second person to ask me not just what I thought of India, but what I thought of her people.

'Some are good, some are bad,' I smiled diplomatically.

He laughed and said, 'Most are bad I think.' I looked surprised, and he went on. 'Most Indians are, how to say it? Outside the law.'

Now it was my turn to laugh. I told him of my experience of corrupt coppers and bent guards at the state border crossings while he nodded knowingly.

'India is by no means the only country where we've seen corruption,' I added thinking of Mr Benn's magic shopkeeper back in Syria. 'But it's definitely taken it to a whole new level.' It reminded me of that conversation with Dhan Chatri, the mechanic in Pune, a man whose kindness and honesty shone like a beacon. He was a troubled man. He too had wanted to know how I was finding India, then spoke with such passion and vigour about the country's rotten corruption, I almost found myself defending the place. It was a short-lived sentiment, however, as while leaving Dhan's garage with his brother Vinod, I was stopped by a policeman for 'being left-hand drive'.

The truth is we met some great people. As well as Dhan, Vinod and Raj, there was Praveen in Pushkar, who showed us how to make chapatis, the Mumbai model I was chatting to on the Bollywood film set who surprised me with his vast knowledge of literature and film, and many other friendly faces who more than made up for the difficult encounters we had. And isn't it interesting that those difficult encounters, the ones that were abrasive, hostile or confrontational weren't with beggars, as we might have mistakenly anticipated, but with men (*always* men) in positions of power? From the state border guard who wouldn't raise a barrier until we paid him 100 rupees, saying, 'It is not a demand, I would just like it,' down to the cab drivers who tried to double the charge, 'Because it is busy'.

A lot of these encounters were undoubtedly because we were such an obvious target. Even without the van, seeing five white faces, three of them blonde-haired girls, was like the circus coming to town for many of the small communities we drove through. The unflinching attention, the gazing and gandering that we all became used to was best acknowledged with a friendly smile, at which point a huge toothy grin was returned, and possibly a handshake and a conversation. In that respect India felt so much friendlier than Syria, for example, where - for reasons that only became clear with the passing of time - the same level of attention felt sinister and icy. Those wide Indian smiles outshine the darker moments in our memories.

The tastes and smells stay with us too. The highlight flavours, the things we long for now we're home, are Rajasthani parathas - savoury breakfast pancakes mixed with chilli, coriander, potato and onion. Yum! And pickle made with tiny lemons that are the size of a small lime. They were super-sweet but packed a punch. India's fresh produce was amazing too. Even the tiniest roadside stall boasted an impressive array of fresh fruit and veg, and the flavours of things like tiny oval grapes or huge peas in pods were so much better than we're used to in Europe.

The fresh coconut milk, so prevalent the length of the country, was also delicious. Roadside sellers, usually clattering hundreds of fresh green coconuts tied to their bicycle, would hack the top off the huge pale-green nut with the expert swipe of a machete, pop a straw in the hole revealed and everyone from kids to commuters would enjoy slurping the refreshing juice inside. It's not as 'coconutty' as you'd think. More like the kind of coconut juice you'd introduce to a shot of vodka in a cocktail shaker. Once the liquid is consumed, hardened locals will ask the vendor to hack the nut in half, and with a precisely chopped sliver of husk they then scoop the innards to eat. Don't be fooled into thinking this is like the delicious white coconut you'd break in chunks from the inside of those brown, hairy things you knock off a shy at the village fête. In a young green coconut, all you can scoop is a translucent membrane of gelatinous goo that tastes a bit salty and is, I can confirm, even less appetising than it sounds.

Another thing we found ourselves talking about in the closing days of our time there, was India's popular culture. It's particularly fitting that, as I write this, my Bollywood movie *Ra.One* has been enjoying lots of attention in the UK. Its other star has been doing lots of press interviews, but more on my old buddy Shahrukh in just a moment.

What seemed intriguing to us was that in Britain, with a population of about 60 million, there are far too many famous people to list. If we sat here now naming British celebrities, whether of cinema, TV, music, theatre, art or sport, we'd be here long enough for Katie Price not to be one any more. But in India, with a population of over one *billion* we calculated that there were approximately six famous people. The same Bollywood stars cropped up again and again and again, presenting TV shows, appearing on each other's TV shows, on posters, promoting products and doing magazine interviews. The biggest glutton for this gorging on limelight was the aforementioned Shahrukh Khan. As well as finding time to be in my film *Ra.One*, he was hosting the primetime TV show *Wipeout India*, presenting a film awards ceremony, appearing on daytime TV chat shows and promoting Nokia, Tata, furniture, toothpaste, watches, a fountain pen and *Fair & Handsome* skin-lightening cream. And they're just the ones we noticed.

Which brings me on to one of the more disturbing aspects of the young stars on India's TV and cinema screens: their blatant promotion of skin-bleaching products. Our girls were shocked at how open the message being promoted across all India's media was: to be white is to be successful. Household names we knew from home were all at it – Ponds, Garnier, Olay. The female focused adverts showed a beautiful Indian model holding a gauge to her face – a paper colour-matching chart. See how in just seven days her skin pales! But it wasn't just aimed at women. *Fair & Lovely*, the biggest brand in the skin-lightening field, had started aiming at butch go-getting businessmen. (A tough sell given the brand name.)

In one advert, an Indian man is at a high-pressure job interview at a law firm. He looks smart, stylish and … white. The elder partner leans to his fellow interviewer and says, 'I think he's perfect.' He gets the job because he's white! Except, of course, he isn't. Presumably his torso and legs are about as 'fair and lovely' as Mahatma Gandhi's were, but the message, in all its appalling bluntness, was 'dark-skinned Indians fail'. While I'm not so naïve as to be oblivious to racism, and its prevalence in the media, this campaign to make dyeing your own skin white the acceptable standard was shocking. I felt sorry for any young kid dreaming of becoming a star in India. It would take immense willpower *not* to resign yourself quickly to being the wrong colour - and the wrong Khan.

So with Penny tucked in a box awaiting her sea passage across the Bay of Bengal, we once again honed our packing down to just five backpacks *plus* a bag of instruments. We would fly to Brisbane, full of excitement about meeting some great friends who'd offered to put us up more or less indefinitely. 'Dangerous words,' Jill had warned them, after reminding them how exhausted we all were, but they seemed to mean it.

'Before we leave India,' I said to the four tired faces in our room at the YWCA, 'I need to sum up India for the blog. Tell me how you'll remember your time here.' Chins were stroked, brows furrowed, and I prepared to type. Bethan was first.

'An experience. I'd come back.'

'Great. I'm surprised,' I said, tapping at the laptop.

'But just to Mumbai and Goa,' she quickly added. I laughed. We had had the most fun in those places.

'Let's see,' pondered Ella. 'An emotional rollercoaster. I've been very glad to be in India, but also sometimes I've just wanted to leave.'

'Very honest. Thank you,' I said. 'Edie?'

'One of the most eventful countries we've been to. Its ups, its down, its smells. The Taj Mahal was beautiful.' There were nods all round in agreement. We all looked at Jill, who was composing her thoughts.

'Without doubt the most interesting country we've visited on our trip. I'm really glad we came and glad we spent as long as we did here. To fully understand the country and people you need to spend time here. Frustrating and fascinating in equal measure.'

I don't think any of us could have put it better. I doubt the India Tourist Board would go for it, but it's the most honest catchline you'll find: *India – frustrating and fascinating in equal measure.*

India

"Taxi!"

India's kindest mechanic

The Dhobi Ghat
laundry, Mumbai.
Our undies are in
there somewhere.

India

What can possibly
go wrong?

... oh.

Sugar cane,
anyone?

"Good evening Goa!"

India

Braced for
Bollywood!

Penny's spring-clean
for shipping to Oz

Australia

"Say cheese!"
(I was talking to the fish)

Busking in
Grafton

Hard at work in the
Australia Planning Office

Our route from the airport through the beautiful, serene, clean suburbs of Brisbane was such a stark contrast to the dirt and noise of Chennai that we were temporarily stunned by the reverse culture shock of Western-world-re-entry. We landed late on Sunday night, picked up a borrowed car (thank you Berners) and drove, sorry, *glided* to our friends Berners and Leona's home on roads so smooth that we might as well have been floating on air.

'The roads are so quiet,' cooed Beth in awe. 'Look. Pavements!' It was such a different world to the one we'd left just a day ago. We drifted along, consumed by the silence.

'I haven't heard a car horn since we landed,' I whispered.

'And where's the litter?' added Edie.

'Can we live here?' asked Beth.

Our friends spoiled us, cooking sumptuous meals and letting us simply collapse and decompress for a few days, which was bliss. We got to know my three-year-old godson, Ewan, whom none of us had seen since he was just three months old, and his one-year-old sister Cara previously only seen on Skype.

All this joy was quickly overshadowed by a major news event. Just weeks after Brisbane had suffered its worst flooding in living memory, the Queensland coast was about to get battered by Yasi, the biggest tropical cyclone to hit Australia since records began. It was a truly unique time for us to have arrived in the land down under, sandwiched as it was between two massive and profound weather events. Yasi had been a minor news item since before we got there, and I recalled watching a BBC weather report while in Chennai which briefly mentioned a major cyclone forming near Fiji. As it grew, fuelled by the warm Pacific Ocean, it travelled west, and by the time we landed, Australian forecasters were reporting the threat of a Category 4 cyclone hitting Queensland.

The number four is from the Saffir-Simpson Hurricane Scale. Cyclones, hurricanes and typhoons are the same thing - they just have different names depending on where in the world they happen. Mexico's 'hurricane' is Japan's 'typhoon', while on the Indian Ocean and South Pacific it's the 'cyclone' that's feared.

'Is category four bad?' Ella asked Leona, who was getting visibly more worried as each news report put more weight on the story.

'Yeah. We've had threes before,' she explained. 'I think the scale only goes up to five, though, so it's pretty bad.'

In Britain, our trusty old Beaufort Scale goes up to 12. If British sailors tuned in to the shipping forecast to hear they were facing a force four wind on Tyne, Dogger or Cromarty, they'd know that was a moderate breeze. But when structural engineer Herbert Saffir and his meteorologist mate Bob Simpson created their scale in 1971, they thought 12 was far too many categories. Even ten seemed extravagant. When you look at the simple (and slightly scary) Saffir-Simpson scale below, you can see why a 'Cat. 4', as it was being referred to, was very quickly Australia's top story:

Category One Hurricane - Damage: minimal
Winds 74-95 mph. Storm surge 4-5 feet.
Damage to unanchored mobile homes, shrubbery, and trees. Also, some coastal road flooding and minor pier damage.

Category Two Hurricane - Damage: moderate
Winds 96-110 mph. Storm surge 6-8 feet.
Some roofing and window damage. Considerable damage to mobile homes, shrubbery and some trees blown down.

Category Three Hurricane - Damage: extensive
Winds 111-130 mph. Storm surge 9-12 feet.
Structural damage to small residences. Large trees blown down. Mobile homes are destroyed. Evacuation of low-lying residences within several blocks of the shoreline may be required.

Category Four Hurricane - Damage: extreme
Winds 131-155 mph. Storm surge 13-18 feet.
Complete roof structure failures on small residences. Shrubs, trees and all signs are blown down. Complete destruction of mobile homes. Major damage to lower floors of structures near the shore. Massive evacuation of residential areas as far inland as 6 miles.

Category Five Hurricane - Damage: catastrophic
Winds over 155 mph. Storm surge greater than 18 feet.
Complete roof failure on many residences and industrial buildings. Some complete building failures. All shrubs, trees and signs blown down. Massive evacuation of residential areas on low ground within 10 miles of the shoreline.

On Wednesday morning we woke to the news that Yasi had become a Category Five cyclone. While Leona made urgent phone calls to her parents, who were near Cairns and in Yasi's predicted path, Jill made me close the Internet page showing the Saffir-Simpson scale, in case Leona should read the damage description for a 'Cat. 5'. Its size and force had newscasters wearing earnest frowns, meteorologists reaching for record books and politicians doing almost round-the-clock press conferences updating people on the threat to property, land, and of course, life.

The best illustration of Yasi's magnitude was demonstrated when the local *Herald Sun* newspaper super-imposed the satellite image of the sinister spiral over a same-scale image of North America. Yasi would have covered the entire United States from Mexico up to Canada and from coast to coast. The eye of the cyclone was an estimated 100 kilometres across. That was just the *eye*, the dormant peaceful lull at the centre of the carnage. Forecasters predicted it would take up to an *hour* for the eye to pass over those in its path. This remarkable phenomenon, the peaceful calm that is so often the cause for false hope, usually lasts just moments, a few minutes perhaps. The fact that some people could suffer six hours of 170 mph winds, then an hour of calm, knowing they had another six hours still to bear was incredible.

The flurry of calls from family and friends throughout the day reassured Berners and Leona that their loved ones were fully prepped and braced for the worst. The advice from the authorities was initially to leave the coastal towns in Yasi's path, but from about midday they advised it was too late to evacuate - the winds were already too strong. 'Now it's a case of batten down the hatches and sit it out,' said the Queensland Premier Anna Bligh, whose hourly updates were broadcast live across TV and radio. Relatives and friends had stocked up on food, taped or covered windows, fuelled up the generators and gathered in groups and communities at each other's houses. Strength in numbers. Besides, they all knew the power and phones would soon be knocked out, so the easiest way to know you're all OK is to gather in the same shelter.

Even in the face of this onslaught, Aussies weren't easily fazed. I heard a guy on the radio being interviewed about his night ahead. 'Well, we've followed all the advice,' he said. 'Got a few friends here, a fridge full of beer and few nice bottles of wine too. She'll be right, mate.' I wondered who he was talking about until Leona informed me that 'she'll be right' is a generic Aussie term meaning 'not to worry'. The safest cyclone shelter in most houses, we learned, is the bathroom because it's small and usually tiled giving it extra strength, so we heard Anna Bligh reminding people to prepare for a long night in the bathroom.

By 9pm all contact was lost with our friends in the north. Berners and Leona both had parents hunkered down in their homes near Cairns, though thankfully a good few miles inland – the coast, of course, would receive the worst battering. Leona's brother Mark was in Towsnville, also in Yasi's path, though on the southern edge, and he was joining his neighbours for an all-night cyclone party, so without power or phones, we hoped they were having a night of fun, not fear.

By 11pm the first edge of the spiral touched down on the coast. News channels transmitted uninterrupted shots from anchored down cameras and it quickly became clear that, apart from the wobbly, grainy shots of dark streets being slammed by horizontal rain and occasional debris, there really wasn't going to be much to see until dawn. At one in the morning we all went to bed, the girls to their bedroom and Jill and I to a tent in the garden. Brisbane was completely calm. It was weird. How could the largest storm in generations be hitting our state, yet leave us without a whisper of wind? It was a peculiar reminder of just how big Australia is, that catastrophic destruction was taking place up the coast, in the same state, rent by a cyclone as big as North America, yet we were utterly untouched by it.

At daybreak Northern Queensland picked itself up to face a morning after like no other, and as news crews eventually found their way to the heart of the most devastated towns - they had to cut their way into Cardwell, Mission Beach and Tully with chainsaws - the biggest story was that of survival. The storm - the biggest and strongest to hit Australia in living memory - claimed just one life, a man who suffocated on the fumes from his generator. Two people were reported missing but soon turned up without injury. One of them, a fisherman I heard interviewed on the local ABC radio, summed up the Aussie attitude. He'd been reported missing after failing to return to his Cardwell home when Yasi hit. He explained how the wind picked up his ten-metre boat, with him in it, and dragged it about a kilometre inland into a banana mangrove where it was stranded. Faced with abandoning his boat and using his small dinghy to get back to shore through the croc infested mangroves – a prospect that would involve swimming the last 30 metres - he sat tight in his tin boat until Yasi blew over. 'Weren't you scared?' asked the radio presenter.

'Not at all,' replied the gruff voice on the phone. 'I had some beers and a bit of food, so I had everything I needed.' Note his order of priorities, in which food came second.

Our friends made contact with their respective families up near Cairns who'd survived unscathed, losing power, phones and a few trees, but nothing worse. Thousands of people sheltered in school halls and shopping malls, and the story of a baby girl born in an evacuation centre in Cairns as the cyclone roared overhead became the powerfully emblematic headline of hope and survival.

Hope and survival. Themes we too found ourselves clinging to. Just a few days after Yasi moved inland we faced a family Category 5 cyclone of our own. While we were plotting satellite images, calculating storm surges and bracing ourselves, 10,000 miles away my Mum was being dealt a worse blow: her breast cancer had returned. Over a year since she'd been given her ten-year all clear, the breast cancer cells that were seeded during surgery a decade earlier were growing in her spine and abdomen. We were shocked and reeling. Mum's email had been very positive about her treatment plan - six bouts of chemo, no radiotherapy or surgery - but even with the stoicism and strength so visible in her email it was impossible not to feel the gut-punching blow that goes with such news.

I wrote earlier how, regardless of our gallivanting travel plans, life went on for the rest of the world and sometimes that meant dealing with bad news. Since arriving in Australia we'd heard the sad news from Ty in Kansas that our friend Lisa had died.

But *this* was a lot closer to home.

As the shock-fog cleared, Jill and I found a private moment to grapple with some difficult questions. 'Should we fly home?' she asked. 'We can if you want to.'

'I don't know,' I replied, which was true. We both knew that, financially, five flights home would signal the end of our journey. 'She wouldn't want us to. But ...'

'But?'

I sighed deeply. She probably knew what I was thinking. 'Remember Liz,' I croaked, trying not to cry. Six years earlier a very dear friend who was about our age got breast cancer which, after being beaten by surgery and chemo, returned over a year later. Liz had gone to the doctor with stomach ache. The cancer was in her liver and 13 days later she was dead. It was the worst fortnight of our lives, and drawing a comparison was inevitable. '13 days, Jill. What if it's worse than Mum's making out?'

Jill held my hands tightly and her slate-blue eyes looked at me earnestly. 'She'd tell us, Sim. Your mum wouldn't mess around on a subject like this.'

This was true, but it didn't stop me feeling horribly guilty for dragging all of us to the opposite side of the planet on a stupid whim. 'I ask myself would she want us there? And the answer is yes, she probably would. But that doesn't mean she'd want us to fly home.'

'Talk to her. Then decide,' suggested my level-headed wife. The modern miracle that is Skype came into its own when an early morning hook-up in Brisbane synced up with an evening in Devon after Mum and Dad had been to see the oncologist. She seemed genuinely positive about her oncologist, her nurse and the treatment that lay ahead. She would start chemotherapy in a fortnight and had been assured that the doctors could stagger it to allow her to go on a planned holiday to France later in the year without her feeling too grotty. 'I can't believe you'll lose your hair, *again*!' I said to her as she smiled back from the computer screen.

'At least I've still got two wigs from last time,' she quipped. She was clearly putting on a very positive front, and wouldn't hear of us flying home, but beneath the surface? I don't think she felt sorry for herself at all, rather she was bloody pissed off, and who could blame her? She thought she'd won that battle. We all did. But she had a steely resolve to fight the cancer once again, and at least this time around my Dad was retired so had more time to care for her. She seemed to have a great support network through their village and church, and my brother lived a couple of hours away if needed. He was a great support to me, too, assuring me that if Mum's condition got worse he'd alert me, knowing how paranoid I was that Mum and Dad might play it down. All of this, though, didn't change the fact that Australia suddenly seemed a very, very long way from home.

It later transpired that Mum had waited until we'd reached Australia to break the news to us, detecting from my on-the-road blog that India was sapping our strength. We were grateful she'd waited. In truth, if we'd had that news in Chennai we'd have come home. Also, you simply couldn't find a more positive place than Oz to help counter a dip in your spirits. The overriding first impression of the people we met was in their attitude. Everyone's default setting is positive. Everything is 'too easy' and 'no worries'. Ask anyone a question as mundane as 'Where's the cinema?' or 'Where can I park that's not gonna cost me 40 bucks?' and they'll give you not just the answer, but a smile, a handshake and all the time in the world. There's a sugary, sickly, fridge magnet/bumper sticker slogan - *A stranger is a friend you just haven't met yet* (to which I say 'blurgh - could just as easily be a serial killer'). Well, Australians seem to live by that slogan, and it's impossible not to be swept up in it, even for a cynic like me.

They're just unstoppably chipper. You can't confuse it with the 'Have a nice day' tick that Americans have developed either. It appears more than just a routine line that's trotted out without thinking. Australians have a reputation for taking people at face value. By their reckoning, unless I did or said something to convince them otherwise, I would be accepted as a decent bloke - a *pommy barrrstud*, obviously, but a decent one. It's a classless society and proud of it.

Aussie equality is unconsciously maintained by the phenomenon known as 'tall poppy syndrome'. Imagine our surprise to discover how little regard Aussies had for super-successful darlings of the UK pop scene Kylie or Dannii Minogue. The mention of Nicole Kidman gets a grudging sneer. And don't even mention Russell Crowe (although, thankfully, he could be blamed on New Zealand). If any Australian appears to be getting a bit too big for their boots, the 'tall poppy' is cut down to the same level as all the others. This isn't the same as the UK gutter-press, building up a star only to tear them down, it's more of a communal socialism dictated by the people. It's what makes the Queensland State Premier, Anna Bligh, hold the attention of millions with her 'leadership in the face of disaster' live press conferences - at which she wears jeans and chunky boots. It's what made it acceptable for a young reporter to embarrass beleaguered Australian cricket Vice-Captain, Michael Clarke, during a press conference we saw, by teaching him how to bat. And it's what made a nation laugh in the face of all nature could throw at it, and salute those who survived it thanks to courage, bravery ... and beer.

While we waited for Penny, whose container was put on Border Processing Hold - a random check a bit like having your suitcases pulled aside by Customs, only with a much, much bigger X-ray machine - we found the enforced break in our travels put us, once again, in holiday mode. 'Reckon we oughta show you guys a bit of Aussie beach,' said Leona one bright sunny morning. 'Waddaya say?'

'Ahhh yes!' said the kids.

'Sounds great,' said Jill.

'A man was eaten by a shark yesterday,' I said, reading the online edition of an Aussie newspaper.

'Really?' cried Ella, leaping over to see any gory details.

'Really. In fact, he was eaten by two. It says here he was an abalone diver. It's a shellfish,' I added, before she could ask.

'Truffle of the sea, they call it,' informed Leona.

'I thought it was earthworm of the sea,' added Berners.

'Sounds lovely,' said Bethan, pulling a face.

'Where was this?' asked Jill.

'Off Australia's west coast near Perth,' I read on.

'Oh that's miles away,' Leona said, brushing it off. 'There's nothing to worry about, girls.'

'According to the only witness, the boat's skipper,' I continued, 'the diver was returning to the surface when he was taken by a great white and what appeared to be the shark's pup. The diver's body hasn't been recovered and the skipper is being treated for shock.' And then I laughed, to questioning faces all round. 'Sorry. It *is* a tragedy, I know, but listen to this. According to the *Perth Now* website he was diving south of Perforated Island near Coffin Bay.' Berners laughed. '*Perforated*?' I asked. '*Coffin*? Did no one see the clues?'

This report was just a week after the local newspaper's front page told of a North Queensland man who had successfully fought off a crocodile attack by punching it in the face. Snatched by the arm he was dragged beneath the surface of the water but escaped after repeatedly bashing the croc in the eyes.

It's not news that Australia has more than its fair share of scary, life-threatening animals, but when I read both of these stories I was struck by the *risks* locals were prepared to take, dicing with nature's angry beasts. The croc socking welterweight, for example, was attacked by the three-metre killing machine while swimming in Beening Creek with his daughters, aged 12 and 17. *Swimming in a creek?* Every Aussie creek I've ever seen looks like a muddy, overgrown death-trap teeming with things that are born to bite. Stumbling upon such a place out in the bush, what possesses a man to leap in for a dip? I imagined him shouting 'Come on in kids! The water's lovely! Oh, hang on, something's got me arm.' I was raised 10,000 miles away, but even *I* saw *Crocodile Dundee*. Everyone knows you don't swim in a creek. You don't even *drink* from a creek. Especially if you're Linda Kozlowski and you're wearing a dangly necklace. What were these people thinking?

But Australia's a big country. All these dangers, though exciting, were a long way from the suburban garden we were camping in, right? Well, no, the threats were very real, as we soon discovered. We drove only an hour up the Sunshine Coast to spend the day at one of our friends' favourite spots, King's Beach. It was gorgeous: golden sand, warm sea, tanned surfers, loud sirens, panicked screams of 'SHARK!' It really was everything you'd want from your Aussie beach experience.

Being the coiled spring of journalism that I am, I almost missed the drama because I was on base camp duty, looking after our pile of belongings spread under a palm tree, and was taking my rôle seriously by dozing off listening to my iPod. Suddenly, something was wrong. The urgent flapping of a child above me interrupted the sublime summer sounds of Jamiroquai.

'Daddy! Get the camera! There's a shark!' shouted Edie, jumping up and down. As I blinked into the sunlight I saw her silhouette racing back towards the scene: one I'd only ever witnessed on screen, when Chief Brody clears the sea of Amity holiday-makers in *Jaws*. Crowds of kids, parents, surfers and pensioners were pouring from the blue

South Pacific, all trying to look calm, but all not wanting to be the person at the back.

By the time I'd found my camera, crowds lined the shore watching the patrolling lifeguards blitzing up and down the empty bay on jet skis. One of the less fortunate lifeguards, who hadn't been given a jet ski to play on, jogged past us on the sand as his radio crackled a report from one of his wave-riding buddies - 'No shark off north beach,' we heard from the tinny speaker. It was all very exciting.

'Does this happen often?' I asked Berners, who'd been coming to this beach since he was a kid.

'I've never seen this happen here,' he replied. 'It's pretty rare.'

'So they're not just being over cautious, then.' (I'd seen Chief Brody make the same mistake.)

'Naaa. They'll have definitely seen a shark out there. They'll just try and drive it back out with the noise of the jet skis.'

After 15 minutes a tannoy crackled saying it was safe to go back into the water and, completely unlike the scene in *Jaws*, everyone rushed back into the surf without hesitation. Remember, these were people who swam in crocodile infested creeks and dived off Coffin Bay. They knew no fear. After about half an hour of blood-free frolicking had passed without incident, I allowed myself a cautious dip with the kids but found I couldn't take my eyes off the horizon, and looked about as relaxed as Richard Dreyfuss being told, 'You're gonna need a bigger boat.'

Some lovely friends in the UK wired us some cash on the strict instructions it was to be used 'only for fun, not food. Or diesel.' which gave us the chance to inspect Australia's wildlife up close at a koala sanctuary. The girls got to hold a koala each, we saw a platypus, dingos, Tasmanian devils (small dogs, big teeth) and prickly echidnas, and spent a happy ten minutes enjoying a Golden Gay Time – a gloriously inappropriately named Aussie ice lolly.

Equally as interesting as the creatures you can pay to see, are the creatures we shared our living space with. And they were free. Tiny geckos wandered the house, too small and too cute to be anything other than adorable, while massive lizards over a foot long were regularly spotted basking on tree trunks. Parakeets flitted among the trees in the garden, kookaburras laughed from the branches and at dusk the night sky was filled with flying foxes - massive bats that I'd previously thought only existed in *Hammer Horror* films.

Then, as Jill and I tucked ourselves up in our tent, the fun would begin. One man and his possum. That's not a euphemism.

Our outdoor bedroom was possum-central once night fell. The nocturnal marsupials are creatures of habit and used regular runs along the fence, across the lawn, past my pillow, past next door's dog ... Normally, they keep themselves pretty quiet, munching leaves, playing cards, doing whatever possums do to while away the night. But every now and then it would all kick off. A highly-charged squabble between joeys over pouch-rights might sound cute to you, but believe me, the asthmatic wheezing squeal of an offended possum is a wake-up call like no other.

So now I was awake, I might as well go to the loo. But that would mean treading into the darkened night-time kingdom of the Cane Toad. This huge, slimy toad is a despised, artificially introduced, poisonous pest. Because its exponential spread across Queensland threatens native wildlife, the Cane Toad had become the focus of a nocturnal Aussie sport played by red-blooded men of the house (and garden) involving stealth, cunning and a spade. I don't think I need to elaborate further. It doesn't end well for the toad. Let's move on.

Australia actively encouraged Brits to help colonise the place through all sorts of schemes over the years. The British judicial system got the ball rolling in the 19th century, as you know, but even back in the 1950s there were the 'Ten Pound Poms' - English families who were offered the chance to relocate to the other side of the world for a tenner. What's now surfaced is the much more unpleasant truth that thousands of care-home children were shipped down under on the promise of 'oranges and sunshine' but found only servitude and abuse – a horror for which both countries' governments have since been forced to apologise. It's ironic then, given the lengths to which Australia went in encouraging immigrants, that by 2010 unless you were young, fit, had a degree in engineering and a part-time passion for hairdressing, you could forget it. A little part of me died when I realised that because I was 40 I was too old to apply to emigrate to Australia. That ship had sailed, and I didn't even hear the boarding announcement. Clearly, 'life begins at 40' is a phrase you don't hear much at the Australian Immigration Marketing Department.

A century of migration means it's not unusual to find you have relatives, sorry, 'rellies' in Oz. If you think you haven't, may I be so bold as to suggest you just haven't looked hard enough? They just don't want to be found. Everyone's got a distant uncle, cousin or grandparent who at some point jumped (or was dragged) aboard a ship sailing for the land of plenty. My own family has two branches leading to Oz, and Jill's father had cousins in Queensland, some of whom he'd never met, so one of our missions while there was to Meet The Moodys. A whole branch of 'brand new' family for us to get to know had arranged to meet us in Yeppoon, a seaside town about eight hours drive north of Brisbane, or as locals would put it, just next door.

We were momentarily held up by Penny, who, having been locked in a box for a month chose to demonstrate her temperamental side. I don't think the old girl had had the smoothest of crossings from Chennai. When I opened the container door for her quarantine inspection, the pristine interior I had confidently looked forward to showing off to the uniformed officials had been replaced by the kind of carnage left by a ransacking pack of angry Tasmanian devils. A cupboard had been ripped from its screws and was across the boot, its contents strewn across the floor. The kitchen had been wrenched out of place, bags, books and cooking utensils had flown across seats, it was as if she'd been hit by a cyclo ... ah.

'She came through Yasi, then,' said the fork-lift driver, raising an eyebrow.

'And there was I, happy it had missed us here in Brisbane,' I replied. 'I hadn't considered the sixth member of the family.' I emptied her contents on to a couple of pallets in the quarantine inspection bay, rebuilt her as best I could, and the uniformed inspector must have felt my pain because he only spent a couple of minutes poking through bags and cupboards, a final run of his fingers around the wheel arches to check for Indian mud, and the crucial 'passed' sticker was slapped on her windscreen.

Remembering the roadworthiness test we'd read about online, I hovered near the office, waiting to see which daredevil was going to take Penny for a spin (hopefully not literally). A lady phoned my shipping agent to confirm the outstanding account, asked me to settle our bill, which I did, then she handed me the keys. 'All good. Have a great day,' she smiled.

'I can go?' I asked, trying not to arouse too much suspicion.

'No!' she suddenly exclaimed.

Damn! She's remembered.

'You'll need a gate pass. Here you go,' she said, handing me a slip of paper.

Without querying any further, I smiled, walked over to Penny, re-introduced myself to her controls and lighter-than-air brake pedal, and gently drove her out of the compound. 'Penny, old girl. Welcome to Australia!' I was talking to the van, but I was in that sort of mood. I could only assume that because the accounts I'd read online were about importing a vehicle at the port in Darwin, the state laws varied. I gingerly guided her, without working brakes, through Brisbane's suburbs to where a full service and the repair of the ruptured brake-pipe and leaky oil seals would be supplied by Laurence, the brilliant local Vee Dub expert. He explained the law regarding imports, and got Penny in full working order. She was certified with a legitimate Queensland Roadworthiness stamp. We were off!

And so was the fan belt.

A roadside repair on the M3 motorway out of Brisbane revealed my back-up replacement belt was too big, but had just enough tension to turn the water pump, so we limped back to the industrial estate home of *German Autos* and a quizzical Laurence. A quick fix was made slightly more complicated by the fact he heard a new noise he wasn't happy with, and discovered a replacement pulley he'd fitted had a slight flange the old one hadn't had, which was prone to rubbing on the tin plate behind. The words 'sodding shim', 'bugger' and 'bloody Germans' emanated from inside the engine bay, until at two o'clock we were finally heading north.

Jill took on the slightly awkward task of phoning family members she didn't even know, to explain we wouldn't be getting to the party on time, or, in fact, *that day*. When darkness fell we camped in Maryborough, our first proper Penny camping night in Oz - a bargain at just 20 bucks (about £12) - and didn't arrive in Yeppoon until about 3 o'clock the following afternoon, almost 24 hours late for our own party. The gathered throng were gracious about our woeful timekeeping and a cold 'stubby' of beer was thrust in my hand almost before I could catch everyone's name.

The general gist of who was who centred around Jill's late grandfather Fred, whose brother Wilf had moved to Australia aged 15 as part of the Big Brother Movement in 1927. Big Brother, before reality TV, or even George Orwell, was a juvenile migration scheme under which Australian men - called 'Big Brothers' - became virtual godfathers to young men, generally 15 to 17 years of age, called 'Little Brothers' who arrived from Great Britain. Obviously this was yet another 'populate Australia' project, but it's unclear why their families sent these boys. No one at the party knew what reason Wilf had ever given for his emigration. Most historical sources seemed to suggest it was with the blessing of parents who'd hoped for a better future for their boys in Oz, but there had been whispers that perhaps young Wilf had been a bit of a tearaway, something of a handful. Still, how fed up with your teenage son would you have to be to send them to the other side of the world? Actually, don't answer that. It's probably quite a common sentiment.

The scheme was suspended with the outbreak of World War Two, by which time Wilf was 27 and promptly signed up for service in the army.

Wilf's three children, Cath, Lorraine and Doug were all there with their respective other halves to meet us, along with so many various friends, offspring and cousins that it quickly became a second party night with a throng of about 30 of us enjoying an al fresco feast of delicious home made food from pumpkin soup to barbecued chicken washed down with endless beer and wine from bottomless 'eskies' – mammoth Aussie ice-box chests. The culinary highlight was a tray of eight massive mud crabs caught by Cath's son-in-law Kris the night before. He'd been out at three in the morning when the tide was right, checking the crab pots he'd set in the mangroves, and cheerfully demonstrated to us how to crack them in the right place to get the meat out. A mud crab might not sound very appetising. They look exactly like huge sea crabs, but with huge vice-like claws that make it look as if it's a regular crab that's been 'pimped' by bolting on a couple of lobster claws. They tasted fantastic - so meaty and succulent. I'm afraid poor old Cromer's boring old English crab has a lot to live up to after we tasted those. They were officially deemed a trip highlight by us all.

We even beat the odds and played a few Beatles tunes for them. Quite a feat given my streaming cold and Beth leaving her music in Brisbane. I felt a bit sorry for our audience; a whole day of waiting and then they got a wheezy version of *All My Loving* with no voice and half a squeezebox. They hid their disappointment well and actually seemed to enjoy it. Their generosity with applause and massive mangrove crustacea was only the start - Doug and his wife Jen had brought camp beds down from Mackay meaning we didn't have to sleep in the van, so we all collapsed into our living room 'campsite' exhausted, full, and very happy.

The next day was Sunday, and as various members of my new family (see how quickly I adopted them?) drifted in and out we relaxed into a chilled-out day of eating, nattering and pottering about. This part of Australia still felt a lot like pioneering country. I don't mean cowboys were riding out into the bush to plant a flag in the ground and claim ranching rights, but even in the thoroughly modern world of air-conditioned homes, glossy cars and hi-tech gadgets (Apple iPhones and iPads had arrived in a big way) there was a 'can do' pioneering spirit that felt rooted in their heritage. Cath and her husband Doc's house, for example, a beautiful spacious two-storey home, was built *by them* on an edge-of-town plot of over 50 acres that climbed to a hill-peak of wild bush-land that was home to wallabies and kangaroos who often hopped past their front door. Their son Casey showed us the house he was just finishing building - another wonderful 'Grand Design' that would have Kevin McCloud, presenter of that UK series, gushing about 'use of space', 'heavenly heights' and 'a sea view to die for'. Later, we popped round to daughter Alicia and Kris's place - the *second* home they've built. Again, it was like walking into a magazine article: polished white floor tiles, wide open spaces, a wrap-around veranda overlooking the ocean. We wandered around, slack jawed. 'Flippin' heck, Jill,' I whispered. 'What happened to *your* side of the family?' Before she could dig me in the ribs, Doc interrupted.

'Come and look out the back. They're putting a pool in.'

A large hole was having reinforced concrete prepared to line it. 'It looks a bit of a mess now,' Alicia apologised. 'But you can see where the rock pools will be around the edge, and the waterfall. She'll be right in a week or two.'

'We only had the idea of the pool a couple of weeks ago,' Kris added.

'Two weeks? And this'll be done in a fortnight from now?! How long did it take to build the house?' I asked.

'About four months,' he said. 'But we took our time with this one. The last one we built in three months 'cause we had a deadline. Alicia was expecting a baby so we had to get a move on.'

'It took us five months just to get our bathroom done,' I said distantly. 'It once took us two years to get planning permission just to change a window,' I added as Jill led me quietly away.

On a nearby paddock of grassland we paid a visit to Doc's livestock - 30 or so head of beef cattle that were the result of a small-time hobby that grew while he wasn't looking. 'I'm thinking of selling them,' he said. 'I want a bigger fishing boat, one I can camp in. It's either sell the shares or sell the cows.' I had visions of our new bovine friends nervously checking the stock market share prices each morning.

Back at the house, Doc and Doug whiled away an hour watching a locally produced DVD of hog hunting. Brawny young men in camouflage vests crept through the bush, stalking black wiry-haired pigs and unleashing a razor tipped arrow from a highly complex looking hunting bow. After each kill, the hunter would squat next to the corpse, describing the approach, the equipment and where the arrow entered (and occasionally exited) the beast. A points score would appear on screen. 'Every trophy animal is scored to a standardised scale,' explained Doc. 'The score is based on length of tusks, that sort of thing.'

By normal TV standards at home, the footage was shocking and gory, but this wasn't deliberately ghoulish television. It was 'info-tainment' to a nation of like-minded blokes. Doc brought out his own compound bow to show me, like those I'd seen on screen. Doug, too, had seen his share of hunting. They told me they had originally planned to bring a freshly hunted wild boar back to barbecue for our party, but the hunting trip had proved fruitless. I nodded my understanding, imagining Beth's reaction to this, and silently thanked the god of mud crabs for his offering.

Hunting, fishing, grabbing some land and building a home - these were the essences of that pioneering spirit I loved so much about these people. That, and their generosity with shellfish, obviously. Further north up the coast, we stayed with Doug and Jen in Mackay for a night, and as we flitted along the seaside, guided by them from one stunning, deserted beach to the next, we were all struck by the apparently endless beauty of this country's coast-line. We stood alone on beaches that, in Europe, would be rammed with people. Beaches certain parts of Italy would have charged for us to step foot on.

'You know what?' I said to Jill. 'I finally get it.'

'Get what?'

'Well, as you go through life you occasionally hear about people who've emigrated to Australia. There was a bloke I worked with in the engineering factory when I was about 17 who upped sticks and went to Oz. I always wondered why. I thought it was like *Neighbours*. I mean, if you're gonna live next door to Kylie, fair enough, but I didn't really get it. Now I see what all the fuss was about. These people have an *amazing* quality of life.'

'Let's live here,' she said, gazing across flat sand that glistened with sparkling minerals, to the wooded, emerald-green island out in the blue Coral Sea.

'It's a deal. Oh, hang on, didn't I tell you? We're past it. Our old-timers' visa expires in eight weeks and the immigration official's wristwatch is ticking.'

'Fair enough. Sand is overrated anyhow. But for the record,' she added, 'this place, right here. This is my favourite beach *in the world*.'

'Duly noted.'

And it remained so, untroubled at the top of Jill's 'beach top ten' by anything the rest of Australia's 2,500 miles of east coast, or even California could offer. Cape Hillsborough near Mackay, a truly heavenly stretch of planet Earth, one which you're more likely to share with a kangaroo than a human. As long as you keep it to yourself, of course, and some fool doesn't publish it in a travel book.

Our onward journey was based on an itinerary that, back in Brisbane, had been the source of some humour. 'What's the plan today?' Leona would ask with a grin each morning, knowing that we were changing our minds more often than our clothes. How were we going to tackle a country as big as Australia? I had toyed with the idea of driving inland to Alice Springs so we could tick the box of seeing Ayers Rock, but close examination of the Aussie map stuck on the loo wall soon dissuaded me.

'Do you realise it would take us a week to drive to Ayers Rock?' I announced, exiting the toilet one day.

'Oh yeah. Easy,' said Berners. 'It's at least four days in a *proper* car.'

'None taken,' I smiled. 'Guess we can rule out Perth, then.' This got hollow laughter and knowing nods from our hosts.

So a two-week mind-numbing drive to see a big rock, albeit a very impressive one, was eschewed in favour of a 'two-leg' journey up and down the east coast. From Yeppoon we would continue north until we reached Leona's parents near Cairns, get to experience the Great Barrier Reef on the way there, see some amazing rainforest in the north, and then return to 'Brissy', about half way down the country, before tackling the southward drive all the way to Melbourne. All of our accommodation on the journey south was to be with people who'd responded to our *Put Us Up Down Under* plea on the blog, so that would be very exciting.

From Mackay, then, we left The Most Beautiful Beach In The World and headed north, our destination being Koah, just inland from Cairns. On the way we would see a barrier reef that is great, visit Leona's brother Mark in Townsville to see how his cyclone party went, and we would be back in Mackay in time to hook up with a Beatles tribute band who were gigging there in a week's time.

Of course, all that was weather permitting.

After what we'd witnessed, wouldn't you have thought we'd have learned by now?

We saw both sides of Yasi's legacy in the next couple of days. First, when we stayed with Mark in Townsville, we heard of its spectacle. His apartment had a balcony on the ground floor that overlooked a coastal inlet - a large seawater lake. This meant he could fish from his balcony, which we did. It also meant that on the night the monster cyclone hit, he and his neighbours had gathered there for a party and were completely protected by the large apartment block to their backs.

'It was the most incredible thing I've ever seen,' he enthused. 'You could actually see the edge of the massive, flat, disc of cloud as it approached. We lost power at about 9 o'clock, but the storm was at its strongest about midnight. The sound was incredible, like a deep, guttural howl,' he went on. 'Debris was flying out to sea, but the weirdest thing was the lake. It dropped by at least three metres at the edge nearest us, and rose by that much on the opposite bank. The wind was literally *pushing* millions of tons of water up against the opposite bank and holding it there!'

The drive further north revealed towns that had suffered a far less entertaining night. I confess that I'd thought seeing the broken trees and bruised buildings of the post-Yasi coast would be quite exciting, but the destruction was so great that it just made us sad. We progressed north from Townsville in the hottest, stillest, most humid weather any of us had ever experienced. Just drawing breath broke a sweat and even the locals were complaining of the heat, so it was strange to see the results of such violently opposite weather.

First there appeared the occasional uprooted tree or pile of debris, which we eagerly pointed out to the kids and explained where we were in relation to where the eye of the storm had been. But further north, driving through miles and miles of 'post apocalyptic' smashed up woodland - *millions* of trees broken, bent, stripped of all their leaves and almost all their branches - the drama lost its lustre. When we reached Cardwell, the seaside town that was the first to face the most ferocious winds at the eye of the Category 5 cyclone, our hearts sank. Lives were going on, a few shops were open again, and diggers steadily cleared up the wreckage, but all around were the scars of what must have been a terrifying night. Roofs had been peeled away - and not just flimsy tin roofs; proper, substantial, fairly recent looking buildings had had entire sections wrenched away. Sometimes a complete corner would be missing, leaving a ragged edge and then a rickety half-house still standing, as if the storm had got its teeth into anything it could and ripped it up like an angry dog. Saddest were the ghost houses that were now nothing but footings at ground level, alongside them a large heap of bricks, beams, furniture and once loved possessions – among the rubble we'd glimpse bookshelves, a baby's high-chair, a fridge, chaotic shattered glimpses into what had once been a home, bulldozed into place for future collection.

'It's a miracle no one died,' we muttered more than once.

We stopped in Tully, another of Yasi's worst hit towns, figuring that at least we could stick a bit of money in their economy by buying some lunch. A friendly woman got chatting to us in the street after commenting on Penny. Beyond the usual pleasantries about our trip, where we were from and Penny being left-hand drive - a *major* attraction in Australia - we asked how things were going. She explained that she'd spent the night of the cyclone with her entire family and a few friends sheltering in the bakery we were standing next to.

'It's much safer than home,' she said. 'I knew our house would get hit hard being high up on the hillside.' She pointed up the street towards the sloping hill of broken trees dotted with distant houses that looked like they were wearing neatly tied blue tarpaulin bonnets.

'Was it damaged?' I asked.

'Yeah. Went back the next morning and the roof was gone.'

'That must have been upsetting,' I said. Stating the obvious is a skill of mine.

'Well, no one was hurt,' she shrugged. 'We'll get it repaired. We've got somewhere to stay until then. Everyone pulls together here, which is great.'

'It's one day at a time,' chipped in her friend, another mum with teenage kids in tow. 'Some days I think "Why me? Why not their house?" but you've just got to get on with it. What else can you do?'

'Reckon we'll move though, once the house is fixed up,' said the first woman. I looked surprised. 'Oh yeah,' she went on. 'We used to live down in Victoria. Came up here for the weather.' She realised what she'd said and they both laughed.

'Well you bloody well got that!' said her mate.

It was all very humbling, and I was secretly glad they didn't ask about the Beatnik Beatles logo on Penny. I felt that saying we were busking The Beatles as we drove around the world would sound rather trite when talking to people who'd just had their home ripped apart. I fleetingly considered some sort of benefit concert but then remembered it wasn't 1985, I wasn't Bob Geldof and we weren't actually very good. So I nipped that thought in the bud and instead chose to benefit a local caff by buying a splendid all-day breakfast.

Long, long before all this, before cyclones, before brake-failures, before Penny had even left Blighty's shores, we had all, of course, discussed our trip at some length. A recurring theme was 'what are you looking forward to the most?' and it's pertinent that I now share these with you. Not only is it an insight into each of our personalities, but it teaches us a worthy truth: as Mick Jagger sang (and George Michael later stole), you can't always get what you want.

Bethan wanted to see glow-worms while floating through caves in New Zealand. I wanted to see Pondicherry, for its faded French colonial grandeur, which we never did because by the time we were in Chennai and within a four-hour drive of Pondicherry, we couldn't face a four-*minute* drive. Edie wanted to see a tornado in Kansas. Jill wanted to see Barry Manilow in Vegas.

See? Told you you'd learn something about us. Ella was the first to get her wish: to snorkel on the Great Barrier Reef.

On the advice of some of Jill's extended family, we found ourselves in Airlie Beach for our leaping off point to explore one of the seven wonders of the natural world. For once, Queensland's extreme weather played into our hands. One of the effects of the blanket media coverage of cyclone Yasi's destruction was a severe dip in Queensland's tourism. This was normally the time of year when holidaymakers from the chilly south made their annual road-trip north to enjoy the Sunshine Coast, and this year, they just weren't coming.

Having found a campsite, we trundled Penny into the little seaside town and pulled up outside a travel agent advertising snorkelling excursions to the outer reef. 'Hey look,' said Jill. 'They're doing a deal.' Recently painted in large letters on the shop window were the words '2 for 1 reef trips'. Perhaps that portion of our credit card reserved for this day wouldn't be too dented after all.

'That two-for-one deal,' I asked the travel agent girl, nonchalantly leafing through the glossy leaflet she'd handed me. 'Does that include the kids?'

'Yeah, I reckon.'

'So we could get two adults, and three kids for the price of one adult and two kids.'

'Yep,' she confirmed with a sunny smile.

And so the following morning we boarded a huge catamaran for the two-hour high-powered blast out into the Coral Sea. None of us had realised quite how 'outer' the outer reef was, but between the cups of coffee and juice to drink, and endless piles of buttered toast to get through, we were kept fairly occupied. It was also a chance for the firm who organised the trip to explain some basic safety rules of snorkelling – rule one, don't inhale sea-water – and also suggest a few other ways to spend your cash, sorry, enjoy this unique once-in-a-lifetime experience.

The big draw was in those five letters that are the key to another world: SCUBA. For a 110 bucks, first timers could be fast-tracked through their Level One SCUBA course to enjoy an assisted dive to 15 metres below the surface, exploring parts of the reef untroubled by those mere snorkellers overhead. I was tempted. I was also about 200 dollars *up* on the deal thanks to Yasi's depressing effect on ticket sales.

'Ella?' I enquired. 'You know it's your birthday in a couple of weeks … ?' You can guess the rest. Soon Ella and I (well, she wouldn't do it without her dad, obviously) were sitting at the front of the boat being drilled through our preliminary SCUBA training. A theory exam was taken, passed, and suddenly we were certified to take our first instructed dive.

Anchored far out at sea is a large purpose-built pontoon complete with restaurant, changing rooms, a full team of dive instructors, bar staff and a chef. It floats above an area of the reef that I couldn't help feeling must get a bit of a battering from the constant conveyer-belt of clumsy tourist snorkellers. As you would hope, visitors are under strict instructions not to touch the delicate coral beneath the water's surface, but our experience was that as the sea level dropped with the tide you simply couldn't help clunking into it from time to time. We reasoned that the authorities had probably figured that the best way of protecting the Great Barrier Reef was to do just that – protect it, or at least 99 per cent of it. Diving was prohibited on most of the reef, so I suppose that by directing everybody to a small section of the 1,500-mile-long living organism, any damage inflicted in that tiny area is a small sacrifice for the greater good.

We donned our quite fetching all-over 'stinger suits' that would protect us from jellyfish and also make us look like the animated super-hero family, *The Incredibles*, and while Jill, Beth and Edie were handed flippers, snorkels and facemasks and took their first tentative dip, Ella and I were further kitted up in wet suits, huge air-tanks and all the necessary pipes, dials and valves that make up Self Contained Underwater Breathing Apparatus.

Descending a set of steep, metal grille steps in the centre of the pontoon, we found they continued beneath the sea into an underwater classroom. Two instructors ensured we were breathing happily through our mouthpieces, and sat eight of us eager divers down on an underwater bench, where we were each required to pass a few essential underwater SCUBA tests – clearing the mask, removing the mouthpiece, unblocking it, etc. One unfortunate hopeful couldn't grasp one of these procedures and never did get their dive. But Ella and I were lucky. We were given the green light and, with our instructor, Ness, and just one other diver, were guided further down through an opening in the floor and into the depths of the wide-open sea beyond.

At first, students are led along tight underwater cables that run alongside the vertical walls of the reef, so that they always have something to grab hold of for a bit of extra security, but we hadn't realised that the bloke who was the third diver in our group of three was a mate of Ness's. After just a couple of minutes underwater, she beckoned us all away from the 'learner line' and we were off. This was one of the most exciting things I'd ever done, and I'd describe my mood as one of breathless glee but for the fact that I was so ardently sticking to Rule One of SCUBA diving: breathe.

As we explored, Ness would stop occasionally and write words on a small, ingenious, underwater wipe board she carried. 'Moray Eel' she wrote, pointing to the large fearsome face of the slippery fellow poking from a dark hole in the reef. We swam further, seeing bright blue brain coral, schools of tiny sparkling fish that moved in beautiful synchronicity, exotic looking fish as big as your head and delicately wafting anemones. Waving us down to join her, she pointed to a thick bunch of translucent anemone tubes, gracefully shimmering in the current. 'Nemo!' she wrote, and waved her arms as if to shout 'Yay!' Enthralled we watched five bright clown-fish weave in and out of the tentacles.

I'd heard people describe tropical diving as finding another world, and I could see why. There was just so much *life* down there, none of it betrayed by the placid-looking water at the surface. The reef, which is roughly 9,000 years old, is the largest structure ever made by life on Earth. It's home to an incredible diversity of life: 5,000 types of molluscs, 1,800 species of fish and 125 kinds of sharks. I was hoping we might see a reef shark, but they're shy and tend to keep their distance. What we all noticed were the sections of the reef that were bleached. These dead areas are caused by warming sea temperature and rising levels of acidity, a deathly combination for coral, caused by increasing CO_2 emissions.

I'm telling you that because it's fact, but saying it in Australia might have got me beaten up. In the country that boasts the highest carbon footprint per capita in the world, carbon emissions, and their link to climate change and environmental damage, is highly-debated. Those who deny the link are plentiful. Research scientists receive death threats and have round-the-clock protection. Some of my own (less dangerous) research revealed that many scientists predict the Great Barrier Reef will be dead by 2050. If you think that's alarmist, consider this: since the mid-90s, mass bleaching has killed 90 *per cent* of coral in the Indian Ocean. It's already happening on the Great Barrier Reef, so if you want to see this natural wonder, get on with it. Meanwhile, buy a smaller car and switch some lights off.

I can only have that little rant with hindsight. I confess that on the day we were nothing short of thrilled by what we saw. That 45-minute dive fulfilled Ella's wish, and then some. After meeting the others for lunch, and then spending another couple of hours snorkelling around the surface, we were beaten by the tide and it was time to head for shore. We'd had such fun, seen incredible things none of us would forget, and Ella and I both came away vowing to get our full SCUBA licence so we could dive together in further exotic locations.

'And that's your problem, right there,' said Jill. 'You've just experienced one of the top dive locations in the *world*. Where do you go from here? The deep end of Banbury swimming pool just won't cut it.' Maybe she was right. It was an amazing day. We found Nemo, for goodness sake! Maybe we should just leave it at that.

We arrived in Koah just ahead of North Queensland's third major weather event in as many months. Admittedly it didn't get as much attention as the Brisbane floods that had swamped the city before we arrived, or cyclone Yasi, but it was major enough to halt our journey for four days, before taking us to new and unexpected parts of Australia.

A day after we arrived at our northern most point in Oz, to stay with Leona's parents for a night at their secluded rainforest-lodge-on-stilts, a huge monsoon moved in from the east, and stalled over Cairns. Australians are more obsessed with the weather than us Brits (and given the extremes they face, you can see why), so almost everyone we met had a rain gauge in their garden. 'A hundred and thirty four millimetres last night,' said Leona's dad, Eric, as we gathered for breakfast.

'Wow! Glad we were sleeping indoors,' said Ella.

'Over 13 centimetres? In one night?' I queried, holding a finger approximately six inches off the table. 'That's … wow … a *lot* of water. Where's it all gone?'

With his wife Kath, they led us down to the fierce, roaring river that yesterday had been a gentle brook at the foot of their land. Now it was three times the width and half way up the surrounding trees. To put 134 millimetres of rain in context, in the UK in June 2007, large parts of the country saw historic, devastating floods, most memorably in Yorkshire and Tewkesbury. The rainfall that June was twice the monthly average – 140 millimetres. In a *month*. Yes, a lot of it fell on one day, but the most that was recorded was a shade over a hundred millimetres. Even the weather-hardened Aussies were going to struggle to shrug off almost six inches of rain in a night.

Sure enough, our main trunk road south – the Bruce Highway – was out, under water and impassable in several places. 'Don't worry,' said Kath, as we gazed forlornly at the TV news. 'We've got plenty of food. Stay another night and we'll check it again tomorrow.' So our massive north-to-south, Cairns to Melbourne road trip was put on hold, but it was really no hardship. The landscape around Koah is incredible, and the chance to stay for an extra day, or as it turned out, three, was an unexpected treat. The terrain is dense rainforest, the aboriginals called it Din Din, which thrives around the Barron river, with the Barron Falls at its heart. This rainforest, I was amazed to learn, is the oldest continually surviving rainforest on Earth. Stick that in your Amazonian pipe, South America. It was also the *second* UNESCO World Heritage natural wonder we'd visited in a week.

A wander through the damp, hot forest to see the point at which the waters of the Barron drop over a massive vertical rocky descent was like stepping into a lost world. Pythons inhabited heather basket clumps high up in the gum trees. Just inches from our path, a scary spider as big as my outstretched hand – shiny, black bony legs and bright red mandibles - sat quietly waiting for the next victim to become tangled in her web - an albatross, or light aircraft judging by the size of the thing.

The previous night's colossal storm had attracted people into the forest to see the effect on the swollen river. We could hear the waterfall long before we could see it. In fact, we could *feel* it. The massive bass rumble shook the air and vibrated through our chests. When we saw it, we soon joined in the chorus of the few locals there saying, 'Whoa!' quite a lot. 'I've lived here 20 years,' one man told me, 'and I've never seen it like this.' I nodded, impressed. 'Seen the old girl dry plenty of times,' he added, which seemed even more unimaginable, as we stood drenched in her mist and deafened by her roar.

Eventually it was clear that the Bruce Highway would remain closed for some time, and that the flooding between us in the north and our rendezvous with *The Beatles Experience* tribute band further south in Mackay was much worse than first thought. Cardwell, one of the small towns on our route, and a community already battered by Yasi, was deluged with 212 millimetres of rain in one day. Keep those statistics I told you about the UK floods in mind: the little Aussie seaside town had *double* the UK's entire 'catastrophic June' rainfall *in a day*. Now brace yourself. While the monsoon stalled, and continued to dump its rain, the weather statisticians in tiny Cardwell, heroes that they are, measured over a *half a metre* of rainfall in five days. It's almost incomprehensible, but it happened. Welcome to sunny Australia.

With a schedule to keep, we waved goodbye to Eric and Kath after imposing on their hospitality for three more nights than they'd expected, and headed south via the much longer inland route to avoid the flooded coast road. By this point in our trip we'd once again started using sat-nav, simply because, for the first time since leaving France, we had individual addresses to find, which would have been impossible with the kind of road maps we'd used over the last five months. As we left Mareeba, the nearest town to rural Koah, the trusty screen perched on Penny's dashboard instructed us to turn left. The countdown to the next instruction showed the figure '540'. Assuming it was indicating the usual 'metres' I did a double take when it didn't click down as we drove. 'Er … I think we can turn this off,' I laughed. 'The next instruction is in 540 *kilometres*.'

And the sat-nav didn't lie. We did the longest, most boring drive of our entire year that day. Ten hours of nothing but scrub-land, a single gas-station where we bought Pot Noodles for lunch, a single sighting of some wild emus, and that was it. Oh, apart from the periodic drama of The Road Train. These inland routes across Oz are used by massive multi-trailer trucks which, despite their size, travel very fast and have right-of-way over everything and anything in their path. Not that you'd ever pick a fight with one. Road warning signs show a silhouette of a huge Road Train in the centre of the road, with a small car tipping off into the verge, to indicate that it's the car driver's job to get off the tarmac when the stampeding, hulking beast approaches. So we did, and we lived.

As we approached our destination, Charters Towers, we had a puncture. Before you ask, yes, Jill *was* driving. That was three out of three – she'd got her hat trick. Charters Towers is a small gold-mining town which, in its late 1800s heyday, was Queensland's second largest town after Brisbane. It still had the charm of one of those 'wild west' prospector towns, so much so that Edie said, 'It looks like you could push the front of the buildings and they'd fall over like a film set.'

In olden days, Charters used to have the nickname 'The World' because its people boasted you could get anything in the world there and would never have to leave. I can confirm that by 2010, getting a tyre at five in the afternoon was impossible. We camped, and first thing in the morning splashed out on two brand new boots for Penny's front-end, finally replacing the last of her original German tyres that must have dated back at least a decade. Then, having travelled far enough south to pass all the flooding, it was off towards the east coast again where we had an appointment to keep.

Meeting up with a professional Beatles tribute band was the brainchild of Jill's Aunty Jen. (By this point she had so many new family members that they were all referred to as cousins or aunties - even the men). She happened to notice that a Beatles tribute band was performing at the MECC, Mackay's theatre and concert venue, on the Thursday. We worked out that we'd be passing back through the town on the same day, so I phoned their manager and arranged to meet them. Even before setting off from home, I'd hoped to find a Beatles tribute band somewhere on our travels, figuring there must be hundreds of them around the world. India would have been best, I thought, not least for the comedy of the Bhangra Beatles, but it wasn't to be. In India, as we now know, beetles are for eating.

The Beatles Experience were playing the penultimate gig of their three-week tour and had agreed we could pop in and say hello after their sound-check at about 4.30 in the afternoon. We only just made it, after our slog from Charters, but as the stage manager showed us into the auditorium all our stress evaporated as we gasped and cooed at the stage set - the instruments, the amps and even the microphones were all authentic replicas of those belonging to the band that had shaped our journey. I suppose because of the era of the music, I expected four middle aged blokes to appear, so when four young lads sauntered from the wings, none of them looking more than about 22 years of age, I thought the roadies had come to ask us to leave.

'Hi, great to meet you,' said one, shaking my hand. 'I'm Paul.'

'I'm John,' said the next.

'George.'

'Ringo,' added the last. A skinny, lofty lad of about 19 who I couldn't possibly believe would be singing *Yellow Submarine* to a packed house in just a few hours. I recorded an interview with them for the radio, and quickly realised that the distances these boys were covering - they'd driven *themselves* to Alice Springs, three days there, three days back, for their opening gig - meant that this was clearly a young man's game as those of us past a certain age might say. The promotion company that puts on these tribute shows obviously wants guys with bags of energy and as few ties as possible to allow them to tour Oz, New Zealand, South Africa, then Canada ...

'Are you coming to England?' I asked. There was laughter from the band.

'God no,' smiled Dirk (John). 'They'd be *far* too demanding an audience!'

They were absolutely brilliant with the girls, asking about the trip, talking to Edie about Beatles songs, giving tips on busking. 'Just have fun,' said Jeremy (Paul), 'because if you keep smiling no one cares how bad you are!'

As much as we were in awe of their ability to play properly to packed houses, they seemed to hold us in as much admiration, saying how cool our trip was and how much respect they had for us being brave enough to busk. Most agonising was that, after we'd all got on so well for half an hour, they offered us tickets for that evening's show.

'Oh, no,' I grimaced. 'I'm really sorry, but we've got plans.' Their faces fell, so I explained that a family get-together had been planned by Aunty Jen so we could meet *even more* Moodys. People were travelling to meet us. We simply had to decline, which broke all our hearts just a little as they'd been so kind.

'Well in that case,' piped up Jeremy, 'Why don't we play for you now?'

While we all chorused 'Really?' 'Wow', and 'Yes please!' they checked the sound and lighting crew were happy to do a run through of their 20-minute 'Hippy' segment of the show, and then said to us, 'Would you like us in costume?'

'Listen mate, it's your time,' I replied. 'We're just chuffed to be here.'

'Right, back in a mo,' they chirped, and they were off, only to reappear not just in full Sergeant Pepper regalia, but wigged up too. We sat in the stalls and sang along to our own private performance of *Come Together, Don't Let Me Down, Lucy In The Sky With*

Diamonds, *Let It Be*, and *Sergeant Pepper's Lonely Hearts Club Band*. The evidence of their skill proved Dirk's earlier comment about a UK audience to be modesty. They were not only very tight as a band, but they sounded damned close to the original and looked that way too. I was very impressed that anyone as young as Jeremy could master McCartney's bass playing while singing those melodies at the same time. I know, I know, McCartney was only his age when *he* did it, but … he was *Paul McCartney*. Edd-with-a-double-d had nailed George's tricky guitar parts and Adam even had Ringo's head wobble down to a tee. They thought they ought to do *Strawberry Fields* for us as that was our destination, so gave us a great version of that too.

As we were saying our goodbyes, Jeremy said, 'Wait! We didn't do *Ob-La-Di*!' We'd talked in our interview about how well the song went live, compared to the original, rather staid recording, and we'd told them that we enjoyed busking it too. So he called the crew back and we all sang through *Ob-La–Di* together. We were utterly blown away by their kindness and generosity with their time, and, for what it was worth, gave them a big plug on the blog, urging readers in NZ and Canada to beat a path to the door of their local theatre when the boys were in town. As a small post-script to the story, Jeremy continued to stay in touch, and followed our journey all the way to the end.

We bounced back to Brissy via a brief stopover at Hervey Bay, where friends-of-friends, Ali and Clyde, had responded to our *Put Us Up Down Under* plea. Their home was Kent in England, but they were embracing an ex-pat life on the Queensland coast for a few years due to Clyde's job. It was a typically English affair: Marmite in the cupboard, boardgames with their kids and a barbecue under brollies in the rain. What could be more British?

The three-day pause in Brissy, ahead of our second big Aussie road trip, was a whirlwind of admin. It was time to look ahead to America.

I was amazed there was a roll-on-roll-off car ferry across the Pacific. Even more amazingly, it was marginally cheaper than shipping Penny in a container, so that was the van sorted. We would fly, so booked our tickets to Los Angeles and, because USA Homeland Security doesn't allow visitors to arrive on a one-way ticket without proof of onward travel, we also booked our flights from New York home to the UK. This was a little alarming. None of us wanted to think about going home, and yet there were essential jobs that needed doing concerning our return. We applied for the girls' school places, and very quickly had confirmation that Edie had been accepted back into her primary school, so she was elated. Getting Ella and Beth back into their secondary school would prove slightly more stressful.

When we had realised we needed to book our homeward flights from New York, we decided to return in time for the last week of the school term. This was a month earlier than we had originally anticipated, but was deemed necessary for several reasons. One was money. We were running out of cash and credit and didn't think we could stretch it all the way into August. Jill contacted her manager at the BBC who was happy for her to return a month earlier than planned, which meant our cash flow on arriving home would be much more bearable. Another reason for an earlier return was my Mum. She would have just finished her chemotherapy by July so we wanted to spend some of the school summer holidays down in Devon with my parents. And a final reason was that by going back to school for the final week of term, the girls could get all that centre of attention spotlight out of the way, and return after the summer break without feeling quite so nervous – especially for Bethan who had not yet set foot in her secondary school.

Communicating all this to Oxfordshire School Admissions Department was quite a challenge. Jill had been in email contact with a woman there since February, yet here we were in mid-April, booking our homeward flights, and still there was no confirmation that Ella and Beth had school places to go back to. The risk that we'd been prepared to take, of the girls not being able to return to their schools, was looking ever more foolhardy.

Again, Jill threw herself into the email equivalent of banging her head against a wall, trying to get the rather obstructive county council employee to process our application forms and confirm the girls' places. What was annoying was that the school in question, The Warriner, had been fantastically supportive of our trip. Teachers had taken time to set work for *both* the girls, and mark it too, which was quite above and beyond their call of duty as neither Ella nor Beth was even on the school register. But we weren't dealing with the school itself. Decisions about places are controlled centrally. All the same, Jill cc'd the email to our contact at The Warriner, the super-supportive Deputy Head (who we only knew as Mr Jordan), and we would wait and see. 'It'll be fine,' I kept reassuring Ella, who was particularly concerned that she would see her friends and familiar teachers again.

'It's just bureaucracy,' explained Jill. 'I'm sure it'll get sorted.' Privately, we both had everything crossed. Having to explain to the girls that they were starting back in a completely new school was *not* a conversation I relished.

Another tough grapple we'd had throughout the couple of weeks leading up to our Brissy 'admin break' was reaching the decision not to go to New Zealand. We realised that the flight costs, plus car hire and accommodation (even with some generous offers from *Put Us Up Down Under* friends) would put a £3,000 dent in our budget. Unsurprisingly, almost eight months into our journey, cash was running low and we calculated that visiting NZ, though possible, would be at the cost of getting across America. That was a trade we seriously considered. 'We could go to New Zealand,' Jill had pointed out, 'and return to Australia with our visas re-set for another three months. That's what happens when you leave and re-enter the country.'

'Then what?' I asked.

'Then we do another three months here, and then go home.' She meant it, too. She loved Oz, and genuinely wasn't too bothered about driving across America. 'I'd regret not seeing Ty in Kansas,' she admitted. 'But we can't do everything. We just don't have the cash.'

This wrangle had twisted and turned in our minds all the way from Cairns down to Brisbane, until I persuaded Jill and the girls that the draw of driving across the USA was simply too great. 'Honestly, you will love it,' I enthused. 'I feel awful about not taking you all to NZ, especially as I've been before and always said I'd take you all. But … America! Are we really prepared to trade that? The one, final leg of the journey? It completes the lap. Liverpool to New York.'

'I suppose it's good to have a country we can plan to visit after we get home,' suggested Beth, searching for a silver lining. The girls were convinced, but I think Jill preferred her plan of an extended stay down under. Whether her opinion could be changed was up to the star-spangled charms that lay 7,000 miles across the Pacific Ocean. So, like Thailand, Malaysia and Singapore before it, New Zealand became a casualty of cash flow - a land to be explored another day. If you're inspired to take on a journey such as ours, heed this lesson: stay flexible and be prepared to let some places go. You can't always get what you want.

On St Patrick's Day, the morning of Ella's birthday, we re-packed Penny and headed south. Ella spent the afternoon in the sea at Surfer's Paradise, which isn't a bad way to spend your 14th birthday, even though the only campsite we could find was little more than a fairly grim car park, overlooked by high-rises all around. Surfer's Paradise is the southernmost beach resort in Queensland before crossing into New South Wales, and seems completely at odds with most of Australia's east coast, in that it's completely built-up and over-developed. Lacking in any charm, or palpable 'big-town' buzz, it simply felt like a small seaside town that had sprawled, and one whose planning authorities had been blinded by dollar signs and thus green-lit any concrete, multi-storey monstrosity which passed under their rubber stamp.

We were pleased to move on into a new state the next day. 'I'm quite glad it didn't work out with Brenda and Michael,' Jill said as we found the open coast road. 'Only because I wouldn't have wanted to hang around there.' Before we'd left England we discovered some friends, Brenda and Michael, were planning a rather luxurious holiday touring Australia, and we'd worked out we might all be in the country at the same time.

'As soon as we have a firm idea of our plans, we'll be in touch,' we had said to each other. Emails followed and, yes, remarkably it appeared we *may* be able to meet somewhere on the east coast, although they were on a strict 'tour party' itinerary so not as flexible as we were. At one point it looked as if we could meet around Ella's birthday in Surfer's Paradise, but then the various flood related hold-ups meant they wouldn't be there. A hurried phone call from a public call-box was the last contact we'd had, confirming that they would be further south than us, and it just wasn't going to happen.

But then it did. Two hours after we left Surfer's Paradise, we bumped into them in Byron Bay. We were pootling through the town in Penny wondering where the beach was, when Jill screamed. I mean *properly* screamed. I thought, at the very least, that a Hunstman spider must have leapt on to her face. As I looked across I saw a woman waving manically at us while rushing into the road. That was our friend Brenda, then, with hubby Michael and two baffled friends in tow. We later learned that, on seeing our van, she had just said to her friends, 'That's the sort of van Sim and Jill have got,' then had spotted the Beatnik Beatles logo and gone momentarily apoplectic.

The coincidence really was enormous. They were only in Byron Bay for two hours, the coach having stopped to allow them a coffee break. We had just got there, neither party had mentioned the place to the other, and yet, in a town as bustling as that, and in a country as *big* as that ... We shared a coffee, swapped stories and basically shook our heads in baffled amazement.

After parting, we bounced from one surreal moment to another. Still unsure about whether to spend the night in Byron Bay, we parked at the beach, made some sandwiches for lunch and sat down on some large boulders, facing the beach and the surf below, to tuck in. A man a few metres away from us reached down into the rocks and appeared to be grappling to retrieve something that was stuck. We watched, intrigued, and then alarmed, as he pulled a five-foot long carpet snake from the rocks. This appeared to be for no other reason than to impress his highly excitable girlfriend who shrieked with delight, held out her mobile phone and took lots of pictures of the tattooed brawn proudly holding the large snake. 'Deep down, all Aussie blokes want to be Steve Irwin,' I mused dismissively, demonstrating how easily I can belittle these macho acts of bravado.

'How's your poorly chest, petal?' Jill teased.

'I've still got a bit of a cough, as you ask. Not that you'll hear me mention it because I'm too brave for that.' I felt sorry for the snake, a relatively benign constrictor with no venom, yanked from its hiding place where it wasn't doing any harm to anyone. I could have made my feelings clear, of course, but the chap was bigger than me - and he was holding a massive angry snake. I may be a coward, but I'm no fool.

As our 'miles since Liverpool' clicked over 12,500, we drove through Liverpool again. Australia does that - keeps throwing British place names at you as if to prove the early settlers' exploration skills far outweighed their creativity with names. 'Hey there, sailor!' Captain Cook must have shouted. 'From where do you hail?'

'Cumbria, sir.'

And so he went through his crew. Able Seaman Scouser, Midshipman Suggs, even Petty Officers Ant and Dec must have had a say. How else would our map of New South Wales now boast Penrith, Liverpool, Camden and Newcastle?

Liverpool is a suburb of Sydney, Australia's most populous city. But it was our journey *to* the state capital, rather than the city itself, that proved most memorable. We were due to meet *Put Us Up Down Under* volunteers, Kerrie and James from the cooking class in Rajasthan, who were now back home somewhere near Coffs Harbour. On the way there, we stopped in a little town called Grafton. It was a pretty town with a plentiful supply of charming 'gold rush' shop fronts and homes - those late 19th century buildings you see in wild west films. We stopped for lunch at the levee, which, as anyone who's ever driven a Chevy to one will know, is a slope or bank holding in a large body of water - in this case the Clarence River.

Edie and I settled down at a picnic table to make some sandwiches for us all, and the only other people we shared the place with was a lady sitting at the table sipping a take-out coffee and gazing across the water, and a bunch of boys down at the riverside having a whale of a time. Some fished from the pontoon, some dived and swam, and some, to our great amusement, rode a bicycle off the end before pulling it back up from the depths with a handily attached rope. 'Have you seen what they're doing?' asked Edie after she'd seen the first mighty splash.

'Cool,' I replied. 'Why did I never do that as a kid?'

'Would you do that?'

'Oh come on, Edie. Surely everyone, deep down, wants to know how it feels to ride a bike off a jetty and plunge into the water, don't they?' She thought about it, then grinned and nodded.

'I'm sure if you ask them they'll let you have a go,' smiled the lady sitting opposite us. She was in her late 40s, smartly dressed with tidy blonde hair and a warm smile. 'Where are you from?'

'England,' Edie replied, politely. And so our conversation with this woman started its familiar pattern – how we'd got to Australia, which countries we'd liked the most and how the girls kept up with schoolwork. Soon Jill joined us and the lady introduced herself. She was called Anne and had come down to the river because it was the anniversary of her mother's death and she wanted to float a rose on the water and quietly remember her. She was waiting for the river to be less full of flying bicycle. This unexpected topic of conversation seemed to trigger Jill to talk to this complete stranger about some very difficult things.

Soon we were spilling our guts about our Kansas friend Lisa's death a few weeks earlier. Then my Mum's cancer treatment came up. We must have sounded like we needed therapy. Soon Anne was telling us all about herself and her mother and it was as if we'd known each other five years rather than five minutes.

Having said that, it was still a big surprise when, ten minutes later, she invited us to stay at her house for the night. Even Jill, normally the first to say, 'We'd love to,' looked a little unsure.

'Why don't you phone your husband and check with him?' she suggested. And Anne agreed that that was probably a good idea. Dave, it transpired, was fine with a family of five landing on them at no notice.

'And you won't have to camp,' said Anne. 'We've got plenty of room in the house.' As if to cement the deal, it started raining.

'A night indoors would be very welcome indeed,' I said glancing at the grey skies. 'Thank you.'

Anne and Dave had moved to Grafton from Sydney a year earlier, in search of countryside and a more leisurely pace of life. Dave had worked 'in the grog game', supplying drinks to major events – he was the guy who got the 'rider' for all those rock bands that came through Sydney. 'Did you have to provide M&Ms with all the blue ones removed?' I asked, jokingly.

'Oh yeah, and lots worse than M&Ms too,' he nodded. But the workdays got longer, the stress got greater, and he figured a heart attack and quadruple bypass were probably his cue to change gear and move to the country.

And what an idyllic life they forged. Dave worked fewer hours, they bought a picture-postcard house overlooking endless countryside and they threw themselves into the community. 'We've started a Sunday afternoon thing at the local hotel - Muso's Corner,' explained Anne. 'An open mic session for local musicians. We're playing tomorrow, actually.'

'You're musicians?' I asked, excitedly.

It turned out they had met playing in bands in the 70s and had never really stopped. The first room they showed us when we got to their house was a small bedroom that was now their home studio. A genuine Hammond organ hogged the space alongside its perfect partner, an authentic Leslie speaker, complete with motors, pulleys and belts to spin its treble and bass horns. I was in heaven, eagerly explaining to the girls how this vintage speaker achieved the tremolo effect by physically spinning the speaker horn. 'It's like the Doppler effect of a car horn going past you, but again and again, every second. Genius.'

'The Hammond's Anne's domain,' said Dave. 'I play guitars, mostly.' He nodded to the various axes leaning against the wall.

'Is that a Dobro?' I asked, picking up the metallic resonator guitar made famous by Mark Knopfler, Johnny Cash and a myriad of blues-men before them.

'Here, take a seat,' he offered, and plugged the guitar into an amp.

'Have you got a …' I gestured my left ring-finger, searching for the word.

'Slide.' He handed me the finger length chrome tube essential for all budding blues-men. The guitar was tuned to an open D chord, so within a few seconds even an enthusiastic monkey could sound like he knew what he as doing, and an enthusiastic monkey did.

'Oh man, I have *got* to get one of these,' I gushed. Jill rolled her eyes.

'Take a look in here,' beckoned Dave, warming to my enthusiasm. He showed me a battered hard guitar case bearing faded shipping-line stickers. Opening the case was like pulling a dust cover off a shadowy object at the back of a garage, and finding a vintage Ferrari under it. Nestled in the fake-fur lining was a 1961 Fender Stratocaster. Red, of course. It had aged beautifully. Its head-stock had a dark amber hue that new guitars never have. Anne had saved up weeks and weeks of wages back in the 70s and bought the guitar for Dave from a musician who'd emigrated to Oz (hence the shipping stickers) and wanted $150 for it. Its value since then had gone, aptly, stratospheric. Dave still played it every other Sunday at the hotel and it sounded awesome.

We were due a band practice so produced our own humble instruments (total value - £100) and set to on polishing our act a bit. They seemed to love it and Anne said those fateful words, 'Won't you stick around tomorrow and play up at the hotel?'

And so the small gathering of regulars at The Australian Hotel enjoyed (or is that endured) a memorable half-hour of Beatnik Beatles shenanigans. We got them singing along, had a lot of fun, and played our first public performance of *Penny Lane*, which gained an extra round of applause halfway through for Ella, who tackled the almost-impossible trumpet solo on her flute. We also raised over 40 bucks for UNICEF, thanks to their generosity. The entire 24 hours had been remarkable, and we promised to pop in and see Anne and Dave again on our way back up Australia in a week or two.

We found Kerrie and James and had a great evening reminiscing about India. It was cathartic to be able to speak so honestly about the place to people who knew what we were talking about. Until then, we hadn't felt we could share the full nitty-gritty with people because, first, it was all so alien to life in Australia that it would sound far-fetched, and second, because it would just sound like we were moaning. But Kerrie and James had had almost as many experiences with dodgy deals and corrupt back-handers as we had, so we spent a happy few hours laughing and swapping tales over a good Aussie barbecue, before settling down in Penny to camp on their drive.

Soon, we were in Sydney. We stayed on the outskirts in Bankstown, camping on a friend of a friend's driveway, and took the train in to enjoy one great day in the city. We headed for the famous harbour, took the ferry to Manly (a brilliant way to take in Sydney's famous waterside view), ate fish and chips on magnificent Manly beach, returned to the harbour to see the Annie Leibovitz exhibition at the MCA – 'Every day's a school day, kids' - and took about 4,000 photographs of a bridge and an opera house.

As dusk fell the harbour lit up. Smartly dressed opera-goers thronged the waterfront, the restaurants swelled, and as the cruise-ship holidaymakers returned to their berths to dress for dinner aboard the enormous *Rhapsody of the Sea*, moored in the most prestigious parking spot in the world, we all wished we were doing the same and not having to return in our smelly clothes to camp in Penny.

Sydney is stunning, of that there's no doubt. But as we boarded the train back out to Bankstown where our own *Rhapsody of the Roads* was moored, I reflected on how it's the people that we'll remember a place by. We didn't get to know any local Sydney-dwellers, so my only impression of the place is that of a sightseer - probably the same impression as that formed by the occupants of the leviathan in the harbour. 'What's Sydney like?' friends ask.

'Stunning,' I reply. End of conversation. But get me on the subject of a little town called Grafton, and there's no stopping me.

As every eager school child knows, because it's a classic 'catch you out' quiz question, Canberra is Australia's capital. Not Sydney. Not Melbourne. And that's why Canberra exists. Sydney and Melbourne had such a battle over which city ought to be the capital that it almost led to civil war. To avert the crisis, a truce was called and everyone agreed that a brand new city would be built halfway between the two. It even has its own mini-state: the Australia Capital Territory.

The A.C.T. is basically, just Canberra. This is where Australia's government sits, where all the Ministry departments are and where all the big decisions are made. As it resides in its own territory, it also has its own state laws. Curiously, it's the state with the loosest restrictions on the sale of fireworks, alcohol and pornography. Politicians, eh?

We stayed on a peculiar campsite on the edge of Canberra that I suspected had once been a military camp that had been rapidly deserted after some clandestine nuclear testing in the 50s. We parked on the edge, so overlooked bush-land and saw our first rabbit in Australia. It looked pretty scrawny which may have been because my theory was true, and the land was harbouring toxic secrets from its past, or because Australia had waged a hundred year war on bunnies by unleashing a constant barrage of new and exciting strains of myxomatosis. The fact we only saw one rabbit in our 5,500-mile journey is probably an indication that the pest controllers were winning.

We froze overnight. The temperature dropped to about 11°C and we realised how acclimatised we'd become to the humid, sticky 30° temperatures of the north. We nicknamed the place Canbrrrrrrrrrrra, and regretted not packing thick socks and long trousers for our road trip south. Apart from a brief drive around its fastidiously planned and neatly groomed roads, we hadn't really planned to do much in the capital, figuring it was full of government offices and not really geared to tourists. That turned out to be completely wrong. Canberra can be a *great* day out, not least because it's all *free*!

Where else in the world can you drive straight up to the Parliament building, park outside and stroll in for a look around? (Well, Arab rebels were doing just that in Tripoli at the time, but discounting Middle Eastern uprisings, it's a rare privilege.) Australia is very proud of its new Parliament building. Its sweeping stone facade is built into a hillside, and the surrounding grass extends all the way across the roof as a deliberate design to emphasise that the Government doesn't look down on the people; the people look down on the Government. So to test the theory we found our way on to the roof and admired the views from *on top* of the nation's Parliament - something you could only do in England if you were a disgruntled Fathers For Justice dad with a head for heights and a Batman costume.

We wanted to visit the Australia Museum before we left Canberra but had a three-hour drive ahead of us if we were to keep to The Schedule (cue hollow laughter, for reasons that will soon become clear). Instead we took the shorter visit to Australia's Royal Mint. I was really keen to visit the Mint for two reasons: first, you can't visit the one in Britain. It's in South Wales somewhere, and I know they don't do tours because I once tried to do some TV filming there, and they were very cagey, almost as if they had something very precious they wanted to keep behind locked doors. The second and biggest reason we all wanted to visit Australia's Mint was because of the tag line on their tourist flyer. 'Australia's Royal Mint - it makes cents.'

A bottle of champagne for the wag who created that catch-line. Take the rest of the day off, your work is done. I mentioned this on our blog, suggesting that perhaps the reason Britain's Royal Mint is so grumpy is because their currency doesn't lend itself to pun-based slogans. The next day a witty reader called Nik posted a response: 'The Royal Mint – the change will do you good'.

The change didn't do us much good at the Aussie Mint because they weren't making any. The huge coin pressing machines lay dormant. Apparently they took Saturdays off - Australia had enough money. Actually, considering the Aussie dollar was at a 28 year high against the US dollar and Britain's feeble pound, they really *did* have enough money. We were finding the prices of day-to-day items like bread, drinks and snacks eye-wateringly expensive – about double the price we were used to back in the UK.

So, on with The Schedule, a set-in-stone itinerary created because Penny had an appointment back in Brisbane with a big ship that would take her to America. We had to be back in Brissie by 5th April, so that the shipping agent could take delivery of her on the morning of the 6th. I'd worked tirelessly in my planning office (Berners and Leona's loo) to create an itinerary that would get us down to Melbourne and back by the 5th, while along the way allowing us to meet lots of interesting new people who had volunteered to *Put Us Up Down Under*. This itinerary also just happened to get us to our southernmost city on something of a red letter day for motor sport fans.

After a two-day hit, splitting the eight-hour journey with a stopover near Albury, we found our way into the Richmond district of Melbourne and I parked Penny on a leafy drive. Knocking on the door of the smart 1930s town house, I found it ajar so pushed it open and shouted into the hallway. 'Hello?'

A tall, lanky man wearing a big grin bounded towards us. 'Hi! I'm Steve. Welcome to Melbourne.'

'Hello, I'm Sim. Can I put the telly on?'

Well, my introduction wasn't *quite* that rude, but Jill would tell you it was close. Through good fortune and wily planning we had arrived in Australia's second biggest city about 15 minutes before twenty-two Formula 1 cars launched themselves around Albert Park for the first race of the 2011 Grand Prix season.

We'd been invited to camp on the driveway of Steve and Megan's house. Steve had responded to our *Put Us Up Down Under* plea after being pointed to it by his brother, our local vicar, Ben. It was funny to notice that, despite the lack of contact between them, inevitable over a 10,000 mile gap, they shared the same boundless enthusiasm, mannerisms and excited, eager eyes – clearly gifted via their shared genes. We were all slightly taken aback that this complete stranger was so instantly familiar.

Richmond, we discovered, is a stylish suburb of Melbourne that had once been the hub of the leather and tannery industry. The only echo of its past was in the red-brick warehouses that were now plush apartments, and road names like Tanner Street that boasted some of the city's most sought-after terraced houses. 'The only "leather-work" you'll encounter round here today,' joked Steve, 'is shopping for designer shoes and bags.'

Furnished with a cup of tea, and flanked by an apologetic wife and a beaming host, I sat and watched the start of the race. The red lights went out, 22 drivers each gunned 20,000 horsepower of carbon fibre up a strip of tarmac, and the familiar screaming roar filled the room. And the back garden. The sound wasn't just coming from the TV.

'You can hear them?' I said in disbelief. The girls ran outside to confirm it. The blistering racket of those engines was echoing around the city.

'Do you want to drive down there?' asked Steve. 'We can get right next to the park.' I can watch motor racing anytime on the telly. It's not every day you get to be right next to one. So we jumped in Penny to go and take a closer look, and Steve, in the passenger seat, directed. 'Straight down - and left at the MCG.'

'*The* MCG?' I asked. '*That's* the MCG?' Melbourne Cricket Ground is not only a very famous sporting arena (home of the first Test Match, the first One Day International, the first Test century), but by 2010 had become even more famous as the home of AFL. Australian Rules Football - that peculiar not-quite-rugby, played-in-an-oval, late-night-on-satellite-TV thing is *huge* in Melbourne. Its popularity peters out further north, where Rugby League dominates, but its heartland is in Melbourne.

As we drove on, still admiring the stadium and its location so close to our hosts' house, another sports stadium loomed. 'There's the Rod Laver Arena,' nodded our guide.

'As in, tennis - the Australian Open?' I uttered, stunned. My brain was struggling to compute a land where you could live in such a lovely home and have all these major sporting venues on your doorstep. It would be like living in Oxford's Jericho, or London's Ladbroke Grove, and yet being just a short walk from Wembley Stadium, Wimbledon Lawn Tennis Club *and* Silverstone. An impossible dream, yet that's effectively what these people had.

'How did Melbourne get all these plum sporting events?' I asked.

'I think it's because of Sydney,' Steve explained. 'There's a lot of rivalry between the cities, and Sydney has all the classic icons. We can't compete with that. So Melbourne did everything it could to attract big events, from horse racing to motor racing.' I'd forgotten about the horse racing institution that is the Melbourne Cup, so mentally added Cheltenham or Aintree to my list of dream sporting locations on my fantasy doorstep.

Within spitting distance of the Albert Park circuit, we parked Penny and jumped out, grinning at the din echoing and bouncing around the city. Access to the track was obviously reserved for fee paying punters, but the girls (and, let's face it, their dad) loved hearing the deafening roar of the race for a few minutes from just beyond the trees at the edge of Albert Park.

It's not just sporting events that the city hosts. We were more than a little peeved to discover that the International Comedy Festival was in town a week *after* we were there. It's one of the 'Comedy Grand Slams', alongside Edinburgh and Montreal. And as we walked around the city, a proliferation of posters and flyers promoted bands, shows and writers' festivals. It took less than a day before one of us said, 'I want to live here.'

It's commonly described as the cultural capital of Australia, but what you can't get from any guidebook or website is the palpable 'buzz' Melbourne has. Every street, every tram ride, every aimless amble we took presented more delights that seemed to merely scratch the surface of what was available if we could only stay a little longer. A train to Flinders Street station, a walk through Federation Square and a look inside St Paul's Cathedral just left us wishing we had time to visit the Australia Centre for the Moving Image or stroll down to the Yarra river front. We wandered through Fitzroy Gardens and saw Captain Cook's cottage. 'But have you seen the botanical gardens?' people would ask. No, we hadn't. Just as we didn't see any cricket, AFL, tennis, horse racing or comedy. We were ruled by The Schedule. Penny had a ship to catch, and as Bethan's lemon drizzle cake cooled we were back on the road, reluctantly heading north, vowing one day to return.

Jill wasn't the only one with a family tree extending to Australia. While our road trip north had introduced us to the Yeppoon Posse - a mass of Moodys who threw open their doors to us more than once between Brisbane and Cairns - our trip south offered us the chance to meet a Courtie. A Courtie is much rarer than a Moody, simply because the surname was only made up five generations ago. If you were collecting us, we'd make an awfully flimsy Panini sticker book. I'd had an email from Jenny (who'd been a Courtie before she got married) years earlier when I was working on the radio at BFBS. A relative of hers had heard me on the radio while abroad, noticed the name and put us in touch. That was ten years ago, and we'd had almost no contact since. I'd dropped her an email as we were heading south from Sydney, completely unaware of whether she still lived in Australia, let alone whether she was within visiting distance. It seemed remarkably flukey, therefore, that she replied with the exciting news that she lived in Pambula Beach, just a day's drive up the east coast from Melbourne.

It's weird meeting a distant relative for the first time. You've never met, yet you have so much in common, sharing a gene pool for one thing. We could all see a similarity in her face with my dad, which was slightly unnerving. And in the evening, after we'd wandered down to the beach she overlooked from her balcony, enjoyed a great meal together and started looking at the family tree research she'd done, photographs appeared of her father, and her father's brother, both of whom looked like two halves of my own dad's dad. Why am I still amazed by genetics? When friends have a baby, I'm always blown away when the months pass and they start to look like mini versions of mum, or dad, or both. Of course they do. It's always amazing, though, isn't it? And discovering the same facial similarities in people who never knew each other, people who lived on opposite sides of the world, people now dead ... well, it's a little moving.

Jen is my second-cousin-once-removed. It took a complicated computer program to tell us that, and neither of us really understood it. She's super-active, plays golf, does Pilates, tap dances and has a fantastic community of friends at Pambula Beach.

One of the things the girls will remember most from our visit is the kangaroos. *Huge* kangas, six footers, hopped on to her front lawn. 'See the way they stand there, on the edge of the grass?' said Jen. 'We say they're waiting for a bus.' It was the perfect description, the marsupial's front paws folded neatly, as if holding a tiny handbag, while they patiently stood there, looking up and down the road.

'I can't believe you have kangaroos in your garden!' Edie kept saying.

'That's nothing,' Jen said. 'You want to see wild kangaroos? Come to my golf club.' So we did. The first fairway must have had 40 or 50 kangaroos on it, grazing, lazily hopping, chatting about bus timetables. Apparently they weren't a problem for the golfers, although kangaroos do grumble a bit if a ball hits them.

'I wonder what the rules say about your ball hitting a kangaroo,' I said.

'Yeah, what if it fell in a pouch?' Edie added.

'Lost ball, I reckon,' said Jen.

'What would Tiger Woods do if he encountered a large marsupial on the 18th?' I wondered.

'Get its mobile number and ask it on a date,' said Jill, proving that in 2011 you were never far from a Tiger Woods joke.

The next morning it was my birthday, and before we left my new-found second cousin once removed, Bethan baked her signature lemon drizzle, Jen found a candle, and we all enjoyed a slice of birthday cake sitting on her bright, sunny veranda, looking down on the sweeping golden bay below. The sea was blue, the beach was deserted, and – in an echo of the sentiment I'd felt up in Yeppoon – I couldn't help thinking that this particular branch of the family had done rather well.

We had one more *Put Us Up Down Under* friend to meet before we got back 'home' to Brissy, but they were north of Sydney, a good two days drive away, so we spent the night of my birthday camping near Ulladulla on a brilliant $20 site that we deemed had The Best Campsite Kitchen In The World. All Aussie campsites have a communal kitchen area – a brilliant idea that I wish European sites would take up. They vary from a couple of benches, a gas hob and a kettle, all the way up to this Ulladulla gem: fully-fitted kitchen, catering pots and pans, microwaves, kettles, two hobs, a coin operated hot-plate barbecue and, in the dining area, a DVD player and massive flat screen TV. It made for a memorable birthday barbie, watching a big-screen movie while we ate.

To the west of Sydney are the Blue Mountains, so called because the eucalyptus trees give the densely forested hills a blue-ish hue. There's a neat scientific explanation for this: the trees fill the atmosphere with finely dispersed droplets of oil which, when combined with dust and water vapour, scatter short-wave rays of light, which are predominantly blue in colour. We drove west of the glitzy city towards Penrith, and quickly found ourselves climbing up a tiny, twisting track into the thick eucalyptus forest. A hut and barrier marked the official gateway into Blue Mountains National Park, where we paid 30 bucks to camp for the night at a secluded spot where the only facility provided was a composting loo and a camp-fire ring to cook over. We were used to the simple life, though, having survived for eight days on Goa's Agonda beach which had zero facilities, so embraced our rural idyll, lit a fire, watched kangaroos grazing at a cautious distance and found ourselves sharing tales with a German couple who arrived in their rented camper. They were living their retirement dream, and couldn't grasp how five of us could survive in Penny. Their rental van was a converted Ford Transit that had a shower! We resigned ourselves to arriving at our next hosts' house, slightly smelly.

Dawn and Laurence lived on a farm near Gresford, just north of Newcastle. You'll recall the Indian cooking class we did with Fiona and Praveen in Pushkar, Rajasthan? Well, Fiona comes from Gresford, and Dawn is one of her good friends, which is how, after an hour of failing to find their house in a part of Australia where sat-nav ends and mobile phone signals are a myth, we eventually took the correct dirt road to the correct farmhouse of another *Put Us Up* friend-of-a-friend.

Laurence had a job in the town - a teacher of kids with special needs – but their home life on the farm was stereotypical of rural Australia: barns, horses, dogs, a veranda, a barbie - everything you'd expect. They were also progressively 'green' – an oddity in a country where energy was consumed and carbon emitted with barely a second thought. They captured solar energy, providing power and heat for their water. They captured their own water, not being on any mains supply. They built their own mini-sewage treatment system so all their 'grey' water was recycled to irrigate the trees and plants in their garden. This meant they paid no water bills at all, and their electricity bills were minimal. This attitude was undoubtedly at odds with the 'plunder and pillage' attitude so visible in Australia's colossal mining industry, where 'green' is a dirty word, but we noticed it *was* becoming more widespread. Anne and Dave, the musos we stayed with in Grafton, had solar cells on the roof and sold power back to the grid. Dawn's brother Joe, just down the road, had installed enough solar panels on his land to be earning four figure sums every quarter from the electricity company. In a country so blessed with sunshine and empty space, I wondered how long it would be before an ambitious government set aside a few hundred square kilometres in the desert to cover in black glass panels with which to power Sydney. Sadly, it seemed that while the mining companies continued to be the goose that laid the golden egg, renewable energy on such a scale would never happen. Not until that goose was cooked.

Dawn had very generously offered to arrange a gig for us in Gresford's Twin Rivers Café, which was great fun. The owner had opened the café especially for us to busk, and although it was a very quiet afternoon with only a handful of customers wandering in, we raised some smiles and got $27 for UNICEF. Importantly, it was good practice for a gig we had coming up in Brisbane later in the week. We had a great couple of days with Dawn, Laurence and their family, and when we left they gave us some wonderful hand-made presents: a recipe book for Bethan, a brilliant 'koala' hat complete with ears and droopy eyes, which Edie now wears through the British winter, and Laurence made the girls a mob of small racing kangaroos cut from local wood, which rock their way haphazardly down a slope. Again, our journey had led us to meet some wonderful, unforgettable people.

After a couple more days and nights of driving and camping, we were back, exhausted and smelly, to invade the lives of our tirelessly patient friends Berners and Leona in Brissie. We'd made it: Melbourne and back in just under three weeks – Penny had clocked up over 5,500 miles up and down the Aussie east coast. The shipping agent needed her by 6th April, and we arrived back on the previous evening. Sure, we'd rushed a bit. In fact we'd rushed a lot. But at least we'd made the deadline. Penny was going to America.

Except, she wasn't.

After we gave her the now familiar pre-shipping spring clean - much easier on a Brisbane driveway than on a muddy YWCA car park in Chennai - we dropped her at the shipping company and waved her goodbye. Then I had a phone call. 'Hey Sim, it's Matt.' This was my always-chipper shipping agent, a man so enamoured with our global adventure that he persuaded his firm, Williams Global, to waive their fee. He was a true gent, and we got on like a house on fire. 'The van's gonna be delayed leaving for a couple of weeks.' I hated him.

The vessel Penny was due to board was still in Japan where, three weeks earlier, there had been a massive earthquake triggering a devastating tsunami. The ship, a purpose-built car transporter, wasn't leaving because the earthquake had stopped all the car factories from working, which meant there were no Japanese cars to export to Australia and America, and there was no point sailing an empty ship. The expected delay was 16 days. This meant Penny's new Estimated Time of Arrival in Long Beach, California would also be delayed by as many days. We *had* to leave Australia as planned, thanks to expiring visas and pre-booked flights, so this delay meant we would have three whole weeks to survive in the States without her, and therefore without our accommodation. Cash was already tight, and three weeks of living in America without Penny to sleep in seemed impossible.

So Matt-the-shipping-agent got on the case. Alternatives were sought. Another vessel was sailing sooner. But not all shipping routes are the same, and the boat departing *sooner* arrived in Long Beach 18 days *later* than the delayed car transporter from Japan! We could ship straight to Europe. That would save the cost of shipping Penny from the USA back to Britain later on. It would mean we'd have to backpack across America (taking much less time than our original planned journey), then fly to Barcelona to pick up Penny and drive home from there. Anguished family discussions took place. A multitude of scenarios were discussed. Many brows were furrowed. I'm sure one of the things Ella, Beth and Edie got from this whole caper was an intense introduction to logistical problem-solving skills.

I paced up and down the kitchen, throwing around 'what ifs'. 'What if we fly to LA, then backpack on Greyhound buses all the way to New York?' or 'What if we fly from LA to Kansas, see Ty, then go back to LA for Penny, then race across the states?' Leona's iPod was providing some background music. Robbie Williams started to sing, 'I sit and talk to God, and he just laughs at my plans.' Well put, Robert.

These dilemmas - whether we could afford to fly to New Zealand, visit Tasmania or even afford to ship Penny to Long Beach and still get her shipped home - seemed endless and unrelentingly changing. Had I bored you, dear reader, with every different plan hatched during our time in Oz, we'd both have lost the will to live several pages ago.

Ultimately, we calculated that we could just about wring the last ounce of cash out of our available credit to get Penny shipped home from New York, so yes, we *would* ship her to Long Beach as planned and would simply have to live without her for three weeks when we got to California. Where we would stay, none of us knew.

'Didn't Brian in Madaba say his parents were in California?' asked Jill. By this point in our year, we'd become completely unfazed by the prospect of living with strangers, and completely shameless about asking.

'I'll email him,' I said. 'See if he can put us in touch.'

Meanwhile, Penny was collected from Brisbane port and returned to our suburban driveway while we waited for a long-lost ship and bought a huge Ordnance Survey map of the United States to work out how we would get from LA to New York in time for our flights home. In a perfect world, we'd be in New York by 4th July, where Edie would celebrate her Independence Day birthday, before flying home two days later.

'You know what's most annoying about Penny not leaving?' said Jill, as we idly smoothed out the enormous map of North America on the living room floor.

'What's that?'

'The comedy festival in Melbourne. We raced away from our favourite city, two days before it started, for no reason whatsoever.'

I shook my head with regret. 'Do you think it's weird,' I asked, 'that Penny arrived here damaged by cyclone Yasi, and now she can't leave because of an earthquake?'

'And that Brisbane got its worst floods ever, two weeks before we got here,' added Ella.

'We do seem to be attracting natural disasters,' I suggested. 'On the bright side, perhaps Edie will get her tornado wish after all.'

The following Sunday was the Beatnik Beatles' 'Day At The Races'.

Brisbane's Eagle Farm Racecourse opened its gates as a busy artisan market, and we'd been invited to busk there by Greg, who ran a shop in Brisbane's West End. Matt-the-shipping-agent knew Greg, and remembered that he'd put live music on in his gift shop window so put us in touch. When we popped in to meet Greg - and survey the window space - he told us about the market. 'It's quite new,' he said. 'Only been running a few weeks but it's super-busy. Reckon you guys'll do better there than here. I've got a stall down there, so I'll talk to the organiser, make sure she's happy. She'll love it!'

So we pitched up opposite the busy Dandelyon Gifts stall and did our stuff. It was great to be proper busking again, rather than doing a pre-arranged 'appearance' because we didn't have to worry about a structured set list, or saying anything entertaining between songs. Best of all, because it was a constantly changing audience, we could repeat our favourites. Poor Greg must have heard the same six songs about three times, but kept on smiling! When we counted up the change in our UNICEF tin we'd raised $28.60 (over £18), which brought our busking total in Oz to over $100. We were pretty pleased with ourselves.

When the day finally came to wave Penny off, her milometer was approaching 14,000 miles since home. That's a fairly average annual mileage for a lot of UK motorists. Ironically, it was less than the distance Jill or I would have driven during those eight months had we been back at home, commuting to our regular jobs. Yet covering that distance in Penny to reach Australia was a huge milestone for us. Long before we left the UK, The Land Of Oz stood as a distant beacon, drawing us from the opposite side of the planet. In fact, during the early, uncertain planning stages of our trip, when one of the children would ask, 'Do you really think this will happen?' Jill or I would say, 'Look, even if it doesn't, we'll use the money we've saved to fly to Australia.' It was our dream to get there, by hook or by crook. (As opposed to early settlers, who got here by Cook or by crook.) We'd made it, and as the final leg of our journey beckoned, we felt sadness at having to leave a land that had promised so much, and delivered even more.

We met nothing but cheerful enthusiasm on our 5,500-mile journey up and down a country that proved more friendly, positive and upbeat than is legal in England. We were entertained by their politicians, constantly bickering over a Carbon Tax that none of them really wanted, enthralled by their abundant natural beauty (the landscape, not the politicians) and awestruck by their extremes of weather. There was just one other thing that almost *everyone* we met asked our opinion on: a thorny and difficult subject that captivated us throughout our time there.

'Bang goes another kanga on the bonnet of the van,' our girls had merrily sung as they played Kate Bush, *The Dreaming*, while we toured Oz. Apart from the demise of an unfortunate marsupial, the song tells of an Aboriginal community, destroyed by mining, with lines like 'Erase the race that claim the place and say we dig for ore'.

The Dreaming is the name of the spiritual belief system of Aborigines – a connection between them, their ancestors and the Earth. And therein lies the topic that proved so spiky: Aborigines. Or more accurately, Australia's indigenous people including Aboriginal Australians and Torres Strait Islanders. The fact that this subject is one to be approached with caution may come as a surprise to you. We were puzzled when we first started to explore the country, first at the lack of indigenous people to be seen, and then at the obvious tension still surrounding the topic when it was brought up. At home, our knowledge of Aborigines is one lacking all context of current difficulties. We think of them as noble, nomadic, tribal people, respected for their history and appreciated for the ancient race that they are. Our kids studied Aboriginal 'dot art' in school, we learned how Aborigines have a spiritual connection with the Earth, like native Americans, and we knew they gave us the didgeridoo (although we couldn't blame them for Rolf Harris). Also, we were aware of the oppression they faced by early settlers, but I'd considered all that to be very much in the past.

How wrong I was.

Our experience in 2011 was that white Australia was treading on eggshells. To fully understand why, and why the issue of its indigenous people was still such a prickly one, you needed to have lived through a generation or two of racism, regret and self-loathing. As visitors passing through, with a cheery smile and a jaunty song, it was a challenge getting a handle on why people kept asking us what we thought of 'our Aborigines' and why, even within families, the ensuing debate was always heated and often divided.

First, some context: in 2011, Government statistics estimated that there were about 400,000 Aborigines in Australia - about 2 per cent of the population. Most of these were in the central and northern deserts, because they were literally hunted by settlers from the south a couple of hundred years earlier. These white hunters hadn't considered Aborigines to be human - you almost need to pause for a moment to take that in - and natives were killed in great numbers. People today still recall that when the killing finally stopped there was only one indigenous man left on Tasmania. When he died, that tribe was extinct.

Now you're starting to see why modern Australia is burdened with more guilt than a Catholic used-car salesman. But there's more. There's 'The Stolen Generation'. It was government policy in Australia between 1909 and 1969 to forcibly remove indigenous children from their families. Under the White Australia and Assimilation Policies, Aboriginal and Torres Strait Islander people who were 'not of full blood' were encouraged to become assimilated into the broader society – the purpose being that eventually there would be no more indigenous people left. Children were taken from Aboriginal parents so they could be brought up 'white' and taught to reject their Aboriginality. Aboriginal children were expected to become labourers or servants, so in general the education they were given was very poor. Aboriginal girls, in particular, were sent to schools established by the Government where they were trained in domestic service.

It seems unimaginable today that supposedly civilised, well-educated British bureaucrats could believe that it was acceptable to breed out a race of people. The systematic extermination of a racial group is genocide. In their defence, the lack of understanding and respect for Aboriginal people meant that many of those who supported the child removals believed that they were doing the right thing. Christian churches were keenly involved in the programme. Some believed that Aboriginal people lived poor and unrewarding lives, and that institutions would provide a positive environment in which Aboriginal people could better themselves. The dominant racist views in society and Government meant that people even believed that Aborigines were bad parents and that Aboriginal women didn't look after their children.

No one knows how many children were taken, as most records have been lost or destroyed. Many parents whose children were taken never saw them again, and when siblings were taken they were deliberately separated from each other. The practice of forced child removal actually continued until 1970. That means there are people my age (42 at the time of writing) who still don't know who, or where, their family is, and have no means of finding out. Aside from the widely reported psychological and physical abuse that these children suffered, the simple fact that such a brutal policy not only existed, but was so slavishly pursued for over 60 years, is still the cause of much gnashing of teeth.

Now set that history against the current state of affairs. Aboriginal communities are commonly viewed as drunk troublemakers by many of the white Australians we met. This opinion, though clearly a sweeping generalisation, was based on some difficult truths. Alcohol abuse was a big problem in indigenous communities. Years of failed schemes attempting to amend for past wrongs led to resentment from both indigenous and white Australians. The Aborigines felt justifiably wronged by their treatment in the past, but also misunderstood about their current needs, while ordinary white Australians saw money (their taxes) being thrown at a problem that seemed unfixable.

Aborigines, with thousands of years of nomadic tribal breeding behind them, did not react well to offers of housing and benefit money. Ownership has never featured in their mindset - no one owned the land, or the animals and plants on it. They were merely custodians of the land, living off it, moving across it, and entrusting it to future generations to do the same. When white settlers put up fences, the divide was both physical, and metaphorical - the two races couldn't be more different. And that divide remains.

'Why don't we ever see indigenous people running shops, or fixing cars, or working in Starbucks?' we asked ourselves. 'I grew up watching South Africa overhaul apartheid,' I explained to some of our Aussie hosts in Yeppoon. 'I'm sure it's no paradise there even now, but I'd expect to see black South Africans doing all those normal jobs. So why not here?'

'You can't compare the two,' I was told. 'The divide here is much more than one of race and colour. It's a total clash of cultures.'

'They don't want to work,' was a line we heard more than once. It sounds horribly like a *Daily Mail* headline, but it wasn't just idle racism. 'It's simply not in the mindset of most indigenous Australians to own anything,' it was explained, 'let alone a shop or a business. To be an entrepreneur is completely alien, because for them it's never been about money or ownership.'

'A garage won't employ an Aborigine,' one of our hosts said, 'because he'll go walkabout. He can disappear for a week or two and think nothing of it. The owner can't fire the bloke for that because it's "in their culture". So what does the boss do? He's in an impossible situation with the rest of his staff. Much easier not to bother hiring one.'

There was that resentment creeping to the surface again. A doctor told me that he got paid more if he treated an Aborigine, so the claims of queue jumping and favouritism that we heard about were not entirely fictional. An artist told me it was *against the law* to do 'dot art' unless you were an Aborigine. She was amazed our girls did it in school.

'No Australian school would be allowed to let their white pupils do dot art!' she said, shocked at the very thought. You can see how that must rile people. In Europe, far-right extremism would thrive in these circumstances, but in Australia the history is so awful, and so recent, that even those who choose to vocalise their thoughts on 'drunk trouble-makers' do so in hushed tones.

Clearly, mine is not an expert appraisal. A totally balanced point of view of this Aussie dilemma could only be reached after spending time with some indigenous people. But the only ones we saw in three months there were in a tiny town called Kuranda, in the rainforest area of North Queensland. Two men and a woman in their 20s were sitting on a street corner, smoking roll-ups and drinking liquor at ten in the morning, sadly living up to the stereotype we'd heard preached so often.

So how do you fix it? It appears impossible to integrate two communities whose entire cultures are poles apart. One requires land without boundaries, the other requires boundaries around land. And if it's impossible, then what? Segregation? No forward thinking democracy, no matter how conservative, could ever condone that. So I'll give you the same answer I was given by every single Aussie who spoke to me about it: I don't know.

It really brought home a couple of important things I was learning from our journey around planet Earth:

> 1. *You can't fix everything.* It was something of a relief to realise that. I was in India, struggling with how they were going to make that country work - fixing the corruption from the top down, welfare support from the bottom up, massive overcrowding, colossal lack of funds. I was shocked to learn that India was the recipient of the largest annual

International Development handout from the World Bank. Those African countries we see on the news suffering droughts and civil wars get millions of dollars in aid. India, so often portrayed as a booming economy gets over a *billion* dollars every year. As I write, the World Bank estimates that the cost of addressing malnutrition in India is $2.5bn. And yet they can afford to host a Formula 1 Grand Prix! The duplicity turned my stomach, and I grappled with it tortuously until a simple but sobering thought occurred to me - it might actually be unfixable.

2. *It's hard to be proud to be British.* In terms of world history, it's not looking good for Blighty. Read about Mahatma Gandhi and his victorious struggle for Indian independence, and then tell me you're proud to be British. Watch Kenneth Branagh's portrayal of Auber Neville, Chief Protector of Aborigines in the film *Rabbit Proof Fence* - the true story of three Aborigine girls forcibly removed from their parents - and see how quickly your Union Jack wilts.

Now that may seem a slightly downbeat way to end a chapter, but if this trip was giving all of us a broader view of our position in the world, and a more informed opinion about some of the big issues we all face, well, that was no bad thing.

Now we were off to the USA, which was a very big deal, first for any Americans who might have been following our trip and were surely bracing themselves for a barrage of natural disasters, and secondly for us, who had so often thought that we would never get as far as the star-spangled land-of-the-free.

Goodbye Australia, home to some of the friendliest, most open-hearted and happy people on this planet. Your wildlife was wonderful, your cities superb and your weather was ... terrifying. But that was all part of the fun. Crazy weather was behind us now. We were off to find friends in Kansas, and what major weather events ever happen there?

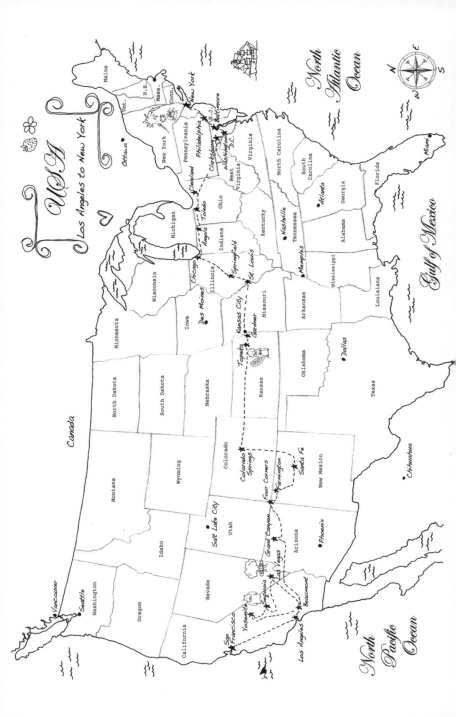

Our arrival in America wasn't half as eventful as you'd expect it to be for a family rocking up at LAX airport homeland security on a plane from China with Syrian stamps in their passports. We'd braced ourselves for a severe grilling. 'What shall we say?' Ella asked nervously.

'Just tell them the truth,' Jill calmly assured her. 'No one would make up a story as far-fetched as ours.'

The reason we were on a plane from China is because we'd bought the cheapest tickets in the world that would get us from Brisbane to Los Angeles; bargain flights that went via Guangzhou in the Chinese Guangdong province. This had its down sides: a 26-hour journey time, a frustrating *glimpse* of China without actually being able to go and *see* China, and a woeful lack of in-flight entertainment, the centre-piece of which was the catastrophically awful Michael Douglas film *Solitary Man*. A project for which writer/director Brian Koppelman should be in solitary confinement.

On the up side, we got to eat real Chinese food in a real Chinese restaurant in a real Chinese airport. And, best of all, we've each got a passport proudly bearing stamps from Australia, China and the USA *all* dated 28th April - a clever trick thanks to crossing the international date line. As it happened, the security checks in LA were smoother than I'd ever experienced getting into America before, and we had nothing to worry about. That may well have been because when the

Immigration Official called us up to his desk, seeing we were one family, the first passport he opened was Edie's. The sharp-eyed fellow saw her birth date. 'Hey, a July-the-fourth baby!'

'Yes,' beamed Edie, turning on the charm as if she were at a Syrian border crossing. 'I'm having my birthday in New York. They're putting on fireworks for me.' The man laughed, gave a cursory glance at our passports and wished us all a happy holiday.

'It's not a ...' I stopped myself. We were in. The final leg of our global circumnavigation had begun.

Predicting we'd be on the verge of collapse after 26 hours of travelling, I'd booked us into a Travelodge at LAX for a couple of nights, where, after checking in, it quickly became clear that we weren't going to get much sleep owing to the excitement of being in America.

'Shall we go out to eat?' I asked the family. 'I know it's ten o'clock, but there's a diner next door. We can live the American dream! A late night burger, then come back to watch the main event.'

The Main Event was the Royal Wedding of Prince William and Kate Middleton. Ella had been very disappointed not to be spending the big day in Australia, it being part of the Commonwealth and undoubtedly geared up for lots of celebrations. But our visas expired on the date set by Wills and Kate. Bad planning on all of our parts, really. 'Don't worry,' I'd said. 'We'll land in Los Angeles in plenty of time. It'll be happening at ...' I did some rough calculations in my head. 'Around three in the morning.'

Any fears that America might not be putting the same emphasis on the event as Australia, were instantly allayed by the receptionist at the lodge. 'Excuse me?' I politely enquired. 'Do you think the Royal Wedding will be on one of the TV channels tonight?' I fully expected the Hispanic lady to not have a clue what I was talking about. She laughed dryly.

'Honey, it'll be on *every* TV channel tonight,' which it more-or-less was.

After returning from our very first experience of a Denny's diner, we found wall-to-wall coverage of the build-up live from the streets of London, the wedding itself, and all the parading and pizzazz that followed. Despite the ungodly hour, we lapped it up, full of burger, but starved of British culture. 'I can't understand why the Americans don't get pantomime,' I quipped. 'They're loving this one. There's a dashing prince, a rags-to-riches bride and two ugly sisters.' It was a cruel joke, but Princesses Beatrice and Eugenie's outfits did raise a smile.

Only after we'd stayed awake long enough to see Kate get kissed on the balcony (twice), did we finally switch off the TV at about 5am and succumb to sleep. The first of us woke sometime in mid-afternoon, and jet-lag's evil spell was cast. We were now horribly out of sync with the rest of LA humanity. Stumbling around the shadowy room, I tugged at the curtain letting blinding sunlight pierce the gloom, getting groans of complaint from the sleeping vampires within. Slowly we surfaced. While I waited for the others to get washed and dressed, I turned on the laptop, which brought tidings of great joy.

'Oh yes!' I shouted. 'We love you Mr Jordan!'

'Are we in?' asked Ella, poking her head eagerly from behind the bathroom door.

'You are in,' I confirmed. Suddenly four bodies, in various states of undress, crowded around me, peering at the screen. An email from Mr Jordan's secretary confirmed that both Ella and Bethan had been given places at The Warriner School, and they would be most welcome to start on their return, a week before the end of term. Apparently, Mr Jordan had seen the fruitless email trail between Jill and the admissions department, and, in a triumph for common sense, had simply stepped in and sorted it. And we loved him for it.

My memories of that day are blurred. I know we got a bus to a shopping mall. I think we had dinner at Denny's - again. But what I *do* remember is all of us saying, at regular intervals, things like, 'That is *so* good about school,' 'Good old Mr Jordan,' and 'That is a right result.' In our jet-lagged fog, it was the sunshine, and it was all we could talk about. The biggest risk Jill and I had taken in the planning of this trip had come good.

It wasn't until the following day that we were able to drag ourselves into the daylight in time to actually 'do stuff'. We hired a car and decided to hit Hollywood (metaphorically, although we all thought it deserved a slap for making that Michael Douglas film).

At this point you might be thinking *Hotels? Hire cars? Had they won the lottery?* I should point out that coming from Australia, we were a bit giddy at how far the good ol' American greenback would go. I told you how expensive Australia was - a combination of a poor exchange rate and high prices (even by the standards of resident Australians) meant everything was almost double the price of its UK equivalent.

By comparison, most things in the US were almost *a third* of the price they were back in Oz. It caught us out a little: I'd bought Greyhound bus tickets online while back in Australia, to get us from LA to San Francisco during the few weeks when we'd be waiting for Penny to arrive. On getting to the States, however, I realised it would have been cheaper to hire one of those grotesquely massive American cars for a week and roll up the west coast in blissful, air-conditioned gas-guzzling comfort. As it was, the tickets were paid for and non-refundable, so we reluctantly accepted that the eight-hour Greyhound bus journey in a week's time would be character-building.

So, for our first week we got some wheels from a car hire depôt opposite our hotel. Having a car is essential in a city where most people's idea of a brisk morning constitutional is a walk to their mailbox and back. In the city of angels, *everyone* drives *everywhere*. Even suburban streets can stretch to eight lanes wide. As a pedestrian in LA, you feel vulnerable, alone, and a bit silly. In that respect it's the polar opposite of New York where you'd be mad to own a car. Only a fool would drive in Manhattan. (A fool was planning to.)

I'd been to Los Angeles many years ago, so I interspersed our drive around Hollywood with priceless nuggets like, 'It's round here somewhere,' and, 'I'm sure this bit wasn't here,' until I'd eventually shown Jill and the girls The Sunset Marquis hotel, where I'd stayed years ago and shared a beer with Slash from *Guns 'n' Roses* (well, he'd been at the next table. I didn't give him guitar tips. Or hair-care tips come to that), the Viper Room ('River Phoenix died there' – 'Who?'), and eventually found Mann's Chinese Theatre with its famous handprints outside.

The strange thing about Hollywood is its lack of glamour. It's a working town and it feels working class. The film stars live in hidden mansions far from the studios. A woman who moved to California from Oregon recalled to me her first visit to LA. 'It was so disappointing,' she remembered. 'I was looking around thinking - they call this Tinsel Town, right?'

Once you've seen the Hollywood sign in the hills, followed the Walk of Stars along Hollywood Boulevard, pointed at the names in the pavement you recognise and smirked at the less likely ones - 'Was Kenny Loggins *ever* that famous?' - and placed your hands in the imprints of those of Johnny Depp or Marilyn Monroe, you've pretty much done it all. You might get lucky and see a famous face - Peter O'Toole was pressing his hands and feet into wet cement when we were there, but we couldn't get close enough to see him. We could only get to admire the result of his efforts after he'd been whisked away in a limo to find a basin and a decent dry-cleaner.

Having our own car meant we could explore though, which was great. We shunned the many 'Star Tours' flyers being thrust our way, promising to show us the homes of the rich and famous, and drove on our own up into the Hollywood hills. Here, tiny single-track roads wind steeply between houses that don't hide behind gates but still have multi-million dollar price tags, and every few minutes we'd get a glimpse of how close we were to those famous white block letters prompting an 'Ooh' or an 'Aahh' from the back of the car.

Later, having cruised the neighbourhoods for a while, we found something unique to our round-the-world journey: a place that we *all* agreed we could move to. In the 30,000 miles we'd travelled from Liverpool, that hadn't happened yet. It's a small pocket of land you probably haven't heard of called the Beverly Hills. We'd travelled the Earth, seen many lands and all agreed that, yes, the Beverly Hills would be a most pleasant place to settle down. Perhaps we'd look into it at a later date, see if we could pick up a nice place before it became too pricey.

At the foot of the Hollywood hills we passed a trestle table laden with bric-a-brac on the sidewalk outside one of the mansions. 'Oh my word, it's a yard sale!' yelped Jill. 'A yard sale! In Hollywood! Pull over.' We parked up, determined to buy something, just for the hell of it. I was tempted by a collection of 1970s *Playboy* magazines until I saw something even more eyebrow-raising. *How To Strip For A Man* was a 1960s photographically (with the emphasis on 'graphically') illustrated guide on, well, just that. It did exactly what it said on the tin. Jill's birthday was a way off, but surely ...? Before I could get my hands on its (well worn) pages, Jill intervened.
'What have you found?'
'Oh nothing. A book about decorating I think. What about you?'
'*Room With A View*. Might as well buy a classic.'
I so very nearly did, I thought.

Remember way back in the first half of this book, when we were in Madaba, northern Jordan and we met Brian, the English teacher, America's third-fastest marathon runner and, by the time we left him, wearer of a plaster-cast and sling? You'll recall how he'd said, 'My folks live in California, so if you're going anywhere near there they'd love to see you.' I doubt he ever thought we'd take him seriously. But we did. And six months, and a few emails, later we were driving inland from the coast to the town of Beaumont, about an hour from Los Angeles, to meet Brian's mum and dad, Julie and Dave, who had generously agreed to put us up for a while. I had put their address in the sat-nav, and then foolishly re-named the destination 'Brian's mum and dad'. This was a mistake, because it erased the actual *address* from the screen. So, having successfully negotiated us out of Los Angeles' notoriously horrible tangle of free-ways, the trusty little screen took us all the way to a smart, suburban street that looked *exactly* like the street in Tim Burton's film *Edward Scissor Hands*.

'Which house is it?' asked Jill.

'I don't know. It just says 'Brian's mum and dad'.' She rolled her eyes.

'Where's their address?'

'On an email. I'll have to get the laptop out.' We pulled up at the kerb and started the rigmarole of retrieving the computer from the back of the car, getting it out of its case, switching it on - a palaver that takes a full six or seven minutes before you can actually read an email. After about five minutes, I smirked at a funny thought. Gazing at the lazy boot-up screen, wedged between my chest and the steering wheel, I said, 'Wouldn't it be embarrassing if we were actually outside their house, and they were watching us?'

'Er … Sim?' said Jill.

I looked up. A smiling man was a few feet away on the lawn of his garden. He was holding a large golden retriever by its collar, and appeared to have been waiting patiently for some time.

'Oh great,' I said through a polite fixed grin. 'You don't think that's …?'

Jill wound her window down. 'Are you David?'

'Yeah! Hi! Ya OK?' As first impressions go, it was special. He must have thought we were nuts, pulling up outside his house, then sitting there ignoring him for so long. Having got that awkwardness out of the way, we endeavoured to convince him that we were basically harmless, and safe people to be around. We met Julie later that evening. Two more lovely hosts you couldn't hope to meet. Both their sons, Brian and Michael, had grown up and left home. Michael was married to Jenny with a little daughter, Audrey, and they lived about half an hour away, while Brian, of course, was several thousand miles away in Jordan. Julie was loving being a grandmother, and seemed to thrive on having our three girls around the house too. Within a very short time we were all so relaxed together we felt like family.

Julie and Dave both went to work during the day, each at different local schools, so we spent our days exploring, guided by their local knowledge. Beaumont is a small town on a flat plain between two mountain ranges and is perfectly situated to experience the vastly different worlds of Southern California - or 'So Cal', as locals called it. At the foot of the hills you have desert, where towns like Palm Springs regularly hit temperatures in the high 30s centigrade. We drove to Riverside, Michael and Jenny's home town which, as the name suggests, is on the valley floor and the thermometer read 36°C. That equalled the highs we'd felt in early February in Queensland, and in southern India before that. The next day, however, we drove just an hour or two up into the mountains to a town called Big Bear, which at an altitude of 8,400 feet (around 2,500 metres) was higher than the Alps we'd driven through and still had snow on the ground.

The girls were thrilled to see some snow, especially as they had enviously sweltered in Mumbai last December hearing from their schoolmates back home how England was knee deep in the stuff. They finally got to make a snowball – on a hot May day in Southern California.

Another mountain village we stopped in had a proper old log cabin coffee house called Annie's. The burly, humourless woman making, serving and refilling our drinks provided service-with-a-scowl - and one other memorable addition. Ella spotted it first. 'Did you see that?' she whispered urgently when Annie had left us.

'What?' I asked, leaning in conspiratorially.

'She's got a gun!' Sure enough, being a mountain gal, livin' among bears an' all, our waitress was wearing a revolver and ammo on her belt. Annie had got her gun. We'd never known our girls drink their juice so politely and with so little fuss or bickering. If you were ever in the position to hire a nanny, I would certainly recommend tooling her up. A Colt 45 says so much more than a visit to the 'naughty step' ever can.

While we were in Beaumont, David arranged for us to talk and play to a couple of after-school clubs at local elementary schools. They were in different neighbourhoods and although they were both groups of about 30 seven to 11-year-olds, they were completely different experiences. At the first school, our audience was quiet, respectful and astonishingly polite. We told them of our travels, about UNICEF and taught them *All You Need Is Love* and *Yellow Submarine*. They joined in, clapped in all the right places and asked intelligent questions.

The second gig at a different school was more raucous, rowdy and confirmed my view that anyone who chooses a career in teaching primary school children deserves a pay rise, a medal and probably some sort of basic armament - a cattle prod at the very least. I held my own pretty well, I think, but more than once I wished I had Annie from the coffee shop on hand, just to discharge a couple of rounds above their heads, you understand.

We went through the same set that had proved so successful at the previous school, and when I got to the place in *All You Need Is Love* where I make the 'Ya, ta da, ta da' bit into a competition between the boys and the girls, they nearly took the roof off. They sang *Yellow Submarine* better than we do, and wouldn't let us go. The questions weren't quite as 'on subject' as at the other school, but much funnier. One boy asked Edie, 'In England do you have those guys in red coats and weird hats?'

'Yes, they're called Beefeaters,' she replied.

'Man, that is sick!' shouted the boy with glee. In case you're not versed in hip-hop parlance, the boy was impressed, rather than disgusted with the notion of Beefeaters. I couldn't help thinking how disappointed he'd be if he ever came to England, wandering bemused from McDonalds to Starbucks, so much like his home, and wondering where all the Beefeaters had gone.

As we were packing our instruments to leave, the kids in the class had a huddle with their teachers and came to us with a bundle of dollar bills. 'We've decided we'd like to donate our snack bar profits to your UNICEF fund,' they said, and gave us 30 bucks. We were so thrilled. Later, we discovered that the donation was an entire term's profits, which only made their generosity even more touching. Nice kids. Sick, even.

Just over a week before Penny was due to arrive at the Long Beach docks, we boarded a Greyhound bus from the less-than-glamorous bus station off South Soto Street, Los Angeles - destination: San Francisco. The boredom of the eight-hour journey was interrupted when the bus suffered a suspension failure half way, catapulting us all up out of our seats quite dramatically. 'You might have noticed something's gone wrong with the bus,' the driver announced. 'A valve has failed, but I've called our technical guys and they said I can still drive it, so you might find it a little bouncy. Don't worry, though,' he assured. 'I'll get you there.'

Several hours of roller-coaster/severe aircraft turbulence/ NASA astronaut training followed, the occasional moments of weightlessness providing great hilarity for the kids. 'No need to bother with Disney,' joked Ella, a careless comment that saved me about 250 quid, so bravo Greyhound!

I'd found an affordable apartment online - just one bedroom but when you're used to a camper van, a palace - in the suburb of Berkeley, home of the famous university. San Francisco is so different from LA. It's smaller, for a start, so getting around on foot is easy -

although those hills are a workout for the thighs - and the people are so friendly and laid back. You don't tend to get chatting to locals in LA because they're all in their cars, but in 'San Fran' you sit next to people on street cars or stand with them on the side of the ancient cable cars and they all make conversation. Once, we were waiting for the subway train to take us back home to Berkeley when a man standing near us asked the familiar question, 'Where are you from?'

'England.'

'Oh right. Which part?'

'Near Oxford,' I replied with a smile that I hope didn't betray it was about the thousandth time I'd said those words on this journey. Then he said something no one had *ever* said in reply.

'I spent some time in Swindon.'

'I work in Swindon!' Jill exclaimed.

'Wow! Really? I saw my first skinheads in Swindon,' he proudly stated.

'Yep. That sounds like the place,' she laughed.

'It *was* 1982,' he added, offering the town an excuse. Then our train arrived and we stepped on, leaving him grinning on the platform.

'Isn't that amazing?' Jill said to him. 'I was there in 1982.'

'Small world,' he said, as the doors slid closed.

'Wouldn't want to drive it,' I joked to the girls. 'Oh, hang on …'

Two essential highlights of a visit to 'Frisco' are a rock and a bridge. Alcatraz, 'The Rock', is one of the most famous prisons in the world. Closed in 1963, it's been a national park ever since, but thankfully preservation hasn't gone as far as renovation. The building is still decrepit. There are some sections where crumbling concrete has made the fabric of the building too unsafe to explore, which, if anything, adds to the eeriness of the place. The award-winning audio tour is led by ex-prisoners and guards, and is so richly produced - with background sounds and real life accounts - you are transported to the days of Al Capone, Robert 'Birdman' Stroud and the famous 'dummy heads' escape that was famously re-told on celluloid by Clint Eastwood in *Escape From Alcatraz*.

You can wander the cells, stand in 'solitary confinement' on D wing and still see the hole, chiselled with spoons, that led to the only successful escape from the island. Here is a great fact about Alcatraz: it was the only US penitentiary to provide hot showers. This was because they didn't want the inmates getting used to cold water, thus hardening them for a potential swim to freedom. It apparently worked, as more than a few would-be escapees got as far as the bay, only to be beaten by the water. One man got to freedom only to be washed up on shore having suffered a fatal heart attack, while another was recaptured after actually calling to the island-prison for help because the sea was so cold. As escape attempts go, that's quite embarrassing isn't it? When you need to ask for help to get back *into* prison, your career as The Great Escape Artist is over. Can you imagine the stick he took in the dining room next day?

The Golden Gate Bridge (which is painted red, not gold), is a landmark I'm sure you've seen a hundred times in various movies and books, but to give our experience an added twist, we cycled across it. There are several bicycle-hire shops around the city which specialise in single-day hire for people brave (or stupid) enough to tackle the ride, and as none of us had ridden a bike for almost a year, the simple offer of a family bike ride was novel enough to convince us. We'd have happily ridden across a canal bridge, and still been visibly gleeful to the point of looking slightly odd.

The novelty of being self-propelled on two wheels rapidly wore off, however, as we slogged our way towards the massive monument which had seemed so close, yet seemed never to get any larger on the horizon. The approach was steep, into a relentless headwind, and exhausting.

'I think I'll go back!' shouted Jill into the gale. I stopped for a rest, and they all teetered to a halt around me.

'You can't go back. We're nearly there,' I lied.

'If you're going back, so am I,' added Beth breathlessly.

'No! Please don't give up,' I whined. 'You'll really regret it. Look!' I swung my arm up to the sky. 'It's The Golden Gate Bridge!'

'Yeah. I've seen it,' dismissed Jill.

'Let's just take our time, plod gently into this hurricane,' I coaxed, 'and we'll get there eventually. Please! You really don't want to quit. You'll regret it forever.' There was a pause while they considered this.

'I think I'd regret it for, like, a day,' Beth shrugged.

'Maybe two,' agreed Jill.

'NO! Come on. We can do this!' I stood on my pedals and braced into the wind, and with an audible sigh, the others did the same. Eventually, the steepest part of the climb afforded us some shelter in the lee of the rock, and by taking regular breaks and me gee-ing them along with over-cheerful zeal, we all reached the bridge.

Without the need for me to say, 'I told you so,' it was agreed that to have turned back would have been madness: the view was incredible. Apart from the wind, the weather was good – blue skies and clear air meant a stunning panorama across the water, looking down on rocks, beaches, the city and over to Alcatraz in the middle of the bay. The camaraderie with other cyclists was memorable, and we stopped a few times and got chatting to people, most of whom were locals who did this ride regularly. The reward for our efforts was that on reaching the north side of the bridge we could all free-wheel down into Sausalito, park up for a pizza lunch, and then take the ferry back to San Francisco – a boat on which half a deck became a bike-park for about 50 bicycles like ours.

We were windswept, but happy. Our calves complained for a few days (as did a few other places - how Lance Armstrong ever manages to sit down without wincing is beyond me), but it was worth it. We all fell in love with San Fran, and none of us thought our week there was long enough. The city has a curious combination of feeling very old, yet very new. It has one of the finest universities, and world-beating silicone valley technology industries, yet at the same time it's

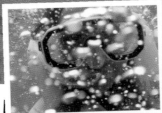

Australia's most patient
hosts – Berners and Leona

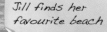

Jill finds her
favourite beach

"Wait! We haven't done
Ob-La-Di!"

Just when you thought it
was safe to go back
in the water ...

Barron Falls
Queensland

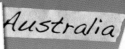
Australia

Sunset at Sydney harbour

It's not a holiday

A day at the races - busking in Brisbane

Catching leaves! Autumn arrives in Melbourne

U.S.A.

Inmate Ella took a relaxed approach to the Alcatraz exercise yard.

"Barry! Over here!"

"And can anyone guess what colour the submarine might be?"

U.S.A.

Our view, camping in Yosemite

"It's a big hole."

More gunge than fuel

Possibly the greatest camping
spot in the world

U.S.A.

Colorado Springs.
Penny splutters.

Busking for friends
in Gardner, Kansas

WEST 70 40
Kansas City

Cubs cap,
Ferris Bueller top,
bandaged finger.
Take me to the
ball game!

My relief, Beth's frustration
after surviving a small fire

U.S.A.

Penny's final camp,
Little Bennett, Maryland

"Nothing to see here, officer.
Lovely day for a stroll!"

The final busk. Not a dry eye
in the place. Or dry clothing.

Last day. Last tenner.
Last person to put in charge
of a boat.

HAPPY 4 OF JULY

got a west coast, laid back, hippy vibe to it. I've never found anywhere comparable. Perhaps it's that uniqueness that made us so fond of the place.

Not all of my advance planning was as successful as our week in Frisco. Using the same 'book direct with the owner' website I had used to find our brilliant apartment in Berkeley, I booked somewhere to stay near Long Beach. I'd done all this from Berners and Leona's kitchen 6,000 miles away in Brisbane, so a certain amount of shot-in-the-dark risk-taking was to be expected. My theory was that we needed to stay near Long Beach because that was where Penny would be arriving, and the accommodation I settled on was a short drive inland from the port in a town called Anaheim.

Anaheim is a completely characterless town, famous for only one thing: Disneyland. Since The Mouse built his theme park in 1955, way off in the distant outskirts of LA, a small town has built up around it to support the thousands of tourists and workers who need places to sleep, burgers to eat and liquor to drink.

I didn't know of Anaheim's Mickey Mouse connection when I booked our rooms in a random stranger's house, and found myself having to remind the girls repeatedly as we drove into the town that, despite a whole week in such a drab place stretching ahead like a prison sentence, on no account were we going to Walt's Wonderful World. Soon enough, though, that was the last thing on their minds. They were transfixed with the much more urgent and potentially frightening issue of our living arrangements.

Rather than having our own apartment, the website's limited choice and our even more limited budget meant we would be staying in a house *with* the owners, who had advertised two of their bedrooms for rent online. We arrived after dark and went through the usual drill with the girls. 'Best behaviour, please. Remember we are guests in someone else's home, so no bickering, no fighting, and *please* remember to smile.'

We trooped up the path to the front door of the large bungalow on a suburban street full of similar houses. I rang the bell, and through the smoke-tinted glass of the door I saw a man approach. We were all smiles as the door swung open. 'Hi, I'm Simeon. I booked the rooms?'

The short, stocky man was about 60, had grey unkempt hair and the rumpled look of long-forgotten chamois leather. A light-bulb of realisation went on behind his eyes. 'Oh, sure! Come in! Come in!' We crowded into the hall and he introduced himself. 'I'm Clifford. This is Max.' A large, friendly golden retriever was wagging its tail on cue. 'I'm afraid Paula is away. She'll be back tomorrow I think. Or maybe the next day.'

Paula was the only person I'd dealt with, so this seemed a bit odd. She hadn't mentioned that she wouldn't be there to meet us, or mentioned Clifford, a husband who had an apparently flimsy grasp on her movements, but we went with it, because that's what you do in these situations. Clifford showed us the two bedrooms we would have, and it quickly became obvious that, far from being 'self-contained' as the advertisement had suggested, we would be living very much 'en famille' with Clifford, Max and (if she even existed) Paula. He seemed like a nice man, retired ex-army, with grown-up children now living far away. But slowly I could sense alarm bells ringing.

Our two rooms, both with double beds, were at one end of the hall, next to the bathroom. He showed us two living rooms facing the large back garden, the kitchen at the other end, and a small study which was full of junk and appeared to be cluttered with prescription medication. This left no further rooms. 'Where are *they* sleeping?' Bethan whispered to me. I shrugged and pulled a face that I hope said *I'm as confused as you – and sorry, by the way, for bringing you here*. Having brought the bags into the house, we found ourselves standing in an awkward gaggle, cluttering up the cramped hallway, trying to make an excuse to head into one of our bedrooms so we could privately swap worried glances about the daunting week ahead, but our host wanted to chat.

'My wife, Paula, you'll meet her tomorrow. Or the next day, I forget. She goes away a lot,' he explained, in a gruff voice not dissimilar to that of TV detective Columbo. 'She goes to prayer-meetings. A lotta prayer-meetings.'

I nodded, wondering whether that was code for something, or whether she really did attend the sort of prayer-meetings that required an overnight stay, and if so, the thought of those prayer-meetings scared me a bit. 'I apologise,' Clifford Columbo went on, grinning at us with his tombstone crooked teeth. He raised a finger and tapped the side of his head. 'I gotta problem, in here. It's like a … waddaya call it … a split personality.' My eyebrows shot up at this candid conversation opener from a man we'd only known five minutes. 'Wadda they call it?' he asked Jill, who hadn't blinked for a while. Then he clicked his fingers. 'Bipolar! That's what it is.'

I nodded knowingly, like this was the most normal ice-breaker for a host to greet his guests with.

'I have these … *episodes*,' he went on. 'Where I don't remember a thing. Nothing. It's all gone. Like I wasn't even there.' Behind me I could sense the girls' mouths forming O shapes. 'I'm OK though as long as I take my pills,' he added with a laugh. Then, suddenly serious, he repeated to himself 'I gotta take my pills.'

It's curious, looking back, how all our minds were racing in different directions. Edie could sense fear but didn't know why. Ella and Beth were mentally building their argument that would plead with me to find somewhere else to stay. I was thinking *bipolar? Is that worse than schizophrenia, or better? I can't wait to blog this! Aren't we having an exciting time?* Jill was plotting her escape.

To Clifford, we were a long-awaited audience for a man who seemed to spend a lot of time alone. 'I got pills for everything. Red ones, blue ones, I forget. Like Max says, girls – it's rough.'

'Hahahahahaha,' trilled the nervous laughter of Ella and Beth, even though this was the second time Clifford had made the old 'rough/ruff' pun since we'd been there. A look of concern spread across his weathered face. 'The police used to be round here all the time, 'cause of my episodes. They know me. They'd pick me up and take me straight to hospital. But now I know ... I *gotta take my pills.*'

An awkward moment of silence hung in the air. Then, suddenly, his mood brightened. 'Anyway, I could talk all night. See you tomorrow,' he said, and with a jaunty wave as he turned to walk away, added, 'Sleep well!'

Incredibly, I can vividly recall putting the girls to bed in their room, insisting they'd be OK, refusing to acquiesce to their pleadings of having one of us in there with them, and assuring them it would all be fine. I feel a bit bad about that now, because it wasn't fine, and they weren't stupid – they knew it was far from fine. I tiptoed into our room and gently closed the door. 'They're OK,' I convinced myself. 'It'll be all right. Won't it?' Jill was checking the windows.

'These don't open. We can't get out if we need to.'

'OK, maybe it's not fine,' I conceded. 'Let's just see how tomorrow goes.'

'If we live that long,' she scowled.

I got undressed and climbed into bed. Jill sat bolt upright next to me, fully clothed. 'Are you ... joining me?' I asked.

'I think when he bursts in here with a kitchen knife, one of us should be awake. "Sleep well",' she mimicked.

And so, with the light off, and Andy McNab sitting next to me like a coiled spring on a special forces 'black op', I closed my eyes.

That's when we heard it. Not the sharpening of a knife, or the starting of a chainsaw, but a sound much more blood-curdling altogether: the gay chorus of Mickey and his friends dancing down Main Street, just a few blocks away. In the dark I lay, haunted by the gleeful echoes of a Disney parade, trapped in the house of an ex-forces bipolar man whose bed we were apparently lying in.

Welcome to Anaheim.

'When is it OK to tell a lie?' Jill asked, as three curious faces looked to me for an answer. I searched for inspiration in my cardboard coffee cup. One of the things about our trip that changed our family slightly, was that there was simply no room for deception. We were all living on top of each other, literally, so the cute little fibs and diversions most parents use to protect their children from life's harsher, more difficult problems were pointless. They'd been party to every single decision we'd had to make, no matter how grown-up the conversation, and this was no different: are Mum and Dad going to lie to get us out of a fix?

It was the afternoon after the night before. No one had died, no police were called, and thankfully no important pills, red or blue, were left un-swallowed.

Of course, in the rational light of morning, we could see we weren't in any danger at all. 'I was thinking of schizophrenia,' I said to Jill, keeping my voice down, as I got dressed. 'Stephen Fry's bipolar and you don't see him wielding an axe.'

'True,' Jill conceded. 'But that doesn't mean I'd choose to share a house with him when he's in his 70s and can't remember which tablets he's taken.'

In the kitchen Clifford was chatty and keen to show Jill and me where the breakfast things were. He still seemed a little confused about when Paula would return, but hoped it would be before that night. He looked a little shabbier than the evening before and I wondered where he had slept. For now, he settled himself in the living room, dominated by a mammoth flat-screen TV showing a highly-charged evangelical minister who seemed to be getting angry about the devil.

Ella appeared, making her way from the girls' bedroom. She scooted apologetically between Clifford and the preacher and found us in the kitchen. She raised her eyebrows, and cocked her head towards the noise from the living room. I smiled. Jill whispered, 'It'll be fine. We'll work something out.'

I didn't know exactly what we would 'work out', but it seemed increasingly clear that, quite apart from the fact that we had found ourselves in the rôle of carers for an elderly man who, by his own admission, had a fairly flimsy grip on his medication régime or the whereabouts of his wife, we couldn't possibly keep ourselves to ourselves here. We'd expected to spend the week in self-contained accommodation getting schoolwork done, which was obviously going to be impossible.

We left the house after breakfast for a day of what amounted to little more than time-wasting. We saw some vast-but-uninviting beaches, drove through Anaheim's endless, soul-destroying, seedy suburbs where nothing thrived more than the fast-food joints and liquor stores, and at one point were so bored that we even played a game where the girls decided which way I should turn the car at each junction. This sounded a blast, but when after 25 minutes we were back in the same run-down backstreet, I lost patience and called time. We all knew what we were avoiding. We were avoiding going back to *that* house. In fact we were avoiding even *talking* about that house. I stopped outside a Starbucks.

'Sod it. I'm spending some money,' I announced. 'Let's get a coffee. While we're in there, we'll have a family meeting about you-know-what.'

'Finally!' exclaimed Bethan from the back of the car. 'I thought we'd *never* talk about it. Right. I'm going first. We … are not … staying there.'

Jill laughed as we climbed out of the car. Apparently this was going to be an interesting discussion. How to extricate ourselves from this predicament, without hurting the feelings of our hosts was a tricky problem.

'I always think it's best to be honest,' I said. 'Even if it's uncomfortable, it's normally the best thing to do.'

'We can't,' Jill said. 'Are you really prepared to go back this evening and say "Sorry we can't stay the week. You scare us"?'

'He's all right,' I said, defending the old boy. The silence around the table told me no one was convinced. 'Look, are we all absolutely sure that we don't want to stay?' I asked the assembly. 'Not even tonight?'

'Absolutely.'

'Oh yes,' replied the girls. I sighed.

'Well, I guess we could cut our losses. We've only paid for half the week, so I suppose they'd be getting a decent wedge of cash for just one night's disturbance.'

'I'll ring Julie,' said Jill. 'We said we'd go back at the end of this week anyway with the van. I'm sure if I explain that we want to come back a little early they'll be only too happy to help. We could find a motel or something until then.'

'What are you going to say?' asked Ella. 'To Clifford?'

'I'll think of something,' I replied. 'It'll be all right - as long as he's taken his pills.'

As we drove back towards Anaheim Jill raised our potential saviours on their mobile. Julie and Dave were away, but driving back towards their home after a weekend break. We heard Jill explain our predicament, using words like 'uncomfortable' and 'awkward', but it was probably words like 'confused about his medication' that got Julie's attention. We were asking to come over in a day or two, which Julie said would be no problem at all, but one minute after Jill had hung up, the phone rang again. 'I've spoken to Dave, and we insist you come over right away.' Politeness would dictate that we should decline this invasion of their privacy, especially as they were hardly prepared to take in guests. But desperation overcame politeness - we were there like a shot, thanking them with gushing gratitude down the phone.

I was relieved to find Paula back at the house, meaning we wouldn't be deserting poor Clifford alone. I opted for the not-quite-white, more grey, lie to Paula that we'd had an unexpected call from some friends we were hoping to see in California who had absolutely insisted we come and stay, and we simply didn't feel we could refuse. She was happy enough to keep the money for half a week, and any guilt I might have felt was vastly outweighed by the colossal sense of relief we felt driving back towards Beaumont. That had been awkward, but sometimes, it *is* OK to lie.

Back in the safety of Dave and Julie's, life returned to normal for a day or two.

It was good fun watching American TV with them. Julie introduced the girls to *American Idol*. Dave introduced me to baseball, watching The Dodgers, but with the sound turned down. 'You can't watch The Dodgers without Vin Scully,' he explained. Scully, 'The Voice of The Dodgers', is arguably the most famous sports broadcaster in the USA, and at the age of 83 was still commentating 'ball by ball' on the radio. Hence - TV on, sound down, radio on, for the full Dodgers experience.

The TV news would generally raise a smile, too. A fringe Christian eccentric claimed the world would end on the following Saturday, and California news channels keenly ran with the 'apocalypse possible' story. As you'll have realised, given you're reading this, Fringe Christian Eccentric was wrong and the world did not end. I already knew this would be the case, however, as I'm certain that when the End Of The World happens, the message won't be delivered by a crazy man who's added up all the numbers in the Bible. It will be delivered in a telephone call from the person most naturally qualified as The Harbinger of Doom - a shipping agent.

A call came from Compton. Hip-hop fans will know this poor South Central district of LA as the home of Doctor Dre, Ice Cube, the setting of the film *Boyz N The Hood*, and the inspiration for countless Gangsta Rap imitators. It was also home to Phyllis, my shipping agent, a polite lady who contradicted all I'd learned about 'the hood' throughout my teenage years of listening to NWA's profanity-laden classic *Straight Outta Compton*; her phone calls required no parental discretion whatsoever. Nor did she appear to have 'an AK on the shelf' or be about to 'squeeze a trigger and see bodies hauled off', which made me wonder whether, as a young and impressionable hip-hop record buyer, I'd been duped.

Penny's ship, Phyllis informed me, was two days late. 'Well, OK then,' I said. 'We can wait an extra two days.'

'But it's gonna be another six days before your van is transferred to the clearance terminal,' said Phyllis.

'What? So when d'you reckon we can get her?' I asked. 'A week from now?'

There was a pause, and I could hear Phyllis tapping a pen on the desk. At least I hoped it was a pen, and not the cartridge clip from her 22. There was a sucking of teeth in Compton. 'Let's see,' she murmured. 'Ship's ETA Friday, weekend nothin' gets done, clearance by next Friday, then two to three days for Customs. I'd say ... maybe ten days from now?'

This was very depressing news, but what could I say? It wasn't Phyllis's fault port authorities operate so slowly. I wasn't about to shoot the messenger. Not when the messenger is from Compton, where that sort of thing is taken very seriously. This meant we faced not leaving LA until the end of May – almost a fortnight later than we'd expected, allowing us just five weeks to traverse the 3,000 miles of North America from west coast to east coast, from where Penny would sail home out of Baltimore, the closest commercial port to New York. There'd be no time to dawdle.

Yet again, for what felt like the one-millionth time, we were confronting a hurdle that would require us to change our plans. So yet again we spread our enormous United States map on Julie and Dave's living room floor and pondered our options. 'It's going to be a race across America to reach Baltimore by the end of June,' said Jill, tracing her finger across one-and-a-half metres of creased paper. On our hands and knees, with Millie-the-dog padding across America wondering what was holding our attention so keenly, we gazed at the map. In our heads we drew a straight line from LA to Washington DC, our last proper 'stop' before we would drop Penny at Baltimore port just an hour north. All hopes of deviating from this imaginary line were extinguished, given the lack of time.

'Chicago seems a long way north,' Jill commented.

'Yeah, and look at Nashville and Mississippi. We can't go that far south,' I said. Then added, 'I can't believe we won't get to boast that we gigged in Nashville.'

'At least Kansas is easy, though,' she said. Kansas City was a must. We'd have found a way to visit Lisa's husband and daughter, Ty and Rebecca, regardless of location, but thankfully they did appear to be bang in the middle of our straight line.

'Will we go to Colorado Springs?' asked Ella. Her best friend, Melissa, had a grandmother there who had offered to put us up. We scanned the map, and found Colorado Springs just below Denver, on the other side of The Rockies.

'It's actually level with Kansas City,' I said. 'If we skirt the Rockies to the south, knowing Penny's aversion to mountains, we could head up to Colorado from Santa Fe, then turn right and drive straight across to Kansas City.' In ten seconds I had summarised over a week of driving. It seemed so simple on paper.

'I think we will,' Jill told Ella. 'Let's wait and see. I don't want to make any firm plans until we actually have Penny back.'

'We can see the Grand Canyon, no problem,' I said, putting one finger on Beaumont, and another on Grand Canyon National Park, 'but Vegas and Zion National Park are out. Too far off our route.'

There was a groan from Ella. She wanted to see Las Vegas. And Jill, you'll remember, had stated long before we left home that seeing Barry Manilow in Vegas would be the highlight of her trip. She liked to give the impression she had said it in jest, but deep down, I suspected she meant it.

So, again, a new plan was born. We decided to spend our enforced week without Penny seeing parts of America we might otherwise have missed. After gleaning some valuable local knowledge from Dave and Julie about which places to pick over others, a week-long road trip in our rental car was hastily concocted - a kooky polygon from Beaumont up to Vegas, back west into California, then north to Sequoia National Park, further north to Yosemite National Park, before finally heading back south to Beaumont.

That evening, as the kids sat glued to *American Idol*, I fired up the laptop. With remarkable ease, I booked a cheap hotel in Vegas, a log cabin in Sequoia and a pre-erected tent in Yosemite – each for two nights. Our accommodation for the week was sorted, and it had cost less than 300 quid. Now, while some all-American young heart-throb with impossibly white teeth sang for her stardom on the box, I had just one more task.

'What are you looking so smug about?' asked Jill as the end-credits rolled and a tearful teen hugged a well-chiselled host.

'Oh nothing much,' I said dismissively. 'I've just … BOUGHT YOU A TICKET TO SEE BARRY MANILOW ON SATURDAY NIGHT!'

As the applause roared from the TV, a tearful woman hugged a less well-chiselled husband.

The next morning we re-packed our bags, loaded them into our hire-car's capacious 'trunk', and waved goodbye once again to our lovely friends. We'd be back with them again in a week - we really were starting to feel like members of the family.

Dave had commented on how boring the drive to Vegas would be. 'Nothing but desert the whole way,' he'd smiled. But to us it was brilliant. American culture is so engrained in us from such an early age, that it's impossible to drive across the Mojave desert without feeling like you're on a movie set. It was nothing like the sandy deserts we'd crossed in Jordan. The ground here was sun-baked dirt. A gritty terrain, punctuated by occasional sprouting bunches of a hardy desert plant that seemed to only stay green for a short time, as most were a crackly brown. Distant mountain ranges drew craggy lines across the clear blue sky. The driest of all North America's deserts, it was the kind of ground on which you'd expect to confront a rattlesnake at any moment. Mojave National Preserve has several ghost towns, the most famous being Calico, and an abundance of something worthless, humble, yet truly iconic.

'Oh my word!' I yelped excitedly as we cruised down a sliver of asphalt dissecting the desert. 'Did you see that?'

'What was it?' the girls asked from the back of the car.

'Actual tumbleweed!' I cried. 'A ball of weed! And it really did tumble! Right across the road!'

They weren't impressed. How many times over the years had I used 'tumbleweed' as a comic device? How many TV prop designers had I tasked with making a fake ball of dead twigs, to pull across the set on a length of fishing line while the sound-effects operater played the mournful clang of a distant tolling bell? It was the standard comic response to a joke you knew would fall flat. And here, for the first time in my life, was the real thing.

Bouncing across the highway came rolling balls of pale brown twigs, just like in the cowboy films. No sound effects tape. No prop guy tugging a string. I was enthralled. We turned off the highway in the middle of nowhere and drove a couple of minutes into the parched desert to stop for lunch. We'd brought sandwiches and drinks, prepared for a lack of amenities. 'Have we got anything for pudding?' asked Edie, wiping her mouth with her sleeve.

'No pudding, but lots of dessert,' I said, shamelessly gleeful. 'Geddit?' The girls looked at me with withered boredom. A ball of tumbleweed rolled past. Damn, that stuff's professional.

About five hours after we left Beaumont, we crested a rise in the desert and saw Las Vegas spread before us. Arriving in Vegas in the daytime is a slight disappointment, because it's a city built to shine in the blackness of a desert night. In the movies, the protagonist's first view of the place is always in the dark, usually from the car he or she has used to flee their humdrum life to seek thrills, spills and usually an inappropriate marriage in Nevada's hotbed of sleaze. Seeing it in daylight is like seeing a TV set in real life - you realise it's just bits of painted hardboard held together with tape: the magic's missing.

'It's not as classy as I'd hoped,' was Jill's first reaction to the place.

'Who's Barry Manilow?' was Edie's, who'd seen a poster bearing the smiling face of what appeared to be a genetic fusion of Rod Stewart and Liza Minnelli. I pointed out that Vegas hadn't gained the nickname Sin City by hosting Ambassadors' cocktail parties and Mozart concerts. It wasn't supposed to be classy.

'Yeah I know, but it's a bit ... tatty,' said Jill.

'Shabby,' I nodded in agreement.

'Downbeat,' she concluded

You might be surprised to learn that Las Vegas has some of the cheapest hotel accommodation in America. That's because they want people to visit for almost nothing so that they'll then spend more money in the hotels' casinos. And *all* hotels have casinos. I'd booked a room at Circus Circus for $45 (about 30 quid), a hotel which prides itself on being the only venue in Vegas aimed at visitors with children. We could have had equally cheap accommodation at the famous pyramid of The Luxor, but did they have a rollercoaster *inside* the hotel? No, they did not, and so it was that our homing beacon at the northern end of The Strip was a towering, 60-foot, brightly lit, happy clown.

The truth is, however, Vegas is no place for kids. Even the best efforts of Circus Circus, with its free Big Top performances in the Midway funfair area don't distract from the fact that to get from your room to the 'child-friendly' funfair you have to escort your little ones through acres of dark, smoky, low-ceilinged slot-machine halls, roulette rooms, black-jack arenas and countless other dimly lit caverns where a strict carpet colour code is policed - kids mustn't tread outside the 'green zone' into the 'red carpet of sin' on either side. A simple stroll to the front lobby is like walking Stephen King's *Green Mile* with hoots and caterwauling not from prisoners on either side, but from glassy-eyed zombie prisoners of Lady Luck.

The atmosphere in these rooms is one of collective hypnotism where players have only the vaguest inkling of how much time has passed or whether the sky outside is lit by the sun or the moon. We quickly discovered it was incredibly difficult to find an exit to the street - a deliberate policy to remove all thoughts of the real world from the minds of the punters. There are no clocks, no windows or doors letting in natural light, and the noise is a constant throbbing drone of electronic beeps and riffs from the ranks of slot machines. It's easy to see how people caught in this unreal world can lose more than just cash. They can lose whole days.

By night, Las Vegas Boulevard, 'The Strip', is a writhing mass of brash, bawdy, brilliantly lit disappointment. Disappointing because each stunning, throbbing, luminescent façade is just the flimsiest of veils before a shoulder-slumping sigh of recognition within. We poked our head into a few different hotels only to find the same acres of slot machines that were in our own hotel up the road. Outside, though, and taken as a whole, the buildings are dazzling and stunning. A cab ride from Circus Circus down to Paris beats Blackpool illuminations by about 40-trillion filament watts.

The choreographed fountains in front of The Bellagio will have you spell-bound. But, for all the beauty in that artistic wonder - and it really is wondrous - there is the ever-present underbelly of sleaze: prostitution is legal in Nevada, so countless 'Girls Girls Girls' cards are handed out on the street, naked girls dance silhouetted against windows, drunk college girls are living it up, throwing up and being propped up by equally unsteady college boys.

'Let's go to The Flamingo hotel,' suggested Jill. 'You can see real flamingos in the garden.' So we fought through the crowds, pushed our way through the front doors to find ourselves in yet another homogenous slot-machine hall, except this one had a couple of unique additions.

'Why are those ladies in cages?' asked Edie. 'And why haven't they got any tops on?'

'Keep moving,' instructed Jill dragging her firmly onwards.

'And where's Daddy?' Edie asked as an afterthought.

'Right behind you,' I said, momentarily distracted.

With the best will in the world, it's difficult to explain caged erotic podium-dancers to a nine-year-old girl, and the worrisome burden of two words weighed ever more heavily on my mind: irresponsible parenting. Mind you, at least the kids were spared the worst: Jill went on her own to see Barry Manilow.

After getting herself about as glammed up as is possible after nine months living out of a rucksack, Jill waved us goodbye at the foot of a fake Eiffel Tower, relishing a night singing along with a living legend at the Paris Theatre. I took the girls for a 'kids eat free' buffet at our hotel. The re-heated favourites were passionately consumed. And our buffet was all right, too.

After collecting Jill, giddy and fizzing, from her Bazzer encounter and fighting our way home up The Strip I dropped her and the girls in our bedroom and stole half an hour to experience a Vegas casino as a grown-up. This was in the name of research for this book, you understand, and I didn't launch myself into such folly without some basic schooling. One of the few things available for free in our hotel's casino was the chance to take proper tuition in gambling. I learned Black Jack from a long-in-the-tooth male croupier who seemed surprised when I asked if, in this game of 21s you had to get over 16 to win. 'Whaddaya mean?' he barked. 'As long as you beat the dealer you win.'

'Well I'm only thinking of Pontoon,' I said defensively. 'That's what we call *this* back home.'

I wanted to tell him that Black Jack is actually an entirely different game involving seven cards and, lo and behold, jacks of a black suit, unlike the ridiculous American casino game where an ace and a picture card together are called a Black Jack. Absurd. But he'd moved on to aid less-troublesome pupils. After a quarter of an hour a paying game started. I made my excuses and left.

Next I sat at a roulette table for my lesson on the spinning wheel of fortune, only to find the same over-tanned wisecracking cowboy was our teacher. He spent 15 minutes making the simplest game of luck in the world appear an application of great skill and strategy, before announcing he would be starting a paying game.

And so, now fully qualified to squander a whole $20 burning a hole in my pocket, I hit the tables. Extensive research from my evening's high-rolling, which I pass on to you at no charge, has revealed this much: roulette is stupid. I'm not letting the fact that I lost 20 bucks playing it cloud my judgement, really I'm not. Just let me tell you *why* it's stupid, in case one day a smartly-dressed cad woos you into a place called The Royale and you find yourself in the awkward position of putting a week's housekeeping money on black.

Each number on the spinning wheel, one to 36 plus an extra couple - zero and double zero - are represented in squares printed on a green baize table. You place your chips (that's real money, kids) on either a number, or a collection of numbers you think the ball might land on. The number of chips (*ker-ching*) you win depends on whether you bet on a single number, or a group of numbers. But here's the thing: the odds you're offered *aren't fair*.

Even the simplest bet - betting on odds or evens, or reds or blacks, will get you a return of one to one (your stake matched) - but the chances *are not* 50/50 because you're betting on 18 numbers out of ... not 36, but 38 numbers on the wheel, thanks to those extra cheeky zero and double zeros. More complex odds are offered on groups of numbers, but always weighted against the plucky player. So even if only *one* person is playing at the table, the house will ultimately win. Now, bear in mind that as many as eight to ten people can play a single spin. As a casino owner, you'd be thinking, 'Well, only one number can come up, yet all these other players have bet on all these other numbers - wahay!'

The house literally 'cleans up' after each spin, sweeping up all the chips from those failed bets for itself. Has no one ever looked at this and thought it might be a tad unfair? That's my cutting edge revelation, right there: the house always wins. It cost me almost £13 to discover that. Don't thank me.

Resolved that Ella, Beth and Edie should get more from our Vegas experience than an eye-popping introduction to gambling and prostitution, we found the perfect 'school day' outing for us all that was both educational and a little alarming: Las Vegas is home to Nevada's Atomic Testing Museum.

Come on, you've got two crazy days in Vegas. What else are you going to do? They tested nuclear bombs here, baby! Right here in the Nevada desert. They built whole towns and blew them to pieces with atom bombs, just to see what happened. Don'tcha wanna see those pictures? Don'tcha? They watched mushroom clouds from wooden benches in the sand, less-than-amply protected by slightly-thicker-than-normal sunglasses! This is a piece of American history you'd be a fool to miss, although you wouldn't think so from the lack of cars in the car park or the immediate ease with which we were welcomed in. No elaborate '45 minutes from here' queueing system needed at the Atomic Testing Museum. Apparently this town had other distractions.

Look, we've all tested nuclear weapons in our time. Maybe not personally, but *as a nation* lots of us have 'gone fission'. In the 50s America had Bikini Atoll and Britain had Christmas Island. Even the French exploded nuclear weapons in, oh, where was it? A tiny uninhabited wasteland ... oh yes, *The Pacific Ocean*! But that was *way* back in NINETEEN NINETY SIX! (That's right France, we haven't forgotten).

The Atomic Testing Museum, an affiliate of The Smithsonian, is a no-holds-barred description of how and why America started decorating the Nevada Desert with radioactive mushroom clouds from the 1940s right up to the 1990s (although latterly hidden underground). The museum includes a concrete bunker from which we experienced a simulated H-bomb blast, loads of real life accounts from the people who carried out these tests and the remarkable story of how Las Vegas turned a potential tourism 'negative' into a marketing 'positive'; we saw flyers from hotels boasting 'See the mushroom cloud from your balcony', photos of smiling families doing just that, and my favourite example of 50s Americana positive marketing - Miss Atomic Bomb 1957. The beaming, buxom blonde looks the picture of health wearing a swimsuit and a cardboard mushroom cloud. You can see for yourself with an online search for 'Lee Merlin', the girl in question.

So it *is* possible to take your kids to Vegas and teach them something educational *other* than the life-lesson of witnessing the extremes of human existence, from penniless vagrancy to hedonistic debauchery. It *is* also possible that this makes me the world's most boring dad, and that years from now, when my daughters are strutting The Strip, expertly schooling their peers in the ways of hedonistic debauchery they will laugh at how I once took them to the Atomic Testing Museum. What can I say? My work here is done.

A sequoia is a giant redwood tree. It's also a panvowel, fact fan – a word that uses every vowel only once. I wonder how many others you'll spot in this chapter, keen-eyed reader? (You never realised this was an interactive quiz book, did you? Your day just gets better and better.)

Sequoia National Park is home to the giant redwood trees that anyone who grew up in 70s Britain will remember Norris McWhirter referring to on *Record Breakers*. I can still vividly remember being amazed at a photo of an arch cut in a giant redwood tree, big enough for a car to drive through. The opportunity to see these monsters was too exciting a chance to miss. The fact that our mountain cabin – a zero-luxury uninsulated shed with beds in - was surrounded by *snow* only added to the thrill.

We had wound our way up twisting mountain roads for almost two hours to get to the heart of the park, and it was astonishing that just a day's drive from the heat of Vegas we found ourselves in a snowy mountain-top wilderness.

A park ranger met us, and showed us which of the small group of log cabins in the woods was ours. Within seconds of dumping our bags in the hut, we were outside having a snowball fight and making a snowman with the kind of enthusiasm only imaginable after not seeing proper snow for more than 18 months.

'D'you remember how hot it was this morning?' Ella asked, shaking her head in amazement. 'This place is brilliant!' The Nevada desert did seem like another world, compared to the icy grandeur of our new surroundings. We explored the park, endlessly astonished by the towering height of the trees around us, and found Major Sherman - the largest tree on Earth.

'That's not a bad day, is it?' Jill asked herself. 'What did you do today? Oh, I saw the largest tree on Earth.'

'That is amazing,' I said, craning my neck skywards, attempting to take in Major Sherman's full splendour. 'What do you think of it, Edie?' I asked.

'Pretty big,' she answered, accurately. I guess when you're nine, you keep your options open. She may yet see bigger.

We drove our hire car under an arch cut out of a tree (I hoped Norris was smiling down at us), walked through the hollow log of a tree *two thousand* years old, and basically oooh'd and aaah'd in tree-inspired wonder. None of this, though, was as adrenaline-inducing as our 4am bear hunt.

National Parks in California are black bear country, and rules are strict on being 'Bear Aware': no food can be left in your car, or cabin, or tent. Bears are curious, brave, blessed with incredible strength and a sense of smell several times greater than that of a bloodhound. I was blessed with a hire car on which I'd signed away an $800 deposit against damage, and my box-ticked-insurance didn't cover 'hungry grizzly peeling door from Chevy to steal nachos'. So we were on high alert.

As darkness fell we had a fun evening, wrapped up against the chill, making smores on the campfire. Smores are an American camping phenomenon – a marshmallow is toasted on a fork or stick over the campfire, then sandwiched between two honey crackers with a chunk of Hershey's chocolate and squished into a warm gooey mess. It's called a smore because you'll want s'more. (See what they did there?)

By about 9.30 it was time to clear up and move from the icy woods into our only-marginally-less-icy shed – sorry, log cabin – for a chilly night of living like mountain-folk. What followed were several hours of broken sleep, punctuated by general complaining from children who were no longer able to feel their limbs, until I was woken sharply in the dead of night by the loud crunching sound of a polythene bag.

'What are you looking for?' I asked into the darkness, assuming one of the girls had got up.

No one replied, and the crinkly crunching continued. I remembered the cellophane wrapper around some logs I'd left outside the door, and, looking at the crooked shed door, could see shadows passing through the moonlight at floor level. I nudged Jill hard enough to wake her up.

'Jill!' I whispered loudly.

'What?' she replied from the other side of the room. That threw me, as I'd definitely nudged someone next to me, and she wasn't where I'd left her.

'Where are you?'

'I'm over here,' she replied from the bed where Edie had been.

'Hello,' said Edie next to me. This sort of midnight-musical-beds happened a lot when we were camping, but I never seemed to be part of the game. Then I whispered the words every wife or daughter wants to hear from the family patriarch.

'Is that a bear?'

Suddenly Ella and Bethan were awake too. I switched a light on, but it was dim and the shadows outside were still clearly visible across the bottom of the door.

'Will it break the door down?' asked Ella, now sitting bolt upright clutching bedding around her.

'Let me go and have a look,' said I, the brave warrior, as I stepped on to the freezing wooden floor and tiptoed towards the window.

As I pulled back the thin makeshift curtain, the family held their breath. 'I can't see anything out there,' I reported, pondering my options.

'I need the toilet,' said a voice from one of the beds.

'Good idea,' I agreed. 'It's a short dash from this door to the loo block. Who's going first?' And so it was that a minute later, or possibly two given the amount of layers we all wrapped ourselves in, all five of us tiptoed into the moonlit snow, in our own nervous tribute to a children's storybook we'd all enjoyed many years ago.

'Hey, *we're* Going On a Bear Hunt!' Edie announced joyfully, remembering one of her favourite bedtime stories.

'You might be,' muttered Jill, breaking into a sprint. 'I'm going to the toilet.'

'The mum in the book doesn't say that,' Edie said quietly to Beth.

Safely back in our cabin, duly relieved (in every sense), we huddled under our icy blankets and I turned out the light. About 30 seconds passed. CRUNCH! The same crinkling plastic was heard from the door. Five pairs of eyes shot open. Under the door I saw a shadow move menacingly. Once again I was at the window. Once again my family held their breath, braced for a slathering eight-foot grizzly to batter down the door.

'I can't see a thing,' I whispered. 'But look at the shadows on the floor!'

'Sim, put the light on,' said Jill, suddenly no longer whispering, and no longer scared.

'Why?'

'It's a mouse.'

'What?' I turned the light on.

'I just saw it under the door,' she said. 'It's about *that* big.' She held her finger and thumb as if gripping an invisible egg.

Ella joined me at the door and held up a carrier bag left on the floor. Inside it were two failed attempts at sticky smores Edie had 'binned' and left on the floor - perfect nosh for hungry rodents. 'So much for being Bear Aware,' laughed Ella.

'Whoops!' shrugged Edie, then as we headed back to bed added, 'Hey, that'd be a good children's book. *Going on a Mouse Hunt!*'

'Yeah, or a film,' replied Bethan dryly. 'You could call it, I dunno, *Mouse Hunt.*'

'Oh yeah,' Edie said, realising it had been done.

'Sleep well,' I ordered, switching the light off.

'Maybe Lee Evans could be in it,' Beth went on.

'Enough!' ordered Jill into the dark. 'Quit troublemaking.'

At least one other person mentioned Christopher Walken before exhaustion beat the game out of us and we finally slept.

Yosemite is a word I knew from a young age, thanks to Saturday morning cartoons featuring the diminutive, hirsute, gun-toting cowboy Yosemite Sam. It's also one of those words that's simply a pleasure to say, although once you've jokingly pronounced it 'Yosser-might' it's hard to see it as 'Yo-semma-tee' ever again. There, now I've gone and put that in *your* brain too. You're welcome.

Describing Yosemite is incredibly difficult, such is its jaw-dropping beauty and scale. Fortunately I have a handy technique for tackling jobs that I find difficult. I delegate. Here is what my family had to say about Yosemite, when I asked them to assist me with a blog entry:

Jill: 'I thought it was the most amazing scenery I've ever seen. Utterly breathtaking.'

Ella: 'I thought the views were incredible. It was a highlight of the trip.'

Bethan: 'I thought it was really stunning. I've never seen anything like it before.'

Edie: 'It was lots of fun and very beautiful.'

We had just one day to take in over a thousand square miles of World Heritage Site, so started at the free Ansel Adams gallery to see the classic views so memorably captured by the famous photographer, before heading out wearing inappropriately flimsy footwear to find those views for ourselves. We walked to the base of the Lower Falls, where the cold air from the mountaintop snowfields plummeted from the heights, picking up spray from the snow-melt waterfall and blasting it into us, reducing the temperature from a balmy 25°C to about 10°C in a matter of a moments.

Then we hiked a few miles up the river to Mirror Lake, where we lost the tourists, and where every turn of the track revealed an oil painting of natural beauty, from the coursing rapids to the deep crystal clear waters of the wider river, with Pacific Dogwood trees hanging bright-white blossom over fallen logs, where Chickaree squirrels would dart and forage. Then, into a clearing, and we were suddenly aware of the colossal towering cliff face of granite that'd been just behind us all along, hiding behind the thick woodland.

'Look at the top,' said Jill, craning her head back, shielding her eyes against the bright blue sky. 'Those tiny bristles are *trees!*' The sheer size of the place is simply astounding.

We were blessed with a lucky pitch on our campsite, deep in the valley, next to the river with a view of Yosemite Upper Falls high on the mountain beyond it. It was lucky, because you can't pick your plot at the Housekeeping Camp. Nor can you pick your neighbours. After being on our own in nature's idyll for the first night, we were joined on the second by a group of ageing bikers, who'd been allocated the pre-made tent backing on to ours.

California has more than its fair share of Harley Davidson riders, most of whom are several decades too old for the Harley image I grew up with – Dennis Hopper and Jack Nicholson in the 1969 film *Easy Rider*. In fact, most of these riders *are* like Jack Nicholson – that is, in their mid-70s. I swear those bad-ass leather panniers they all have slung over their hogs are full of medication and incontinence pads. Rebels with gout and gauze.

Even though all my juvenile dreams of one day owning a Harley had been erased by America's army of wrinkly riders, I was still excited to see three fully chromed hogs filling the space next to our tent where I had earlier parked our thoroughly dull rental car. The total number of guys sharing the three-bed tent eluded me. I think there were six or seven, but we only met four to properly chat to. They quickly came to say hello. The most enthusiastic one, Steve, sported the obligatory bandana on his balding 60-something head and a bone-handled knife on his hip. 'We're gonna be playing some music later,' he said, brimming with excitement. 'Dirtbeard's brought his guitar. Come over if you like.'

I looked at the girls. I was so tempted to say, 'Why Steve, we'd *love* to. Tell me, have you heard of The Beatles?' I could see tense terror in the glares boring into me from Ella and Beth.

'Maybe we will. Let's see how tired the kids are,' I said, non-committal. I'm too good to those girls.

A few Jim Beam-fuelled hours later (on their part, rather than ours) we lay in our beds while, just feet away, Cheezy Riders dragged several once-good songs to the edge of Yosemite's highest peak and pushed them murderously to their deaths. I recognised *Sultans of Swing* (twice), *Hotel California* and, oddly, John Mayer's *Daughters*. Perhaps that one was for me. Most agonisingly, especially for Edie, was their passion for Lennon and McCartney. Hearing *Blackbird* throttled in the dead of night actually made Edie shed a tear, writhing in her sleeping bag. They did *Please Please Me*, or rather, they *didn't*. And they failed to recognise the irony of picking up the guitar to play *I Should Have Known Better.*

'Honestly, kids,' I whispered. 'Aren't ham-fisted amateurs doing Beatles covers tiresome?'

'Now we know how all those innocent people we've played to felt,' said Beth.

'We're better than this!' scolded Ella, then added, 'Aren't we?'

No answer. We lay in the dark, full-to-the-brim with a dose of our own medicine, begging for sleep to take us, or an angry bear to take them.

Back in Beaumont I battled hard with various shipping and port officials to get Penny released before the Memorial Weekend – a three-day holiday when the entire Long Beach port shuts down – which was a stressful but ultimately successful struggle. Penny was back with us!

I had to do a few repairs again. The last time I'd faced this was after cyclone Yasi threw Penny's ship around with such violence that it wrenched a cupboard from its screws. This time it was a cyclone of activity from the US Customs officials, who had gone through everything, and mysteriously forced a cupboard door open, splintering it from its hinges and breaking the latch. What's strange is – the cupboard wasn't locked. You can imagine the choice words I had for the anonymous goons at border control.

So, after three separate stays, totalling about a fortnight, it was finally time to wave goodbye to the wonderful Julie and Dave, who had flung open their home to us, on nothing more than a recommendation from their son Brian who we'd spent a day with in Jordan. It was an emotional farewell, because having left them twice before I don't think any of us could quite believe that this time we wouldn't be coming back. They had been so generous and kind, and we were all a bit depressed as we pointed Penny east, watched the milometer click past 14,000 miles, and drove into the Mojave desert – destination Grand Canyon. Still, it was good to be reunited with the sixth member of the family again.

The Grand Canyon was stunning. Of course it was. It would be a brave travel writer who said 'Grand Canyon – lacklustre disappointment'. Like the Great Barrier Reef, it's one of the seven natural wonders of the world and has been on my tick-list to see since I was about ten years old. I'm pleased to say it *didn't* disappoint. We were driving around the rim when we first saw it. The road cuts through forest for a while, and the trees had been hiding it. I was saying to the kids, 'It's just on our left, honest,' when suddenly the trees opened up ... along with our mouths.

'Wow!'s and 'Woah!'s chorused from all of us. Well, most of us. I pulled over and we walked to the edge to take in our first view of nature's most famous chasm. 'It's a big hole,' said Edie, which I felt did six million years of hard work by the Colorado River something of a disservice.

'Are you serious?' asked Ella. 'A big hole?'

'Yeah,' shrugged Edie. 'Pretty big.' Just as when faced with the world's largest tree at Sequoia, she was keeping her options open. She may yet see bigger.

Keen hikers can yomp all the way down to the river that continues to cut slowly into the bed of the canyon, where the exposed rock is almost two billion years old. *Two billion!* We should just take a moment to let that figure compute. When those rocks were last exposed, there were no animals on the planet. Photosynthesis was new, there were bacteria, single-celled organisms, but that was it. Earth's atmosphere was only just getting *oxygen!* No animals would appear for another one-and-a-half *billion* years. And thanks to the tireless work of the Colorado River, you can just wander down and touch rocks almost half as old as planet Earth itself. The fact I find that so cool makes me wonder why I didn't study harder in Geography at school.

Ella, Beth and I took a narrow trail down into the canyon to just beyond a lookout point known as 'Ooh Aah' (Manchester United fans will be forgiven for wanting to say 'Cantona' after that) where the temperature rose as quickly as the rocks above us. The views were incredible as we descended past layered stripes of crumbling sedimentary rock, all shades of orange, brown and red. Our route was graded as one of the easiest hikes in the canyon, yet the steep climb back to the top, in searing heat, made us realise why there are signposts on the rim warning against any attempt to reach the river and return to the top in a day. An average of 16 people die every year in the Grand Canyon, mostly through dehydration. It's deceptively easy-going to hike down, but life-sapping to climb back up.

We camped in the forest on the southern rim and, thinking we'd stay for a couple of nights, even pitched our tent. This was now our fourth tent, incidentally, since leaving home. Having returned the huge awning to England from a bewildered post office in Greece only a couple of months into our trip, we had since bought and destroyed two pop-up two-man tents. We had slowly discovered that most camping gear just couldn't hack it at our level, being put up and packed away far more often than just the occasional weekend I suspected they were designed for.

So, it was time to use the latest edition, bought from a Target supermarket in Los Angeles. It didn't have a fully fitted fly-sheet, just a half-fly to act as a waterproof 'lid', leaving loads of ventilation mesh exposed underneath. This was clearly a summer-time tent. That night, as Jill and I huddled inside under a quilt and blankets, and the girls slept in the van, the temperature dropped to minus 1°C and it *snowed*. 'I consider us hardened campers, I really do,' shivered Jill, 'but *snow*? That's not really on, is it?'

The next morning, finding the girls had also spent the night wrapping themselves in every item of clothing they owned, we scrapped the idea of staying a second night and re-packed Penny to set off for one last morning at the world's most famous ditch, after which we'd move onwards to the considerably warmer Monument Valley.

But …

Penny refused to start.

We all exchanged worried looks. In all the time we'd owned her, she had *never* refused to start. Fearing I was going to drain the battery turning the engine over, I suddenly had a thought. 'Oh! There's a special lever somewhere for cold starts.' I reached under the dashboard and pulled a plastic handle that had never before been pulled. Edie's face fell.

'Blue told you never to touch that,' she said earnestly.

It was true. I had once asked our mechanic Blue what the mysterious plastic handle was for and he'd laughed and said something about a cold start choke and never to touch it because 'they're bloody temperamental and effing useless', or words to that effect. Edie had clearly been there, and taken in this vital fact. I turned the key. We held our breath. The engine spluttered. I held the key turned.

Soon she was firing on at least two, then three cylinders, until finally in a cloud of smoke she revved her heart out. I pushed the lever back in and recoiled a bit as if prodding away an angry snake. I didn't really want to have to touch that thing again. Penny didn't sound happy and I wasn't sure the lever had helped. As we gingerly left our icy campsite, I pondered the cause of her upset. I remembered the old fuel filter problem Luigi had diagnosed in Italy. Penny lacked a certain 'oomph', so I suspected her fuel filter might be clogged again. A day or two later, at a town called Farmington in New Mexico, I went on to put some Diesel Kleen additive in the tank, put our final new fuel filter on and was reassured to find the old one was visibly full of nasty dark brown gunk. We never touched that lever again. I made the kids promise not to tell Blue.

Monument Valley was even better than the Grand Canyon. Better because hardly anyone goes there, and if you arrive after 6pm, as we did, no one charges an entrance fee. Of all the places we'd set up camp in the world, none could compare with the sunset views of Monument Valley. We sat outside, spellbound, remembering all the inferior places where we'd paid too much to camp, or places like Petra in Jordan, where they wanted £100 entrance fee. 'We bought a week pass to the entire Grand Canyon for 25 bucks,' said Jill, as the girls sat on top of the van in Penny's roof-well, gazing at the towering red columns. 'What's that equal to?' she continued. '15 quid? And that was with all those free ranger talks and shuttle buses thrown in. And then *this* - a night in Monument Valley *for free.*'

'God bless America,' Ella said, without a hint of irony. She meant it. This country, so often reduced to stereotype, and even ridiculed by the more cynical of us Brits (guilty as charged), was winning our hearts. We'd found stunning landscapes, friendly strangers and kindness and generosity at every turn.

Depending on your age, you'd either recognise the towering pillars of Monument Valley, a collection of massive sandstone buttes protruding vertically up to a thousand feet from the Navajo valley floor, from a John Wayne or a Tom Cruise movie.

The Duke made five films there, including *Stage Coach* and *The Searchers*. Tom Cruise was hanging off one of the massive rock-towers at the start of *Mission Impossible 2*, a stunt I would dearly have loved to mimic, but sadly it was only achievable with the aid of several helicopters, some climbing gear, the permission of the Navajo land owners and far more technical support than a 1989 Volkswagen camper van can provide.

We neither stage coached, searched, nor took on missions impossible. We slept peacefully under a starlit sky, woke early and wandered on to the valley floor, enchanted by the majesty of the morning sun slowly warming the striking natural monuments around us. Then the first truck-load of Japanese tourists came noisily chattering past us and the spell was broken. The heat quickly forced us to beat a hasty retreat to the small visitor centre café, where we had the balcony to ourselves, overlooking the splendid vista. The paper-cup coffee may have been nothing special, but, with that view, it remains the best cup of coffee I've ever had. Simply awesome.

As you know, our aim was to drive east towards New York, keeping to as straight a line as possible because of our limited time. Colorado Springs and Kansas, each of which were home to friends (with toilets and washing machines) were both on that straight-line route. However, there was something in the way. It was called the Rockies.

We got as far as Four Corners, the kooky point at which four states meet, when we had to think more carefully about our route. There's absolutely nothing to see at Four Corners apart from, well, four corners. Nicely laid metallic strips on the ground show the only point in the USA where four states collide. Having taken photos of all of us in various positions, including an impressive 'crab' from the girls with each hand and foot in a different state – Utah, Colorado, Arizona and New Mexico – it was time to move on. I feared Penny might kill herself crossing the Rocky Mountains – the most direct route from Four Corners to Colorado Springs – so we spared her and turned right, heading south towards Albuquerque.

In fact, after camping for a night in the very bleak one-horse town of Farmington - and having done those running repairs on Penny – we scooted past Albuquerque and settled for a few days in Santa Fe, right at the southern tip of the Rockies.

Santa Fe is, as well as the name we'd give our friend Fay if ever she dressed as Father Christmas, the capital of New Mexico and the USA's highest state capital at 7,000 feet above sea level. Its Spanish colonial history is obvious in the architecture, especially the many smooth brown Adobe buildings. This doesn't mean they're owned by a software giant, but that they're built using bricks made of mud and straw, and rendered with smooth brown mud by hand. With their rich chocolate colour and sleek, rounded corners they look amazing and, given the fairly severe rain storms these mountains produce, it's a wonder they don't simply dissolve into the gutter.

The city has become a creative hot-spot, and a promotional video I watched at our campsite in the city's mountainous outskirts boasted that Santa Fe was home to 14,000 'creatives'. They meant artists, writers, sculptors, musicians and the like, but I wondered how such a figure was arrived at. Had these people had to sign a register to say they were 'creative'? Where would the line be drawn? I could play Beatles songs on a ukulele but I doubted that would qualify me to be counted as a shining jewel in the 'Land of Enchantment' (New Mexico's bumper-sticker slogan). Conversely, I've known accountants who can be incredibly creative.

Anyway, the city is now something of a Mecca to lovers of art and has more galleries and studios than you can shake a hand-painted-authentic-Apache-cactus-rainstick at. Its distinctive architecture, its classic late 19th century town-square and its surrounding mountainous dusty roads have also proved irresistible to a legion of movie directors. The aforementioned *Easy Rider* was shot here, along with more recent classics such as *Changeling, Crazy Heart, No Country For Old Men* and *Cowboys & Aliens*. (Well … they can't *all* be classics.)

Add to that list *Odd Thomas* which, although not yet released at the time of writing, was most certainly cluttering up Santa Fe's small town centre when we first wandered into the square, and accidentally on to the set.

'Sorry sir,' said a young man in a bomber jacket, baseball cap and holding a clipboard. 'Could you please wait inside this shop for a second?'

He ushered us into the doorway of yet another arts-and-crafts gift shop and clasped his hand to the side of his head, listening to a small headphone clamped against his ear. Then, apologetically into a small microphone he said, 'Yeah. Yeah I know. Sorry. We're good.'

Then, slowly absorbing what we'd stumbled upon, we heard 'Standby!' shouted from a man next to a large camera mounted on a dolly.

'Rolling!' shouted someone else.

'Background!' shouted a harassed looking floor manager, and it took all my strength not to respond to the cue and start juggling a cocktail mixer in the careless and haphazard way that made my

Bollywood performance so memorable. We didn't recognise the actors in this particular scene (Anton Yelchin and Addison Timlin, I can now reveal) but were as transfixed as the many locals who had politely halted their daily routine to allow this tiny slice of make-believe to hold up their day.

To us, the three stars performing for our entertainment were 'Hunky Male' (in dark shirt with impeccably tousled hair), 'Sexy Female' (in denim shorts with impeccably tousled slightly longer hair), and 'Red Vespa' (a highly desirable vintage scooter). We watched the scene - in which H.M. and S.F. cross street, deep in conversation, until S.F. mounts R.V. and scoots off leaving H.M. alone and perplexed - played out several times and, I must say, Red Vespa was a complete professional. I did suspect, though, that the reason for so many re-takes was because the director spotted what all of us onlookers knew from the start: the Red Vespa was stealing the scene every time. Not even a bloke in the background throwing a cocktail shaker in the air could have distracted from its shiny charms. So I walked away, content that my contribution to the silver screen should not be in *Odd Thomas*, but in odd Bollywood sci-fi fantasy. These are the decisions De Niro must make every day.

Santa Fe is a charming, delightful town, but I don't think we got the most out of it. We were all exhausted and a bit depressed. I know it seems highly unlikely (and more than a little self-centred) to be tired and fed up while experiencing such beauty and wonder all around, but it's a fact of travelling that it's very taxing on both body and soul. Really, ask anyone who's done a gap year of backpacking: there are times when your heart's simply not in it.

Weighing us down was the fact that every day we were driving closer and closer to home. That had been the case since LA, of course, but none of us had vocalised it until now. The 'I don't want to go home' conversations were becoming more and more regular. 'If we won the lottery,' asked Jill one day, 'would we keep on travelling, or go back home?'

'Carry on!' was the unanimous reply, and a surprising reaction from the girls. They had changed so much since we left England. Those first few weeks of teething troubles, camping in the rain in Holland and France, missing their mates, doubting the sanity of what we were doing – they were a distant memory. What had once seemed a fantastic adventure had become normal life to us now. Moving on each day, meeting new people, seeing new places, not knowing where we would sleep – this was our routine, no longer special, but simply comfortable. Living hand-to-mouth, eking out our diminishing funds, eating when we were hungry, sleeping when we were tired – none of this seemed unusual anymore. The looming shadow of 'home' made us realise how blissfully happy we had become. The idea of returning to the rigid routine of school, work and the whirlwind of commitments that are normal life for every British family – well, it twisted a knot in the pit of our stomachs.

'Hey, it'll be good to see your friends again, won't it Edie?' I asked, knowing that of the three, she was the one most eager to return to her schoolmates.

'I guess,' she replied wistfully.

'Well, what about you two?' I asked Ella and Beth. 'You must be missing … oh I don't know. Your phones, texting, makeup, the latest goss on who's going out with who?' They raised their eyebrows, as if to say 'Really?' I think I might have insulted them. 'You wait,' I encouraged. 'You'll be straight back into it when we get home. It'll be like we never left.'

'And that's what's so depressing,' said Ella, with surprising insight.

The only way to try to eliminate this encroaching gloom was to keep reminding ourselves of the incredible highlights still to come. We were going to New York! We were going to Washington DC! We looked at the map – hang it all, we might even make it to Chicago too. We had friends to visit in Kansas, and before all that we had friends-of-friends to visit in Colorado Springs. As we drove north, up the east side of the Rockies, and the milometer passed 15,500 miles since home, we still had plenty to smile about.

It's a peculiar feeling, walking up to the front door of a complete stranger in an unknown part of the world knowing it'll be your home for the next day or two. It takes nerve to ring that doorbell. A deep breath and a wide smile help. We pushed Ella to the front. 'Go on,' we urged. 'She's *your* friend. *You* do the talking.'

We were in Colorado Springs, outside the home of the grandparents of Ella's friend Melissa. The girls have known each other since they were four years old, cycled to school together and their emails throughout the year had kept Ella up to date with all the essential news from home; who fancied who, why the new head teacher was a bit scary and what on earth was going on with *The X Factor*.

The events that had brought us to this driveway in the peaceful suburb of Fountain were typically last-minute and impulsive. Before we left home Richard and Debbie, Melissa's parents, had said to us, 'Don't forget we've got family in Colorado, if you go that way,' but we hadn't been sure we'd actually get there until about a week beforehand. Richard and Debbie had been great at keeping in touch, following the blog and commenting on our exploits, so I composed a hasty email back to Banbury along the lines of, 'Remember that offer you made a year ago?' and a day or two later, somewhere in the Arizona desert, in a dust-blown burger bar, I logged on to our emails and got the news: Jackie, Richard's mum, and her husband Chris were expecting us. We had a home in Colorado Springs.

Ella pushed the doorbell and a tall, jolly, bearded man opened the door. 'You must be those crazy Brits!' he smiled. 'Come on in.'

'Hi, I'm Ella. I'm Melissa's friend,' said our eldest daughter leading the way.

'Hi, I'm Chris, this is Jackie.'

'Hello,' we all chanted cheerily, bustling through the door.

'D'ya miss Melissa?' asked Chris.

'Yeah, but we email loads so ...'

I didn't hear what Ella said next because of the screaming. From the kitchen walked Melissa, and behind her, as large as life and with a grin like the Cheshire Cat was Richard! I couldn't have been more surprised if I'd pulled the head off a cow and found my mother inside.

Back in the mid-90s I'd presented a Saturday morning kids show on ITV. One week, the wacky production crew devised a cunning wheeze to play a prank on me. At a particular point in the madcap, slightly anarchic live show a pantomime cow was to plod on to the set. I was to pull the head off the cow revealing a top TV star inside - except when I got to that part in the programme and I whipped the head off Daisy, the top TV star was replaced by my mother, wearing a grin not dissimilar to the one I described on Richard a moment ago.

I remember reeling a bit, genuinely shocked at finding my Mum on my TV show - inside a cow. Mum recalls that she saw me go visibly grey. Instantly she remembered how, when I was a kid, if I got a massive surprise I'd throw up. Suddenly, she realised the cow prank might have more dramatic results than the production team wags had bargained for. I attempted to find some words and a camera to say them to, got through the show in a daze (I still can't remember any of it), and as the credits rolled walked casually to my dressing room, closed the door and threw up. Happy days.

Back in the house, Jill was still screaming. I was stunned. Suddenly we were all hugging and crying. It was like the final shocking guest being introduced on that old 'Big Red Book' show *This Is Your Life*. As you can imagine, me vomiting would have sullied the moment, somewhat. After a few minutes, the hysteria subsided (along with any risk of a shock-induced mishap on my part), and we pieced together how we'd been set up. A flurry of last minute web surfing and flight booking at home had miraculously coincided with us *not* changing our plans, breaking down or arriving a day late (all of which we'd done before), and culminated in the most elaborate sting I've ever been on the receiving end of. Cow included.

And so, with Richard and Melissa in jolly holiday mood, and us lot still elated that they'd gone to the trouble of flying out here to meet us, we all set off in high spirits on Saturday morning to tackle Colorado Springs' highest summit, Pike's Peak. The gruelling hike takes nine hours, or you can drive the twisty mountain road all the way up to the 14,000-foot (4,300-metre) peak. Thankfully for Penny, we planned to take the 'cog railway', which takes just over an hour to reach the summit and saves unfit hikers and old VW engines from an untimely death.

We'd just left the town's look-out point, Palmer Park, where we'd been taking in the splendid vista of the Rockies and the snow capped mountain we were about to scale, when Penny suffered an untimely death.

Well, no. She suffered a minor collapse. While climbing one of Colorado's steep hills in busy traffic, her engine died. I could just about get her running after turning the starter motor over for a long time, but as soon as she had to do any work pulling her own weight, she'd die again. I looked in the rear-view mirror, waited for a gap in the traffic and freewheeled backwards a few hundred metres to a point where I could pull off the road. Melissa, our new passenger on board, was having a hair-raising first glimpse of what Ella's year had been like.

I suspected a fuel problem, unloaded the boot to get to the engine-bay and as Chris and Richard re-joined us in their car we watched nasty tell-tale air bubbles coursing along the fuel pipe into Penny's engine. The last time this happened was in Italy owing to a blocked fuel filter. 'That's weird, though,' I explained to my new VW apprentices, 'because I've only just changed the fuel filter. Maybe it's not fitted properly.' I dismantled it, found it was clean, re-tightened all the hoses, checked all the seals and still the stream of air bubbles stopped her having any power.

We zipped into town in Chris's Jeep to try to find a VW garage to replace the filter in case it was dodgy, but failed. Then, a weird thing happened. We got back to Penny (and Jill and the girls) empty handed and were pondering what to do next, when Chris's Jeep broke down. It was haemorrhaging fluid on to the road and refused to start. Now, we had *two* stranded vehicles and no hope of making the mountain day trip. It was ridiculous. We laughed at the improbability of it all. Well, Jill, Rich and I laughed. Chris seemed a bit cross, which is understandable when you own a proper car, rather than a vintage camper van.

Then, the weirdness got weirder. We planned to move Penny off the road and into a car park from where we could arrange to get her towed to a garage. We left the Jeep to cool down because Chris identified the fluid on the road as engine coolant. I re-packed the van, turned the key and she started first time. I drove her straight past the car park, up a very steep hill and she didn't falter. She was, apparently, cured. I returned to the throng and announced that she was back to her old self. Chris turned the key on his Jeep and it started first time. It too behaved impeccably from that point on.

Had we somehow stumbled into Colorado's own Bermuda Triangle? Well, no. In fact what had happened is that I had parked Penny on a ferocious slope overnight with very little fuel in the tank (breaking my own rule from Italy) and some sludge in the fuel tank had blocked the pipe. All my revving and wriggling had simply cleared the blockage. Admittedly I have no idea why the Jeep had a funny turn. I've never owned one. Perhaps they do that sort of thing. It's all I can do to keep up with the mood swings of a Volkswagen. Penny had given us a scare, but she appeared to be back on track. I filled her fuel tank to the top, as Luigi had told me to many thousands of miles ago in Italy, and she continued to behave properly. With a three-day drive across the sparsely populated fields of Kansas ahead of us, we'd be keeping more than just our legs crossed between loo breaks.

We missed the last train up Pike's Peak so resolved to do it tomorrow. Besides, Chris had a package to collect from the airport in the afternoon so it all fell into place quite nicely. We all trundled off to the small airport in Colorado Springs to discover that 'the package' was in fact, surprise number two: Richard's brother Ari and his girlfriend had flown in from St Louis in his own small aeroplane! So, Richard got a taste of his own medicine, more emotional hugs all round, and then we all got a go at sitting in Ari's cockpit and pretending to be Spitfire pilots (or perhaps that was just me).

It was quite a party that night. We even got the instruments out and performed a rather shambolic set of Beatles songs. Perhaps it was the lack of practice, or perhaps it was the free-flowing Californian Syrah. Personally, I blame the altitude. Honestly, at 6,000 feet – over a mile above sea level – nothing works as you'd expect in Colorado Springs: cars need re-tuning to cope with thin air, kettles boil under boiling point at 95°C, cakes rise too quickly in the oven and ukuleles don't play very well.

It must have been the altitude that made me wake up with a headache the next morning too. Weird, huh? We fired up Penny who started after a few seconds and rewarded us with an unproblematic drive into Manitou Springs, the arty, slightly hippy village from where super-fit climbers and less-than-fit rail passengers start their journey up Pike's Peak. Barely breaking a sweat, we successfully made the rack-and-pinion powered climb to what is the highest point on Earth I've ever stood. The air at 4,300 metres is quite thin, and combined with the strong painkiller I'd taken for my hangover, sorry, altitude-headache, my entire time on the summit was spent in a gloriously giddy head-spin.

To demonstrate the effects of these great heights, and explain a bit about athletes training at altitude, boosting their red blood cells and all that, I persuaded Ella and Beth to join me for a gentle jog around the mountaintop. It was amazing. After about 20 seconds of relaxed jogging we were shattered. I looked back to see they'd both quit, slumped on rocks, laughing uncontrollably. I tried to say, 'Isn't that incredible?' but all that came out was 'Idadatikedaber,' because my mouth had stopped working. My legs were wobbly so I staggered towards the hilltop café for a much needed sugar-hit.

The view from Pike's Peak was impressive, but seriously hampered by haze. We'd left Santa Fe with our clothes smelling of smoke, and all the way up to Colorado Springs we'd been followed by the haze and smell of ash from a wildfire that was sweeping Arizona some 600 miles to our south-east. By the time we were leaving Colorado for Kansas, it had become the largest wildfire in Arizona's history. Our track record for leaving disaster in our path was as glittering as ever.

People would gasp. Burly men would wince. Eyebrows would be raised in alarm and disbelief. 'You're driving from Colorado Springs to Kansas City?' they would ask, as if everything we'd previously told them about driving around the world and busking The Beatles had seemed utterly sane by comparison. 'It is so *boring!*' they'd continue. 'So … *brown*. And so *flat*.'

Perhaps it was because we were braced for several mind-numbing days of 55 miles-per-hour nothingness that we found ourselves quite enjoying Kansas. It wasn't boring at all. It wasn't flat, and it wasn't brown. After a damp spring all the fields were green, and they rolled with enough undulation to be not dissimilar to the fields of Essex that border the M25. I realise I'm the first travel writer to compare Kansas with Essex, a ridiculous statement, but I'll stand by it.

We came off the main Interstate 70 a few times to break up the journey, dawdling through tiny middle-of-nowhere farming villages, and eventually found ourselves camping in Topeka, the state capital. It was a weird place, frankly. It felt like the sort of place where you marry your cousin's niece only to find she's your sister. In the days that followed, everyone we mentioned Topeka to was horrified we'd stopped there. 'You were only an hour or two from Gardner,' our friends would say. 'Why didn't you keep going?' But we weren't expected in Ty's town of Gardner until the next day, so we found a campsite with a lake, pitched up and went for a swim/wash.

We were just getting used to the water, confident that we could put our feet on the muddy bottom without treading on anything nasty, when I saw a large animal coursing quickly through the water towards us. 'Woah! Is that a croc?' I yelled, pushing children out of the way to get to the bank. Jill and the girls were surprisingly swift at finding their way to the shore too. We watched as the vee-shaped wake came closer.

'That's not a croc,' said Ella. 'It's too small.' The creature came under the trees near us and two large teeth were visible at the crest of its wave.

'It's a beaver!' squealed Edie.

'Hmmm. Scary,' said Bethan, nudging me.

'Er, you were pretty keen to leave the water too,' I said defensively. We watched as it swam among the branches in the water, enthralled by its paddle tail, thick wet fur and webbed paws. It gnawed a long thin branch off a tree and then swam away with it in its mouth, back the way it had come.

'Would you look at that?' I cooed. 'He's off to do some building.'

'And scare swimmers,' added Beth. 'Are you all right now, Daddy?'

'Very funny. Right, who's going back in for a swim? No? Me neither. Let's get dressed.' We weren't very good at close encounters with wild animals. It was no man-eater, but as swimming pools go, this had one too many three-foot rodents for our liking.

Our evening in Topeka got more unusual. We had pitched our tent and were apparently settled, when I drove with the girls to a supermarket to buy some veggies and pasta for tea, leaving Jill reading in the tent. We returned to find her slightly stressed. 'We've got to move!' she hissed in a hoarse whisper.

'What? Why?' I complained.

'Shhhhh. It's the neighbours.' Unaware that Jill was just feet away in the tent, both couples from either side of us had got together to swap stories of their time in prison. I'd already got to know the gap-toothed, bearded man with cauliflower ears. He was called Ray and I'd lent him our air-bed pump. His rugged-faced girl Darleen was sweet enough too. Sure, Jill had heard how Ray had beaten Darleen up once or twice. And, OK, so he'd done time for it. But tonight that was forgotten. Tonight was about beer and laughter ... and us moving to the opposite side of the campsite. So, as if it was the most normal thing in the world, I nonchalantly collapsed our tent, threw it in the back of the van and tootled across to a distant part of the site in the hope that I wouldn't cause offence to the chaps on D Wing.

Our new home was among the wealthy retired RV folk whose biggest crimes were those against fashion. Our neighbours Sandy and Colleen proudly showed us around their palatial trailer, but were rudely interrupted by a siren from a small plastic box in their kitchen. 'Oh that's just the tornado alarm,' Randy casually said. Suddenly the retractable queen-size bed and en-suite didn't seem quite so engaging.

'The what?' we chorused in unison.

'It's this storm system here,' he explained, pointing to a built-in LCD TV showing a live weather satellite feed. 'It's heading our way. Could be a rough night.'

Sure enough, our own lo-tech AM radio carried local weather warnings, and we ate our pasta listening to a sports show constantly interrupted by weather updates and the regular three beeps every two minutes alerting listeners to be on tornado watch. It was all very exciting.

The girls reccied our escape plan should Edie's trip-long wish come true and a tornado touch down: we were all sharing a cubicle in the ladies loo block apparently, should the sirens wail. We went to bed, all five in the van as it was already too blustery for a tent, and as the battering started and the van shook we realised at about midnight that Penny's roof was probably going to be torn off. Against the howling, buffeting gale we collapsed the roof, sacrificing the two high-level beds, and somehow all of us endured the storm curled into impossible, back-breaking positions in the tiny space left alongside all our bags.

At daylight I released the door and staggered into the morning calm. I expected to walk into a post-apocalyptic landscape of splintered trees and upturned motor homes. Instead, the only evidence of our deafening, sleep-starved night of twister terror was a tiny snapped twig, sitting gently on the windscreen wiper.

'Is that it?' I demanded, examining the flimsy shoot. 'No carnage? No devastation? It's hardly *Perfect Storm* is it?'

'Which is a good thing, right?' said Jill.

'Hmmm. I guess.' Apparently we'd survived 65 mph winds, but I couldn't shake the feeling that my sleepless night had been without the reward of any drama. I'd had visions of local news channels running the story 'Beatles tribute band swept away in tornado' under the headline 'Twister Shout'.

Our visit to Gardner was always going to be bitter-sweet. It was Jill's friend Lisa, whom she'd met while running the New York Marathon back in 2004, that drew us here. We had entertained Lisa, her husband Ty and their two teenage children Matthew and Rebecca when they'd visited us in the UK in 2006, and this was our chance finally to see their home and meet their friends. But then we had that email from Ty in January while we were camping on an idyllic beach in south Goa telling us Lisa's health was failing and we weren't going to get there in time to see her. She lost her fight against cancer a month later.

What might have been a sad time, though, seeing Ty, Rebecca and her husband Nathan (Matthew was away in Germany with the US army) was actually a highlight of our year. Lisa's absence was obviously palpable, and she was such a vibrant and popular woman that of course people kept talking to us about her, and sometimes we all got a bit choked up. But the overwhelming sentiment was one of joy at a life lived so fully and so generously in the service of her community and church.

Ty, the lively and witty pastor of the church, had arranged a 'cook-out' gig for us at the home of his friends Phil and Debbie. About 40 people gathered to share a barbecue (a Kansas staple), teach us Kickball - a kind of baseball played with a football that quickly becomes ferociously competitive - and hear us play.

Two distinct things contributed to it being our favourite gig of the year. First, we practised, which always helps. And second, the audience was fun, friendly and up for it. They sang, they clapped, they even laughed at my rubbish jokes. We romped through eight songs, recruited extra help on percussion – a tambourine appeared, the frog did the rounds while ambidextrous Edie mastered the complexities of two-handed egg shaking. One of the brand-new friends we'd made, Darrin, joined us on his guitar for the sing-along tunes of *Yellow Submarine* and *All You Need Is Love* and we had such a fantastic evening that none of us wanted to leave. Almost as an afterthought we shook the UNICEF tin and raised another $42.50 (£26).

Back at the house that night, as we settled down in our beds in the comfortable self-contained flat that was Ty's basement, we looked back on all those tortuous moments busking around the world. How we'd gritted our teeth and blagged our way through half-learned songs in horribly public places, wondering if the whole busking idea was really very bright. That evening in Gardner was the reward. It had been worth it for that. Lisa would have loved it.

With the pressure of the performance behind us we were free to relax and enjoy whatever 'The Wheat State' could throw at us. Kansas is famous for more than just twisters and Dorothy dancing her ruby slippers down the yellow-brick road. They cook meat, they cook lots, and they cook slowly. In fact they cook it sublimely. 'Barbecue' in Kansas isn't what it is in Australia or the UK – standing outside cremating sausages or shrimps on a slightly rusty grill. It's an entire food group, prepared and served in 'smoke house' restaurants at every turn. At this stage, we were all still carnivores apart from poor Beth, who would have her veggie willpower stretched to the limit.

To visit Kansas and not eat barbecue would be like visiting Harry Ramsden's and asking to see the healthy options menu.

First we all went to Oklahoma Joe's - a funky barbecue joint that's got mod cons like cutlery and beer served in a glass - for our first taste of succulent hickory-smoked ribs and 'pulled pork' by the pound. But on our last evening together Ty took us to LC's, a tiny downtown caff that's always heaving when there's a ball game on, and where the 'burnt ends' are legendary. Burnt ends are a Kansas delicacy. The crispy edges of a smoked, roasted beef brisket are piled high and smothered in barbecue sauce. Serve on a paper plate with white bread, fries, onion rings and bottomless soda - welcome to Kansas. It was sensational. These days I'm a vegetarian, but as I write my mouth is watering remembering it. If another trip to LC's were ever to be on the cards, the vegetarian me would have to take a day off. Those burnt ends are just too good.

Kansas is the home of basketball, and James Naismith's original hand-typed rules are still displayed in a museum in Kansas City. Rather brilliantly, they show that he typed 'a goal is scored when the ball is thrown or batted from the ground', before adding in pen above it, 'into the basket'. From these tiny details did a multi-million dollar sport grow. It's massive at college level in America and huge rivalries exist between fans of Kansas University's team, the Jayhawks, and the 'K State' university team, the Wildcats.

But this is nothing compared to the rivalry that simmers between Kansas and their neighbours Missouri: it's historic and huge. These days it's crystallised in sporting battles, but at its worst, pre-civil war, when both states held different views on slavery, violent tit-for-tat exchanges escalated to the point where disgruntled activists from pro-slavery Missouri marched across the border and sacked the tiny Kansas town of Lawrence before burning it to the ground.

Kansas City itself epitomises the divide, being bisected by the state line. Even today there are sports coaches who, when the rival teams meet, will refuse to enter the opposing state until the very last minute so to avoid spending a single cent in the heartland of their sworn enemy. Locals in Kansas freely admit to the dilemma they face when filling up their cars - fuel is cheaper across the state line, but it pains them to put money in Missouri's pockets! All this might explain why Kansans pronounce the home of their neighbour 'Misery'. It also explains a *Simpsons* joke I'd never fully understood, where Marge notices Grandpa Simpson's American flag has only 49 stars. He proclaims, 'I'll be deep in the cold, cold ground before I recognise Missoura!' – a clip that regularly entertains KU fans in the local basketball stadium, played on huge video screens and edited to end with the words 'Grandpa Simpson – Jayhawk fan'.

It was with some trepidation, therefore, that we left our friends and drove further east across the state line, heading for St Louis where we would turn north towards Chicago. Driving away from Gardner was like driving away from the sunshine towards a bank of grey cloud. All the gloom descended again when, as Penny approached 17,000 miles since home, we realised we only had three weeks left before our flight back to reality. In a strange reverse of Dorothy's experience at the start of *The Wizard of Oz*, we'd enjoyed a Kansas that glowed in Technicolor, only to be picked up and dragged into a world of grey. It was a huge testament to our friends and the people of Gardner that, with even the heady delights of Chicago, Washington and New York still ahead of us, none of us wanted to leave.

Admit it, you were too swept up in the story weren't you? I understand.

In order they were sequoia (well, I gave you that one), troublemaking, exhaustion, unproblematic, cauliflower, tambourine and ambidextrous.

Did you spot the panvowels?

Our trip was blessed with thankfully few medical incidents. Edie had a cast on her arm for a couple of weeks in India after slipping and walloping her elbow on some marble stairs in the Mumbai YWCA. Beth had stitches in her foot after her Evil Knievel stunt show in Goa. And me? Nothing worse than a broken nail.

We'd camped outside Chicago and I was re-packing the van for driving mode in exactly the same way I'd packed her hundreds of times before. The crate of schoolbooks was in the boot, I was stacking the pillows above it and, as on every other occasion, I stuffed the final pillow against the ceiling, sliding my hand over the top. But this time, some stitching had opened up in the roof lining, allowing my thrusting hand to hit a steel roof-seam, which caught the nail of my right ring finger.

You know how much it hurts when you snag a nail? Perhaps you've experienced how much it hurts to get a splinter *behind* your nail. Well, feeling exactly that sort of pang, I yelped and yanked my arm out to see that my familiar hand - the one I'd known for 41 years - had been replaced with a prop from a horror film. My nail had peeled entirely from the finger and was standing vertical, at 90 degrees, upright and bloody.

'Tish and fip,' I exclaimed calmly. 'I appear to have wrenched an entire finger nail off.'

Of course I didn't. I howled like a wounded dog and clutched the deformed digit in my left fist. 'OOOOOHHHHHH LORDY THAT'S A BAD ONE!' I hollered.

Jill and Edie were away dealing with laundry, and Ella launched into rescue mode. 'What's happened?' she barked. 'Do you need an ambulance?'

'No, but it's not pretty,' I winced. Before she could establish what I'd actually done, she ran off to get Jill, leaving Beth my only companion. I was quite proud of the measured manner in which I composed myself at this moment.

'Beth, I've torn a complete nail off and I need you to get some stuff for me,' I stated calmly. 'Because in a minute I'm gonna go into shock, start feeling really sick, and then I'll be useless.' I could sense the panic in her as she shouldered the responsibility. 'Get the silver medical box out of the cupboard,' I instructed. 'I need gauze, tape, antiseptic spray, scissors and painkillers. Lots of painkillers. Paracetamol, Ibuprofen, Syndol, whatever we've got.'

'Right!' she said and started rummaging away in the van. I was hunched over outside the back of the van, trying to keep my head from spinning, looking at the cupboard in the boot containing the medical supplies, wondering why she wasn't dashing to my aid. I could feel the oh-so-predictable 'shock' symptoms of plummeting blood pressure circling impatiently for their evil moment of glory. Beth was inside the van, pulling books and presents from the darkest depths of the *wrong* cupboard.

'What are you doing?' I panted.

'Oh. Have we moved the silver box?' she asked innocently.

'Yes. About a week after we left England.' She raced round to the boot to start searching for the necessary supplies. She found a bag of cosmetics.

'Nail strengthener?' she quipped. I didn't laugh. 'Too soon,' she confirmed. The first wave of nausea hit me.

I've already mentioned my inability to cope with shock. It's an affliction, to be honest. I should be pitied. There's simply nothing I can do about it. Whether it's discovering my mother inside a pantomime cow on live TV, or rushing Beth to an Indian hospital with a gaping wound that happened on my watch, once the adrenaline has subsided, the rather embarrassing side effects will have their wicked way. It happened after every motorcycle accident I had as a teenager, after a clumsy kitchen-knife-sharpening-error in which I sliced through my thumb to the shiny white joint - it's as predictable as it is horrible.

Assuming you've never been victim to a shock system as flimsy as mine, here's what happens: first, you get the queasy stomach and the giddiness, just like when you've drunk far too much booze, but with none of the earlier fun. Then, in an instant, you're rapidly overheating, you're burning up and your mouth is charcoal dry. Your heart is banging away hopelessly in your chest wondering why it suddenly seems to have been caught napping. By this time I'm normally lying on the floor in an attempt to remedy the malaise - utterly pointlessly. Now your head spins and you lose peripheral vision. A kind of blackness pushes in and you're looking at the world from the bottom of a well. Then the incessant whistling in the ears begins and the stomach cramps start. All of these symptoms will now collide and have a happy party together for anything from two minutes to quarter of an hour. You'll wish you were dead, or at the very least that you'd just black out so you didn't have to be present for the ordeal.

As I say, it's all a bit embarrassing, particularly because this now infamous 'Courtie Collapse' never happens in the privacy of one's own room. It tends to be a horribly public affair. So, as I lay sprawled on the gravel next to the van door, with my feet up on her raised floor, my bloody hand held aloft, my groggy head retching into a plastic bucket, what were my family doing to ease my pain?

Edie, having run to the scene with Jill, swiftly ran away again because the sight of my finger made her gag. Ella kept declaring I'd fainted, even though I was just having tiny naps, Beth wiped my head with a wet cloth saying, 'I've done imps.' I had no idea what that meant*. Jill tried to put soothing music on the iPod, but accidentally kept finding 120 bpm dance remixes.

No one would go near my wounded finger. In fact, just looking at it made them clutch their hands to their mouths and recoil. In short, it was later agreed that my family are useless in a crisis. So I lay there in the dirt, waiting patiently for my head to reconnect to my body, deafened by a soundtrack of flapping, shouting and random bursts of drum and bass.

Like I said, nothing worse than a broken nail. Most of the root of the nail had pulled away from the finger but one corner was still attached beneath the cuticle, so I took the 'bandage it up and pretend nothing's wrong' approach, thus cleverly avoiding America's worst medical problem: a bill.

Our two biggest concerns during the nail episode were, 1) missing the ball game, and 2) having to go to Chicago's County General Hospital only to discover that it's not, in fact, staffed by Noah Wyle and George Clooney. My outstanding bravery, however, meant we never had to shatter the E.R. illusion, and could still get to Wrigley Field in time to see The Chicago Cubs take on The New York Yankees.

This was our Olympics. Despite the fact that our dwindling funds were at the perilously low point and we felt like we were coasting to New York on little more than fresh air and a winning smile, we had put aside some money earlier in the year for London 2012 Olympics tickets. Back in the comfort of our friends' living room in Brisbane we had, like thousands of other Brits, grappled with the Olympics ticketing website and committed several hundred pounds of credit card cash against tickets we may, or may not, be allocated. And, like so many other Brits, we waited forlornly for confirmation that we were

*Injury Minimisation Programme for Schools. Thank you NHS Oxfordshire.

all going to The Greatest Show On Earth, only to find we'd been overlooked for every event but tennis, and we'd only applied for those on behalf of someone else.

So, with those few hundred pounds still intact, untroubled by even a morning ticket for rhythmic gymnastics, I was able to justify our purchase of Cubs tickets as 'out of our Olympic fund'. I realise this seems a very irresponsible approach to personal finance, but when you've managed to get almost the entire way around the world on a budget that didn't even get as far as being scrawled on the back of a paper napkin, little things like tickets for premier sporting events appear trifling hurdles to overcome.

The Cubs haven't won the World Series for over a hundred years, but have America's second oldest, and most charming stadium, dating from 1914. Our entire, brief time in Chicago was a catalogue of movie references, and Wrigley Field was the first. From *Blues Brothers* to *Ferris Bueller's Day Off*, I've grown up knowing this stadium as an American sports icon. From high up in its riveted wrought iron stands we watched, we chanted, we sang *Take Me To The Ball Game* (a tradition at every match, apparently), we bought beer, nachos and hot dogs from vendors who passed their wares along the row to our seats, just like in the movies. Basically, we lived the dream. And a crash course in the rules from our friends back in Kansas meant we even understood what was going on.

At a baseball game opposing fans all sit together, so there was plenty of banter. We had some young and witty Yankees fans behind us. 'Are you Cubs fans?' asked one of the men.

'Actually we're English,' I replied. 'We support the underdogs ... so, yes, we're Cubs fans.' They laughed, but not as much as when they asked how we knew *Take Me To The Ball Game* and Ella told them we'd seen it in *The Simpsons*.

The Yankees are the baseball equivalent to Chelsea, or Manchester City football clubs, in that they've bought their way to the top. Because of that, the Cubs hadn't played the Yankees since 2003 as they're in different leagues, and this meeting was like the UK football equivalent of an FA Cup giant-killing fixture. The atmosphere in the stadium reflected that it was a big day, and thanks to our expert chanting and distracting of the Yankees star A-Rod (Alex Rodriguez, ex-Cameron Diaz squeeze and highest paid player in the US) we watched him fail to get a single hit and saw the Cubs score a historic 3 - 1 victory.

A-Rod? Pah! The New York visitors would have been better off letting Andy Roddick take a swing. As we left, the highly disgruntled Yankees fans behind us had the good grace to shake our hands and wish us a pleasant stay, in much the same way that English football fans don't.

Ferris Bueller, we established, simply couldn't have fitted everything into his Day Off that the film suggests. I suspect that the John Hughes classic is *not* a documentary. The 1986 story of one boy's final fling before leaving high school, and his best friend Cameron's personal triumph over the fear of his father, has long been a Courtie family favourite since I first showed it to our girls at an inappropriately young age given how much swearing I'd forgotten was in it. Our attempt to re-capture some of Ferris's day in Chicago was scuppered early on by a 90-minute wait to get to the Skydeck at the top of the Willis Tower (once the Sears Tower). Instead of queuing we headed straight to the Chicago Institute of Art and were thrilled to discover they still exhibit most of the classic pieces we've watched Ferris, Cameron and Sloane view so many times over the past 25 years.

Jill had emailed an ex-colleague from the BBC who now lived in Chicago and so, after taking in some art, we headed to *The Bean* - Anish Kapoor's 110-ton polished chrome droplet in Millennium Park - to meet Shelley and Rob who'd moved to Chicago a couple of months earlier.

Shelley and Jill nattered about work, Rob and I nattered about our trip, and all of us seemed to revel in the novelty of hearing other English accents – something we hadn't realised we'd all been missing. After leaving Wiltshire they'd lived in Hawaii prior to moving to

Chicago, so shared a lot of our experiences of leaving home and friends behind. Over some classic Chicago pizza, we swapped stories of friends who'd surprised us with their lack of contact, and of others who'd amazed us with their support. It was quite cathartic to share these common experiences that had all of us saying, 'I thought it was just us!' with some relief.

Tapping their local knowledge, we walked the Magnificent Mile from the Chicago River as far as the glittering Trump Tower, where Rob used his expert blagging skills to get us into an exclusive rooftop bar, simply to take in the views. Chicago is Gotham City in the *Batman* films, the 'L' elevated train is the same one that web-slinging Toby McGuire saved in the second *Spiderman* movie, and the same one in which Tom Cruise and Rebecca De Mornay got hot and bothered in *Risky Business*. Looking down on Chicago is like looking down on a film set, its mix of modern sheen and gothic towers making it arguably the most photogenic city in America - after Manhattan.

But *that* was for another day.

After driving away from the windy city on the appallingly potholed Interstate 90 – ironically our first toll road in the US, and yet the one most reminiscent of all terrain India – the road eventually smoothed out into open countryside and we enjoyed a blissful drive from Illinois through Indiana where we found ourselves in Amish country. We regularly passed horse-drawn buggies on their own special inside lane carrying families dressed as if from a century ago – the men in wide-brimmed hats, the women and girls in bonnets, and all clothed in monochrome. It was fascinating, but hard not to stare. The girls were transfixed. 'It's like looking at an old photograph,' Ella said. 'Even the carriages are in black and white.'

We stayed at West Otter Lake campsite near Angola where the owners Don and Theresa explained how most of the construction work in that area, in north Indiana and Pennsylvania, is done by the Amish. 'But how do they run a building firm, if they believe in shunning modern technology?' I asked Don, a warm, smiling man who had quickly insisted we camp on his own personal fishing spot next to the lake, where he still had a campfire burning.

'Ah,' he grinned. 'Some aren't as strict as others. They get around that by not actually *owning* the equipment. There's good business in these parts hiring construction gear to Amish builders. Most Amish families round here don't own a car, but *do* employ a driver ...'

'... who comes with his own car,' I concluded.

'Exactly. And for most, as long as the vehicles and machinery aren't kept on their land, they can reconcile using them and still remain faithful to their custom.'

Don and Theresa wouldn't take any money from us for the camping pitch and, a day after we'd left, donated to our UNICEF fund online. We had only known them for a matter of hours. We didn't even busk for them. Come to think of it, perhaps that's why they donated.

We'd left Indiana, passed Toledo and Cleveland in Ohio, and were just about to tick off another state as we crossed into Pennsylvania when, somewhere near Austintown, Penny conked out.

It was the old 'air bubbles in the fuel pipe' issue again, and I became convinced it was a blockage, not in the filter, but back where the fuel-pipe joined the diesel tank, where sludge in the fuel tank was blocking the tube. So I cut a meter of garden hose off the pipe we used to fill our drinking water-tank, wedged it on to Penny's fuel pipe and blew. I could hear bubbles gurgling away in the diesel tank at the front of the van, so let the thing settle for a minute, then carefully sucked fresh diesel back up to the fuel filter, misjudged it, drank a bit, coughed, spluttered, reconnected everything and she ran perfectly. Hooray!

Then she caught fire.

Well, not immediately. We were leaving one of our regular McWifi stops some miles later. By this stage I was no longer buying a coffee in return for McInternet use, having developed the cunning ruse of taking an empty McCoffee cup with me to plonk on the table each time we needed to get online. All seemed well, Penny started first time, and then as we drove away the first acrid smell of burning hit us.

'Is that outside?' I asked, sticking my head out of the window. 'Yep,' I confidently assured my passengers. 'It's not us.' Then, as I drove on, Ella raised her voice from the back of the van.

'Lotta smoke! Lotta smoke in the front!'

She was right. I didn't know *what* was on fire, but suddenly every air vent was blowing white smoke at us. I pulled over and yanked the key out, hoping that killing the power would kill the fire. The kids had slid open the side door and were on the verge almost before we'd even stopped moving. They'd been in a car fire years earlier, so had well-honed reactions.

'Calm down,' I said as we gathered in front of Penny. 'It's probably nothing.' We still couldn't see any flames, but smoke continued to waft from her windows.

'Shall I get the fire extinguisher?' Beth asked hopefully.

'Go on then,' I agreed.

She was on it, at lightning speed. That last-minute safety addition, bought in Essex the day before we caught the ferry from Harwich, and not once disturbed from its bracket near the door, was finally getting its day in the sun. Beth read the directions on the red cylinder eagerly, her finger poised on the safety pin, but before she could have her fun, the smoke thinned. 'Hang on a sec,' I said. 'I think it's going out.' Her shoulders slumped with disappointment.

I got back in the driver's seat, turned the ignition key and heard a fuse blow. 'Ah ha!' I proclaimed, victorious. 'I know what it is,' I

announced to Jill, who would take some convincing. 'It's the blower. I was fiddling with the blower switch in the McDonalds car park.'

'The blower that doesn't work?' she asked.

'Yes,' I admitted from under the dashboard, where I was inspecting the fuse box.

'The one that hasn't worked since India?'

'Hmmm,' I nodded. She rolled her eyes.

'OK,' she went on. 'Disregarding *why* you started fiddling with something that broke six months ago – why should it choose *now* to burst into flames?' It was a fair question.

'Well,' I began, 'here's my theory.' All four of them seemed to wither slightly. 'Ever since the blower stopped working, the switch has been in the "off" position. Today, I fiddled with it, just casually in case a miracle happened, and accidentally left it in the "on" position. Now, if the fan motor has jammed, when I turned the ignition on a fuse should have blown. But it didn't.'

'Why?' asked Beth.

'Don't know. Not important,' I dismissed. 'Anyway, the fuse didn't blow, the switch was on, electricity poured through the motor coils, it was jammed, it caught fire, but now it's out. When I turned the ignition back on just now, I heard a fuse blow, and, lo and behold, which fuse had gone?'

'The blower?' suggested Ella, as if this was the most boring science lesson she'd ever been subjected to.

'Yes!' I beamed. 'Proving my theory!' There was no applause. I wondered whether Einstein ever had difficult days with such a tough audience.

After a beat of silence, Jill asked, 'Is it safe?'

'Yes, yes, completely safe, but aren't you impressed with my diagnosis?'

'I just don't want us to die in a burning vehicle.'

'It's fine,' I smiled. 'Come on kids, jump in!' They looked at each other warily. 'No one's going to die in a burning vehicle,' I assured. 'Mummy's just being dramatic.' Ella poked her head inside and sniffed. With a shrug she said, 'There *is* less smoke. Seems OK,' and climbed in.

Beth joined her, muttering, 'I can't believe I didn't get to use the fire extinguisher.'

Without further incident we made it to the east coast of America. It was still another six days until Penny's appointment at Baltimore docks, but it felt somehow momentous to reach Maryland, where we would spend five days exploring Washington DC. It was only an hour's drive from Washington to Baltimore, and as far as Penny was concerned, she couldn't drive further east: she'd reached the North Atlantic, the next land in that direction was Liverpool, our starting point 11 months earlier.

She'd made it.

This was cause for great relief and much nostalgia. 'D'you remember when we first got her?' recalled Edie. 'She was *horrible*.'

'I didn't like her,' admitted Bethan. 'I didn't say anything, but I thought she was nasty.'

'Same here,' chipped in Ella. 'She stank.'

'She was in a bit of a state,' I remembered. 'Can you believe that the ratty old van we drove home from south London that day has just driven us all the way around the world?' Heads shook in disbelief as we all absorbed what an amazing achievement we'd been part of.

'She *did* break down this morning,' said Ella.

'And then caught fire,' added Beth.

'Maybe she's trying to tell us something,' said Jill with a smile.

I patted the steering wheel. 'Just one more week, old girl.'

'I know,' said Jill, 'and stop calling me "old girl".'

For five days we camped outside the US capital, in a wooded state park in Maryland. It was cheap, beautiful, had great amenities and was almost empty – a happy way to round off our year of camping with Penny. We pitched our small tent for Jill and me to sleep in, and each morning we'd throw all our bags in there, fold up the beds in the van for a fairly brisk getaway, and drive towards Washington DC. It was a 20-minute drive to Shady Grove train station on the edge of the city's Metro system, then a half hour train ride into the centre.

Curiously, that daily drive we did was on a freeway sign-posted 'Damascus', a small rural town outside the capital. I'd been slightly let down by our original 'road to Damascus' experience eight months earlier. The journey from Aleppo to Syria's capital brought no epiphany, no blinding flash of truth. I didn't find myself. I just found myself complaining about the litter.

How bizarre then, that here, on the other side of the planet, 18,000 miles beyond that first road to Damascus we should all experience such a revelation: a momentous life-changing realisation struck all of us during our visit to Washington DC. The unforeseen thunderbolt that changed our lives struck just outside the Smithsonian Museum of American History halfway between the Capitol Building and the Washington Monument. Before I tell you about it, and how it was actually caused by Edie, her Beatles obsession and a really bad hotdog, let's pause a moment to behold the mighty Smithsonian museums.

The American capital is blessed with a gift from us Brits. Admittedly, we did also burn down the White House and the Capitol Building during the 1812 revolutionary war, but we'll gloss over that. It was essentially a misunderstanding. A few years after all that ugliness an English scientist, James Smithson, who had never set foot in America, left a fortune to the US to found 'an establishment for the increase and diffusion of knowledge'.

One of his conditions was that it should always be free. Hooray for James Smithson! As a result of his forward thinking, world-weary and increasingly-poor global travellers who have reached Washington more by luck than judgement are rewarded with a week of free stuff to do!

And it takes at least that to explore the collection of Smithsonian museums. They are vast, and they are awesome. What strikes you about each museum is the jaw dropping 'wow factor' of the exhibits. If all the world's museums were the football league, Smithsonian would be Manchester United. Take the Air and Space Museum. They don't tittle-tattle around with reproductions of this or artists impressions of that. Walk through the front door and - boom - there's a piece of the moon. Touch it - you're allowed to.

'Look, girls! There's an Apollo command module,' I said dragging them onwards. Er ... not just *an* Apollo command module. This is the Smithsonian. 'No way,' I gasped, pressing my face to a triangular window in the massive, grey charred cone. 'This is *the* Apollo 11 command module.' The girls weren't getting it. 'Neil Armstrong?' I prompted.

'Ohhhh!' they chorused.

'Neil Armstong, Buzz Aldrin and Michael Collins sat right there!' I gushed.

'Oh, that's the man who had to stay in the spaceship and didn't get to walk on the moon,' Edie remembered. She peered into the command module, its three seats lying snugly nestled between a dazzling array of buttons, dials and levers. 'Whoaa,' she sighed. 'D'you think Michael Collins was cross?'

'Well, someone had to stay on board,' I said. 'What do you reckon?'

'I think he was probably acting like it was no big deal but he was secretly cross.'

'Awkward journey home,' commented Beth, gazing into the confined gloomy module.

Upstairs, we walked right up to, and around, the Wright Flyer. Not a model, not a copy, the *actual* aircraft with which Wilbur and Orville made the first powered flight and in one faltering lunge changed the world. Do museums get any better than this? As you might imagine, I was very excited to be there.

And if all this sounds a bit 'boy's toys', the 'wow' factor is maintained from one museum to the next. Jill and the girls cooed over every single First Lady's inaugural ball gown, from Martha Washington's rather drab, grey frock to Michelle Obama's sparkly white creation of princess fluffiness. The potentially sombre Museum of American History panders to showbiz geeks like me with the chance to see Judy Garland's *Wizard of Oz* ruby slippers (tatty enough to have been through a tornado) and Jim Henson's first ever Kermit (which weirdly had human feet instead of webbed, which came later). A leather jacket in a glass case caught my eye. 'Is that …? It is!'

'Daddy can die happy,' said Jill as I gazed at an icon of my TV childhood: Fonzy's jacket from *Happy Days*.

The free factor makes DC a brilliant place to visit. We toured Congress and even got passes to sit in on a Senate debate - all for zero bucks. Before touring the historic Capitol Building we were ushered into an auditorium to sit through a beautifully-shot film explaining Congress, America's 'brave political experiment', how it survived being torched by the British (we gave you the Smithsonian - stop going on about it) and how, narrator Whoopi Goldberg explained, it continues to shape the country 'through free and lively debate'.

Yeah. Right.

We queued for a spot in the Senate's public gallery to watch the lone figure of the Senior Senator for Arizona make a considered half-hour argument on how Obama's economic measures weren't working - to whom? To nobody. The place was deserted. The Senate President who chairs proceedings, normally the US Vice President, was away and his stand-in spent the entire time rummaging in his bag for packed lunch items and texting his mates. The few other staff on duty on the Senate floor seemed similarly consumed with their phones, texting faster than the stenographer could type. Every other seat in the Senate was empty.

Afterwards, as we made our way out, an American family rather sheepishly asked us, 'Whaddaya think of our Government?'

'Er … quiet?' suggested Jill, diplomatically.

'Surely you need at least two people to have a debate?' I enquired. 'That guy had even gone to the trouble of having a chart printed. He'd brought an easel and everything.' They nodded their agreement, slightly embarrassed.

Now, I can't actually *prove* that the American family we spoke to were planted by the CIA, but strangely, just two days later, President Obama made a highly critical speech to The Senate, the gist of which was, 'If you want to get anything done, you lot have to actually *be here.*'

I like to think we gave the world's biggest superpower a helping hand - a wake up call when it was needed. No thanks necessary, American reader. Sorry, again, about all the fires in 1812. On the plus side you *did* get a good National Anthem out of it.

Happy in our daily routine of commuting from our rural campsite, we absorbed all DC had to offer, from seeing where Abraham Lincoln was shot in the Henry Ford Theatre to wandering through Arlington Cemetery. From a traumatic but memorable day at the Holocaust Museum to lazy coffee stops on the benches outside the White House, humming the theme to *The West Wing* like fools. We really enjoyed Washington, and I'd thoroughly recommend it.

Oh, I almost forgot to tell you what our life-changing decision was. It was during our time there that Bethan *finally* got some solidarity at mealtimes: we became vegetarians.

It was Edie's doing. Towards the end of our DC week we noticed the central grass mall that leads from the Capitol Building west towards the huge Washington Monument obelisk was becoming a village of stalls being erected ahead of a big weekend event. While we were taking a break between museums, eating some over-priced-but-below-par hotdogs, Edie spotted something. A young lady in her early 20s was handing out free magazines, and they had a free Paul McCartney DVD on the front. The bright showbiz magazine had movie star Natalie Portman on the cover and was in fact a publication by PETA – People for the Ethical Treatment of Animals, campaigning because of the huge Barbecue Festival that was about to begin.

The Paul McCartney DVD wasn't music, but a documentary called *Glass Walls* about the industrialised meat industry – the famous vegetarian once said, 'If abattoirs had glass walls no one would eat meat.' The magazine was an easy-to-read, celebrity-endorsed guide to becoming a vegetarian – well, actually a vegan.

The DVD wasn't watched until long after we got home when I stuck it into my computer: horrific. But the magazine stayed in our bag and as we took that half-hour train ride home, and back, and home again it was read by all of us, mainly because we had nothing else to do.

Turning veggie wasn't a huge family decision, but basically, PETA's propaganda worked. I was the first to say, 'You know what? I don't think I want to eat meat any more.' Then Jill jumped on board. She's always erred towards vegetarian choices and we'd been living on cheap veggie dishes while we were travelling all year anyway. Ella pooh-poohed it. Then she read the magazine. She wrinkled her nose. She grimaced. She jumped on the veggie-bus. You've gotta hand it to those PETA writers.

It wasn't just the animal cruelty aspect of the factory meat industry that persuaded me. I'd long been wondering what I could do that would make a difference to the conservation of the planet, since we had witnessed so many ecological difficulties on our journey: the critical lack of water in Jordan, the pollution in India, the carbon footprint of energy-hungry Australia. I really felt that the planet was being plundered.

There are many eye-popping statistics about the huge resources it takes to produce meat, but two leapt out at me: it takes 2,400 gallons of water to produce one pound of meat – whereas a pound of wheat requires 25 gallons, and the meat industry produces more CO_2 than all the vehicles in the world *put together* – cars, planes, ships, the lot. These mind-boggling facts are just that – *facts*, arrived at by neutral organisations like the United Nations. The message was simple: if you care about the environment, one of the single most effective things you can do is to stop eating meat. It seemed like an easy 'tick' for my conscience. Even Edie was on board!

She lasted a day.

'That's fine,' I said, announcing my intentions to the family. 'I'm not gonna get all militant about it. It's a personal choice, not a family rule. Eat meat if you want to. I'm not going to be one of those bores who preaches about it.' And, as if to cement my intentions, I've just spent 500 words preaching about it.

Here endeth the lesson.

We drove to Baltimore with heavy hearts. This was it: the beginning of the end. We hired a car from the airport, arranged for a one-way hire to Manhattan, and drove in convoy to the docks to meet the sixth shipping agent of our journey. Penny's fan-belt was squealing. She was overdue a service, but so close to the finish line it was hardly worth it. Baltimore was the most straightforward 'drop off' of them all. I parked Penny on the dockside in a row of vehicles destined for Bremerhaven, Germany, from where she would 'trans-ship' to Southampton on the south coast of England. The vehicle was checked, paperwork was stamped, and I was escorted out of the port. Penny had finished her journey.

I was dropped back at the car park where I had met the agent earlier that day, but Jill and the girls had gone to get some lunch. While I waited for them to return and pick me up, so we could find a campsite (all five in the two-man tent tonight) I waved goodbye to the shipping agent – a woman I'd only known for two hours and would never see again – and sat on the kerb. Inevitably, I started reflecting on the significance of what, for the people I'd just been dealing with, had been a fairly humdrum morning.

I was stunned that our old VW had made it. Her primitive milometer had clicked round 18,500 miles since Liverpool. Recollections bounced around my head: dragging her over the Alps, cursing her as she died in Italy, the anguish of being expensively marooned in Alessandria, the punctures, the faultless thousands of miles she'd carried us through Jordan, Syria, India, Australia, the beautiful home she made on Agonda beach in Goa. She'd been so much more than transport. She'd been bedroom, kitchen, cinema, disco, A&E gurney, and hilariously slow getaway car from Indian police. *One complete lap of the planet*, I kept thinking, hardly able to take it in.

Our own journey wouldn't be complete until we'd made it to Manhattan, and busked in Central Park. But with New York only a few hours up the road, that was just a formality, right? We had the hire car, we had a tent to sleep in, we even had an apartment booked in the Big Apple. The final chapter of our epic quest would be a cinch, I was sure.

What was it they said in Australia? Too easy.

There had been relatively few occasions throughout the year when one of the kids had asked that clichéd old question from the backseat – 'Are we nearly there yet?' I suppose when you're driving round the world, 'there' is almost always an unfathomably long way away, and not worth the enquiry.

And yet, with Penny on a freight ship to Europe, and the rest of us heading to Manhattan, 'there' was almost here.

Thirty-eight thousand miles after our journey began, we reached New York. The opportunity actually to answer 'yes', should one of the girls ask if we were nearly there yet didn't arise because we were all so excited at the first sight of the Manhattan skyline. We were driving north up the New Jersey Turnpike when the distinctive island of skyscrapers appeared to our right.

'There it is, girls,' I declared. 'New York City!'

There were sighs of wonder, and possibly relief, as they all twisted and craned to get the best possible view from the backseat of the hire car. Manhattan's distinctive silhouette, like grey stalagmites reaching skywards, had us immediately in her spell. This was the sixth visit for Jill and me, having adored the city since we first came on our honeymoon, and the thrill of glimpsing New York's outline rising from the Hudson River was as potent as ever.

We turned right between Jersey City and Union City (of the Blondie song, pop-pickers) and descended into the Lincoln Tunnel beneath the Hudson. And stopped. The first, inevitable, traffic jam we encountered was ten metres into the tunnel, meaning that, teased by the sight of our destination, we were forced to spend an agonising *half hour* in the dark, tutting, huffing, and sighing impatiently. Eventually we climbed into the sunlight. We were in Manhattan!

The traffic system delivered us on to 42nd Street. I headed west. The brilliant thing about New York City's grid system is that you don't have to be a native to get your bearings. Even *I* knew that if we were on the east of Manhattan on 42nd Street and we drove west, we would encounter one the city's most famous intersections.

'Girls, we're about to cross Times Square. I can't stop, so take a good look.'

The scramble to press their faces to the windows wasn't without occasional yelps of complaint, mainly aimed at Edie who was stuck in the middle and didn't seem to mind who she climbed over to get a decent view. Traffic cops held back dense crowds of tourists and New Yorkers and waved us through. I crawled as slowly as I gauged I could without being arrested. The acres of flashing lights, the towering video walls, and the fact that almost every other vehicle was a yellow taxi had the desired effect: the girls were in their own movie. That's what NYC does to first-timers – transports them into a world only ever seen on the big screen. It's intoxicating, and the girls were under its spell.

Having lived the dream (though for many it would be nightmare) of driving in Manhattan, we wasted no time in finding the tiny apartment we'd rented on the corner of Lexington and 71st, just a few blocks from the park, before dumping our bags and negotiating the hire-car over to the rental depot on the upper east side. There was an unexpected feeling of relief in handing the car back.

'Wow, that feels good, doesn't it?' I said to Jill as we walked away from the cramped garage, with our deposit intact.

'It really does. I hadn't realised how stressed I was about getting the car here in one piece until now. It's like a weight's been lifted from us.'

'This is *not* a city to drive in. From now on, girls, we're walking.'

'Or taking cabs,' added Bethan, hopefully.

'Possibly. But mainly walking,' I assured her.

The few days we had in New York were quickly filled with a schedule that left almost no single minute un-allocated. We arrived on Saturday and would fly home on Wednesday. Monday was Edie's birthday, and being 4th July would culminate in the World's Biggest Firework Display. Tuesday was chosen for her extended-birthday trip to Coney Island fun fair, which would be offering super-cheap tickets in an attempt to counter the post-Independence Day slump. This left Sunday as the obvious day to do what we actually came here for.

It was time to busk in Central Park.

This was the big one. The one we'd driven 18,500 miles from Liverpool for: from outside the bright-red wrought-iron gates of Strawberry Field on Beaconsfield Road, L18, to the equally iconic Strawberry Fields memorial garden, the most visited corner of the most visited city park in the United States. A year earlier, our only audience had been Linda and Joan, who contributed the first two-pounds to our UNICEF fund. Now, almost £3,000 later, we were in Central Park. There'd be joggers. There'd be tourists. There'd be ... rain.

Lots of rain.

To be honest, we shouldn't have been surprised. All the signs that this might be a tricky gig were there from the start. First, when we reccied the place on Saturday afternoon, we approached the famous tiled 'Imagine' mosaic, surrounded by fans and curious tourists, to be confronted with lots of official 'Central Park Police' rules bolted to the lamp-posts.

'Er, Sim?' said Jill, beckoning me over to one.

The metal sign boldly stated 'Quiet Zone. No musical instruments'.

'Oh dear,' I replied, reading the list of things that were banned. 'And what's worse, I won't be able to do my cycling, rollerblading and skateboarding extravaganza either.'

Jill leaned towards me, and in a stage whisper said, 'There are no buskers here. I think they mean it about the musical instruments.'

'Well, strictly speaking,' I argued, 'we're not *actually* musical.'

'Are we still gonna do it?' asked Ella, looking at the sign from under furrowed brows.

'Of course,' I said. 'We'll come and do it first thing. That way we get it over with and we can relax and enjoy the rest of our Sunday.'

'Plus it gives us a full day to talk our way out of jail,' added Jill as we walked away. The other sign we should have noticed, that foretold of our meteorologically-challenged gig, was a mammoth 40-foot poster in Times Square promoting a Beatles Tribute Show on Broadway. The title of the show, named after the B-side to *Paperback Writer*, was one word in colossal white letters: *Rain*.

New York was quiet, overcast and a little chilly as we left the apartment at nine o'clock on Sunday morning. The park was peaceful, although we would soon put a stop to that. 'I think we might be too early,' I said. 'It seems awfully quiet.'

'There are a few joggers,' Jill pointed out. 'And a man walking a dog, look.'

'One man and a dog,' said Beth. 'That's our kind of audience.'

'It's raining,' announced Ella, as we strode west. I felt the first spitting drops of water and looked earnestly towards the sky. The slab of grey was menacingly dark. We marched on. No one spoke as the shower got heavier. By the time we reached Strawberry Fields, near the entrance opposite the Dakota Building, the sky had unzipped. The dog walkers, joggers and tourists vanished in the flash of a lightning bolt. We huddled under a leafy archway that offered no shelter whatsoever. The sky grew blacker, the thunder shook and the pathways turned to rivers. From nowhere, something lunged at us. It was fast, it was big and it was black. We all jumped. Jill screeched. A huge rat brushed past her foot as it scarpered from a flooding drain. It was the biggest rat I'd ever seen, and given some of the specimens India boasted, that was quite a feat.

Jill ran headlong into the storm, doing that 'yucky, squealy' run girls do when they flap their arms and pick their feet up as high as they can. Through the pummelling rain and the clattering thunder I didn't catch what she said, but the gist of it was, 'Sod this, I'm off to find a Starbucks.'

Clinging to the far-from-weatherproof instrument bag (a woefully inadequate French hypermarket shopping bag) and desperately failing to protect its contents, I led the charge after Jill. We crossed, sorry, *forded* Central Park West, and with the rain stinging our faces looked wistfully into the dry archway of the Dakota building. The home of Yoko and the location of John Lennon's murder normally holds more sway with me, but at that moment all I could think was how unfair it was that a uniformed guard stood between us and shelter, and how I felt sure John would have let us in if he'd been there. We ploughed on until we found the inevitable Starbucks (one of 174 branches in Manhattan, so not a long walk) and collapsed, dripping and freezing in the normally-so-welcome air conditioning. Huddled around hot chocolates, we waited for the storm to pass.

But it didn't. An hour later we were back in the park, ruefully hoping that the weather was changing for the best, hurling well-practised English phrases into the pounding, watery onslaught, such as, 'the worst is over', 'the sky's brightening up' and, 'it's definitely easing off'. All of which were incorrect.

We stood alone in Strawberry Fields, wet to the bone, and looked at each other in drenched and exhausted disbelief.

'It can't end like this!' I said. The kids looked resigned to it. They'd been through a lot on this trip. This was a fairly standard day for them. Jill laughed.

'I think it's perfect,' she said. 'Let's end as we began. We played at Strawberry Field in Liverpool to nobody. Let's do the same here.'

'But we were rubbish then,' I whined. 'We know eight whole songs now!'

'Let's just do a song right here at the memorial. At least no one can tell us off. And in a way, it's symbolic.'

'It's *sham*bolic.'

'Exactly. Like I said, it's perfect. Very *us*.'

I knew she was right. The only sign of life was a cop car sitting at the park entrance, so, after dispatching Bethan and Edie to check that New York's Finest were facing the other way, we gathered at our final destination and, through driving rain and claps of thunder performed the weirdest rendition of *All You Need Is Love* we've ever done. Our only audience was a hastily trotting pedestrian completely wrapped in a massive polythene bag. He, or possibly she, cast us a puzzled glance and kept running.

I shouted, 'Thank you New York!' after them. You've got to live your dreams.

For the sake of our website, we recorded the spectacle as best we could on a rapidly-malfunctioning video camera that clearly didn't appreciate being asked to operate beneath what it considered to be a waterfall – a closing message to our faithful followers from what looked like a family of half-drowned refugees. Hardly the grand finale I'd hoped for.

The rain was dogged and unrelenting all day, and our own anti-climactic cloud hung over us. We must have been the only tourists in New York with long faces. Jill and I were very excited about showing off our favourite city to the girls, but you couldn't say that for any of us our hearts were in it. Resigned to 'indoor amusements' we toured the shops from Bloomingdales to FAO Schwarz, taking window-shopping to Olympic levels until, late in the afternoon, we returned to the apartment and everything changed. I turned on the laptop to check our emails and idly checked our UNICEF donations page. We had received two new donations equalling almost £1,500!

The first was from one of our closest friends, Fay, who'd been following our progress closely throughout the year and felt moved enough by our adventure to add £500 to the pot. Amazing. The second was from an old friend of mine, Colin, who I hadn't seen for about 20 years. He'd been the drummer in a band I played in when I was a teenager, and although we'd never been very good at staying in touch he'd found our website early in the trip and followed our exploits all year. Impressed with our efforts, he persuaded his church youth group to do a sponsored '24-hour fast and sleepover' and donate the resulting cash to UNICEF in our honour. Incredibly, they raised almost a thousand pounds.

When Colin posted the news on our Facebook page we were gobsmacked. We didn't even *know* these kids, and yet somewhere in a church hall in the English market town of Rushden they had gathered, got hungry, slept on a hard floor, and passed the time by making a huge collage on one wall. A photo of it was posted online for us to see: a huge picture of Penny. We were so moved by their generosity we completely forgot our depression – the timing was impeccable. It made our underwater-scuba-busk in the park seem worthwhile, after all.

We'd been looking forward to 4th July for ages. The idea that Edie would be celebrating her birthday in America had been exciting enough in the early planning stages of the trip – the fact that it became a birthday celebration in *New York* only ramped up the anticipation. Back in Colorado, while we'd been sitting on the cog-train climbing Pike's Peak, Jill got into a conversation with the woman opposite us. She and her husband were from Texas, and looked in their late 50s. The all-too-familiar conversation about our trip and the lady's unbelieving amazement at our 'vacation of a lifetime' (it's not a holiday) led to its customary conclusion – 'And we end in New York for Edie's birthday on Independence Day' Jill said.

'That's great,' said the woman. 'Have you seen many Independence Days around the world?'

I considered this a surprisingly good question, partly because no one else had asked it, and partly because, well, she was from *Texas*. The generalisation I was guilty of was that everyone from the southern states had practically no knowledge of world politics, or indeed *any* events beyond their own frontier. Jill warmed to the opportunity.

'Well yes, we have as it happens. We were in Turkey for their Republic Day in October.'

'And we were in India for their Republic Day – 26th January,' I remembered.

The lady listened, then said, 'And when do you have your Independence Day in England?'

Jill couldn't help herself. In her finest BBC announcer's voice she leaned forward and said, 'Actually, we don't have one. *You're* celebrating independence from *us*. We don't mention it at home.'

'It might upset the Queen,' I added, in a hushed tone.

'Ya don't say!' whispered the lady, slightly awestruck.

We started Independence Day with a walk into midtown, dazzled by the sun and mystified by the remarkable change in the weather. It's true that 4th July should really be a dark day to be a Brit in the USA, what with it commemorating their independence from us - an independence we refused to acknowledge until a war had been fought, a capital had been torched and a damned fine National Anthem had been penned. Thankfully, all that was water under the Brooklyn Bridge by 2011, because we were greeted with cheery 'Happy 4th July!'s all day long, even though we were quite clearly from the side of the evil oppressor. The fact we lost probably helped.

The firework display over the Hudson River is legendary, and is regularly listed as the biggest display in the world, thanks to its trick of actually being several identical displays that all simultaneously launch from barges positioned all the way up the river. It closes 30 blocks of 12th Avenue and attracts about three million people to what quickly becomes a summer street party. It was memorable and bizarre to spend a couple of hours chatting to strangers having bagged our spot on the wall of a central reservation, while hip-hop music throbbed, kids played games and picnics were eaten - all on the tarmac of what is normally a busy dual carriageway.

Finally, after nature had provided us with her own stunning display, turning the heavens bright orange as the sun slid below the horizon, the sky grew dark, somewhere on a distant stage Beyoncé started singing the *Star Spangled Banner*, and the blackness burst into light. From out on the water, 40,000 shells were unleashed at a rate of 1,500 a minute. The breathtaking scale of it is only bettered by its inventiveness. We 'ooohhhh'd and 'aaaahhhh'd as *shapes* appeared in the sky. D'you remember when fireworks went up, went bang and that was that? These were *amazing!* Three-dimensional 'planets', complete with 'Saturn' rings, exploded before our eyes. Red heart shapes burst forth and hung in the air just long enough for three-million people to say, 'Did you see that?' And Edie's favourite - bright, glowing, smiley faces periodically punctuated the blinding array of sparkle and colour. Her face was a picture of delight. As birthday celebrations go, it was off the scale.

Twenty-six minutes later we joined in a live experiment to see what happens when you simultaneously release three-million pedestrians on to Manhattan's roads. Traffic stops, is the less-than-surprising result, I can reveal. We bustled our way west, grabbing hands, keeping close, jostling with the crowds until we reached Broadway and took a right. This was a trip down memory lane for Jill and me, that the kids were polite enough to look vaguely interested in.

'This is the hotel we stayed in on our honeymoon!'

'This is where we first ate sushi!'

'This is where David Letterman's show comes from!'

'Who?'

'Letterman. Comedian. Had an affair. Got blackmailed. No?' Jill's bullet-point summary was ringing no bells. Then I remembered something.

'Edie, you know when The Beatles first came to America they appeared on the Ed Sullivan Show? It was here!'

She looked up and read the words up in lights above us: The Ed Sullivan Theatre. She shook her head in disbelief.

I can't remember a thing about my tenth birthday. Can you remember yours? I *really* hope she remembers hers.

We walked on, with the only-slightly-thinning crowds, towards Times Square. It was 11 o'clock at night and *heaving* with life. We stood, we watched, we absorbed the incredible spectacle that it is, and then after a few photos we suddenly felt very tired and treated ourselves to a cab back up to 71st Street where comfy beds were calling our names.

Our final day in the Big Apple was spent in two halves. In the morning we visited Coney Island which, despite a much-publicised refurbishment, was reassuringly 'beaten up' and 'run down' – in other words, exactly as I'd hoped it would be. They've installed a couple of new rides there but, importantly, you can still see masses of faded charm in the peeling paint of many decades. The highlight was The Cyclone – at almost 100 years old, the oldest rollercoaster in the world. It has no pneumatic safety barriers, no head restraints - in fact you basically sit in a tiny two-seater bench – and it throws you around its corners and humps with such vigour and G-force that coming off it with whiplash is considered a triumph; at least you haven't lost a limb. We went on it twice.

We spent the afternoon in Central Park, messing about on the boating lake and wandering around the edge of the zoo, too skint to go in, but happy to peer through the fence at the sea-lions and polar bear. We were tourists. We wore no badge, no uniform, no medal of honour that proclaimed us as global travellers. While Jill and the kids were in a rowing boat on the lake I sat in the beautiful arched pavilion and listened to a busking trio – cello, violin and tenor - great musicians whose talents were sublimely supported by the hard, tiled building's natural reverberating acoustics. I blended in. I wasn't the white face in Aleppo's busy souq, or the only Westerner in Mumbai's dockyard. I wasn't standing in Istanbul's Taksim Square explaining to locals who The Beatles were, or forging a path up the steep, dusk-lit side of Jordan's Mukawir mountain to find where King Herod imprisoned John the Baptist. I was just a bloke, in a park, listening to some buskers.

It was over.

That night, I made a list. All boys love a list. Soon we'd be back in England, soon this whole trip would be behind us, the entire experience consigned to the past tense. Before that happened, I had to capture a few travellers' truths, some salutary lessons we'd learned from our voyage. Something I could look back on years later, when the jaded routine of normal life had dulled the memory. Maybe even something I could share with others. When people asked, 'What did you learn? What did you *discover*?' wouldn't it be nice to have a few examples that were more significant than, 'I discovered it's not great to be a goat in Jordan at Eid'?

As I opened the laptop I recalled an annoying number one novelty-record from the late 90s in which movie director Baz Luhrmann read pithy words of advice, borrowed, supposedly, from a school leaver's graduation speech. As well as advising the listener to wear sunscreen, he summed up a multitude of eternal truths, such as, 'Do not read beauty magazines - they will only make you feel ugly.' Hardly Neitzsche, but he had a point.

I didn't want a whole novelty record's worth of one-liners, but I wanted ... *something*. At best, a declaration of what I'd learned from my adventure, a reminder of all those lightbulb moments I'd travelled so far to find. At worst, an embarrassing letter to myself that amounted to little more than 'a list of stuff'.

It read like this:

Sim,

You're reading this because you're bored with life, fed up with your lot or you just found this piece of paper at the bottom of a box. Either way, read on, and let the next two minutes remind you how clearly you saw the world from the front seat of a Volkswagen camper van.

Taps.

No one ever thinks about them. Remember how during nine weeks in India we became wedded to plastic water bottles? We watched countless women and children pump muddy water into buckets and carry them to their homes. You vowed never to take our drinking water for granted again. But of course, you do. Bless the tap, my friend. It's more valuable than any of us give it credit for.

Some problems might be unfixable.

This tormented you for a while, you'll remember. Australia's white community had about as much in common with its Aboriginal community as Father Chalk does to Mistress Cheese. They share a land-mass, but that is all. That two such contrary ways of living, such opposite mindsets, will ever merge seems impossible to comprehend. Also, look at India. Remember how full it was? Over a billion people live there, dude! That's one in six people on Earth. Yet most of the wealth is shared between about seven of them. Possibly eight if Shahrukh Khan gives his cousin a job. It's corrupt, Sim. These are things you can't fix. If you want to fix something, sort out that dripping tap in your bathroom. And while you reach for a spanner, remember what Reinhold Niebuhr said: God grant me the serenity to accept the things I cannot change *(India)*, courage to change the things I can *(your bathroom)*, and the wisdom to know the difference *(one is an unimaginably crowded place monopolised for the sole benefit of the lucky few, the other is India).*

No one explores their home.
We met lots of Australians, but few who'd been to Ayers Rock. We met lots of Americans, but few who'd been to Yosemite. You could criticise, but you live half an hour from Shakespeare's birthplace. Have you been yet? Probably not. When was the last time you went to Stonehenge, the British Museum or visited Parliament? Exactly. Too busy. Too this, too that, too whatever. You have some astonishing treasures within an hour or two that you've never seen. Go. Be a tourist. One day they'll be gone, or more likely, you will.

A Volkswagen T25 is a wondrous machine.
It oozes charm, turns heads and looks great. So, you might argue, does Keira Knightley. But will Keira carry you around the world in return for nothing more than a regular oil change and keeping her belts tensioned? Exactly. Look after Penny.

Everyone wants the same stuff.
And weirdly, it's not money. We were struck by the similarities we saw in people from such diverse cultures. The overwhelming friendship and generosity we received on our journey was humbling, and everywhere we found the same home truths. From Muslims in the Middle East to Hindus in India, people put family first. They want the best for their kids, they want a safe home and they want a happy home. The world really isn't a dark and scary place. It's full of people like you. People who smile first, ask questions later. They look for friendship rather than barriers. Remember this when the TV news shows protesters chanting in a foreign tongue, crowds in burkas or slum dwellers in Mumbai. We all want the same stuff.

It's good to do something scary.

No one likes being outside their comfort zone. The fear of failure and the fear of the unknown are stifling. But really, Sim, remember to take a risk once in a while. What about that woman you're married to? She would never have considered quitting jobs, schools and a home to travel around the world in a camper van. It's still a mystery why she agreed. But she'll tell you that doing something scary always reaps rewards. Almost all the memorable, happiest moments of our journey, and the great new friends we made, can be traced directly back to the fact that we chose to put ourselves out there and take a risk. Whether it was busking (which was terrifying), or asking to camp in someone's drive or car park, if we'd kept ourselves to ourselves and checked into a hotel, none of these brilliant things would have happened. The point is, doing stuff that scares you always reaps rewards. Fact.

Don't trust an Italian mechanic.

Well, don't trust an Italian mechanic in a Volkswagen dealership.

Well, more accurately, don't trust an Italian mechanic in a Volkswagen dealership in Alessandria called Zentrum VW.

They are bad people.

All other Italians, to my knowledge, are bella.

Look after the Earth.

When was it you first heard about global warming? 1988? And yet 23 years after first being aware of environmental issues we watched India pollute with gay abandon, America still drilling for oil (at the cost of Alaska) and Australia spending weeks wringing its hands over a green Carbon Tax while, unfettered by conscience, its economy boomed selling billions of tons of coal to China, the world's biggest polluter. If we want to save the planet for our grandchildren, we've got a long way to go. And if all these issues seem too big, too vast, and too far away to be bothered with, remember what Gandhi said - 'You must be the change you want to see in the world.'

Wise words, Mahatma.

Do not *refer back to my message about unfixable problems. I was talking about something else then. This is one you can fix. Or at least help with.*

Family matters.

No, you can't choose them. Yes, they drive you insane. Seeing the importance that other cultures put on family made us aware of how disparate our community has become, especially with regard to our own flesh and blood. Remember that magazine article you read, where they conducted an international poll asking people to define 'integrity'? Western people said it meant being honest and straight, especially in business - not being 'two faced'. Whereas in the Middle East 'integrity' meant providing for your family, caring for your brother if he's sick or providing for his kids if he dies. Their priorities are completely different. It was amazing how well we all rubbed along as a family for a year, especially in such a small living space, and we resolved that we mustn't simply drop back into only having one meal a week together (Sunday lunch) and passing each other like ships in the night. I know that's easy to say, and an idealistic dream, but it's worth the effort. Look after your family. They're the only one you get.

Respect the sun.

Australia is so acutely aware of skin cancer that often sunscreen is available free at public pools and beaches, and massive sails are always erected to create shade. A car park without shade is unheard of in Oz. But in the States - nothing. 'Park in the shade,' we would quip, entering yet another sun-baked barren parking lot. Pink babies cooking in prams, peeling backs on fair-skinned mothers, hoards of 'summer camp' teens char-broiling on campsites with not a hat between them. I can't believe I'm saying this, I'm aghast that my whole year of worldly wisdom might be reduced to these two words, but Baz Luhrmann was right all along.

Wear sunscreen.

Epilogue

We landed to find England's weather hadn't changed a bit – it was July, it was 15°C and it was raining. Although our unforgettable adventure was over, I didn't want this book to end in New York. There are just too many loose ends, unresolved questions that I'm sure you demand an answer to, like 'How's your Mum?' 'Were the girls bottom of the class after a year out of school?' and 'How many litres of diesel did you burn, Mr *I became vegetarian to save the planet*'?

All valid questions, so first, stat fan, here are some numbers:

- Total miles travelled - 38,814
- Miles driven in Penny - 18,261
- Days on the road - 333
- Countries visited - 17
- Litres of diesel bought - 2,594
- Tents destroyed - 4
- Punctures - 3
- Laptop chargers and iPod leads broken - 7
- Number of times we asked someone, 'Do you know your wifi key?' – 123.

We spent the summer continuing to 'camp' in the UK, living out of those same rucksacks that we'd dragged all the way around the globe, but camping in other people's homes. Our own house wasn't ours again until our tenants left at the beginning of September, so for six weeks we roamed from home to home, imposing on many very generous friends, and house-sitting for a few who went on their summer holidays. The best two weeks of this time was spent in Devon at my parents' new place. They'd moved house after we left the UK, so although they'd lived in Lympstone for nine months it was all new to us. My Mum had endured her chemo, survived some compulsory R&R in France, and was in great form. Even in the two weeks we spent with them, we could see her energy levels increasing all the time.

Today, she's as bright as a button, back to her old self. She takes daily medication and gets plugged into a monthly 'bone strengthening drip' at her local hospital, but neither has any nasty side-affects, so she's very happy about that. She'll never be rid of the cancer, but she can keep it at bay for many years yet. Best of all, she fought the disease, survived the treatment and battled back to full fitness just in time to help me edit this book, which was awfully considerate of her, don't you think? I can't thank her enough. Even when she brutally chops my words. (I wonder if she'll leave this bit in?)

Ennas, the student who so helpfully guided us through Damascus has been in our thoughts. Since we arrived home, what started as street protests in Syria's towns and cities has descended into daily violent clashes which, as I write, look certain to degenerate into civil war between the Free Syrian Army and President Assad's troops. I emailed Ennas, and was relieved to get this reply:

Thank you very much for the email.
I'm still alive, and so happy you still remember me. Syria is bleeding. Our life's become totally

horrible. Al Assad government is very bad and they kill people every day. I will send you another email later.
Take care and keep in touch. Thank you again.

That really struck a chord: Syria is bleeding. What a powerful line from a girl who learned English at school, and only *once* met English people – us. The fact she opens her reply by saying 'I'm still alive' tells us something about the daily horror of life in Damascus. I think of Ennas if I'm having a bad day. It gives me some perspective. Certainly makes minor worries like getting the rent money seem rather trivial, doesn't it?

However, I'm sure you're curious. Well, after all the stress of *late* rent money and *missing* rent money, we reclaimed our house with relative ease. In fact, with the deposit held to cover the missing month's cash, and nothing worse than slight wear and tear to the house, we were owed nothing in the end. Having said that, it was a terribly stressful way to fund the trip. That's something I'd change if we did it again – get an agent and a guaranteed rent agreement.

And the girls? Ella was most nervous about her return to school, even more so than Beth who took joining a brand new school in her stride. I'm sure there were a few naysayers who thought the kids would be so utterly derailed by our year away that they'd fall into drink, drugs and be running the local mafia by now. And although the latter will always be a risk where Edie's concerned, I'm pleased, almost embarrassed, to tell you that they are all Grade A students whose teachers can't speak highly enough of them. Especially their Geography teachers, funnily enough.

I know. I can't believe it either. We got away with it. The whole crazy, bonkers scheme came off, and it's left an indelible mark on us all.

Just the other day Bethan said, 'I've had a brilliant idea about what to get you both for your next big wedding anniversary.'

'Oh? What's that?' we asked.

'A city break to Alessandria.'

Not even funny.

Acknowledgements

As you'd expect, none of this, neither the trip nor the book, would have been possible without the generous help of lots of lovely people. Top of my 'thank you' list are five women without whom it couldn't have happened: Jill, who I still can't believe agreed to it. I love you for running with the idea, even when it looked doomed. Ella, who went into the camper-van-cocoon a grumpy teenager and emerged one year later a beautiful, intelligent young woman. How did that happen? Bethan, who chose to face her fears and defeat her dread, rather than simply divorce her parents, which would have been her first choice. And Edie, whose unwavering enthusiasm for the adventure, for the busking, and for the lack of washing facilities was wondrous to behold. I love you lot. Thanks for humouring your old man.

Then there's the legend that is Brenda Courtie – writer, editor, granny and cancer-cruncher. Thank you so much for all your help, your encouragement and your hours of Skyping, and all so soon after doing another twelve rounds with our old enemy. We love you, Mum.

What is it they say about 'behind every great woman'? Thanks Dad, for having a proper education when it comes to grammar, resisting the temptation to inflict it too heavily over mum's shoulder during the edits, and for the many, many ink cartridges.

A big gift-wrapped, air-mailed Thank You to all the people who put us up around the world. Thank you for your generosity, your warmth and most of all, your toilet. (I hope you didn't pay for this book. What? But you're in it! That bloomin' Courtie, eh? Is there no end to his cheek? Come and stay any time. We have room for five in a van on the drive.)

Thanks also to patient friends who've helped with the nitty-gritty of publishing a book: Peter Unsworth, Sarah Meyrick, Ben Phillips and Lynne Wilson.

Thanks again to the army of 'friends back home' who supported us around the world, all of them named-and-shamed on the 'End Credits' video at www.beatnikbeatles.com

And thanks to the blog readers for following our journey and spreading the word. Now, if you can just work your magic once more, I know a great book you can recommend …

See more photos, video and donate to UNICEF online at
www.beatnikbeatles.com

Contact the author - sim@beatnikbeatles.com